MEDIA, NATIONALISM
AND EUROPEAN IDENTITIES

MEDIA, NATIONALISM AND EUROPEAN IDENTITIES

Edited by
Miklós Sükösd,
Karol Jakubowicz

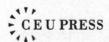

Central European University Press
Budapest–New York

Published in 2011 by
CENTRAL EUROPEAN UNIVERSITY PRESS

An imprint of the
Central European University Share Company
Nádor utca 11, H-1051 Budapest, Hungary
Tel: +36-1-327-3138 or 327-3000
Fax: +36-1-327-3183
Website: www.ceupress.com, *E-mail:* ceupress@ceu.hu

400 West 59th Street, New York NY 10019, USA
Tel: +1-212-547-6932, *Fax:* +1-646-557-2416
E-mail: mgreenwald@sorosny.org

ISBN 978-963-9776-74-6 cloth

COST is supported by
the EU RTD Framework Programme

ESF provides the COST office
through an EC contract

LIBRARY OF CONGRESS CATALOGING-IN-PUBLICATION DATA

Media, nationalism, and European identities / edited by Miklós Sükösd, Karol
Jakubowicz.
    p. cm.
Includes bibliographical references and index.
ISBN 978-9639776746 (hardbound)
1. Mass media—Political aspects—Europe. 2. Mass media and nationalism—Europe. 3. Mass media policy—Europe. 4. Group identity—Europe. 5. Europe—Economic integration—Political aspects. I. Sükösd, Miklós. II. Jakubowicz, Karol.

P95.82.E85M426 2010
302.23094—dc22

                        2010036919

Printed in Hungary by
Akaprint Kft., Budapest

Table of Contents

COST—the acronym for European Cooperation in Science and Technology—is the oldest and widest European intergovernmental network for cooperation in research. Established by the Ministerial Conference in November 1971, COST is presently used by the scientific communities of 36 European countries to cooperate in common research projects supported by national funds.
Web: http://www.cost.esf.org

The COST A30 Action *"East of West: Setting a New Central and Eastern European Media Research Agenda"* was a 4 year long (2005–2009) COST research project that has established an outstanding network, bringing together approximately 70 distinguished media and communications researchers from 27 countries in Western and Eastern Europe. The main objective of the Action was to increase the knowledge concerning media production, media reception and use, and the political implications of the transformation of the media landscape in the Eastern and Central European context. The Action aimed at organizing a European social science research network with a clear focus on emerging problems of Central and Eastern European media in a comparative perspective. The Action also aimed at building a network of media studies and communication research centers, higher education programs and departments in Western and Eastern Europe.
Web: www.cost.eu

Six Communicative Deficits in the European Union

KAROL JAKUBOWICZ AND MIKLÓS SÜKÖSD

New Sense of Place

The central question of this book and at the same time the fundamental question at the heart of the European Project, as the European Union is often called, is as follows: can this top-down, elite-led process make further progress without the added impetus of greater unity also in the sphere of social consciousness and ultimately culture which would help make it more of a bottom-up project? Undoubtedly, this fundamental question has to do with communicative processes, media, public opinion, and identity formation.

This question is often asked. What is perhaps unusual about this effort to develop an answer is that it emerged out the (European Cooperation in Science and Technology) A30 Action of the European Union, entitled "East of West: Setting A New Central and Eastern European Media Research Agenda," launched at the Central European University in Budapest, Hungary. In 2005, we set ourselves the task of "developing a cutting edge, joint European social science research agenda with a clear focus on newly emerging problems of Central and Eastern European media in a comparative perspective," but also of developing "a joint European media research agenda, and the related theoretical conceptualization, at the frontiers of knowledge."

Before we proceed to a presentation of the book's contents, it is interesting to trace shifting geographical identities revealed by Action participants. The title of the Action itself would place it "East of West" One of the books that came out of the Action was entitled "Finding the Right Place on the Map: Central and Eastern European Media Change in Global Perspective" (Jakubowicz and Sükösd, 2008). That already showed that "East of West" was not, perhaps, where

Central and Eastern Europe wanted to be, but it also revealed a certain ambivalence or uncertainty as to just where the region belonged. But when it came to the Action's final conference in 2009, things had clearly changed, because the title of that conference was "Beyond East and West. Two Decades of Media Transformation after the Fall of Communism."

From "East of West" to "Beyond East and West" in just four short years?! These are more than word games: they speak to a new confidence among Central and Eastern Europeans and a rejection of old divisions, once imposed by the Cold War.

This book is testimony to the new mindset. Central and Eastern European media scholars had spent years morbidly reporting, blow-by-blow, on the latest twists of the never-ending story of what it was that the politicians had done to the media in their countries. Now, we decided to broaden our horizons and take a look at another "emerging problem of Central and Eastern European media," i.e. the European Union. In this, we were aided by Western European participants in the Action. In addition to the present book, also another collection that came out of the COST A30 Action (Klimkiewicz, 2010) reflects this approach.

Altogether, contributions to the present book do not seem to provide an unequivocally positive answer to the question about the EU's future posed above.

Legitimation Deficit in the European Union

The book is divided into three sections: "The European Public Sphere and European Integration," "National and Transnational Identities" and "European Media Policy: Boon or Barrier to European Integration?." Normally in such an introduction, the contents of the three sections would be presented briefly. What we would like to do instead is to problematize this introduction by explaining how the particular contributions throw light on what we regard as five different, but interrelated deficits in the EU that are related to communicative processes, mass media, and public opinion: 1) media deficit; 2) communication deficit; 3) media policy deficit; 4) democratic deficit; 5) identity deficit. As result of these factors, we see 6) the persistence of a legitimation deficit regarding the EU and blocking its further integration. Successive rejections of the various treaties in popular referendums particular countries indicated that the EU has been and remains less of a "community" or "union" than it needs to be to enjoy full legitimacy in the eyes of its citizens. All these issues are thrown into sharp relief by the EU's handling of Hungary's media legislation of 2010 and the worldwide storm of criticism provoked by these laws. In Hungary, the government passed a media law that created a pro-government, partisan media oversight authority, put public service media and frequency distribution for commercial media under government control, and also widely regulated press and Internet content (for details, see OSCE, 2010 and Hume, 2011). *The Economist* regards this legal package as evidence of the "Putinisation" of Hungary. "Laws like this have only been known in totalitarian regimes where governments are restricting free speech," according to Dunja Mijatović, representative on Freedom of Media of the Organization for Security and Co-operation in Europe (OSCE) (quoted by Bajomi-Lázár et al., forthcoming). Mijatović wrote to the Hungarian Foreign Minister that "The media package is cause for very serious concern. If left unchanged, it can impose a serious chilling effect on media freedom and can drastically curb freedom of expression and of the media in the country." We will return to this case below.

MEDIA DEFICIT

The European Project and its various ramifications are not represented adequately in issue agendas, frames of interpretation, information provision, content of media organizations in national media systems. In other words, the democratic performance of the media in terms of European integration remains insufficient.

This media deficit could be broken down into deficits of a) the performance of individual media organizations (that have a deficit covering transnational European politics and common themes in Europe), b) national media systems (that are still by and large dominated by "banal nationalism"), c) the deficit of the European media system (marginal existence or elite character of pan-European media institutions).

Creation of a European public sphere would be a crucial way of promoting integration. This was recognized by the European Commission itself in 2005, when it launched a "Plan D for Democracy, Dialogue and Debate." Its goal was to "reinvigorate European democracy and help the emergence of a European public sphere, where citizens are given the information and the tools to actively participate in the decision making process and gain ownership of the European project" (European Commission: 2005: 2–3).

For a "European public sphere" to function properly, a "supranational political culture" and a range of European publics are needed. That, in turn, would require—according to Philip Schlesinger—(a) the dissemination of a European news agenda, (b) need among citizens of EU countries to become a significant part of the everyday news-consuming habits of European audiences, and (c) "that those living within the EU have begun to think of their citizenship, in part at least, as transcending the level of the member nation-states" (Schlesinger, cited after Golding, 2006; emphasis added).

Several chapters in this book deal with these issues. Slavko Splichal discusses at length "The Transnationalization/Europeanization of the Public Sphere/s" from a conceptual and theoretical point of view and concludes by saying that there is no substitute for the public sphere in both national and post-national democratic constellation. "Improving our capacity to articulate ideas about public sphere—he says—will help make it more relevant for democratic processes. This is particularly vital in order to dealing better with transnational consequences of transactions among either national or transnational actors."

Dominic Boyer and Miklós Sükösd in their contribution "European Media and the Culture of Europeanness" discuss *inter alia* European media in the context of global media. So does Farrel Corcoran in "The Politics of Belonging: Identity Anxiety in the European Union."

István Hegedűs and Peter Varga examine the operation of European media and the contribution that they make to the development of a European public sphere. Hegedűs concludes in his chapter "Media Representations of EU Matters in National Media Systems: The Hungarian Case" that content analytical studies can convincingly show a national bias in reporting about the EU in all member states. Varga in "Pan-European Media: Attempts and Limitations" seeks to identify the strategies used by the few print media that target pan-European audiences to report politics and public affairs to the populations of Europe, which are characterized by multinationality, overlapping identities and interests.

Inka Salovaara-Moring describes in "What is Europe? Geographies of Journalism" how journalists are struggling with the concept of Europe and how their journalistic discourse constructs three different "Europes": a) Territorial Europe in constructing 'Otherness;' b) Institutional 'Fortress Europe;' and, c) Historical Europe as an experience.

Peter Gross together with Katerina Spasovska in "Aiding Integration and Identity" look at minority media and their impact on prospects for the integration of national and ethnic minorities with their nation-states and with the wider Europe. The question is: are they a force for integration, or for disintegration?

COMMUNICATION DEFICIT

As already noted, several EU treaties have been rejected in popular referendums in particular countries, to mention only the Danish "No" to the Maastricht Treaty of 1992; the Irish "No" to the Nice Treaty in 2001; the Dutch and French "No" to the Constitutional Treaty in 2005; and the Irish "No" again to the Reform Treaty in 2008. Seeking to explain the reasons for this last development, Crum (2008: 17) has described it as a "case of drifting political elites that, once brought face to face with their democratic principals again, failed to convincingly justify their actions." Krastev (2008) has sarcastically described the European Commission's "default attitude" as one according to which the EU "never has political problems—it only has communication problems."

That was confirmed when the Commission sought to rally after the 2005 debacle by proposing "Plan D for Democracy, Dialogue and Debate." Its effectiveness remains in doubt because three years later, in 2008, the Irish said "No" to the "Reform Treaty," since known as the Lisbon Treaty. This time, as before, it was more than a communication problem: "the promoters of the Constitutional Treaty, then redrafted into the [Reform] mini-treaty, are incapable of explaining to European nations what the benefits of the new institutions envisaged by the treaty would be [...] The expected benefits are not easy to describe. Faster decision-making—yes, but what decisions and for what purpose? There is no answer" (Sorman, 2008). Even very slick and expensive communication campaigns will not do the job if they provide unsatisfactory answers to the citizens' questions. And these—as

Sorman suggests—reach into the heart of the democratic (or other-wise) operation of the EU.

The communication deficit is thus clearly related to democratic deficit and media deficit—and they are all a barrier to further European integration.

A good illustration of this deficit, provided by Ms. Neelie Kroes, Vice-President of the European Commission responsible for the Digital Agenda, communicated the European public opinion on the Hungarian media package. Early on in the story, she dismissed the matter: "the situation regarding the media in the various Member States does not fulfill the conditions necessary to trigger the Article 7 procedure" [of action against EU member states in violation of fundamental EU values]. Then, under pressure from Member States (with Germany, Britain and France particularly outspoken) and the European Parliament, as well as countless articles in the European and American press and statements of protest by journalism associations around the world, she admitted that "the new [Hungarian] Media Law raises broader political questions concerning freedom of expression." A few days later, she noted that "it may contravene EU laws on press freedom and broadcasting" and she had been in touch with the Hungarian authorities "to raise specific points on which the media law does not appear at first sight to be satisfactory." What certainly does not appear to be satisfactory is the EU mincing its words in the midst of a general out-pouring of condemnation of the Hungarian government's authoritarian media package.

Efforts to bridge the communication gap are discussed in this volume by, among others, Karol Jakubowicz in "European Melting Pots? European Integration and EU Audiovisual Policy at a Crossroads," where he discusses at some length European Commission communication efforts aimed at promoting integration and the development of a "European identity."

As already suggested above, the development of a European public sphere require "the dissemination of a European news agenda." According to Brüggemann, Sifft, Kleinen-von Königslöw, Peters and Wimmel (2006), "Europeanization" of European publics requires what they call "discursive integration" through the media, as shown in Table 1.

Table 1. Discursive integration

DIMENSION	RESEARCH QUESTION	INDICATOR
Discursive exchange	To what extent are public spheres permeable for discursive exchange with fellow Europeans?	Direct and indirect quotations from foreign actors
Collective identification	Is a sense of belonging to a common European discourse developing?	"We"-references

Thus, by communication deficit (or otherwise) we could also understand the flow of media content between and among EU member states. As shown by several chapters (e.g. those by Boyer and Sükösd, Jakubowicz, Salovaara-Moring and Corcoran), the level of such communication and interchange of information and other media content is by no means sufficient effectively to promote not only political, but also cultural integration.

MEDIA POLICY DEFICIT

EU media policy focuses primarily on issues that are relevant for the media as a commercial industry (to promote competition with Hollywood and other overseas imports, and to support major European companies in the media and information sectors) in the European and the global markets, respectively. The main foci of interest are the single market and protection of competition. Issues of European culture, and news media or public service media in the member states and at the EU level remain secondary, or neglected. The Hungarian media package case illustrates a major issue in this respect. It is the EU's helplessness in addressing—precisely in media policy terms—a situation in a Member State which is widely seen as contravening the values of media freedom and pluralism enshrined in the Charter of Fundamental Rights of the European Union. As the EU institutions have no clear independent mandate to deal with media policy issues, it lacks a framework of criteria to apply in assessing, and responding to, such a situation.

One may distinguish two major areas of media policy deficits: media culture and media institutions. On the one hand, the deficit in media policies in the area of European media culture contributes to the weakness of cultural mechanisms in creating European identity, i.e, identifying with the European project symbolically and emotionally. On the other hand, the deficit in the institutional area harmfully impacts on the public's factual knowledge about European matters. As public service media bring more factual information and hard news and contribute to the build-up of more citizen knowledge than tabloid commercial media, the weakening of public service media in the member states and their non-existence at the EU level also weakens prospects of the European project.

The EU media policy is discussed at length in a number of chapters. Monica Arino in "Which Frontiers for EU Media Policy: An Assessment in the Context of the European Project" believes that all in all "EU action in the sphere of media has had an overall positive effect." However, she warns, "there is a danger that the drive to develop a pan-European culture and a pan-European identity might conflict with, or even fundamentally compromize, the diversity within the individual national cultures, thereby undermining the competence of national governments in this field."

Judging by the conclusions of other authors, there seems to be little prospect of national policies being overshadowed by EU ones in this field. Jakubowicz argues, in the context of the debate on the Audiovisual Media Services Directive, that the audiovisual policy of the EU is primarily economically-driven and is not diversified and sophisticated enough to respond to the complexities of the clash between "European" and national identities, all the more so that it is separate from the European Commission's "communication policy" which appears to be more attuned to these needs. Jakubowicz looks especially at the EU's audiovisual policy to see how consistent the EU has been in this endeavour and finds that the revision of the TWF directive has handed a number of (primarily symbolic) victories to Member States and their ability to use media policy to achieve cultural goals. The practical impact of this in terms of national integration is bound to be limited, however.

Boyer and Sükösd provide a detailed examination of the EU audiovisual policy and show that it has "failed to generate the culture of Europeanness that it seeks." Beata Klimkiewicz in "The Clash of Resonance: Media Pluralism in European Regulatory Policies" provides a detailed analysis of the stance of EU institutions on media pluralism. She concludes that "The policy concerning media pluralism has been seen as one of the biggest failures of EU institutions (both the Commission and Parliament). Despite the increasing need for harmonized European rules on media pluralism, the EU still lacks the formal powers (especially if member states' interests strongly diverge) and the institutional capacities necessary to enforce the compliance with the rules and their transposition in the member states."

Finally, Petros Iosifidis examines the EU policy on the digital switchover in terrestrial television He seeks, first, to establish whether the proliferation of digital services can enhance programming diversity. This, he says, would be very difficult without the contribution of public service broadcasting. The second goal of the study was to investigate the potential influence of the new digital channels to European cultural integration and the establishment of a "European public sphere." In terms of covering EU-related issues, the findings suggest that the new digital services of all EU countries under scrutiny, with the exception of France, lack a clear commitment to European content. European affairs, culture and politics are marginally represented in national digital networks, whereas the amount and prominence of American programming genres is more visible. The negligible coverage of European affairs reflects the absence of a communal and shared European culture and citizenship. One may conclude that Europe has made its presence felt only on an economic and monetary level, rather than on a cultural and social level.

IDENTITY DEFICIT

For citizens of EU member states, national identity remains a basic framework of social, cultural and political worldview and references. This "banal nationalism" (Billig, 1995) is ubiquitous and expressed by many unrecognized symbols that surround us: flags on public buildings, on the street on holidays, and behind the president; coat of arms and historical references on coins and bills we use every day; sports events in which the nation unites in friendly (or less friendly) competition with other nations; of or even the weather reports that use national maps as units. Both in the family and kindergarten, from early childhood we also are socialized into deep emotional identification with the symbols of the nation, especially the flag and the anthem. In short, the nation remains the hidden frame reference and the source of emotional community, reinforced by unrecognized and invisible routine practices of "banal nationalism."

Through mass media dissemination, banal nationalism defines "markets for loyalty" (Price, 1995). In this context, Europe remains secondary as an invisible frame in banal everyday practices and communication. Europe rarely manifests itself as a unit in contemporary popular culture or sports (the Eurovision Song Festival is the only all-European entertainment media event; and Olympic medals by European states are only rarely counted together as "EU medals" against the Chinese or US medal hauls). The emotional connection to the European flag and the anthem also remains limited. To create a European culture in this strong emotional sense is an extremely challenging task without the necessary corresponding processes and practices of "banal transnationalism."

This set of issues has received extensive treatment in a number of chapters. Sabina Mihelj deals with "The Media and Nationalism, East and West" and points out that nationalism and nationalist media coverage of European affairs can and indeed often do function as an obstacle to European integration. However, numerous cases from the peripheral members of the European Union also suggest that when "Europeanization" becomes a national project—as was the case across Eastern Europe in the early 1990s—nationalism can have the opposite effect.

Farrel Corcoran contrasts two approaches to conceptualizing European identity: the ambition that emerged in Brussels in the early 1980s to establish a European consciousness through media policy, and a more contemporary emphasis on fostering forms of "constitutional patriotism," not cultural homogenization, across all member states. That was supposed to be the answer to "identity anxiety" when the decline of the nation-state and "post-nationalism" were all the rage. Whether it has worked is another matter. Gonzalo Torres in "Pan-European, National, Regional and Minority Identities in the Eurovision Song Contest" provides an account of the interplay of European, regional and national identities, as European television audiences select the winner.

Karol Jakubowicz in his contribution "European Melting Pots? European Integration and EU Audiovisual Policy at a Crossroads" deals with the cross-currents in European identity policies (both the EU and member states have, in recent years, sought to reinforce

"European citizenship and identity") on the one hand, and national identities on the other. He argues that the hidden agenda of EU policy—namely that strong national identities are a barrier to "post-national" European integration—is wide off the mark. In fact, the reverse may be true: the more secure a nation is in its identity, the more open it may be to forms of advanced integration, without fearing the loss of its own national and cultural identity. However, given that both the EU and member states seek at the same time – partly in response to immigration and the failure of multiculturalism – to bind their peoples closer to the EU and to their nation-states, they are at cross purposes and success may be partial at best. European and national "melting pots," and "European" and national identities are on a collision course.

DEMOCRATIC DEFICIT

Few diagnoses of the situation in the European Union are better known than the view that it suffers from a "democratic deficit." Jürgen Habermas (2008a), the German philosopher, has called for a "citizen-friendly" way of conducting politics inside the European Union. In his view, pro-European elites should no longer treat representative democracy as an excuse for disregarding popular will. The gap between decision-making powers transferred to Brussels and Strasbourg, and prospects for democratic participation solely at the national level, is too great. Political parties should roll up their sleeves and get to work, so that Europe becomes a subject of lively, engaged debate among citizens.

The EU decision-making system is perceived by citizens as being too remote and too complex, not to mention the fact that EU institutions are largely unelected. The shift of power and regulation from domestic governments and national legislations to the European Commission, the European Parliament and other European institution is not underpinned by the legitimacy of European institutions and not recognized by public opinion. Related to that, the growing importance of external national representation in and through EU organizations, as well as the shift towards common foreign policy is not reflected in domestic public opinion. To a significant degree, the public perception in member states remains focused on national legislation as the major of source of legislative power, and national governments as the major executive power. The powers of the European Commission and the European Parliament are downplayed in the media as compared to their real competences. Both in domestic and foreign policy making, the public image of sovereign nation states is alive and well in the public opinion of the member states.

The European Commission has acknowledged that "the gap between the European Union and its citizens is widely recognized. In Eurobarometer opinion polls carried out in recent years, many of the people interviewed say they know little about the EU and feel they have little say in its decision-making process. Communication is essential to a healthy democracy. It is a two-way street. Democracy can flourish only if citizens know what is going on, and are able to participate fully" (European Commission, 2006: 2). But when the democratic provision of the Lisbon Treaty (signatures from 1 million EU citizens on any issue obliges the Commission to consider a legislative proposal in the area) was about to enter into effect in 2010, the Commission proposed a set of rules that make practical use of this provision very difficult.

As mentioned before, this democratic deficit of key European institutions has also been related to their legitimation deficit. When national publics still see national parliaments and governments as the major *loci* of power, they tend to downplay not just the importance of EU institutions, but also their relevance and legitimacy. In a way, when Dutch, French and Irish publics refused to provide support for deeper integration in decisive referendums, their choice may be considered logical. If European institutions and matters are perceived as not truly relevant in the life of the member nations, why would national publics press for, or agree to, further European integration?

According to Eriksen and Fossum (2007), there can be three ways of reconstituting democracy in the EU, as shown in Table 2.

Table 2. Three possible democratic orders in Europe

Audit democracy	Federal multinational democracy	Regional-European democracy
The Member States are formally sovereign entities The Union is derived from the Member States	The Union is recognized as a sovereign state, in accordance with international law	Polity sovereignty is multi-dimensional and shared among levels, subject to cosmopolitan principles of citizens' sovereignty

Regarding the second model, we might do well to listen to Günter Verheugen (2008) who has acknowledged that the European Union is not a unified state and will not become one in the foreseeable future. If anyone has dreamed of a European federation, he says, they should stop dreaming. No European nation, according to Verheugen, is ready to give up its identity in favor of some European superstructure. In his view, the answer is more democracy: "We are Europeans, but we are not a European nation. This is why decision-making processes in the EU are so time-consuming and laborious, and it is impossible to directly to replicate the national democratic process at the European level."

If Verheugen is right, then both the second and the third model of reconstituting democracy within the EU are pipe dreams. We are left with the first model and here little headway can be made without clear progress in overcoming all the deficits discussed in this "Introduction" and throughout our book.

Across much of the non-European world, the resurgence of ethnic nationalism and of religion is having a growing impact; and these forces are also more present within Europe itself. In such circumstances, it is not difficult to predict that the crisis of the universality of the European model can become a profound crisis of Europe's political identity. With European citizens experiencing rising psychological insecurity about their future, Krastev (2008) points out, European elites will soon find themselves at the epicenter of an ideological earthquake. Therefore, he concludes, "the future of the EU will be determined not so much by its success in finding a workable compromise; it will be determined by its success in finding new social, political and intellectual energy ... Europe is in urgent need of alternative sources of energy. And this time it is about human energy." This, in turn, will, as is clear from the reasoning developed by several authors in this book, depend on the outcome of several structural and discursive processes related to media systems and organizations, communication processes, and media policy.

In short, the democratic deficit may be seen as resulting from several sources: media deficit, communication deficit, media policy deficit, and identity deficit. The situation with the Hungarian media law package may point to yet another reason for this democratic deficit: uncertainty, in the light of experience, as to how far "the EU," including its diverse actors and institutions, is prepared to go in practical political terms to defend democracy and media freedom in the Member States.

LEGITIMATION DEFICIT

The legitimation deficit appears to be the original sin of the European Community and the European Union. Paradoxically, the founding fathers seem to have wanted things to be exactly that way.

Pomian (2006: passim) notes that European integration has long been the work of politicians representing very different political and ideological orientations who therefore "took great pains to avoid any discussion of values" as this might have bred conflicts. They worked behind closed doors in order to avoid excessive public attention. However, in Pomian's view, already the 1992 Maastricht Treaty "put an end to conducting the process of integration in such a way as to prevent the patient from noticing what was happening ... and the time has come to put fundamental questions on the table." Clearly, the "patient" (i.e., the citizens and peoples of EU member states) has woken up and does not like what he/she is seeing—that, in the words of the Commission, they still do not have ownership of the European Project.

According to Andreev (2008) at least four main types of EU legitimization have been identified:

1) Output legitimacy: Support, granted on the basis of improved efficiency in provision of goods and services, as well as an increased European problem-solving capacity—government for the people.
2) Input legitimacy: Direct legitimation through the elected European Parliament; citizens' participation and consultation; better transparency in taking decisions-government by the people.
3) "Borrowed" legitimacy: Indirect legitimation through the Member States and their democratic representatives operating at different levels—government of the people.
4) Constitutional legitimacy: Formal legitimation through European and international law-government by the "rule of law."

Research on democratic legitimacy in the EU has concluded that supranational authorities have traditionally relied on the first and third types of legitimation.

Clearly, this is no longer sufficient today, as several chapters in this book indicate. One of the fundamental barriers must be that of the cultural framework within which the process of integration is taking place.

The pursuit of further European integration is facing more and more hurdles as we go along, one of the main reasons being that it "is reaching a stage where it encroaches on core national sovereignty" (Wanlin, 2006). It has come to a point of intrusiveness into the operation of nation-states and the lives of their people where there can be little expectation of popular support for further steps without genuine emotional identification with, and commitment to, the whole process. In reality, "th[e] energy for change is missing in Europe. There is no alternative that can mobilize the sentiments of the people. The very strength of the European project—its focus on piecemeal engineering and institutional reforms—can also become (and be seen as) its key weakness. This makes Europe boring and unattractive" (Krastev, 2008).

Habermas (2008b) seems to believe that removing cultural barriers is not impossible: "During European championships, the rituals and reactions of both the players and the fans show that nations are not opposed to one another like blocks of rock. Also the flags on cars show that drivers often need more than one to display their identification with "their" teams. The question is not whether a nation is ready to give up its identity, but whether a European public opinion can develop. If that happens, holders of EU passports will also share a determination jointly to face up to the challenges thrown at them by world politics and to other threats to them all."

If we are to believe Torres in the present volume and his analysis of the regional and national divisiveness that the European Song Contest breeds (as one of the results of the ESC he mentions the fact that "Regional collusion shatters the illusion of One Europe that the ESC has striven to promote"), then Habermas' opinion and hopes may not be confirmed.

As several articles in the present book show, the EU seems to be plagued not only by a "democratic deficit," but also by a "deficit of commitment" to the organization and its goals among the citizens and peoples of the European Union, arising out of insufficient identification with it: "the problem is less that Euroscepticism is on the rize as that Euro-enthusiasm has disappeared" (Krastev, 2008). Robert Kagan (2008) notes that over the years he has seen the EU lose self-confidence, close in on itself to shut out the outside world, and fall prey to growing pessimism. One of th EU's founding dreams has been the conviction that globalization is synonymous with the decline of the nation-state and of nationalism as a political force. The European Union was, and perceived itself, as a "foretaste" of the way the world of the 21st century would be organized. The European elites were tempted to read their own experience of overcoming ethnic nationalism and political religions as a universal trend. Europe's postmodernity, post-nationalism and secularism was to make it a "model" for the rest of the world (Krastev, 2008). It remains to be seen whether this will indeed be so.

REFERENCES

Andreev, Svetlozar (2008) "Legitimating the Union: Dilemmas of Citizens' and National Elites' Inclusion in a Multilevel Europe." *Journal of Contemporary European Research*, 4(3): 209–223, http://www.jcer.net/ojs.index.php/jcer/article/view/70/106.

Bajomi-Lázár, Péter, Vaclav Stetka and Miklós Sükösd (forthcoming) "Public Service Television in the European Union Countries: Old Issues, New Challenges in the 'East' and the 'West'." In: Just, Natascha and Manuel Puppis, eds. *Trends in Communication Policy Research: New Theories, Methods and Subjects*. Bristol: Intellect Books and Chicago: Chicago University Press.

Billig, Michael (1995) *Banal nationalism*. Sage: London.

Brüggemann, Michael, Stefanie Sifft, Katharina Kleinen-von Königslöw, Bernhard Peters and Andreas Wimmel (2006) *Segmented Europeanization. The Transnationalization of Public Spheres in Europe: Trends and Patterns* (TranState Working Papers, 37). Bremen: Universität Bremen, http://www.staatlichkeit.uni-bremen.de.

Collins, Richard (2006) *Misrecognitions: positive and negative freedom in EU media policy and regulation, from Television without Frontiers to the Audiovisual Media Services Directive*. Paper presented at a conference on European media, democracy and Europe, Copenhagen.

Crum, Ben (2008) The EU *Constitutional Process. A Failure of Political Representation?* RECON Online Working Paper 2008/08. Oslo: University of Oslo.

Eriksen, Erik Oddvar and John Erik Fossum (2007) *Europe in transformation: How to reconstitute democracy?* RECON Online Working Paper 2007/01. Oslo: Center for European Studies, University of Oslo; http://www.recon-project.eu/projectweb/portalproject/RECONWorkingPapers.html

European Commission (2001) "Communication from the Commission on the application of State aid rules to public service broadcasting." *Official Journal of the European Communities*, 2001/C 320/04: 5–11.

European Commission (2005) *The Commission's contribution to the period of reflection and beyond: Plan-D for Democracy, Dialogue and Debate*, COM(2005) 494 final. Brussels: European Union

European Commission (2006) *White Paper on a European Communication Policy*. COM(2006) 35 final. Brussels: European Union

Golding, Peter (2006) *European Journalism and the European Public Sphere: Some thoughts on Practice and Prospects*. Paper presented at a conference on European media, democracy and Europe, Copenhagen.

Habermas, Jürgen (2008a) "Europejska bezsilność [European impotence]." *Dziennik/Europa*, July 5, http://www.dziennik.pl/dziennik/europa/ article203042/ Europejska_bezsilnosc.html

Habermas, Jürgen (2008b) "Zrozumieć Irlandczyków" [Let's Understand the Irish]. *Dziennik/Europa*, July 12, http://www.dziennik.pl/dziennik/europa/ article206116/Zrozumiec_Irlandczykow.html

Hume, Ellen (2011) Caught in the Middle: *Central and Eastern European Journalism at a Crossroads. A Report to the Center for International Media Assistance.* Washington, D.C.: Center for International Media Assistance. http://cima.ned.org.

Jakubowicz, Karol and Miklós Sükösd (2008) (eds.) *Finding the Right Place on the Map: Central and Eastern European Media Change in a Global Perspective.* Bristol: Intellect.

Kagan, Robert (2008) "Irlandzki cios" [The Irish Blow]. *Dziennik/Europa* June 28, http://www.dziennik.pl/ dziennik/europa/article199860/Irlandzki_cios. html

Klimkiewicz, Beata (2010) (ed.) *Media Freedom and Pluralism. Media Policy Challenges in the Enlarged Europe.* Budapest–New York: Central European University Press.

Krastev, Ivan (2008) "Europe's trance of unreality." *openDemocracy*, http:// www.opendemocracy.net/article/europe-s-trance-of-unreality.

Kroes, Neelie (2008) *Broadcasting Communication Review*. Speech during the French presidency conference on public service media in the digital age. Strasbourg, http://www.ddm.gouv.fr.

OSCE (2010) *Analysis and Assessment of a Package of Hungarian Legislation and Draft Legislation on Media and Telecommunications*. Prepared by Dr Karol Jakubowicz, Commissioned by the Office of the OSCE Representative on Freedom of the Media. Warsaw, Poland, September 2010 (57 ps) http:// www.osce.org/fom/71218.

Pomian, Krzysztof (2006) "Nikt nie rodzi się Europejczykiem" [No-one is Born a European]. In Conversation with Jacek Żakowski. In Jacek Żakowski, *Koniec*, Warszawa: Wydawnictwo Sic! 219–244.

Price, Monroe E. (1995) *Television, the public sphere, and national identity*. Oxford: Clarendon Press; New York: Oxford University Press.

Sorman, Guy (2008) "Dwie Europy" [Two Europes]. *Dziennik/Europa*, June 28, http://www.dziennik.pl/dziennik/europa/article199861/Dwie_Europy.html.

Verheugen, Günter (2008) "Nie zatrzymujmy integracji" [Let's Not Halt Integration]. *Dziennik/Europa*, July 12, http://www.dziennik.pl/dziennik/europa/ article206115/Europa_krok_po_kroku.html.

Wanlin, Aurore (2006) "Adieu, Europe?" *openDemocracy*, http://www.opendemocracy.net/democracy-europe_constitution/adieu_3694.jsp.

Section 1

THE EUROPEAN PUBLIC SPHERE
AND EUROPEAN INTEGRATION

CHAPTER 1

Transnationalization/Europeanization of the Public Sphere/s

Slavko Splichal

> The European peoples form a family in accordance with the
> universal principle underlying their legal codes, their cus-
> toms, and their civilization. This principle has modified their
> international conduct accordingly in a state of affairs [i.e.
> war] otherwize dominated by the mutual infliction of evils.
> The relations of state to state are uncertain, and there is no
> Praetor available to adjust them. The only higher judge is the
> universal absolute mind, the world mind.
>
> Hegel, *Philosophy of Right*

This chapter is not devoted primarily to the developments that *may*
lead or *do* lead to a genuine European public sphere, or that may or do
prevent its formation. My main interest is rather in conceptual modifications, innovations and aberrations—or more generally, attempts at
deconstructing and reconstructing the concepts of publicness and the
public sphere in a contemporary European (or even global) context, as
well as the reasons for those formulations.

Differences in conceptualization of the public sphere refer to its
ontological status (that is, how does the public sphere exist), its epis-
temological status, and its methodological implications (the key questions here being whether the public sphere is conceivable as an object
of empirical research; and if so, in what way should the concept be
made operational). Specifically, the differences may be outlined by
demonstrating how the concept of the public sphere is related to those
of the public(s), public opinion, and publicness in general.

The intellectual diversity in conceptualizations of the European
public sphere is certainly related to specific traditions that grasp the

phenomenon uniquely. The notion of a public sphere is largely rooted in democratic political theory but there are other important areas and lines of thought highlighting the processes constitutive of the public sphere. In addition to democratic theories, I list several approaches developed in communication and media studies, such as the political communication tradition (closely connected to democratic political theories), the political economy (of the media) and cultural studies, and I could also add others, such as feminist theories. In the first place, however, I should refer to the founders of the modern concept of publicness, Jeremy Bentham and Immanuel Kant, who have "encumbered" the intellectual history of publicness since its very beginning with antithetical conceptualizations of "the principle of publicness."

The concept of publicness that represents the very heart of the concept of the public sphere is in its strict sense a product of the Enlightenment and since its first appearances had a clearly critical sting—having been directed against the social and political structures of the traditional, pre-modern or pre-bourgeois society, and certain hereditary and authoritarian powers. The concept of the critique was central to the idea of publicness and to the ideas of Enlightenment in general.

In Kant's interpretation, the principle of publicness is not only fundamental to *citizen rights*, but also represents the fundamental principle of *democratic order*. Any regulation of relationships in (political) community would contradict the public interest and the citizens' freedom, if citizens cannot be convinced of its expediency by reason in the public realm, or if they are kept alienated and isolated from public communications that would enable them to discuss matters of common concern in public. The legitimacy of the state can only be grounded on the principle of publicness because the government can only hold authority over people if it represents the general will of the community.

In early debates, the idea of publicness pointed toward freedom of the press as a natural extension of personal freedom of thought and expression. However, soon after the press had been liberated from external censorship, it became an instrument of power based on property rights. With the discrimination in favor of the power/control function of the press embodied in the corporate "freedom of the press," the struggle for press freedom digressed from the Kantian quest for the public use of reason and his idea of publicness as a personal right and the basis of democratic citizenship. Moreover, privatization of the press largely removed the ground for a public discussion about what had been appropriated.

Since the beginning, however, publicness never referred only to one thing. It was always constituted by, and conceptualized to include, a number of competing and often contradictory tendencies in political, economic and cultural processes. It should be no surprize then that different conceptualizations of the public sphere and the public led to different (even opposing) answers to the question of the viability of the general concept of the "public sphere," and specifically of a "European public sphere." In contrast, with the growing role of the media, conceptualizations of publicness and public sphere became increasingly media-centric. Conversely, the idea of citizens' public use of reason—a critical indicator of autonomous power vested in the public sphere—was shoved off. It was the idea of publicness (including personal right to communicate) as the defining principle of the public sphere, which remains a blind spot in contemporary debates about European public sphere(s).

Key Issues in the Debates about the (European) Public Sphere

Except for its close connectedness with publicness, there are not many things that can be reliably said today about the public sphere in general, and even less about the European public sphere. The concept of the public sphere is no better defined than it was perhaps in the early Habermas' period before the translation of his *Strukturwandel der Öffentlichkeit* into English. The most obvious thing is that there is no consensus among scholars and practitioners (e.g., politicians) concerning what the constituents of the public sphere are; how it is or could be established; who may or should participate in it and how; and whether the public sphere is a cause or a consequence of democratic developments. The differences further extend in conceptualizing the role of communication—and specifically, the media—in democratic processes and defining publicness as the fundamental principle of the public sphere.

In the conceptual diversity of theoretical traditions, we can identify four major dimensions of the debates about the (European) public sphere:

(1) The structure of the public sphere and the constitution of the public/s which constitute the groundwork of the public sphere, in terms of technological and political *infrastructure*.

(2) The nature and functions of publicness and the communicative processes taking place in the public sphere and specifically, the nature of contents produced and publicized (broadcast) by the media (cultural and ethical "*infrastructure*").

(3) Linguistic tools that enable individuals to participate in the public sphere. The issue of a natural language seemed to be irrelevant as long as the public sphere has been technologically, politically and culturally limited to individual nation-states, i.e. the publics and the public sphere were considered strictly a "national matter." With economic, political and cultural processes of globalization, the question of language became part of the quintessential question of individual access to and participation in the public sphere.

(4) The development of a European public sphere ought to enable national publics (and perhaps a European public) to become visible on a larger scale through (a European) *public opinion*, which makes clear the difference between an authentic public communication and its power to discipline the people.

These issues are associated with three different intentions and discussed from three partly interwoven perspectives:

(1) Normative-theoretical perspective;
(2) Historical-empirical perspective;
(3) Practical-political perspective.

I will concentrate on these three perspectives referring primarily but not exclusively to the institutional (infra)structure of the public sphere.

1. Of all three intentions associated with the concept of public sphere at present, its *normative–theoretical meaning* seems to be most significant. As a normative-theoretical concept and project, the public sphere is a counter-factual ideal central to contemporary critical theory and political critique. In Europe, the notion of the European public sphere is deeply rooted in a rather general (political) dissatisfaction, both in theory and practice, with the neoliberal domination of economy and

global supremacy of corporate capital over political issues essential for democratic citizenship. It theoretically underpins critical reactions to, "[a] disproportion between the dense economic and rather lax political connectedness on the one hand, and the democratic deficit in the decision-making on the other hand" (Habermas, 2001: 63). The kind of elitist neglect of civic engagement Habermas is referring to is certainly not a specific European problem. It rather characterizes global political developments of the 21st century where, "[t]hose now attempting to implement a new world order seem to hold in disdain the unending and continuous civil discourse and dialogue in which we all can participate" (Shotter, 2003: 2).

As Benjamin Barber put it in a recent interview for *Logos*, "[w]e've got doctors without frontiers, we've got criminals without frontiers, we have capitalists without frontiers, and we have terrorists without frontiers. The one thing we're missing is: citizens without frontiers. The Democratic project, I believe, should rest on finding ways to create citizens without frontiers" (Barber in Aronowitz, 2004: 136-7).

There is only a handful of those believing that, "[i]n light of the possibilities and dangers posed by the new digital technologies, [...] critical and democratic theorists [should] jettison the idea of the public sphere and adopt a more complex model of civil society" because "the regulatory fiction of the public sphere privileges a theorization of political norms [while] struggles that contest, resist, or reject its idealizations are excluded from the political terrain as remnants of tradition, say, or manifestations of a terroristic irrationalism" (Dean, 2001. 247). Such position is similar to that of Niklas Luhmann who, more than thirty years ago, argued unconvincingly that the concept of the public was merely an "agrarian-historic concept" without any reference to practical existence or practical object" and thus "too undetermined, and for analytical and critical purposes an inappropriate category" (1974: 339-401).

I should add (in brackets) that the rejection of the concept of the public sphere as an irrelevant dimension of civil society or irrelevant concept compared to that of civil society, is "countered" by a denial—marginal again—of theoretical validity in the concept of "civil society" suggesting that it is merely a descriptive category. To be exhaustive, I should also add that for some others, civil society and the public sphere are essentially synonymous, or the public sphere is considered simply "a role" of civil society which thus "becomes the arena for argument and deliberation as well as for association and institutional collaboration" (Michael Edwards 2004). Yet all these "resistance movements" are of marginal relevance.

2. As a *historical–empirical category*, the concept of the public sphere is used to analyze and theorize social changes (in Europe and elsewhere) initiated by Enlightenment. However, the concept of the public sphere is more widely contested when applied to specific historic circumstances. Habermas himself warned against too extensive a use of the concept "the public," by suggesting that its full validity is limited to its historically specific meaning in England at the end of the seventeenth century, and in France of the eighteenth century (Habermas 1962/1995). In other words, the concept of public has a distinctive conceptual heterogeneity that is not defined only (or not primarily) by specific theoretical positions but is specifically defined *historically*.

I insist on the normative dimension of the concepts of the public sphere and publicness primarily—but not exclusively—for *historical reasons*. In a way, the normative-critical dimension of publicness is a modern "substitute" for the divine dimension once associated with the public, which the concept of the public sphere does not comprize any more.

When public opinion—or public opinion *tribunal* as it used to be called in the 18th century—became the superior authority and replaced in that position the king himself, it was considered, in empirical terms, a process in which individuals incorporated in the public, expressed approval or disapproval of an action in particular places. There were some references made to the concrete bearers of public opinion of the time. The public was not the people or citizenry at large but rather a small fraction, such as the men of letters, newspapers and their editors, and the bourgeois class, with specific tasks of public opinion such as surveillance of the execution of power. But public opinion and the public were never exclusively and exhaustively defined.

Yet the concept of the public and that of public opinion were not used primarily as descriptive concepts—to identify its concrete constituents or bearers; they had primarily a polemical, normative character. The public had challenged and eventually replaced the monarchic power but it retained the transcendental nature of the supreme authority. Public opinion was considered an almighty impersonal "tribunal," and the voice of public opinion, or the public voice, was nearly identical to the divine voice once exclusively belonging to monarchs. In theory, public opinion "replaced the powers of heaven and earth in returning men to possession of their decisions," but it had also preserved appeal to a divine authority that can never be disrespected (Ozouf, 1988: S11, S13). It is not by chance that Ferdinand Toennies in the 1920s compared the role of public opinion in *Gesellschaft* with that of religion in *Gemeinschaft*, as did many scholars before him.

Similarly to the "divine dimension" of public opinion, by using the concept "the public sphere," we also make suitability and necessity claims for certain regulation and conduct rather than merely describing the ways in which we in fact behave in empirical discursive situations. The *norm* of critical publicity is *the* fundamental and organizing principle of the public sphere. As I will try to show later, the dimension of normativity may also help us to draw clear distinctions between the critical-theoretical concepts of "publicness" and "public sphere," and the more descriptive, empirical concepts of "public" and "civil society". Public opinion, in contrast, was captured by both "sides," and not surprisingly so, as I will try to demonstrate.

A normative-historical approach is productive inasmuch as it links the present and the future. The results of a historical inquiry have to be tested—in terms of theory and practice—against the existing reality, from the point of view of its hypothetical future development, and alternatives in the past. It may help us to see what *could* have happened and what *can* happen due to specific circumstances. As Kant suggested in his defense of the "Platonian Republic," we should carefully follow up the ideas past, even if the past thinkers "left us without assistance," and "employ new efforts to place them in clearer light, rather than carelessly fling them aside as useless" (1781/1952, 174).

The normative dimension implies a *critical look* at intellectual and material *history* of publicness. This is particularly important because at present, the fascination with new information and communication technologies can easily veil their deep embedded character in the social structure, and also their ambivalent potential in relation to social visibility and publicness. It is important to realize that without an enhanced citizens' capacity to gain access to information and to communication media, they will remain deprived of opportunities to make democratic decisions. Yet the capacity of citizens to acquire information they need is largely a question of regulations and laws, not only of technology. The capacity of citizens to communicate with each other is largely a question of an appropriate media, but also of education and development of virtual or physical public spaces. The technical capacity of information and communication technologies has not totally transformed and devalued the importance of our generic ability and need to communicate, central to which is the capacity to communicate face to face. In a way, I think that those who call for alternative media today often fail to rediscover the potential of what we already have, in principle, available to us.

One of the reasons of controversies about the historical-descriptive and explanatory value of the public sphere among historians—and at large—is the troublesome translation of the German word *Öffentlichkeit*. The concept of the public sphere was introduced into English with the translation of Habermas' book *Strukturwandel der Öffentlichkeit* (1962), translated as *The Structural Transformation of the Public Sphere* (1989), and it rapidly and almost completely eliminated the traditional concept of "the public" from critical-theoretical discourse. The once prominent concept of "the public" that dominated for three hundred years—think of Dewey, Park, Lippmann, Blumer, Mills, not to speak of Bentham!—almost disappeared from theories dazzled with the splendour of the new concept. Of course, Habermas himself cannot be blamed for the confusion deriving from the translation, and even less for casting out the traditional concept of "the public."

Darnton suggests that the translation of Habermas' book *Strukturwandel der Öffentlichkeit* into French had an important negative consequence. The French word '*public*' has been largely 'replaced' by '*sphère publique*' which is, according to Darnton, a mistranslation of Habermas' concept '*Öffentlichkeit*.' As a result, 'French historians have attributed agency to this 'space' and made it the crucial factor, more important than ideas or public opinion, in the collapse of the Old Regime. In fact, spatial metaphors have proliferated so much in historical writing that they are choking out other modes of analysis' (Darnton, 2000). As Darnton ironically states, "A researcher who sets out to discover the public sphere is likely to find it wherever he or she looks and then perhaps to reify it—that is, to construe it as a force at work in history, an active agent which produces palpable effects, possibly even the French Revolution."

3. Finally, the concept of the public sphere also has *practical–political relevance*, which effectively refutes the argument of the "regulatory fiction" supposedly associated with the concept. This is particularly clear in the contemporary European political context.

According to the Treaty on European Union (2008), the European Union is normatively becoming a genuine way to create a transnational public sphere at least sub-globally. In Art II-10 and II-11, the Lisbon Treaty declares the principles of participatory and representative democracy. Specifically, the Constitution provides the right of European citizens "to participate in the democratic life of the Union" (I-46, Para 3). It further stipulates that EU institutions shall "give citizens and representative associations the opportunity to make known and publicly exchange their views in all areas of Union action" (Art II-11, Para 1). "Open, transparent and regular dialogue" by the Union institutions with representative associations and civil society shall take place (Para 2). However, the declaration of these principles and rights in the Lisbon Treaty is not followed by any more detailed provision aimed at enhancing European democracy.

Nevertheless, the idea of the (European) public sphere has an increasingly important legitimizing function in building (pan-European) democratic institutions. Some politicians and officials are still fearful that public engagement might comprize a threat to effective policy-making and good governance. But given an overwhelming evidence of public distrust of national and particularly European political institutions after French and Dutch citizens having voted "no" on the proposed EU Constitution, they are recognizing that "democracy can flourish only if citizens know what is going on, and are able to participate fully," as the European Commission claimed in the White Paper "On a European Communication Policy" (COM(2006)35 final, February 1, 2006).

The Commission attributes "a sense of alienation from 'Brussels'" that has been identified among citizens with "the inadequate development of a 'European public sphere' where a European debate can unfold." While the Commission seems to have found *the* solution to close "the gap between the European Union and its citizens," it obviously still feels uneasy about the European public sphere. Throughout the White Paper, the expression "European public sphere" (in contrast to the public sphere in general) is used in quotation marks.

If this "fundamentally new approach—a decisive move away from one-way communication to reinforced dialogue, from an institution-centered to a citizen centered communication," as described by the Commission, will indeed materialize, remains to be seen. Only half a year earlier, the Commission similarly had expressed a "renewed commitment to communication with Europe's citizens" in its "Action Plan to Communicating Europe by the Commission" (July 2005), and drafted 22 specific actions to achieve that goal. However, 19 of them merely comprized measures to be taken by the Commission to make its communication (or "public relations," strictly speaking) more noticeable and effective (including "cooperation with journalists"). Only three actions were planned to step up citizens' participation.

Public Sphere/s in the Era of Globalization

Declared efforts to enable European citizens to participate in the democratic life of the European Union beyond their respective national institutions bring us to the question of the nature of the public sphere that would pave the way for such participation. In theory, this practical question may be decomposed into three subsets of questions related to:

(1) decentralization,
(2) transnationalization of the public sphere,
(3) the development of a "strong" public sphere and its relation to "the public".

DECENTRALIZATION OF THE PUBLIC SPHERE

One of the first critiques of shortcomings of the early Habermas' work on *Öffentlichkeit* was that he misconceived of the public sphere as having one single authoritative center. Rather, it was suggested, the ideal of equal participation in public debates is better referred to by thinking of a "plurality of competing publics." "Publics" (not: "public spheres"!) in plural may indeed better represent the diversity of interests in any given society. But a "plurality of competing publics" does not necessarily entail the "plurality of public spheres" as the critic suggested (Fraser, 1992: 116–7), even if the relation between competing publics is conflicting. Yet public(s) and public sphere(s) are not the same thing!

There is no public without a public sphere, and no public sphere without a public. They are inseparably connected to each other—like a system and its component which must produce results congruent with the defined goal, or else they are "dysfunctional." But nevertheless, the difference between the two is important and we have to draw a clear analytical distinction.

The (political) public sphere is defined by Habermas (1992/1997: 446) as "all those conditions of communication under which there can come into being a discursive formation of opinion and will on the part of a public composed of the citizens of a state." It is a specific sphere, domain, or imagined space of social life existing between and constituted by the state and civil society, which represents an infrastructure for social integration through public discourse—a kind of "opinion market." In contrast, a/the public is a specific grouping that appears or is imagined as a social actor or agent (once a "tribunal") in relation to some important and controversial social issues (traditionally conceptualized in contrast to the crowds or the masses). The existence of a public sphere is vital for a public to become visible through public opinion, and an acting public is a necessary condition for a public sphere to really exist. The public sphere is safeguarded only when economic and social conditions give everyone an equal chance to meet the criteria for admission to the public sphere.

It is important to keep in mind that both a public and a public sphere are established in communication among strangers and even enemies, as Toennies wrote, only "if the need to talk is strong enough." There can be various circumstances for a conversation in community or society, which may help bring about "a public." But "a public" is always distinct from community and society. Most importantly, without newspapers and other large-scale communication media, communication "from stranger to stranger," a true publicness would never be possible.

Publicness is a creature of 'stranger sociability' and relatively large-scale communications media, starting with print. Publics connect people who are not in the same families, communities, and clubs; people who are not the same as each other. Urban life is public, thus, in a way village life is not. Modern media amplify this capacity to communicate with strangers. And communication itself is vital, for it both creates shared culture and enables debate (Calhoun, 2005: 5).

It goes without saying that a plurality of publics has always existed, as Toennies has suggested. With the proliferation of communication media, there are more and more opportunities for the formation of new publics and "counter publics" associated with specific social issues. Some social scientists suggest that there are as many publics as there are different social issues. To the extent that social issues are partly individually constructed, we could end up with as many publics as individuals, or at least as many as the number of "site[s] of a temporary intersection of two 'network domains,' which may be individuals" (Ikegami, 2000). Such a "deconstruction" of the concept shifts it from the public-political life to "any intersection of two individuals" as the smallest "micropublic" tracks, for all intents and purposes. The empirical sociological tradition tried to reduce public opinion to the smallest possible entity—any public expression of an individual opinion, and eventually even a private expression in a "public opinion" poll. In both cases, the idea of an understanding that is formed in public deliberation is completely discarded, and accordingly, the concept of either the public sphere or public opinion depoliticized. Without the political dimension, however, the two concepts are simply irrelevant for democratic theory "for the promize of the public sphere is in part to shape a common understanding of how different issues relate to each other and what priority they should have in public action" (Calhoun, 2005:5). While, with some reservation, we may think of multiple publics as independently existing (forming opinions about different issues) or even competing actors in the public sphere (similarly to civil society in singular which includes many different groups, arenas of activism, and social networks), "deconstructing" the public sphere into many spheres is a much greater trial. The public sphere is [t]he structured setting where cultural and ideological contest or negotiation among a variety of publics takes place" (Eley, 1992: 306). It is a kind of communication network radiating public opinion—

a social phenomenon just as elementary as action, actor, association, or collectivity, [which] eludes the conventional sociological concepts of "social order." The public sphere cannot be conceived as an institution and certainly not as an organization. ... Just as little does it represent a system. ... The public sphere can best be described as a network for communicating information and points of view [...]; the streams of communication are, in the process, filtered and synthesized in such a way that they coalesce into bundles of topically specified *public opinions* (Habermas, 1992/1997: 360).

The public sphere is thus the context of public opinion, its "infrastructure" rather than its generator, which is always a public. Thus according to Calhoun,

> [t]he public sphere is thus a crucial dimension of civil society. Civil society without a strong public sphere lacks opportunities for participation in collective choice, whether about specific policy issues or basic institutions. The public sphere is also a medium of social integration, a form of social solidarity, as well as an arena for debating possible social arrangements. People are knit together not only by cultural similarity, in other words, but by the opportunity to discuss issues with each other and even to consider differences (Calhoun, 2005: 4).

"Dissection" of a public sphere into a multitude of public spheres would put civil society—and society as such—at a radical risk.

A fundamental difference between the public and the public sphere is in their relation to the organized power (e.g. the state). The public sphere is inseparably connected with the organized power which is one of the actors in the public sphere and, at the same time, its legal guarantor. In contrast, a public is formed more or less *in opposition* to the organized power—an idea inscribed both in Bentham's concept of the public opinion tribunal and Kant's concept of the public use of reason.

A public sphere of multiple publics is always charged with dynamics of power. Some authors tend to speak of "strong" and "weak" publics according to the amount of decision-making power they accumulate. "Weak publics" are characterized by deliberative practice which "consists exclusively in opinion formation and does not also encompass decision making." It is a sound idea to analyze the interrelationships and hierarchical structures of publics to understand their efficacy.

We shouldn't tacitly assume that publics are not interrelated, or—if an interrelation is recognized—that differences between them are independent of power relations. Whether the proper measure of efficacy of publics is their decision-making power is another question.

But more importantly, the validity of the efficacy claim is not transferable to public spheres. What is "good" for a public is not necessarily "good" for the public sphere. Unfortunately, the difference between the public and the public sphere is often blurred in the efficacy discourse. It is suggested that with the emergence of parliamentary sovereignty, parliaments have been constituted, "as a *public sphere within the state*. ... [S]overeign parliaments are [...] strong publics, publics whose discourse encompasses both opinion formation and decision making" (Fraser, 1992: 134; emphasis added). This radical turn that somehow follows Dewey's idea of the public incorporation of the state (1927) is strongly opposed not only to Habermas' conceptualization of the public sphere but also to the first indigenously defined concept of the public—that of Bentham.

If we follow this dichotomy, we can only conclude that, with the establishment of the European Parliament and–to a limited extent because of its limited mandate–the Parliamentary Assembly of the Council of Europe (PACE), a "strong European public (sphere)" came into existence. Unfortunately, I'm afraid that there is a much longer way to get there.

TRANSNATIONALIZATION OF THE PUBLIC SPHERE

One of the fundamental questions in contemporary debates about the European public sphere is about the nature of the relationship between "national" and "European" public sphere, if they indeed should be conceived of as two different entities.

The ideas of transnational public sphere and cosmopolitan democracy are obvious reactions to the development of a complex, interconnected but at the same time diversified and hierarchically stratified world in which we live. Local, national, regional (subglobal) and global issues, policies and actions affect us individually and collectively, but mechanisms are lacking that would enable citizens to act effectively beyond the national frame. The normative requirement of the public sphere to be both a forum for citizens' deliberation generating public opinion, as well as a medium for mobilizing public opinion as a political force, makes it necessary that a public sphere and a sovereign power correlate with each other.

Traditionally, national public spheres were dominated by the pursuit of national interests, eventually supported by force. This may well remain into the future but nevertheless, the relation between the nation state and national public (sphere) is significantly changing. In the period of globalization, conceptualizations of the public sphere are challenged by a tacit assumption implicitly woven into the concept of the *nation-state*. Paradoxically, this is less true of the more traditional concept of the public.

While Dewey could have conceptualized the public as a political state, as "the organization of the public effected through officials for the protection of the interests shared by its members," the states of the 21st century definitely lost the exclusive power of "guardians of custom, as legislators, as executives, or judges" who may effectively protect the interests of the public by regulating actions of individuals and groups. Traditionally, the state was indeed able to regulate direct and indirect consequences of transactions to which people not directly involved were exposed, but today states are not the exclusive regulator of those transactions. But while they lost this exclusive "privilege," they also acquired a new one: today decisions made by states have implications not only for their own citizens but also for others who can hardly act as a public in a Deweyan sense in relation to a "foreign" state. In others words, while formerly there was a symmetric relationship between national public(s) and the nation state which was held responsible to and by them, in a "postnational constellation" the state and public sphere became much more vaguely associated.

An often implicit understanding of the public sphere as a national phenomenon prevailed throughout history. Or rather, due to empirical circumstances, this question never attracted theoretical concern. On the one hand, such a tacit assumption implied that a large number of publics may have existed—in principle, there may be as many publics as there are nation-states. On the other hand, it implicitly denied the possible existence of publics not correlated to the state. Why should a nation have the privilege of generating the public? Why can't other types of collectivities also have their own publics and/or public spheres?

Although there is no doubt that the public—and similarly the public sphere and civil society—has generally retained a tacitly assumed national label until very recently, it is hard to find any author for whom the state, and particularly the nation-state and national boundaries, would have a constitutive role in theorizing the public (sphere). I would argue that the international dimension was not really a blind spot in theorizing the public and public opinion for a long time. On the contrary, and explicitly, the public was not seen as existing exclusively under the safeguard of a nation state.

Let me briefly refer to three outstanding theorists who grappled with the international dimension of public opinion already a century ago.

For Gabriel Tarde, a proponent of the "European federation" in the late 19th century, it was precizely the permanent tendency toward internationalization—similar to that of human reason—which significantly differentiated public opinion and public spirit from tradition or "traditional national spirits". Tarde argued that journalism succeeded "to nationalize the public spirit little by little and internationalize it even more and more" (Tarde, 1901: 44), and that the newspaper "finished the age-old work that conversation began, that correspondence extended, but that always remained in a state of a sparse and scattered outline—the fusion of personal opinions into local opinions, and this into national and *world* opinion, the grandiose unification of the Public Spirit" (p. 83).

Following Tarde, Ferdinand Tönnies discussed explicitly opinion formation by the international public, and even public opinion representing "the entire civilized humanity" (Tönnies, 1922: 137). As a matter of fact, the earliest experiential forms of the publics in the Middle Ages were typically "transnational" (or transregional, i.e., traversing administrative units). This was largely enabled by Latin as the *lingua franca* among intellectuals and brought about by the scarcity of literate individuals. A clear example presented by Tönnies was the theologians who represented an international, educated public with internal differences of opinion. Like religion, *"Zeitgeist,"* which in Tönnies' theory "moves between liquid and firm states" of public opinion, is an exemplary form of public opinion that transcends national borders and is international by its very nature.

Similarly to Tönnies, John Dewey emphasized the time and space variability of the public, caused by differences in "the consequences of associated action and the knowledge of them" and in "the means by

which a public can determine the government to serve its interests."
Dewey conceptualized the public as a consequence of transactions between individuals and (nonpolitical) groups that affect individuals and
groups not involved in these transactions. The public therefore occurs
because of the need for the (legal) regulation of such consequences,
and regulation is only possible through the political organization of the
public—which was, in concrete historical circumstances, the state.

Even if Dewey defined the state as an organizational form of the
public, and the public as "a political state." The state only meant political organization with the task "to care for its special interests by
methods intended to regulate the conjoint actions of individuals and
groups" (Dewey, 1927/1954: 35). According to his definition, the state
"is founded on the exercize of a function, not on any inherent essence
or structural nature" (p. 77). The public always implies the state, according to Dewey, but only in the sense by which also a war or an
earthquake "includes in its consequences all elements in a given territory." This means that they have immense consequences for an entire
territory, but this does not imply that the inclusion is "by inherent nature or right" (p. 72).

According to Dewey, history clearly reveals that diversity rather
than uniformity of political forms is the rule, which demonstrates that
the nature of consequences and the ability to perceive them and act
upon them varies with time and space. The loose status of the (nation-)
state in his conceptualization of the public is quite clear from Dewey's
observation that "in no two ages or places is there the same public"
and that "states may pass through federations and alliances into a
larger whole which has some of the marks of the statehood" (Dewey
1927/1954: 48, 88).

In other words, either explicitly or implicitly, a higher level of regulation and decision making than the nation state was foreseen as correl-
ative to the publics long ago. Dewey's concept of the public, for example, directly calls for an appropriate deliberative and decision-making
(infra)structure beyond the nation-state retaining "some of the marks
of the statehood" to be used by those significantly affected by transnational consequences of (inter)national transactions, which would constitute them as a transnational "public." Thus we could speak of (the
possibility of) a transnationalization of publics that parallels the formation of transnational political communities with their own regulatory

means (e.g., the European Union), although such means do not imply that nation-states are dying out.

Nowadays the general public is loosely associated with the *national* population primarily for empirical reasons—because this is the only "definition" that makes survey research and polling based on random sampling possible, and because the most powerful actors "appearing *before* the public," such as large interest groups and political parties, draw on this type of research as a resource of their power. We can identify in such practice a "tacit assumption of nationalist rhetoric [that] reinforces our acceptance of state-centered conventions of data-gathering that make nation-states the predominant units of comparative research—even when the topics are cultural or social psychological, not political-institutional" (Calhoun, 1999: 218). Even "European" polls, such as 'Eurobarometer' conducted on behalf of the European Commission, are focused on the comparison of "national public opinions" rather than on processes of "Europeanization" of public opinion. The aggregation of individual opinions is still confined to the level of the nation-state. Similarly, analysis of media contents must focus on national media because only a handful of genuinely transnational media exist.

But this is not to say that other forms of communication particularly relevant for the public sphere are not being inter- and transnationalized to a much higher degree. With new forms of communication that are emerging, citizens' involvement in public debate may become more spontaneous and less rigid than before. Internet is the prime example, with recent developments—such as blogs, wiki sites and collaborative filtering tools—empower individuals to make possible the construction of new communities and spaces of shared interest.

A telling example of opening up opportunities for transnational debate in Europe is *Eurozine*. By translating texts from approximately one hundred cultural periodicals from almost every European country into one of the widely-spoken European languages, and presenting them together with some original texts on controversial issues on the web site, *Eurozine* creates a possibility for texts to be understood and valued outside of their original national context. *Eurozine* stimulates a common cultural discourse among an international readership in pretty much the same way as newspapers of the 18th century helped to create "literary publics" that easily gained in terms of political significance.

The loose association of European cultural journals and their readers perhaps most closely resembles a definition of the European public sphere. These journals stimulate a genuinely international debate, spreading political, philosophical, aesthetic, and cultural thought between languages. They reflect the multiplicity of issues, questions and problems which affect and bind people together irrespective of whether they are in one nation-state or another. But we also need to develop democratic political institutions that would parallel this process and respond to and regulate consequences of transnational transactions by which trans-border or transnational groupings are affected, and which lower (national) levels of decision-making cannot manage to regulate effectively.

Since we increasingly live in a world of "multiple citizenships"— both national and transnational or cosmopolitan—and there exist, as I indicated, public spheres that are not confined to national borders, it is necessary to distinguish between different levels of the institutionalization of public debate. In the European context, this primarily calls for a clear conceptualization of possible forms of Europeanization of communication and discursive mobilization. Three forms are suggested (Koopmans and Erbe, 2004):

(1) The emergence of a *supranational European public sphere* constituted by the interaction among European-level institutions and collective actors around European themes, ideally accompanied by (and creating the basis for) the development of European wide mass media.

(2) *Vertical Europeanization*, which consists of communicative linkages between the national and the European level. There are two basic variants of this patterns, a bottom-up one in which national actors address European actors and/or make claims on European issues, and a top-down one, in which European actors intervene in national policies and public debates in the name of European regulations and common interests.

(3) *Horizontal Europeanization*, which consists of communicative linkages between different member states. We may distinguish between a weak and a strong variant. In the weak variant, the media in one country cover debates and contests in another member state, but there is no linkage between the countries in the

structure of claim making itself. In the stronger variant, actors from one country explicitly address or refer to actors or policies in another member state.

This is an accurate description of the Europeanization processes on the level of "institutions and collective actors," but a less appropriate account of citizens' capacities to transcend national borders in public debate. This discrepancy brings us to the question of what actually generates the strength and effectiveness of the public sphere. Is it indeed the decision-making power as some theorists suggest?

A "STRONG" (EUROPEAN) PUBLIC SPHERE

Marx Ferree et al. (2002) grappled with the intellectual diversity in theoretical definitions and operationalization of the public sphere in political theory by identifying four "traditions of democratic theory": Representative Liberal, Participatory Liberal, Discursive, and Constructionist. These competing traditions in their conceptualization of the public sphere are restricted to the ideas prevailing in the second half of the 20th century and focused on "mass media discourse in 'actually existing democracies.'"

In short, four operational criteria were used to identify the differences: (1) *who* should speak, (2) the content of the process (*what*), (3) style of speech preferred (*how*), and (4) the relationship between discourse and decision-making (*outcomes*) that is sought (or feared). As Marx Ferree et al. (2002: 316–17) suggest, different normative criteria for "a good democratic discourse" are decisive in different traditions. For the representative liberal tradition it is the question of expertize (elite dominance). For the participatory tradition it is the question of what the process of engagement in public debate is and does (empowerment). For the discursive tradition it is mutual respect and civility of the dialogue. Finally for the constructionists it is the expansion of political community and the avoidance of exclusionary closure of debates. It is only "the representative liberal tradition "valuing *elite inclusion* over stronger and more active versions of *popular inclusion*" (p. 317). In other words, popular inclusion is among those normative criteria widely accepted and least resisted by democratic theorists (Splichal, 2006).

This analysis of democratic theories brings us close to Barber's concept of "strong democracy". The key dimension of Barber's conception of "strong democracy," as contrasted with traditional concepts of liberal democracy, is in the emphasis on citizen participation in central issues of public debate. Barber argues that the conceptualization of democracy should not be reduced to its institutional forms, but should rather take into consideration the participation of people in the process. In other words, Barber's "strong democracy" presupposes a developed, and I may say, *"strong" public sphere.*

This of course is far from being an idea distinctive of the second half of the 20th century. Barber himself explains what he means by "strong democracy" by quoting what Dewey said of democracy: "Democracy is not a form of government, it is a way of life." Thus popular inclusion is essential for Barber's concept of "strong democracy," which emphasizes opportunities for different kinds of citizens' participation and civic engagement at the national and the local level. It is fundamental for "strong democracy" that civic participation and engagement spread across the borders and across different sectors of society.

With *no* public use of reason in the media, which is based on the right of citizens to be heard, there is no democracy. With public use of reason *only* in the media, there is no democracy either. Democracy also rests on the principle of dialogue, not only mass dissemination. As Habermas states, "[p]arliamentary opinion- and will-formation must remain anchored in the informal streams of communication emerging from public spheres that are open to all political parties, associations, and citizens" (1992/1996: 171). The informal sphere of opinion formation and expression, which influences political decision making, has to be separated from the institutional sphere of formal political proceedings aimed at reaching decisions. The two spheres have to be constitutionally protected as autonomous spheres enabling discursive formation of will. Neither of them must be, as Habermas emphasizes, "organized like corporate bodies," but they should differ in conditions of communication, which also lead to differences in terms of accessibility of the two spheres.

In particular, as Habermas emphasizes, "we must distinguish the actors who, so to speak, emerge from the public and take part in the reproduction of the public sphere itself from the actors who occupy an already constituted public domain in order to use it," or between the actors, usually only laxly organized, who "emerge from" the public and those merely "appearing before" the public (Habermas, 1992/1996: 364, 375). For Habermas, this is not just a difference between endogenous and exogenous actors. He assumes that "the public sphere together with its public must have developed as a structure that stands on its own and reproduces itself *out of itself*"—which is *per se* a valid assumption—*before* actors with strategic intent can illegitimately capture it, which would always enable those "latent forces" to recapture it. It is not clear, however, how could "strategic actors" be excluded from the *constitution* of the public sphere? If we only take the example of the press, this assumption seems untenable. The *constitutional guarantee* of (negative) freedom of the press also gives constitutional protection to private business of publishing newspapers. There is no public sphere without the press; thus historically, the public sphere was "infected" by strategic (profit) interests almost with the very act of its constitution.

Nevertheless, taking Habermas' juxtaposition of "legitimate influence" vs. "actual influence" seriously, the question appears as how to bring "actual influence" closer to its "legitimate" model? Habermas' judgment seems to be too optimistic: "[p]ublic opinions that can acquire visibility only because of an undeclared infusion of money or organizational power lose their credibility as soon as these sources of social power are made public. Public opinion can be manipulated but neither publicly bought nor publicly blackmailed" (p. 364).

The trouble is that those "public opinions" are legitimized by the very fact that they appear in the mass media—the most trustful actor of all the actors appearing in front of the public! It makes sense, as Habermas proposes, to test empirically "the relation between actual influence and the procedurally grounded quality of public opinion," since actual influence of public opinion does not necessary coincide with legitimate influence. Yet his conclusion about incorruptibility of public opinion refers only to the extreme case of immoral power sources, whereas—as the *empirical* evidence shows—at the same time the whole advertising and public relations industry is based on a now legitimate "infusion of money or organizational power" to promote opinions. Habermas's optimism assumes, as in a fairy tale, that justice eventually always wins out. My experience (more than mere pessimism) is saying that even in the long run this may not always be true.

A European Public Sphere—Can We See It?

The confusion about the nature of the European public sphere becomes even greater when one tries to answer such a "simple" empirical question, as whether or not a European public sphere does (already) exist. Obviously, different conceptualizations would lead to divergent assessments of empirical evidence in favor or against a European public sphere. Similarly to what has happened with the empirical concept of public opinion in the 1930s, more empirically oriented approaches toward the European public sphere tacitly assume a sort of "lowest-common-denominator" when defining the European public sphere. This approach seems to be more "rewarding" than grasping the concept of the public sphere "as a crucial category for a critical examination of the contemporary situation" (Hohendahl, 1992: 100).

Some social scientists, for example, draw a distinction between two models of the European public/ness that either (1) *transcends* individual countries or (2) *integrates* or "*Europeanizes*" national publics (Gerhards, 2000). The latter seems to be more realistic, according to Gerhards, because it does not imply the necessity to surmount huge language differences within the European Union (which is implied by the first model), but involves only: "(1) thematization of European themes and actors in the national public spheres on the one hand, and (2) assessment of themes and actors in a non-nation-state perspective on the other" (p. 293).

Others operationalize the European public sphere as "political communication about the same issues under similar aspects of relevance" and "as a watchdog of policy making and politics" (Eder and Kantner, 2000), thus reducing it to the circulation of the same issues in different national public spheres and mass media with a more or less explicit European frame of reference—i.e., a kind of "uniformities" observed in the media.

Such media-centered operationalizations of the (European) public sphere may help in collecting some useful data about the images of Europe in the media, editorial gate-keeping and agenda-setting, but they are clearly limited. It is exactly the way how "a researcher who sets out to discover the public sphere is likely to find it wherever he or she looks and then perhaps to reify it" (Darnton, 2000). Furthermore, the critical question remains to what extent the European public sphere which should be shaped by, or help give rize to, democratic developments in Europe depart from the nation-state "model" supposedly hidden in the original concept of the public (sphere).

As long as conceptual differences are considered only "a matter of theoretical definition," *any* operational definition may be attributed some validity because it *seems* that the "objective" empirical world is less complex than its "subjective" theorization. It is true that a "more empirical concept" usually "encounters fewer problems," as it is argued (van de Steeg, 2000: 507), but unfortunately this is not to say that it is more valid. The reduction of the empirical concept of the public sphere to what one can find in the mass media because, as it is argued, "[i]n the end, what the general public gets to see of the public debate is that *which* is reported by the media, and, especially, *as* it is reported by the media," tacitly (but wrongly) assumes that what is reported by the media is genuinely discussed in the public sphere. Arguably, in this way "the public sphere is studied to the extent that the mass media is a forum for it" (van de Steeg, 2002: 507), but such a by-passing of conceptual problems cannot eliminate any peril of theoretical uncertainty that would be greater than the reduction itself.

For the same reason for which "public opinion" should not be confused with polling results, "public sphere" (and also "public opinion" for that matter) should not be confused with the results of media analysis. This kind of results may provide a certain reflection on the public sphere only if "they have been preceded by a focused public debate and a corresponding opinion formation in a mobilized public sphere" (Habermas, 1992/1996: 362). Media content is not representative in a statistical sense of either "what the general public gets to see" or of "the 'texts' emanating from the interaction of people in public debate." Not only members of the public(s) may use, in addition to the general news media, other and different sources, but also each member interprets what s/he uses (sees and hears) individually. Otherwize, the public is considered as if it imploded into a mass audience of media consumers. In addition, as Dewey (1927/1954: 35), suggested, the themes themselves do not determine what is of concern to the public; but actions, which are evaluated and have consequences. These determine the way in which the public sphere develops.

To make it worse, if following Habermas' distinction between the loosely organized actors emerging *from* the public and much more re-source- and powerful actors merely appearing *before* the public (p. 375), it is everywhere the case that indigenous actors who alone can repro-duce the public sphere influence the contents of the media much less than powerful commercial groups and political agents. Rather, as Niklas Luhmann suggested, in such circumstances public opinion becomes an "inner media" of political system, a mirror "generated by mass media to regulate the watching of the observers." With its help, politicians ob-serve themselves, their adversaries, and ordinary people, who are mere observers (Luhmann, 1994: 63). As a consequence, the picture we get from quantitative or qualitative media analysis only is distorted—the only question is, by how much—and thus media contents cannot be considered a valid operationalization of the public sphere.

I would conclude by suggesting that although the public sphere has been challenged and compromised there is no substitute for it nei-ther in national nor post-national democratic constellations. Improv-ing our capacity to articulate ideas about the public sphere will help to make it more relevant for democratic processes. This is particularly vi-tal in order to deal better with the transnational consequences of trans-actions among either national or trasnational actors.

References

Aronowitz, S. (2004) "A Conversation with Benjamin Barber." *Logos* 3, 4, 127–139.

Calhoun, C. (1999) "Nationalism, Political Community and the Representa-tion of Society. Or, Why Feeling at Home Is not a Substitute for Public Space." *European Journal of Social Theory* 2, 2, 217–231.

Calhoun, C. (2005) *Rethinking the Public Sphere*. Presentation to the Ford Foundation, 7 February 2005.

Darnton, R. (2000) *An Early Information Society*. Online Discussion Archive: Topic and Reply 2, available at http://www.historycooperative.org/ahr/darnton_files/darnton/discussion/d02.html.

Dean, J. (2001) "Cybersalons and Civil Society: Rethinking the Public Sphere in Transnational Technoculture." *Public Culture* 13, 2, 243–265.

Dewey, J. (1927/1954) *The Public and Its Problems*. Athens: Swallow.

Eder, K. and C. Kantner. (2000) "Transnationale Resonanzstrukturen in Eu-ropa. Eine Kritik der Rede vom Öffentlichkeitsdefizit." *Kölner Zeitschrift für Soziologie und Sozialpsychologie*, 52(Sonderheft 40): 306–331.

Eley, G. (1992) "Nations, Publics and Political Cultures: Placing Habermas in the Nineteenth Century." In C. Calhoun (ed.), *Habermas and the Public Sphere*, 289–339. Cambridge: The MIT Press.

European Commission. (2005) *Action Plan to Communicating Europe by the Commission* (July 2005).

European Commission. (2006) *White Paper "On a European Communication Policy"* (COM(2006)35 final, February 1, 2006).

Fraser, N. (1992) "Rethinking the Public Sphere: A Contribution to the Critique of Actually Existing Democracy." In C. Calhoun (ed.), *Habermas and the Public Sphere*, 109–142. Cambridge: The MIT Press.

Gerhards, J. (2000) "Europäisierung von Ökonomie und Politik und die Trägheit der Entstehung einer europäischen Öffentlichkeit." *Kölner Zeitschrift für Soziologie und Sozialpsychologie* 52, Sonderheft 40, 277–305.

Habermas, J. (2001) "Warum braucht Europa eine Verfassung?" *Deutschland* 6, 62–65.

Habermas, J. (1962) *Strukturwandel der Öffentlichkeit*. Neuwied: Luchterhand.

Habermas, J. (1962/1995) *The Structural Transformation of the Public Sphere: An Inquiry into a Category of Bourgeois Society*. Cambridge: MIT Press.

Habermas, J. (1992/1996) *Between Facts and Norms. Contributions to a Discourse Theory of Law and Democracy*. Cambridge: Polity Press.

Hohendahl, P. U. (1992) "The Public Sphere: Models and Boundaries." In C. Calhoun (ed.), *Habermas and the Public Sphere*, 99–108. Cambridge, MA: MIT Press.

Ikegami, E. (2000) "A Sociological Theory of Publics: Identity and Culture as Emergent Properties in Networks." *Social Research*, Winter 2000, available at http://www.findarticles.com.

Kant, I. (1781) *The Critique of Pure Reason*, trans. J.M.D. Miklejohn, available at http://www.e-text.org/text/Kant%20Immanuel%20-%20The%20Critique%20of%20Pure%20Reason.pdf.

Koopmams, R. and J. Erbe. (2004) "Towards a European public sphere? Vertical and Horizontal Dimensions of Europeanized Political Communication." *Innovation* 17, 2, 97–118.

Luhmanm, N. (1974) "Öffentliche Meinung." In W. R. Langenbucher (ed.), *Zur Theorie der politischen Kommunikation*. München: R. Piper Verlag.

Luhmann, N. (1994) "An Interview with D. Sciulli." *Theory, Culture and Society* 11, 2, 37–69.

Marx Ferree, M., W. A. Gamson, J. Gerhards, D. Rucht. (2002) "Four Models of the Public Sphere in Modern Democracies." *Theory and Society* 31, 289–324.

Ozouf, M. (1988) "'Public Opinion' at the End of the Old Regime." *Journal of Modern History* 60 Suppl., S1–S21.

Shotter, J. (2003) "In Defense of Public Spheres and Public Goods." *Concepts and Transformation* 8, 1, 1–23.

Splichal, S. (2006) "In search of a strong European public sphere: some critical observations on conceptualizations of publicness and the (European) public sphere." *Media, Culture & Society* 18, 5, 695–714.

Tarde, G. (1901) *L'opinion et la foule*. Paris: Felix Alcan, available at http://pages.infinit.net/sociojmt.

Tönnies, F. (1922) *Kritik der öffentlichen Meinung*. Berlin: Julius Springer.

van de Steeg, M. (2002) "Rethinking the Conditions for a Public Sphere in the European Union." *European Journal of Social Theory* 5, 4, 499–519.

CHAPTER 2

What is Europe? Geographies of Journalism

Inka Salovaara-Moring

Introduction: Manufacturing Europe

The extraordinary political changes of the last decade were but the visible element of a massive re-organization of European power geometry in which all the countries were forced to seek their place in a new setting.[1] An enlarged European Union saw its border shift a considerable distance eastwards, as it simultaneously began to negotiate its southern frontier. This new territorial order reignited discussion on the nature of "Europe" as a territorial, cultural, and institutional entity, a discussion in which radical alterations in thinking on what Europe could be as a cultural area were particularly prominent. As French historian Jacques le Goff remarked, "Europe has had a name for twenty-five centuries, but it is still in the design stage."[2]

Territorial transformations have been comparatively intensive in Central and Eastern Europe. Thus the construction of this part of Europe is particularly interesting because many of the new member states are still both in a state of genesis and of liminality (Schöp-flin, 2000: 174). Genesis in this case implies that the nature of the new order (symbolic, power-formation and ideological) is fluid with many options available to these societies. Liminality as a concept refers to the cultural sphere where old and new elements are reconfigured, leading to the rules and norms organizing society that are very elusive. It is clear that in Europe, as well as its constituent regions, all

---

[1] Doreen Massey's concept 'power geometry' refers to a spatial matrix of power relations in which regions evolve as physical and temporal processes (see Massey 2005).

[2] See Garton Ash 2004: 63.

these territorial transformations can be seen as historically contingent processes that are part of larger-scale economic, political and cultural transformations.

The role of journalism specifically, and political communication in general, is at the core of manufacturing narratives on cultural identities and the new sense of space. Media representations, by and large, translate and interpret the fluid elements by planting new elements of narratives into people's minds. Consequently, journalism is an activity that intensifies the formation of knowledge about territorial entities in order to clarify what gets excluded from, and included in, these entities. The function of social communication, and hence journalism is to re-produce cultural orders, and organize them around value systems and common meanings to produce what is considered to be preferable and "normal."

Journalists themselves can be seen as important actors in the formation of narratives on new spatial imageries. The role of journalistic actors, the positions they take in various cultural constellations, and especially the value systems that imbue them are salient in understanding cultural change in a broader comparative European framework. Thus, domesticating Europe is not only translating transnational processes for a domestic audience but also creating an understanding of European issues and what "Europe" means as an organized experience.

This chapter asks "What is Europe?" following the redefinition of the Continent's centers and peripheries in the last decade. Its main focus is on articulations of new spatial imaginaries formed by members of journalistic elites in Brussels and the capitals of new Europe. To analyze complex relations between new discursive formations and changes in spatial imageries, Europe as geographical imagery will be explored through three different concepts: 1) Europe that is understood as a physical territory and a structural body; 2) Europe as an institution with set structures; and 3) Europe as a socio-spatial experience (see Lee, 1985; Paasi, 2001). These discourses are constitutive of each other and, especially in journalism, often intertwined.

Empirically, however, it is also interesting to analyze how territorial, institutional, and experienced dimensions of space carry separate meanings. The article builds on analysis interviews carried out with journalists from Eastern and Central Europe (Estonia, Latvia,

Lithuania and Hungary).[3] The focal questions are on how the frontiers and contours of Europe are articulated (what is included in, and excluded from, "Europe"), and how the territorial unit is defined in the evolving spatial and symbolic practices of journalists. In this, "Europe" is constructed through three different discourses: a) Territorial Europe in constructing "Otherness;" b) Institutional "Fortress Europe;" and, c) Historical Europe as an experience.

Europe as a Territory

Europe as a unified space has very strong discursive and narrative dimensions in "bordering". Klaus Eder (2006: 225) argues that the social construction of the borders of Europe could be "understood as the combined effect of a historical trajectory in which the construction of its outer and its inner boundaries interact. These boundaries make sense to the people only if they are credible, i.e. if they in some sense have a perpetual feature". In such narratives territorial borders are grounded in a way that the narratives and their trajectories have "hard" ideological and political implications.

Geographically "Europe" is, in many ways, straightforward as the synonym for the Western peninsula of Eurasia. In the north, west, and south, the peninsula is delimited by the sea. However, the Eastern land border lacks a firm and continuous physical feature and has been ambiguous and shifting. It can be claimed that Europe, as a region, has been in a constant crisis of border definition in the East (Davies, 1995 7–9). Part of the power politics of border-formation related to discursive representations of what constituted "East" and "West," and that still continues today. This representational struggle has a long history. Although the term "Eastern Europe" did not rise to prominence until the eighteenth century, when it was used to describe an area of economic stagnation, it could be said to mirror Western Latin-Roman propaganda towards the "decadent" Greek-Roman Empire centered

---

[3] The qualitative data consisted of 46 interviews with Central and Eastern European Brussels-based correspondents and foreign journalists in Budapest, Riga, Tallinn and Vilnius. The interviews were conducted during spring 2007.

on Byzantium (modern day Istanbul) of the early medieval period.[4] It
was always a vague notion, however, and many countries did not fit the
stereotypical view. Before the development of an East/West axis, Europe had been largely divided between Mediterranean states and a barbarous North, and then along Catholic/Protestant/Orthodox fault lines
(see Wolff, 1994, Hefferman, 1998). Interestingly, journalists seem
to rely on the old geography book version of Europe, with bordering
influenced by cultural intimacy. This cultural closeness is articulated
through affective exclusion more than inclusion what Europe is and
how it should be defined.

> Europe? Well what is Europe on the map—everybody knows the Ural
> Mountains form the Eastern border. That's the geographical Europe
> but I think that with this enlargement we have set the true Europe.
> Even if geographically half of Russia is in the European continent,
> Russia is not in Europe at all. As you know, geography is not actually
> the criteria here. In addition, I don't think Turkey is part of Europe,
> despite being a candidate country for a few years, Turkey is not part of
> Europe. However, maybe Ukraine is. (Lithuanian journalist, Brussels)

> I think that in regard to this district (Europe), we can feel where the
> border is. That is why the Turkey issue is coming up; we feel that it is
> artificial. It is not Europe anymore, not because of religion or because
> only five per cent of territory is in Europe but because there is this
> feeling. In Latvia there were Swedish times, German times, Russian
> times, of course, but before that, Polish: everywhere is related and we
> feel like we belong. In Soviet times it was the same situation, we were
> in the same Union with absolutely different cultures (Kazakhstan,
> Uzbekistan). We didn't understand each other and it was an artifi-
> cial situation. It was easier to understand Russians because, of course,
> they are Europeans as well, or at least more European than Turks.
> My feeling is that this enlargement should be the last one: no Tur-
> key. There have to be borders, it is like family. I can say that everyone
> who enters my house is part of my family, maybe distant relatives but

---

[4] "Eastern Europe," in this new divide, was seen as a region where serfdom
and reactionary autocratic governments persisted long after those things had
faded away in the West.

family is family. Western Europe it was natural but now we are going further East and I think the same thing will happen as to the Soviet Union: it will break-up. (Latvian journalist, Riga)

I think this idea shouldn't be forgotten because of countries like Turkey and Ukraine, or Belarus—sometime in the future when and if it becomes a democratic country—it's maybe a good idea because it is a country which is surrounded from all sides by the European Union. It should be included because, you know, it is European in some way. It's like the Balkans, if they stop killing each other sometime, then they are Europe too. (Hungarian journalist, Budapest)

As Morley and Robins (2001) have argued, it seems cultural identities can mostly be understood in and through their relationship to "Others." Consequently "what is Europe?" would be difficult to understand without drawing borders as to what is not Europe. For example, Russia and Turkey serve as European "Others" for defining what is inside and what should be outside, and they can act as cultural and political regions against which "Europeanness" is measured. Current definition of the "Other," however, is much more complicated than it was during the Cold War when the inner German border between NATO and the Warsaw Pact offered a "natural" Eastern border. When historical and ideological camps and fault lines start to fade, new values have to be evoked in order to articulate difference. Thus, the political variant of Europe is increasingly revolving around the triumphal march of liberal democracy that has, over the last decades, become the only "game in town" and the mode of European governance. Its recent and rapid conquest of Central and Eastern Europe has been portrayed as a victory over more authoritarian governments.

As a result of these factors, public discussion to define "Europe," especially in the borderlands, i.e., former Soviet republics, often revolves implicitly around an East/West ideological axis. This East/West geopolitical position or borderland predicament provides shared elements of identity politics that according to certain analysts has translated into a borderland identity position.[5] The inner core of identity

---

[5] See Herb, G. & Kaplan, D. (eds.) (1999) Nested Identities: Identity, Territory, and Scale, 123–150. Boston: Rowman & Littlefield Publishers, Inc;

in borderland areas is always created through difference, through exclusion: what we are not, rather than what we are. Therefore, in these countries, identities and cultural measures are often constructed around questions of political subjectivity, power, and language, which also create conditions for public opinion formation that differ from other European countries, but differ also through liberal political culture from what is concerned East, i.e., Russia.[6]

> That's a complicated thing—I think that Russia could be Europe but currently its political culture definitely is not. Russia has been struggling as to whether it is European or not for centuries and my feeling is that Russian identity has somehow been weakened; they feel very strongly what is alien to them. We are very secure and can accept other cultures but they are very insecure, for some reason. That's why they need to brag about their culture and power: it's a lack of confidence, an inferiority complex, actually. It finds different expressions: some are masochists and say there is nothing in Russia, nothing will ever grow here; others say in Estonia you have nothing—you are too small a country, with no oil, no Dostoevsky. You have nothing, we have oil, we have Dostoevsky, and we have everything. Both are wrong attitudes completely, they just haven't regained their self-confidence for some reason. (Estonian journalist, Tallinn)

Kaplan, David & Jouni Häkli (2002) Learning from Europe? Borderlands in Social and Geographical Context. In Kaplan, David & Jouni Häkli (eds.) Boundaries and Place. European Borderlands in Geographical Context. pp. 1–18. Lanham: Rowman & Littlefield Publishers.

[6] All these countries have been spaces of passage during the upheavals of Europe. Lacking natural borders, those geographical spaces now called Estonia, Latvia and Lithuania have had very different names and been subject to conflicting laws over the centuries. After a rude introduction to European Civilization, courtesy of the crusading Teutonic Knights, the Baltic peoples have suffered the visitations of near neighbors such as Sweden, Denmark, Poland and Russia. Hungary has demonstrated that even strong physical borders such as the Carpathian Mountains and the mountainous regions of the Balkan Peninsula and Styria do not guarantee a stable frontier. Indeed the frontier of 1914 encompassed twice as much territory as that of modern Hungary. As a strategic node, it has been central to European power politics and has formed part of various Empires including those of Byzantium, Ottoman Turkey and Austria.

Yeah, geographically I would agree with De Gaulle who, when asked "where are the borders of Europe?" said "Europe starts at one end and ends at the other." It means that, for me, the European Union and Europe can go further than the border of Europe. It means, I'm not against the accession of Turkey—for instance—and I'm not against former Soviet countries like Uzbekistan, joining the Union— later on. I was not against it when Israel asked to join the EU in '96 and everybody said "what a stupid thing for Israel to ask for member- ship" but Israel has always considered itself to be a European country. It's not because of geography but a way of thinking and the level of the economy and everything. (Lithuanian journalist, Vilnius)

Although European states have long been obsessed with delineating their precise boundaries, it is obvious that Europe as a larger cultur- al entity is appearing in the minds of the interviewees. According to Agnew (2004:19), the answer lies in competition between emerging national elites who justify their claims to superiority over one another by positioning themselves as the most qualified agents in a struggle for power and wealth that increasingly extends beyond the political bor- ders of Europe. This requires a clear sense of where Europe begins and ends. With the EU mostly administered through elite networks of politicians and civil servants, it shouldn't be surprising that these new European elites have the same task of delineating what is Europe territorially.

Europe as an Institution

Europe today is dominantly understood as an institutional body by media, that is to say, as the European Union. The EU is defined through institutional structures that are constitutive of European cul- tural and economic integration (Paasi, 2001: 11). This institution has its genealogy within different historical narratives, where the econom- ic dimension has often been emphasized (McLean, 2003: 502). How these institutional narratives are born and mediated is largely in the hands of national and international media. The institution itself also strengthens these narratives through its anniversaries, symbols, and stories that circulate within the press corps and civil servants.

The EU as an institution has a history that is marked by the constitutive treaties of Paris (1951) and Rome (1957). These treaties gave birth to the European Economic Community, which preceded the European Community, and, through the 1992 Maastricht Treaty, the European Union. As an institution, the EU can primarily be seen as an intergovernmental body whose members have rationally bound themselves to supranational institutions. Moravcsik (1993: 3) argues that the broad line of European integration since 1955 reflects mainly three factors: commercial advantage through European economic space; the relative bargaining power of the governments of big member states; and, the incentive to enhance the credibility of interstate commitments and regulations. Most fundamental of these were commercial interests and, although the language expressing the existence of the Union is rather technocratic, giving priority to cooperation against crime and illegal immigration, and emphasizing internal security, Europe as an institution is understood as a regulative body with governance from the center. However, the EU as a structural body is not very visible in the minds of journalists, unless it helps in the process of inclusion/exclusion at the core of European identity.

I think a very useful definition of Europe is provided in Article 49 of the basic Treaty of the European Union—which isn't very popular these days because of the problems with enlargement and the borders of Europe—but I think Europe is really a state of mind rather than something pre-given. To be honest, from my point of view Israel is Europe. I don't think it would fulfill the Copenhagen criteria at this stage but in terms of their state of mind—they're European. Whether that's a sustainable path for the European Union to take—to admit, for example, that Armenia is European or whatever, is a different matter. I mean that's a political consideration but I would like to think that, culturally at least, Article 49's definition on what I think is an emphasis on the state of mind is, possibly, the best way to define Europe. (Hungarian journalist, Brussels)

It's a spot on the map and then—what is more relevant is 'what is European Union?' and how we within the European Union and countries who wish to join European Union are defined because I am certain some will continue to join. Define our common goals and economic alliance and so on. This is a more important question than just this definition of Europe. (Hungarian journalist)

It is, however, very clear that as a prerequisite to membership, EU institutions implemented new socio-spatial and material practices that were not limited by the political borders of earlier territorial units. Thus institutions produced spaces of a more or less durable sort: territories of control (1985 Schengen Agreement), terrains of jurisdiction (European Court of Justice), and domains of organization and administration (European Commission). In this sense, the West had defined the social model, forms of democracy, and a desired value system for those who might subsequently want to join the club. All that was left for "New Europe" was to adjust itself to the stipulated structure. Hence Europe as an institution is often referred to as a collective actor, a super actor that monitors development and controls deviations from the norm.

> The way Eastern Europe fitted into or latched onto Western Europe—of course these ways differed—but overall the framework was there: the conceptual framework, the institutional framework, I mean. The European Union accession talks, for example, were all about how to apply the European Union to those countries. There was no negotiation and there was one basic tenet from Day 1: This is not about negotiation. These countries were not negotiating how to change EU law; they were only negotiating how to apply it. So what basically happened was these countries entered a space delineated, demarcated, and arranged by the European Union and they had to make themselves fit. However, they obviously made themselves fit in different ways depending on the national, cultural and social backgrounds. (Estonian journalist, Brussels)

In Central and Eastern Europe, the EU was mostly regarded as a "test" to measure how new countries were able to adopt and adjust to the rules of "the West," i.e., the EU. The journalists who were interviewed for this study articulated the role of Europe as an institution that through its regime was forcing accession countries at the European level to conform. Europe as an institution set a benchmark for those who wanted to be inside.

Throughout those 10 years, we so much wanted to be part of Europe or part of NATO that we would do whatever we were told. It's a good thing that the West actually told us those things, I don't know where the country would have gone if they hadn't said "clean up," "fight corruption" and "do that kind of thing," but it created certain type of mentality: you don't make trouble; you say "yes" and you do it. We grew up with this mentality and we didn't have the transition period when one turns from teenager into a sensible adult. We came from teenager immediately into adulthood—all with the different rules of the game when it comes to your self-esteem, when it comes to your self behavior, and we are still thinking with this "Yes, Sir" mentality. We don't think very often "What do we gain," we think "What are the others going to think of us." (Latvian journalist, Brussels)

We did many things during our accession period that we would never have done otherwise and life would have been much worse. The environment, for example: it is hugely expensive to try to keep the environment clean, and difficult to be aware of what can be done. The environmental projects were hugely expensive—due to the Soviet legacy in North-Eastern Estonia. There you can see what kind of environmental catastrophe went on in the Gulf of Finland. We would never have addressed these issues so soon. The EU forced us to do it in order to get in and we were desperate to get in. Who would carry out reforms which are harsh on your people, which create unpopularity, who would do that? But if you want to get into the EU, then you have to do that and then you speed up your own development. That is what happened in Estonia; probably we wouldn't have clean water to drink otherwise. (Estonian journalist, Tallinn)

The institutional regime forced countries to "clean up" their territories both ecologically and socially. The economic variant of Europe is, however, produced by neo-liberal economic theories and "economies of scale" in order to make European space capital-friendly. Thus, Europe as an institution was often articulated through excluding people from the "third and second World" by strict immigration controls. In this case, Europe was depicted as affluent and self-possessed with a "Fortress Europe" counter narrative developing as part of the whole.

"Fortress Europe" was a counter narrative describing a rather elitist, very affluent and inward looking club.

> Europe is a continent, a very rich continent. It doesn't know or care much about other countries. Although all European Member-States give aid and charity, there is no systematic approach to those things. Even if they give some money to fund African Union soldiers, for example, or if the Belgians take care of the Congo, an ex-colony, in reality nothing is changing there. Europeans want to live well in Europe. Also immigration policy is exclusive, it is better without immigrants. I would connect Europe to the European Union, economically, and even from a political point of view. But I wouldn't say that Europe is very open. (Lithuanian journalist, Brussels)

> I think it's arbitrary to define Europe in geographical terms. So all you can do to define it in cultural and political terms. If you consider the world population as a whole, we are very lucky to be here, even if we are Hungarian or Polish or Latvian, which means we are poorer than the Austrians, the Finns, and the Swedes. This is a privileged part of the world and we are just not aware of it. We have no idea how the East Asians, the South East Asians, and the Africans, the South Americans—tens of millions of South Americans and hundreds of millions of Africans live day to day. We just can't imagine it—the poverty and the... it's just too comfortable a place. We are just living in a too comfortable place of the world. That's what the European Union is. (Hungarian journalist, Budapest)

In the articulations of the journalists, Europe as an institution has inner and outer circles, peripheries and cores, and first and second-class status countries: it is hierarchically constructed and its architecture is based on the institutional power geometry of EU dominated by the West.

> This "inner circle" of insider members: let's take the Euro zone—now twelve countries—and the thinking is: don't enlarge the Euro zone, this is going to be our club—we are "one-Europe." The larger Europe, you know, the outer circle, which are out of Euro zone, well, it's also Europe but it's a little bit of a 'different Europe' because of different

interests. Different levels of development, but actually it's true, it's true—why not." (Lithuanian journalist)

Although geographical understanding should be seen as a central element in forming the consciousness of political rationalities through which individuals and collectives organized their behavior in new situations, this is not the whole picture. Especially for the younger journalists, "freedom" in the context of the EU as a geographical entity was about mobility, unrestricted communication and rights to use and roam space freely. Both economic and political restrictions and rigid nation-state based geography were experienced as outdated and criticized as belonging to the past.

> I'll give you an example: in Central Europe we are not a very big country and if you go from Budapest to Krakow, if you go by train at night, there is border control on the Hungarian border and then the Slovak will come and again the Polish guy will come—and that's a short trip to Krakow. We have this wonderful Visegrád cooperation among the four countries and our example had always been the Benelux countries but in the Benelux you don't have that. If you go from Amsterdam to Luxemburg by train nobody will wake you up in the middle of the night to say "Hi, I'm the Belgian controller." (Hungarian journalist)

> But as a European citizen I would be very happy if I didn't have to pay the roaming prices in Holland or in France or in Germany, in Hungary—wherever—just because I happen to use a Belgium mobile. You need people to exert economic pressure for that to happen, you know it's a slogan "Bring Europe closer to the people" it's a slogan but eventually that is what you really have to do." (Estonian journalist)

Whether the European integration process is a continuation of an old narrative or whether it points towards a specific discontinuity in the further telling of Europe's story, is still historically contingent. Europe just has to continue to tell a story about itself that makes narrative sense.[7] This pragmatic narrative supports Kristeva's (1999) argument

---

[7] The etymology of the word "frontier" has been interesting in the European languages. According to Febvre (1973: 210), by 1773 the expression

that, at a deeper level, Europe as a Union is still seen by Europeans as more useful than meaningful. The institutional articulation's pragmatic approach remains vital among the interviewees, and Europe is seen as space for accumulating wealth, to roam and travel freely, and to be economically protected within the institutional borders.

Europe as an Experience

Europe as an experience is mostly constructed as temporal narratives: what Europe has been and what it will be in the future. The idea upon which experiencing Europe is generally based is a relatively modern idea. This idea gradually replaced the earlier concept of Christendom in a complex intellectual process lasting from the Fourteenth to the Eighteenth Centuries.[8] Therefore, the cultural variant of Europe has its roots deeply entwined in the union of Christendom and emerging Protestant ethics that enabled a thriving market economy to expand across the Continent. Hence, one of the strongest networks is a religion that has power over space and has retained that over centuries. In some accounts Europe was seen as being weakened from inside by "religious diversification" that could not be controlled. Many of the journalists were not interested in the narcissism of minor differences of what Europe could be, as Freud would put it. Thus, the narrative leaned heavily on the broader traditions of common history, Christianity as a shared religion and a new dilemma of Islam that multi-cultural Europe has brought to the fore.

"démiliter une frontiére" (to mark a frontier) had come into common use in the French language. Until the 1789 Revolution that "frontiére" existed only for soldiers and princes, and then only in the time of war. (Agnew, 2004: 21)

[8] The Treaty of Utrecht of 1713 provided the last major occasion when public reference to the *Republica Christiana,* the 'Christian Commonwealth' was made. In 1771 Rousseau announced: "There are no longer Frenchmen, Germans, and Spaniards, or even English, but only Europeans." The final realization of the 'idea of Europe' took place in 1796, when Edmund Burke wrote: "No European can be a complete exile in any part of Europe" (Heffernan, 1998: 140)

Well in a narrow sense, Europe is whatever its geographic boundary is and then you can start revolving about a common culture and
heritage—if any. You cannot even really refer to Christianity because
there are Muslim countries in Europe such as in Former Yugoslavia,
which was one of the issues of the civil war there. Well you cannot
deny that this European part of Russia is Europe—well, I would be
glad to do that, but I cannot. Culturally and so on it's—as I said it's
hard to refer to Christian culture, to a white race, if you want—well,
we have that here—and so on, but, therefore, this is another reason
why I wouldn't care too much for a definition of Europe. (Estonian
journalist, Brussels)

Europe is not strong enough to stop this, so I think that in fifty years
there will be a Muslim majority in Europe. Europe is very weak and
ill—we don't have the power because of globalization, the effects of
multi-national companies. Europe is not strong, there are no…that's
the problem with the European Union: there is no strong image,
nothing which shows that Europe still exists. In my opinion, the last
thing Europe gave something to the world was the Beatles—it was the
Pop Music. They keep saying "innovation" but where is the innovation? Innovation is in Far East, in United States, not here. (Hungarian journalist, Brussels)

In these socio-geographic constructions, borders and frontiers articulate cultural intimacy and belonging. Defining something is basically
an exercise in articulating *la différence* through such things as attraction
and repulsion, distance and closeness. These "common cultural spaces" are part of the geographical imageries of the time and are, therefore, immensely revealing. From time to time, the European narrative
has to redefine itself in relation to America as well as to the Far East
and, through that exercise strengthen, internal "borderless" cultural
belonging.

The situation that we are belonging to Europe officially, without borders, is very natural for me. I think that the opposite was quite un-
natural. It is interesting that if you read Hungarian literature at the
turn of the last century, the last century, not this one, poor guys, poor
intellectuals—there was no money—could travel to Paris to have a tea

with Hemingway, to London or to Berlin. Many of the great Hungarian scientists came from middle level bourgeois families, but they were not rich men. They were not affluent, but they could study in Berlin, Vienna, Prague or anywhere and I think that this is natural—this is the natural situation and I think Communism was very special. It has a deep...the legacy of Communism is the division of Europe—rupturing these natural links. (Hungarian journalist, Budapest)

Noticeably Europe as an experience refers to the structures of feeling coined by Williams (1961). These structures of feeling are shaped by time and space, and by different modes of social communication. Structures of feelings are being constructed as space(s) of ideologies, emotions, and memories through which people move, and these spaces are shaped by prevailing economic, political relations as well as imagined or documented recollections of "European" history. Although personal experiences may vary, a given generation often faces similar large transformations. Also journalists as a group do have many shared ideas although they are forced to live in different social frames and political realities in their own societies. The Central and Eastern European experience differs greatly, however from the Western counterpart, both in its recollection of the past and formation of possible futures because of the heavy historical legacy.

We are very "rooted in the past." Very often, we can't look forward if we haven't looked backwards. It's not only us—I think it's the whole of Eastern Europe is the same. You feel that you've been betrayed and that that hasn't been acknowledged properly because take a look at those debates last year; for the first time that I can remember in EU history, people were speaking about Communism being as evil as Nazism. Still, you know, breaking their arms over each other—what was worse and how Europe has to commemorate et cetera. I think that it was very important to, it is very important for Europe to have a collective memory. To accept that these New Member States have a different history; that not everybody was liberated in 1945. (Lithuanian journalist, Brussels)

...Hungarian history in the Twentieth Century is a horror story. Like my family, for example, my mother was an orphan because the rest of the family was killed. On my father's side, they were nearly all interned and displaced within the country to somewhere else, because they were German speakers—it is a horrible story. If you read the opposition's newspaper, every single day it's complaining about the fate of Hungarians and, I think, that the experience of the last fifty years is that the general line, the mainstream line is that it's not a big trauma, it's not good but it's not unbearable. We can just make it, we live poor but nobody is in prison for political reasons, nobody is killed, nobody is sent to Siberia—it's a good period. We can live with a beer or something. (Hungarian journalist, Brussels)

As Paasi argues (2001:10), identity is, therefore, not only an individual or social category, but also, crucially, a spatial category. In a local context, identity may be based on social interaction, but large-scale territories are often imagined communities, that is to say solidarity units that can be understood as units and are often communicated through national media. Although the media are inventing and constructing communities, they cannot be constructed without a cultural basis and the structures of feelings attached to that. Communities, whether concrete or invented, have to resonate "genetic," i.e., cultural intimacy so that they have become the social facts of the people.

> This collective memory basically defines Latvians on a genetic level to think of themselves as Western Europeans—full stop. It doesn't matter: New Europe/Old Europe, whatever, just on genetic level you have to be there. Just away from Russia—the only thing which we are concerned about, honestly, and it goes through many generations already. (Latvian journalist, Brussels)

At the same time as when being part of a concept where (Western) Europe is seen as something profoundly natural and genetically "determined," a possible and shared European identity has not yet gained a foothold. The clean break with the East wasn't only an ideological or historical issue—by and large it was a question of belonging to a West that is ultimately a diverse mosaic of cultures.

> The very motto of Europe, as we well know, is "United in Diversity" and while that remains Europe's motto then I think it removes any possibility of there being a shared identity—going beyond this

recognition of diversity. You can recognize any diversity, there's no limit to diversity, so it's not a positive force—if you see what I mean. So, no, I don't think that in the foreseeable future you will have a European identity. (Estonian journalist, Brussels)

I don't think that finally East (Europe) can meet West or West can meet East—not for the moment at least. They must meet at some time and they will meet—but not soon. (Hungarian journalist, Brussels)

What is Europe?

Paasi has pointedly argued (2001: 9) that the challenge for any research is to reflect on how regions and places mesh together and what kind of spatial imaginaries and ideologies are involved in this process. In other words, there is a need to historically contextualize diverging spatial imaginations in order to understand their contested and also contradictory nature. Journalists as actors can easily capture the ruptures and contested structures attached to European "mental geographies." In articulating these geographies each generation has the autonomy to remake history. The upcoming generation takes its inheritance from its predecessor and can react against it; creating a new environment that again is the object of reaction for the following generation

Remaking history also has to do with the daily practices of news production. In their professional context, journalists act by creating and organizing the spatio-symbolic exchange between the main political, cultural, and economic discourses. Therefore, journalism itself can be seen as a "super discourse" that moulds structures, experiences, and physical territories into narratives. At the same time journalists participate—willingly or unwillingly—in a process of modification of values, democratic ideals and political aspirations; reconstructing their surroundings and larger geopolitical entities in accordance with the economic and cultural interests of their origin. When journalists act as symbolic producers, therefore, how they imagine and define "Europe" is not without importance.

When asked, Central and Eastern European journalists defined "Europe" through a wide array of answers, ranging from historical narratives of a common history to structures of feelings in flux. Europe seems to be "a summary of events and ideas, political, religious, military, pacific, serious, romantic, near at hand, far away, tragic, comic, significant, meaningless, or something else" depending on the interviewee (see Hrytsak, 2005). Thus it seems that Europe is under construction and is still a product of relations-between, relations that are necessarily embedded material and historical practices that have to be carried out (Massey, 2004, 9).

This squares with Eder's (2006) idea of narrative boundary construction that is embedded in a process of identity claiming, in which anything could serve as a boundary within a historically specific situation. In line with this perspective, Europe is "Europeanness" and cannot be defined only in space. Its value, as a coherent region, is assessed through its flexibility to unite internal diversity as well as serve as a coherent unity within the larger geopolitical constellation. Therefore the Other(s) are defined mostly by their willingness not to question the historical narrative, i.e., impose their own cultural heritages and codes too strongly on it. In the following table, in the form of "discursive grid" the different dimensions of constructing Europe are presented.

Table 1. "Discursive grid" of understanding Europe by journalists

	Cultural dimension	Socio-political dimension	Economic dimension
Europe as a Territory	East and West; religion, cultural histories, internal divisions; mental maps of occupied space; (borderland areas and disputes) soft and cultural borders; construction of "tradition"; historical spaces of repression, freedom and belonging	"New and Old Europe" newly defined political borders towards East/South; hierarchies within EU, forms of social control (surveillance and policing), social networks of communication	Common borders and neighbors, core states and peripheries and semi-peripheries with emerging economies (alternative capitalisms); Flows and mobility of money, ideas and people, Euro-zone as an "exclusive club"
Europe as an Institution	Political and regulative "hard" borders against "Others," common understanding of shared values and future trajectories	Safety, mobility, social communication over the borders, new policies of levelling off social differences;	Affluence, Fortress Europe, internal divisions and cleavages, Single Market, mobility of social labor

	Cultural dimension	Socio-political dimension	Economic dimension
Europe as an Experience	Temporal narratives; history of the present; Common cultural heritage; social, psychological and physical measures of "we" and the "other"; legacy of communism; II World War and stolen time	EU citizenship; Freedom to cross the borders; systems of mapping, critical counter-discourses on Europe as form of "Fortress Europe"	Capital for building infrastructures; new economic order, colonizing of new territories; Europe as closed economic space; flows of capital, information, people and ideas from West to East

How then is "Europe" constructed through these three different concepts, i.e., territory, institution and experience? Three categories evolve as follows: a) Territorial Europe is activated through constructing "Otherness"; b) Institutional "Fortress Europe" is constructed in shared discipline, regulation and co-operation and, c) Historical Europe as experience moulds spatial, temporal and collective trajectories into one.

Europe as a Territory and its internal divisions still carries a spatial and ideological heritage that has at different times defined what Europe means geographically. Europe and liberal democracy are often seen as synonyms, as well as the continent's legacy as the birth place of modern capitalism.

European cultural space is understood as a form of cultural solidarity and a collective mode of accommodating to a changing cultural and political environment. The counter-narratives criticizing the closed and selfish nature of "Fortress Europe" are also notable. Europe as territory is produced in the narratives of the "Other" but it is also in counter-narratives that the limits of cultural intimacy of what is thought as "Us" is tested. That has led to an extensive debate on whether all Eastern European countries (such as Russia, Belarus and Ukraine, for example), and especially Turkey, are suitable and "European" enough to become Members of the EU.

European territorial solidarity is based on geopolitics, dominant cultural values, and stability of the national economies. In addition, as a territorial unity, Europe is mostly a mental "state of mind," applying exclusion and inclusion as strategies to define the content of the category itself. Thus it is, perhaps, useful to bear in mind that, in an understanding of territorial experience, space is not an independent category but an ever-changing product of economic, social and political processes constructed in discursive formation. Those formations tell about the current fears, needs for security but also uneasiness about the inevitable cultural encounters of new types of European diversity.

Europe as an Institution is intertwined with pragmatic genealogies of the EU as a body of governance and the newly learned bureaucratic discourses of the institutions. Europe exists not only as physical idea, but also mostly through the intensified networks of interaction between people, technologies, institutions and legislation that form an experience of Europe. Institutional imagery evokes mainly pragmatic claims and imageries of mobility, unity, economic effectiveness. Institutionally Europe also means a Foucauldian regime imposed from the regulative center with Brussels serving as a modern day *Panopticon*.

The territoriality of the EU itself is a mode of social organization which operates by delimiting geographical spaces and controlling the movement of people, goods and ideas between them. It is a spatial strategy that uses territory and borders to control, classify and communicate in order to implement relationships of power. These power relationships can be peaceful or imposed from above, repressive or productive (for example, including or excluding people from the same social space, supporting some rights to specified groups of people but not to others) or supporting or muting expressions of cultural diversity. (Barnett, 2004: 185). Hence, Europe as an institution is often understood as administrative principles supported by benchmarking, regulation and regime imposed from the center, i.e., from Brussels.

Europe as an Experience is an emotional container of both collective and individual histories and the emotions of Europeans. Hence experience is always emotionally charged (with fears or hopes). It has an interactional character in the sense that it is knit together through narratives and discourses. Affects, memories, norms, practices of power and governance are all conceived through symbolic practice and, therefore, under constant reconstruction. The structure of a (master narrative) is specific to local transformations although the deep structure of binary opposed concepts that are important to European culture seem to be similar according to the interviews. In these discourses, "Europe" is constructed through two different narratives: a discourse on exclusion, where ethnic European identities are the prevalent point of definition; and, Europe as an ideological space, where the main organizing principle is economic pragmatism in its historically nested context. However, more that being two separate discursive formations, Europe is constructed as part of a symbolic grid from which certain features are used and others are left out depending on the individual questioned.

To understand that the symbolic boundaries of territorial histories, spaces and meaning-makings are producing communities is an essential part of understanding that all territories—whether Europe or national spaces—are not only geographical sites. Eder (2006: 257) pointedly argues that the new symbolic space of Europe should be therefore bordered by "shared stories" in order to gain vitality. Manufacturing the narrative plausibility of these shared stories has to do with adding new elements to the evolving stories in a way that they can configure new socio-spatial orders. Thus, we have to analyze stories that are constituted by shared histories in order to make sense of the embeddedness of cognitive projects of constructing boundaries and collective identities. These stories also have their "dark" side or side of exclusion, for example stories of those non-Europeans that may threaten the narrative plausibility in the future.

The cultural approach to spatial change starts thereby with the realization that the essential and unvarying elements of human experience are not only empirical, but the social facts of life. In this context, theoretically, cultural change and the transformation of society in those countries that form the focus of this study (Estonia, Latvia, Lithuania and Hungary) may be seen as an "adjusting process," which in a subtle way relates to the Habermasian "learning" processes for a new set of practices for a formation of narratives. Therefore, the transformation of Europe as an institution required not only "the change of formal, institutional, and governmental links—or formal definitions of European citizenship—but also changes in the abstract, psychological and symbolic links, and institutions in which the production and reproduction of spatial loyalties and sentiments occurs" as Paasi (2001, 25) has written. (See also Hassner, 1997; Linklater, 1998)

When Marx and Engels, writing about Europe in 1848,[9] famously celebrated capitalism's creative destruction of established structures as

---

[9] See Marx and Engels, 1968: 38.

a process though which "all fixed, fast frozen relations are swept away" and "all that is solid melts into air," (1968, 38) Europe was only at the beginning of its capitalist journey. Today's contradictory narrative of Europe reassembled by journalists creates almost a unified cosmology of Territory, where the history, culture and solidarity are still part of the European picture. It seems that the narrative structure that keeps the continent together is solid, after all.

> My personal view...I'm struggling for a visual metaphor here, but my personal view is that what happened after 1989 and 1991—obviously it happened gradually and the countries only became part of it in 1991 properly—was a bit akin to a large body...a large foreign body entering a stellar system from outside and re-arranging the way everything else in that system rotates and revolves and what not. So essentially, you could say that once Eastern Europe was free, it had no other option: the magnetic pull of Western Europe was so strong that there really wasn't other option than to fit themselves or itself to spaces provided and shaped by Western Europe beforehand. (Estonian journalist, Brussels)

REFERENCES

Agnew, J. (2004) "The civilisational roots of European national boundaries." In Kaplan, David & Jouni Häkli (eds.) *Boundaries and Place. European Borderlands in Geographical Context.* 18–34. Lanham: Rowman & Littlefield Publishers.

Ash, T. G. (2004) *Free World.* Penquin Books: London.

Davies, N. (1997) *Europe: A History.* Pimlico: London.

Eder, K. (2006) "Europe's Borders: The Narrative Construction of the Boundaries of Europe." *European Journal of Social Theory* 9(2) 255–271.

Febvre, L. (1973) *New Kind of History: From the Writings of Febvre.* Routledge & Kegan Paul: London

Hassner, P. (1997) "Obstinate and Obsolete: Non-Territorial Transnational Forces versus European Territorial State." In O. Tunander, P. Baev and V.I. Einagel (eds.) *Geopolitics in Post-Wall Europe.* London: Sage.

Heffernan, M. (1998) *The Meaning of Europe: Geography and Geopolitics.* London: Arnold.

Herb, G. & Kaplan, D. (eds.) (1999) *Nested Identities: Identity, Territory, and Scale.* Boston: Rowman & Littlefield Publishers Inc.

Hrytsak, Y. (2005) "The borders of Europe—seen from the outside." *Eurozine*. http://www.eurozine.com/articles/2005-01-10-hrytsak-en.html (retrieved 2008-04-23)

Kaplan, D. & J. Häkli (2002) "Learning from Europe? Borderlands in Social and Geographical Context." In Kaplan, David & Jouni Häkli (eds.) *Boundaries and Place. European Borderlands in Geographical Context*. 1–18. Lanham: Rowman & Littlefield Publishers.

Lee, R. (1985) "The Future of the Region: Regional Geography as Education for Transformation." In R. King (ed.) *Geographical Futures*. Sheffield: The Geographical Association.

Linklater, A. (1998) *The Transformation of Political Community*. Columbia: University of South California Press.

Marx, Karl (1867/1968) "The Eighteenth Brumaire of Louis Bonaparte." In K. Marx and F. Engels (eds.) *Selected Works*. London: Lawrence and Wishart.

Massey, D. (2005) *For Space*. London: Sage.

Morley, D. and K. Robins (1995) *Spaces of Identity. Global Media, Electronic Landscapes and Cultural Boundaries*. London: Routledge.

Paasi, Anssi (2001) "Europe as a Social Process and Discourse: Considerations of Place, Boundaries and Identity." *European Urban and Regional Studies* 8(1)7–28.

Schöpflin, George (2000) *Nations, Identity, Power: The New Politics of Europe*. Hurst & Company: London.

Williams, R. (1961) *The Long Revolution*. London: Chatto:Windus.

CHAPTER 3

Media Representations of EU Matters in National Media Systems: The Hungarian Case

István Hegedűs

It has become commonplace to say that European citizens look for and receive information about the European Union in general, as well as about European events, policy issues and debates in particular, over-whelmingly from national media sources. In national media, European matters are discussed—when they are discussed at all—foremost in a context of domestic public debate within member states. The coverage of all-European matters on a national level differs in each country reflecting both the historical-cultural heritage and lessons learned from the past in the respective member state as well as in internal cleavages and the logic of partisan competition. Although dissenting perceptions and views exist inside the pluralist democracies about EU related topics, the dominant framework of public discourses vary characteristically amongst the member states.

The main reason for this situation is the lack of a common European public sphere. Whether it is constituted as an emerging "ideal," autonomous pan-European arena or conceptualized as the European-ization of current spheres of public in the member states and beyond, the European public sphere exists just in an embryonic form. Beside other important organized players and participants, the European in-stitutions make definite efforts to widen the scope and influence of all-European debates. Their own top-down communication, however, faces obstacles like a lack of financial resources, a lack of professional-ism combined with institutional inertia, as well as ideological reserva-tions of some national political groups against the "propaganda coming from Brussels."

National conditions inside the EU-27–in "old" and "new" mem-ber states–might explain divergent political and cultural assumptions about the European Union. (For the sake of the argument being made, but also because of the subject matter, Europe and the European Union will be taken to be synonyms in this analysis.) The historical packages, including the specifics in the development of a national identity and in the process of state-building, the socio-cultural experiences of citizens, and the domestic party political contexts, result in divergent issue framing and agenda-setting mechanisms concerning EU matters in the national media of the member states. The impacts of path-dependency in the coverage of European issues are mixed with the general cultural norms, professional values and patterns of national journalism in the process of news selection.

All member states have long-lasting European stories. The European "adventure" has become a special challenge for the post-communist countries in Central Europe. In Hungary, during the 1990s and at the beginning of the new millennium, the dominant media narrative about EU membership and the European Union shifted from early Euro-enthusiasm to pragmatism, even to a fuzzy "Euro-pessimism"– hand in hand with the changes in the rhetoric of mainstream political parties and with the general shift in the public mood towards more negativism. Although the project of joining the EU was not openly questioned by any important political actors and hard Euro-skepticism did not find ground in the country, fears about a second-class membership spread throughout the public. After joining the European Union in 2004, common wisdom perceptions about the European Union still suffer from old-fashioned national stereotypes, provincialism and the lack of all-European approaches in this relatively new member state.

The European Public Sphere and the Communication of European Institutions

European public sphere, Europeanness, Europeanization, European identity–all these notions, intertwined with each other, used in social sciences and in politics, describe crucial social and political changes on the European level as well as inside the individual states of the old European continent. In the case of these terms, the meaning of Europe has become overwhelmingly equivalent with the European Union parallel to the process of how the EU gradually obtained a single representation of a European idea through the implementation, development and extension of its political-economic regime.

As for the concept of the European public sphere, "a central precondition for a democratic order is a viable public sphere–namely, a communicative space (or spaces) in which relatively unconstrained debate, analysis and criticism of the political order can take place. This precondition applies as much to the EU as it does to any nation state" (Fossum and Schlesinger 2007: 1). The notion of public sphere has a strong universalistic element. "In the public sphere, citizens could recognize each other as free and equal, engage in democratic learning processes and subject each other's claims to the very universal principles which they endorsed patriotically" (Müller 2007: 31). However, both the original idea on the public sphere proposed by Jürgen Habermas and the normative assumptions of liberal democracy in social sciences has been elaborated under the circumstances of a dominant (nation-) state. Therefore "searching for a nation-state model of public sphere in the European Union, and then claiming that there is no European public sphere would be to state the obvious" (Sicakkan 2007: 2). Moreover, according to critics of the old model, instead of one single sphere, it seems to be better to talk about different "spheres of publics" in order to avoid the impression of one homogenous spatial and cultural entity on the European level. "Thus, an important challenge for theorists and media researchers working within a political communication perspective has for some time been to reformulate the critical potential of the public sphere model to a complex and constantly changing European system of transnational, democratic governance" (Slaata 2006: 10).

Realizing that the European Union is not a traditional state, the European public sphere(s) might appear autonomously on the European level (this is the ideal version), or, it/they can be constituted through the Europeanization of national politics and discourses. A strong all-European media or, at least, the Europeanization of the national media, would be a decisive factor for the implementation of such a concept. In the first case, the overall European perspective on common political issues would characterize public discourses. According to the second scenario, the dense intensity of Europe-related topics, the high appearance of EU-protagonists, and a broad coverage on other member states (Machill, Beiler and Fischer 2006) would constitute a victory of the new approach in the national media.

There are empirical signs for both tendencies towards the creation of a European public sphere: the emergence of pan-European discourses and an increasing salience of political actors representing European institutions and thoughts, on the one hand; and the growing importance of EU matters in the national media, hence the Europeanization of national public debates in the political life of member states, on the other. This shift has occurred parallel to the hectic, but continuous deepening and widening of the integration especially in the last twenty-five years. There is nothing like a blueprint or "finalité" agreed upon regarding a desired political-institutional set-up for a united Europe and recent debates have shown the very pluralistic character of visions on the future shape of the European Union. The EU project has been a "moving target" for observers: especially from the beginning of the early 1980s, the European Union functions under the circumstances of an ongoing institutional reform period.

Without going into details about the results of this gradual change (Laffan and Mazey 2006), it was the growing significance of the European Parliament—the direct representative body of European citizens—in the decision-making procedures and its increased strength amongst the European institutions that should be highlighted from the perspective of the formation of a European public sphere. By now, the political groups of trans-national European parties in the European Parliament show bigger coherence and they gained more room for manoeuvre in all-European power games.

"Supplementary" European identity, without replacing the national and local feelings of people, reached a relevant, sometimes even high level in most of the member states according to numerous surveys (Kohli 2000). Recently a campaign called "One Seat" having the objective to end the European Parliament's monthly Strasbourg session and to relocate the institution full-time to Brussels successfully gathered more than one million individual signatures from all over Europe showing the strengthening of political Europeanization on the continent[1]. Fifty years after signing of the Treaty of Rome in 1957, the EU ceased to be an elite-project: the degrees of public support, citizens'

---

[1] One-seat Parliament campaign in EU Treaty pitfall. *EurActiv*, 21 September 2006, http://www.euractiv.com/en/opinion/seat-parliament-campaign-eu-treaty-pitfall/article-158058

participation and the transparency of decision-making processes have become crucial issues in European and national discourses concerning the feasibility of the historic program.

Nevertheless, European elections are often described as second order events compared to the importance of the partisan competition on the national level of member states, not only because of the lower turn-out, but also because they lack the primacy of European issues in the campaigns of (national) political forces. Consequently, in 1999, in the national media of the member states "the majority of news items relating to the elections did not deal with any central EU policy issues" (Kevin 2001a: 225). For the voters, "[w]hile the elections represent a process of political participation outside the national sphere, there is no corresponding common sphere of debate, which can be examined in relation to this exercise of citizenship" (Kevin 2001b: 21).

The sessions and debates in the European Parliament practically do not reach those, the European citizens, who elected its members. The European Union is far from being perceived as an existing political community in the eyes of most Europeans. "If there were different candidates for the Commission President before the elections we could ask our party leaders who they support for the most important post in EU politics, and why. The media would also have some European personalities to write about in the build-up to the elections, and we could all watch the winner and loser on election night" (Hix 2009). On the long run, a truly European contest of European transnational parties can fundamentally change the current characteristics of European elections.

In 2005, the victory of negative votes on the draft European Constitution in two founding member states, France and the Netherlands, showed–beside other problems–the broad communication gap between elites and citizens. In the absence of a European-wide referendum, European matters have been discussed–and not only in these two countries–overwhelmingly in a national context with little overlap with the public debates in other member states. The lack of a strong European public sphere compared to the strength of national ones is a crucial issue also because "[a]t the heart of the EU's "democratic deficit" is the discrepancy between its increasing competences over the lives of Europeans, and the continuing dominance of national politics as the space for public debates and as the source of collective identities" (Statham and Gray 2005: 61).

The European public sphere is still "in the making." The EU "is rather an increasingly interconnected grouping of overlapping communicative communities with the potential to become a loosely integrated communicative space, not just for élites but also for entire peoples" (Schlesinger 2003: 5). Today, "what makes an arena a public sphere is first and foremost the existence of diversity" (Sicakkan 2007: 3). According to this concept, the notion of otherness signifies both disparities and commonalities between individuals and groups represented in the various discourses. For the European Union, under the conditions of dynamic change in identity patterns and interest-wielding configurations of the people, the interplay between citizens might constitute new communicative public spaces "relatively separate from the state" (Sicakkan 2007: 11) as well as a common public sphere, where citizens as "co-Europeans" confront their views with representatives of other communicative public spaces and also with "central" European actors. The real challenge for the European institutions is exactly how to increase the degree of interaction with European citizens and how to listen and react to the voice of autonomous groups, representatives of civil society and individual European citizens.

"One of the main reasons of the low degree of mediatisation of the political processes in Brussels compared to individual member states of the EU is the basic relationship of the European Union with the media" (Huber 2007: 6). Namely, there is a "limited penetration of European institutions as a visible and "active" actor, even in the field of claims about European integration. The EU/EEC appears to be a poor communicator within national public spheres, though it could also be the case that the media are poor in picking up EU/EEC demands" (Statham and Gray 2005: 69). Historically, the everyday working of the European Community—perceived as a regulatory body dealing mostly with narrow "common market" issues—was not supposed to be covered regularly by journalists. Today, Brussels is a media center: "Considered Europe's most important media hub, Brussels boasts the largest press corps in the world, with the Belgian capital home to over a thousand journalists covering EU issues"[2]. Still, all-European issues

---

[2] "National angle" continues to dominate EU news reporting. *EurActiv*, 26 November 2007, www.euractiv.com/en/pa/national-angle-continues-dominate-eu-news-reporting/article-168626 Last access on 2 March 2008.

cannot be simply "sold" from a single perspective to professional media people proud of their editorial independence. "62% of the journalists surveyed believe that their main role is providing analysis and commentary, rather than "raw" information, which comes notably from institutional and online sources."[3] In fact, there is an ongoing competition between and within European and national politicians as well as journalists for agenda-setting priorities and how to frame the news having in mind the presupposed attitudes and interests of the citizens/audiences "back at home" in their country of origin. The conflict between information-suppliers and information-consumers is built-in to the system regarding the currently dominant communication methods of the European institutions.[4] At the same time, "[i]t must be stated firmly, that a natural consensus on what Europe is, and how the EU is representing European interests and societies does not exist. Thus, the media should not be expected to be this neutral, mediating platform for information and debate. The media are themselves structured according to political and economic structures in society, and are consciously or unconsciously participating in the constant negotiation and contestation of what kind of Europe we might be asked to imagine" (Slaata 2006: 21).

European organizations also lack financial resources for direct communication to citizens; meanwhile institutional inertia hinders their representatives to become pro-active in the member states. In some of these countries, however, supranational actors participating in a national discourse probably would give arguments mostly to Euro-skeptics in their fight against the influence of "Brussels." This negative image of the European institutions might become stronger because of the low degree of salience of European-level partisan pluralism. Certainly, the ignorance of European citizens about the real role of the common institutions, the sharing of competences between national and European levels, and the ways and means of decision-making processes

---

[3] EurActiv survey reveals shift in focus of EU media. *EurActiv*, 29 October 2007, www.euractiv.com/en/pa/euractiv-survey-reveals-shift-focus-eu-media/article-167904 Last access on 2 March 2008.

[4] See EU Communication and the media: allies or enemies? *EurActiv*, 1 December 2006, www.euractiv.com/en/opinion/eu-communication-media-allies-enemies/article-160157 Last access on 2 March 2008.

inside the European Union creates another obstacle, which cannot be simply overcome with better communication methods. By way of contrast, multi-level governance makes politicians acting on the European field comfortable with the situation. They are much less under the control of journalists than their colleagues competing in the national arenas.

The European Commission seems to be aware of these difficulties. Its representatives continuously urge for institutional innovation that would increase transparency in the European decision-making processes and would decrease the gap between European political elites and citizens concerning both everyday policy issues and the debates on the future of Europe. The European Commission also stated the need for more partisan mobilization on a European level, arguing that "[i]t is precisely the contested and often polarised nature of the exchanges between political parties which generates interest and a demand for greater levels of information on the issues concerned" (European Commission 2007a: 11). After the shock of the victory of "No-Sayers" in France and the Netherlands, the European Commission and the European Parliament made efforts to modernize communication between European elites and citizens which became manifest in speeches and documents. Margot Wallström, then Vice-President of the Commission responsible for institutional relations and communication strategy, reacted with the declaration of new principles and methodological improvements regarding the communication of European institutions:

> Our new approach to communication will be built on the following underlying principles. First, communication is not a one-way monologue; it is a two-way dialogue. The Commission has to listen to people, seriously and attentively. We must make more systematic use of opinion polls, focus groups and citizens panels to find out the concerns and attitudes of specific groups of people in each EU country. Second, the EU needs to explain its aims and policies clearly and comprehensibly. We in the Commission have to speak in plain simple language, avoiding jargon. We must spell out the ways in which our proposals will actually affect people's daily lives. We must not limit ourselves to the conventional channels—press releases, press conferences and booklets. We need to find new ways, working closely with the other institutions, the national parliaments, civil society and the

media. And I believe the internet is THE new channel for debate and for communication (Wallström 2005).

During a reflection period after the failure of the two crucial referenda, an Action Plan, the so-called Plan D ("for democracy, dialogue and debate") and a new White Paper on a European Communication Policy have been produced by the European Commission in order to find the way out of the crisis.

The White Paper argues that the new approach means a shift from an institution-centered to a citizen-centered communication paradigm: "Communication has remained too much of a "Brussels affair." It has focused largely on telling people what the EU does: less attention has been paid to listening to people's views" (European Commission 2006: 4). The European Commission realized that "the "public sphere" within which political life takes place in Europe is largely a national sphere. To the extent that European issues appear on the agenda at all, they are seen by most citizens from a national perspective. The media remain largely national, partly due to language barriers; there are few meeting places where Europeans from different Member States can get to know each other and address issues of common interest. Yet many of the policy decisions that affect daily life for people in the EU are taken at European level. People feel remote from these decisions, the decision-making process and EU institutions. There is a sense of alienation from "Brussels," which partly mirrors the disenchantment with politics in general. One reason for this is the inadequate development of a "European public sphere" where the European debate can unfold" (European Commission 2006: 4–5).

The European Parliament also claimed its crucial role in building contacts between the European institutions and the people starting to organize new Citizens' agora on the future direction of the EU, saying, with a strong mission zeal, that "[b]ecause it is directly elected, Parliament is the European Union institution best qualified to take up the challenge of keeping open the channels of communication with European Union citizens."[5] In a draft report entitled "On journalism

---

[5] http://www.europarl.europa.eu/parliament/public/staticDisplay. do?id=66&pageRank=1&language=EN – The official website of the European Parliament. Last access on 25 February 2008.

and new media—creating a public sphere in Europe" to the Committee on Culture and Education, the rapporteur, Morten Løkkegaard, Danish liberal MEP found positive development such like "the use of social media platforms by Parliament in the 2009 European election campaign successfully increased the number of active users, especially among young people." Still, he argued, "[t]he aim of creating a European public sphere is one that must be achieved on several levels. This task does not belong solely to the media but also to politicians and public institutions" (Løkkegaard 2010).

There have been strong reactions to one of his main points—at least in the Danish public debate: "Most interesting for a Brussels audience is probably the draft's suggestion to find EU funding for the Brussels based team of journalists covering European affairs. They should have a contract of editorial independence and the team should consist of an elite of top-level journalists, Løkkegaard explained on Danish Radio. 'This is both provocation and experiment from my side,' the MEP explained. 'It would be a fantastic step ahead, if they dare do it,' he said" (Alfter 2010).

Nevertheless, the core challenges concerning the distance between European citizens and European politics are mostly beyond new communication ideas and methods implemented by the European institutions. "I don't claim that it is wrong that the EU institutions try to improve their transparency policies and routines as well as their more proactive information strategies; however, I think the political aspects of their information become neutralised and naturalised in the process, and that the information then becomes adequate in some respects, but systematically inadequate in other respects" (Slaata 2006: 21). This happens because of two reasons. First, the media reporting about EU affairs have a focus dominantly influenced by the national context. Second, interested citizens usually learn just about the outcome of European decision-making and cannot follow the whole process. "Individuals have small room for manoeuvre in the political communication process to Europe, until the structure of reporting on Europe is not fit to the importance of the political project of European integration" (Huber 2007: 7–8). The current institutional reforms of the new Lisbon Treaty—including a stronger personalization of European leaders, effective from 2009—might help in making the political offer from the side of European actors more citizen-friendly.

Today, the relatively fragmented elements of spheres of publics in Europe become more and more visible. The European Commission has placed videos on YouTube, whilst some local teams across Europe, "[b]ringing together young people from across the continent, this network aims to contribute to the construction of pan-European public opinion through the cafebabel.com magazine,"[6] and "supranational" pro-European groups have been formed spontaneously on Facebook, one of the biggest international on-line social communities. There are new techniques presumably able to deepen a European-wide debate: "the use of hyperlinks is not only a way to create connections to others. Hyperlinking allows completely new forms of writing about European politics, and those who understand this can actively contribute to the creation of a European public sphere, both within the institutions and in the wider public" (Frisch 2009).

Definitely, the borders of European and national media are not made of an iron curtain. "Both national and European discourses co-exist. 'Europe' is inside the nation-state as part of the domestic political agenda and also as a constitutive part of the broader politico-economic framework; yet, it is also still another place, a different political level and locus of decision-making that is outside. In the EU, given this ambiguity, the national, state-bounded context no longer completely defines the political scope of communicative communities" (Schlesinger 2003: 11). Moreover, the fragmentation of the national media and the diversity of their national audiences express the imperfectness of the dominant public spheres. Paradoxically, "[i]t is this unfinished and unsatisfied nature of the project of the public sphere, which becomes the seed of its potential transnationalisation" (Trenz 2008). From a normative, but probably a realistic perspective "[c]ontinued support for the European project requires adaptation of national institutions to the European governance system and an open discourse where issues related to change are confronted and discussed both at the national level and in cross-border dialogue, before being implemented in Brussels. Broad-based discussions including critical stances are necessary in order to clarify the issues and modify positions of power elites" (Ruth 2007).

---

6 http://www.cafebabel.com/en/infos/networks.asp - last access on 9 March 2008.

There is a strengthening European public sphere on the horizon, based on a new narrative: "our identity will not be constructed in the fashion of the historic European nation, once humorously defined as a group of people united by a common hatred of their neighbors and a shared misunderstanding of their past" (Ash 2007).

Dominant Discourses about EU Matters in a National Context

Historically, the conceptualization of the question "What is Europe?" has always had "a temporal dimension meaning that the answer changes over time depending on various contexts. Europe means variety" (Malmborg and Stråth 2002: 4). Philosophers and politicians, movements and parties have conceptualized the European idea in different parts of the continent. In the last two-hundred years, nation-state building was the dominant, but also a parallel—although ostensibly often a contradictory—process to the formation of Europe. Europe was invented, used and misused in the political ideological views of competing elites and individuals. The different meanings of Europe are still with us, as older and newer member states of the European Union have brought their own historical-cultural perceptions about the integration project into the common club. "The term 'Europe' has been–and is–full of political content in each national setting. The conceptualization of Europe varies and contested within—as much as among—nations" (Malmborg and Stråth 2002: 4).

In the individual member states, dominant attitudes of the public to current European affairs are based on "common wisdom" experiences from the past–certainly, this "public knowledge" might differ significantly from one place to another. The number of European citizens who proclaim their European identity in European-wide surveys, for example, is also an indicator of a more pro-European or a Euro-skeptic character of each country. Internal political differences, on the other hand, make the picture inside these democracies more colourful. Conservatives, socialists, liberals and other political groups–represented both on national and trans-national levels–have their own narratives of Europe. It is an important question: to what extent do widely shared national assumptions on European matters frame the discourse in a member state. Or, in the absence of such a general interpretative scheme, to what extent do partisan cleavages and conflicts matter more in structuring debates about European politics. In the latter case, differentiated views of groups might even fit into the ideological dividing lines on the supranational European level.

"In contemporary societies, for the vast majority of the population the mass media are the one and only source of information on EU political processes" (Oberhuber, Barenreuter, Krzyzanowski, Schönbauer and Wodak 2005: 229). The national media of older and newer, bigger or smaller member states that reflect the path-dependency of their respective country when placing European news and issues into a specific national context.

Path-dependency is not cultural determinism: "Patterns of history are in no way deterministic, but Europhile versus Europhobe national discourses can predispose some nations to react mainly positively and others rather negatively towards the imposition of a European polity on the nation states... It must be emphasized, when we talk about the French, Austrian, Russian, etc. image or meaning of Europe, we do not ignore the fact that France, Austria and Russia are abstractions.... With the French image we refer to one image with particularly great influence in the French debate, an image which contributed highly to the self-understanding of France as a nation, but it does not mean that this image was uncontested" (Malmborg and Stråth 2002: 13–14).

Because of the different national contexts, comparative studies on the Europeanization of the national media face a serious methodological problem:

By focusing on how the same, predefined EU news discourses are filtered and reformulated, the comparative research design risk leaving out all the complexities of various discourses and discursive orders surrounding the selected news story. By doing this, one easily mistakes a predefined category of EU-related news discourse with a nationally representative discourse on Europe, disregarding the fact that the selected discourse is a pre-structured discourse.... In their domestic and historically constituted political cultures, European integration and the political institutions and initiatives within the European Union takes on different symbolic meanings in each nation state" (Slaata 2006: 13–14).

Intertextuality in national discourses, divergent meanings of European issues, ideas and expressions in the internal cultural-political contexts of member states are especially relevant, since "as soon as a particularly large amount of reporting is devoted to one event in a state, the respective authors of the studies justify this with reference to *national* events or debates connected with the particular EU topic" (Machill, Beiler and Fischer 2006: 70). The case of a non-member state, Norway shows a similar pattern: "Slaatta has for instance studied how news production strategies among Norwegian correspondents on the "Brussels beat" changed as the Norwegian membership debate ended and the EEA agreement was implemented. In the Norwegian situation, the institutionalization of European politics and the EEA agreement at the national political beat was much more important for defining news production strategies than what happened in the EU" (Slaata 2006: 15). In general, "Europeanization of national television news is considerably lagging behind the Europeanization of the economy and politics" (Peter, Semetko and de Vreese 2003: 320).

From a supranational normative perspective, "EU-related information provided by national media is insufficient" (European Commission 2007: 11). Empirical data support this statement. The meta-analysis of 17 comparative studies on how the national media of the EU-15 between 1994 and 2003 dealt with the European Union points out that "the media in the individual states examined name protagonists from home much more frequently than players on the EU stage." Moreover, "EU reporting only accounts for a small part of total reporting... it can be established as a rough tendency that German, Danish and Netherlands media devote themselves more to Europe than the media in other countries... The UK represents a special case because in the British media attention focuses especially on Europe's currency policy issues, with highly personalised reporting of the EU protagonists. By contrast, only a small number of reporting is devoted to other EU topics and states" (Machill, Beiler and Fischer 2006: 71, 75). As for the German case, according to another study, just 5 percent of all the news coverage was focused on EU topics in main news programs and non-regional newspapers between 1998 and 2004 (data quoted in Huber: 2007). In 2000, according to the results of a comparative study in Germany, Denmark, France, the Netherlands and the United Kingdom "the share of EU stories in the entire coverage did not exceed 4% in any country, except Denmark (10%)." Still, there was a paradox in the representations of the EU, what might be called, as the authors argued, the invisible importance of the integration: "EU affairs are obviously considered important because they are prominently placed" in the sequence of the news (Peter, Semetko and de Vreese 2003: 313–414, 321) Actually, the intensity of reporting about the European Union grew significantly in Germany and in the United Kingdom already by the early 1990s, when the former elite-driven project received more and more public attention at least at European summits (Hodess 1998). Since then, it has become more and more complicated to define and separate European news from national ones in the media: "What were once domestic issues is now some combination of *domestic* and *European* issues" (Semetko, de Vreese and Peter 2000: 131).

Although EU events are still handled as foreign news in many editorial rooms in national capitols and cities, the twinning of the two levels is often simply unavoidable. The process of Europeanization, sooner or later, challenges old patterns of cleavages amongst and inside the member states. The changes are also technologically driven: "National cultures are usually permeable, however much they are censored and controlled, and in the age of the Internet and satellite broadcasting that relative openness is necessarily greater than ever before" (Schlesinger 2003: 10).

The process of domestication, namely when common European issues are translated and fit into the national context by professional gatekeepers, has another unavoidable consequence. Different segments of the whole information package become salient and available to each national media audience. The differences in the ways and means how professional gatekeepers select and frame the news coming "from Europe" can be contribute to the lack of a uniform European journalistic tradition and media culture, as well as to the characteristics of functioning media systems—the relations between the media and politics—in the member states. Perhaps different media regimes—whether they belong to/stand closer to the liberal, the democratic-corporatist or the polarized pluralist model (Hallin and Mancini 2004), or in the case of the post-communist countries, presumably to a fourth type of media system—also play a role in how European topics reach the stimulus threshold of the national media elites and when they get politicized. During the European elections of 1999, "[t]he expansion of the EU was not a major election issue but given more consideration in Germany and Sweden (probably for geographical reasons) and in Ireland (possibly as regards the potential loss of structural funds). Common foreign policy issues hardly surfaced in the UK media in relation to the EU elections but seemed a relatively important issue in the Swedish media due to neutrality" (Kevin 2001b :28).

Focusing now on individual cases and starting with the United Kingdom to illustrate the peculiarities of representations of EU matters on a national level, this country is certainly a special case. "In everyday English, the most striking feature of the way in which 'Europe' is used is the manner in which it has often become synonymous with 'continental'–i.e. a geographical area which does not include the British Isles" (Ludlow 2002: 101). According to the allegory of the historian Timothy Garton Ash, Britain has four faces: "The back and front faces can be labelled 'Island' and 'World'; the face on the left says 'Europe' and that on the right 'America'" (Ash 2004: 18). The two big parties, the conservatives and the Labour Party changed roles in the last fifty years concerning their willingness to support European integration and especially its political dimension. Liberals/liberal democrats continuously proclaimed their pro-European platform. But even the political attitudes and ambitions of a strongly committed politician, former Prime Minister Tony Blair, who "wanted to overcome for once and for all, a half century of British ambivalence about the European project" (Ash 2004: 46) can be characterized with the "Janus faces" of his country. "[Blair's] keynote European speeches, even when they were delivered in the continent, tended to turn into speeches about why Britain had to be in Europe rather than about Europe as Europe" (Ash 2004: 47). During the first period of the Blair government "Britain did indeed seem to be moving towards the heart of Europe, or at least towards shedding its image as the 'awkward partner'." Still, comparing original commitment and real performance, the record of the New Labour's European policy is "at best mixed" (Smith 2005: 721). Some policy areas remained taboos in the British approach: common foreign policy must exclude supranational players; taxation must be in national competence. Nevertheless, the political line of Blair's government fits into the political tradition of the EU-friendly part inside the elite, hence, "to feel that Britain should play an encouraging role from the sidelines" (Ludlow 2002: 114). Cautious attitudes of politicians are also to be explained with an overwhelmingly anti-European yellow press. In 1999, "*The Sun* was far more explicit in its suggestions for '10 (alternative) uses for a load of Euro ballot (papers)' including suggesting they be used as confetti or as draught excluders" (Kevin 2001b: 30). "But even among the broadsheet publications, several with less important circulations but reaching an influential readership, particularly the *Daily Telegraph* and *The Times*, are overtly hostile to European integration" (Bond 2001: 260). On the other hand, in the British media "European integration appears to be an especially elite-dominated public debate... While Eurosceptics have been making political arguments against Europe for years, pro-Europeans have not provided political justifications for European integration to the same extent" (Statham and Gray 2005: 71, 76). The room for victorious pro-European political action–for example a call for referendum in order to introduce the euro as a single currency in the country—remained limited taking into account the general ambivalence of the "islanders"; their "us and them" perception about the UK and Europe. So, according to Chris Patter, the existential question still sounds like that: "Will Britain ever 'actually' join the EU?" (Patten 2004). The new coalition government of the conservatives and the liberal democrats formed in 2010 brings politicians with very different prepositions on the European Union into one team. Yet, Britain's Foreign Secretary William Hague used a pro-European language in one of his first articles after taking up his new post: "The EU's new External Action Service is going to have considerable bearing on the future success of Europe's global role. It is true that we in the Conservative Party were not persuaded of the case for the new EEAS as a service, but its existence is now a fact... Nevertheless, we now look to the smoothest possible establishment of a service that must play a positive role for the EU and have the confidence of its member states. Britain's Conservative government will work closely with the High Representative, whom we wish well" (Hague, 2010).

In France, Europe has been the name of the concept to implement liberties derived from the Enlightenment and the Revolution outside the boundaries of the country. For most French intellectuals and politicians, this was rather the idea of a French Europe and not a Europeanized France. As for the attitudes of General Charles de Gaulle to Europe, to the Commission and Britain's entrance into the European Community, the view to defend French national interests overruled

any other concerns. Since the beginning of the late 1970s, "a gradual Europeanization of French nation state identity took place among
elites which came about as a result of French experiences with European integration as well as two more 'critical junctures'–the utter failure
of Mitterand's economic politics in the early 1980s and the end of the
Cold War in the late 1980s" (Marcussen, Risse, Engelmann, Martin,
Knopf and Roscher 1999: 62). The original "little Europe" has gradually enlarged to a European Union in the 1990s and to the EU-27 by
2007. So the French dominant perception had to start to accommodate another reality, where France—or the French-German political-
economic tandem—has no longer the final say about the direction of
the integration process and its speed in the European debates. The assumptions about the EU are changing: Europe has become much less
simply a space for French influence–as a solution after the decline of
French global "gloire"—but a space for a new French identity. This
shift means that "national identity is capable of evolution and of new
connections with European identity" (Frank 2002: 324). The process
is seen as far from complete. Although the negative vote on the draft
European Constitution in 2005 might be explained first of all with domestic reasons, the majority of French citizens seemed not to accept
the offer of pro-European elites (Schild 2005). "The legacy of the old
ambitions of French leadership has not entirely disappeared" (Frank
2002: 325) in high political circles, either. However, an expanding view
that even bigger nation states cannot solve problems of our global age
moved French attitudes from the idea of French centrality in Europe
to European centrality in France. Although Europe seems to be a new
fortress against the political power of the United States of America in
the eyes of many French people, Nicolas Sarkozy won the presidential elections not only with a pro-European, but also with a rather pro-
American program in 2008.

Whilst during the Franco-dictatorship "Europeanism" of the regime was limited to the economic ties to the European Community,
after the death of the General, Europe has become a symbol of modernity and democratic renewal in Spain (Jáuregui 2002). This function of
the European integration shows similarities to many post-communist
countries. The Spanish political elite learned how to transfer its own
(foreign) policy ideas to the European level (Torreblanca 2001). Differentiation in attitudes towards Europe developed between the two

big competing political camps—between the more national and pro-American political line of the conservative and the more all-European approach of the socialist governments—which have been represented in the partisan press, too. After the failure of the European leaders in agreeing about the final text of the European Constitution in December 2003, "while the social-liberal *El País* seems to take a more neutral stance on Spain's position, blaming Aznar for isolating Spain within the EU and considering the negative implications for the EU, the conservative *ABC* defends the position of the Spanish government and is mainly worried that Spain will lose the power gained through the treaty of Nice" (Oberhuber et al. 2005: 248). Still, in spite of partisan cleavages on EU matters, Spanish "membership of the European Union remains a fundamental uncontested dimension of the national self-image in the world" (Jáuregui 2002: 96).

Current Polish attitudes towards Europe show the legacy of the long-lasting historical fight for independence. For the representatives of the Polish state, for its noble-gentry elite, their homeland was the last defender of Western Christianity on the eastern periphery for many centuries. After the collapse of the sovereign Poland in 1795, intellectuals and politicians created and represented new Polish ideologies about Europe. Pro-European concepts about the modernization of Poland competed with Slavophile ideas and Romantic messianism—all of them, nevertheless, contributed to the national resistance against Russian, German and Austrian oppression. The ideological differences grew between "occidentalism" and a new "ethnocentrism," which was based on the assumption that national culture should be defended from the liberal, "degenerate West." This was the birth of the recurrent and later wide-spread view "to treat the relations between Poland and Europe in the terms of creditor and debtor. In the eyes of the Poles it is Europe that has a dept to Poland, 'the knight of Europe' and the 'Christ of nations', a debt never paid back" (Törnquist–Plewa 2002: 222). In the inter-war period, the new independent Poland brought dominance to the occidentalists after the successful battle against Bolshevik Russia. However, the feelings of alienation towards the western European countries did not disappear and they were strengthened after the Second World War, when—partly on new territory—Poland became a victim of big powers' bargaining and found itself in the position of a satellite communist country. Although one of the most characteristic slogans of the regime-change in 1989 was Poland's "Return to Europe," increasing Euro-skepticism and rising populism at the beginning of the new century (Michnik 2006) showed in a bitter way that "Polish attitude to Europe presents whole emotional syndromes described by psychologists as 'the complex of an unwanted child.' There is longing and unrequited love, distrust, fear, inferiority feelings and a compensatory need for self-assertion" (Törnquist–Plewa 2002: 239). Poland has become an example for the crystallization of competing pro-European and anti-European political forces as well as a clear differentiation of the media coverage of European matters, just to mention *Gazeta Wyborcza*, a liberal daily on the one side and the fundamentalist Catholic *Radio Maryja* on the other.

Slovenia is widely seen from outside as one of the most successful new member states, which was the first amongst the new democracies to be able to adopt the single European currency already in 2007. "Throughout the late 1980s and early 1990-s, the political elites and the mainstream mass media in Slovenia—the only former Yugoslav Republic that survived the violent break-up of the federal state without much scarring—were framing the process of gaining independent statehood in terms of exiting 'the Balkans' and entering 'Europe'" (Mihelj 2004: 165). But in a couple of years, the language of media reports changed and a much more negative picture was painted about the European Union: "Contrary to 1992, when the prevailing connotations connected with Europe were positive, in 2000/2001 the West was presented as ambiguous. This is most clearly evident in print media, where the words 'Europe' and the 'West' regularly appear together with the adjective 'promised' or the phrase 'promised land' put into question marks ... The main argument appearing alongside such attitudes is that 'the West' no longer keeps to its own standards of democracy and liberalism" (Mihelj 2004: 183).

The Visegrád countries, feeling economically, politically and geographically less peripheral, especially wanted to present the significant differences inside the candidate countries, foremost the gap between Central and Eastern Europe. The political project of this image-building effort has been mostly addressed to Western Europe. Still, all East-Central European countries—not only their national media, but their elites and population—have showed a lot of similarities in their more and more ambivalent relationship to the European Union since the collapse of communism. "For us from the East, after the crumbling of the Iron Curtain, Europe came to symbolize not only a promise, but also a latent neurosis" (Plesu 1997). Around the turn of the century, soft and hard Euro-skepticism emerged in public discourses (Szilágyi 2002). Beside blaming the old member states for alleged mistakes and sins, the newcomers' obsession—to use another strong psychological term—was to prove the full Europeanness of their own catching-up country during the accession talks and right after gaining membership. Just to illustrate such claims with a Slovak example: "A year and a half after the EU entry, former Slovak Prime Minister Mikuláš Dzurinda could state in front of the members of the parliamentary European Affairs Committee that Slovakia had shown it was not just a consumer but also a creator of EU policy" (Bilčík 2007: 328). This sort of political communication also refers to the illiberal regime between 1993 and 1998 when "Europe was shocked from Vladimir Mečiar' Slovakia and the nation lived through the exclusion as a deep trauma. That is why it is such a good feeling to be accepted as one of the others. But the relief has a serious disadvantage: it makes the debate about Europe, the essence of Europeanness and about our Slovak specificity inside this framework impossible" (Simecka 2003). In Slovakia, which entered the Euro-zone in 2009, the political forces in the coalition government created in 2006 sustained the European orientation of the country with a strong pro-European rhetoric: "Ironically enough, among them there are two parties which systematically destroyed fundaments of liberal democratic regime while serving as ruling parties in mid-90s (HZDS/ Movement for a Democratic Slovakia of Vladimir Mečiar and SNS/ Slovak National Party, the radical nationalist formation) and the biggest political formation, the self-declared social democratic party (Smer-SD), which blamed the previous government in betrayal of national interests during the accession process, accusing then the ruling coalition of doing integration policies being on its "knees" under the dictate from EU. Among the most "pronounced" Slovak Euro-optimists are nationalist and populist formations… 'Euro-optimism' can be labelled rather as the 'situational quasi-Euro-optimism'" (Mesežnikov 2009).

Twenty-five newspapers of six post-communist countries, Bulgaria, Croatia, the Czech Republic, Hungary, Poland and Slovenia, throughout their accession negotiations to the EU (except Croatia, which did not conclude the talks until 2006) were the subjects of critical discourse analysis that was published in a summary article (Vidra 2007). In spite of the cultural-historical differences, "one of the most striking observations was the structural similarities revealed in the studies. Apparently, the accession process generated discursive positions in all the countries included in the analysis regardless of their position in the region, their date of accession, and their 'individual story' in respect to the countries' specific relationship to the EU." The discourses had a dominant pro-European stance in each country, and the EU issues were domesticated for national use and purposes. During this historic period, when a once perceived fast "re-unification of Europe" gave place to a long-lasting adjustment process, it was not surprising that a differentiation in positions took place in these new democracies: "The representation of the EU reflected the political party divisions and the ideological cleavages typical of the given country… The pro-EU discourses were mainly found in left wing and/or liberal oriented quality newspapers" (all quotes in Vidra 2007).

The summary study uses the concept of self-colonization as a starting point. This "infamous theory" can be criticized because of "[r]allying the metaphor of trauma, self-colonization theory actually doubles the trauma by essentialising and fixing the binary opposition, closing the door at the more nuanced critique and analyses" (András 2004). However, this framework is able to express, according to the author, the voluntary aspect of the accession process and allows "to apply some psychological and social psychological terms to deconstruct the images and discourse types" in the pro-EU coverage as well as in the negative reactions to this dominant narrative published in the analyzed newspapers (Vidra 2007). The categories used in the study contradict the common wisdom views that the media of applicant countries simply supported European Union membership in a sort of propaganda manner. Just the opposite: the comparative study shows that national press expressed—often in an unconscious way—the ambiguity of the historic project in the eyes of the newcomers. Three common major attitudes and emotions were found in the reporting about the accession process: *obedience*, *resentfulness* and *fear*. The 25 newspapers gave colourful examples for national perceptions of a subordinated, inferior position to the EU, which was portrayed as an omnipotent figure. Self-criticism and shame about the country's political and economic culture was elaborated probably the best in the Slovenian *Delo* in 1999: "The EU can actually protect us from ourselves!" Resentfulness and suspicion are mixed in the report of *24 chasa* in 2000, saying that "the EU swindles Bulgaria with membership." The following quote from the Croatian press—published in *Globus* in 2003 - shows again the psychological position of an underdog: "It's good to be highly suspicious of the EU. You cannot believe everything they say. Very often they do not know what they are really talking about. To be very precise, even in this very moment they do not know who they are, where they are going and how all that will end. Even when they're talking in a way which you can understand, the message: 'Come here, come inside!', is only a catch-phrase, a learned manner." Fear of the unknown started to grow before the day of the entry to the club everywhere in the region, and Euro-skeptical language strengthened–and not exclusively in the rhetoric of nationalist and new populist political groups. The feeling of being second class citizens inside the European Union became a typical complaint all over. One of the main conclusions of the comparative study is that "self-blame and an enhanced vision of our backwardness are core elements of the identities of the Central and Eastern European countries and the only existing response and reaction to this attitude is an ill-defined national interest position" (all quotes in Vidra 2007).

Hungary: Media Representations of EU Matters

Like other nations fighting against the Turks in the middle ages, Hungary also has a self-image once being "the last bastion of Christianity." The attitudes, views and opinions of Hungarians on Europe have been largely influenced by previous historical lessons like failed, but glorious revolutions, two lost world wars and their consequences, the secession of 2/3 of the country's former territories and Hungarians living beyond the borders. The "Trianon syndrome" (Kende 1995) contributed to the public imagination that today's Hungary is a small state—although it is now one of the mainstream medium sized member states of the European Union. Hungary shares with other post-communist countries the political and psychological impacts of a forty year long isolation from the "West" until the regime-change in 1988–90. The "soft" dictatorship under János Kádár following the 1956 revolution and its brutal oppression—"the most joyful barrack inside the peace camp" as the position of the system under Soviet dominance was satirically formulated—tried to depoliticize the society. "There seemed to be no real need for a past while the actual system of conditions for the Kádár system to develop remained: the psychological aftermath of a social capitulation in 1957–8, a milder, but persistent Cold War, and partial legitimacy won by inflating the standard of living" (Rainer 2002). When this construction finally collapsed because of its lack of a moral basis and the increasing economic hardship, a dominant western orientation emerged in the country, however, often mixed with traditional nationalism as well as with romantic concepts about a "third way" between capitalism and socialism in the rhetoric and program of new democratic political leaders (Bozóki 1992).

During the 1990s, the new-born democracy successfully solved the tasks of economic transformation and the institutionalization of the rule of law, whilst ensuring stability under the circumstances of fresh, competitive party pluralism. Citizens, however, were not satisfied with the price of adjustment to the world of market economies and to a hectic democratic life, especially because of the pain of the fall-back in economic performance for almost a decade, as well as the over-ideological character of sharp partisan fighting between representatives of political elites. Just like in other post-communist countries, the media has become immediately one of the most significant battle fields after the regime change (Jakubowicz 1996). The new media law was approved only after the end of the (first) media war between 1990 and 1994, when the struggle for influencing media contents involved all political forces, the Constitutional Court and street demonstrators, whilst the question of showing loyalty or being in opposition to the first conservative government deeply divided the journalistic society. Still, political manoeuvres in order to control the mass media did not disappear at all even when commercial media was introduced into the media system after the end of open fighting. Especially in the case of public media, both the former reform-communist, now socialist party and the conservative forces had a hidden political agenda: "The essence of the left-right platform was to secure direct participation by parliamentary political parties in media supervisory bodies" (Molnár 1999: 95). One of the most important ideological objectives of the right-wing parties concerning the media was "to counter-balance" the perceived power

of the left-liberal media. This view flourished especially during the period of a second right-wing coalition government in 1998–2002, led by
Fidesz, which wanted to change media relations through governmental
interventions (Bajomi-Lázár 2003). Around the turn of the century,
parallel to the polarization of Hungarian politics and the strengthening of citizens' partisan identification that helped to create the overall dominance of party politics in public life—which became "the only
game in town" (Enyedi and Tóka 2007)—the political dailies showed
more and more partisan affiliations than ever before, even if the degree
of loyalties differed when comparing the sovereignty of papers supporting one of the two antagonistic political "sides" (Gordon 2007). As political tension still grew and led to violence on the streets in 2006, the
coverage of a highly divided and bias press reflected the negative consequences of "over-polarized" pluralism. At the same time, the most
important nation-wide commercial media channels were able to keep
political distance from the events, mostly because of their overall tabloid orientation.

This background seems to be important when talking about the
country's changing relationship towards the European Union. The
distorted political agenda that dominated the political arena—like the
traditional ideological conflict between "national" and "urban" intellectuals raised on party political level in the early 1990s, later the re-
emergence of a communist–anti-communist divide as well as the rise
of new populism—might be the main reason for the lack of any sophisticated debates about the future of Europe, and especially about the
potential role that Hungary should play inside a united Europe. Immediately after the regime-change, there was a declared consent amongst
the parliamentarian parties concerning desirable membership in Eu-
ro-Atlantic institutions and a high public support to this orientation.
The main content of this general wish, however, gradually moved from
"idealist" emphases on the re-unification of Europe as well as from optimistic proclamations that Hungary could join the democratic community of nations with a "luckier" historical past. The new, pragmatic
attention was now focused exclusively on another important aspect of
belonging to the West, namely to catch up with the economic space
where individuals had a higher living-standard. To be more precise, the
pro-European argumentation in favor of accession to the EU started
to concentrate on the financial advantages of membership and almost

stopped talking about the importance of European values. This mental drift around 2000, concerning the actual objective of joining the integration also expressed a disillusionment about the alleged motivations and behaviour of old and rich member states. These countries, in the eyes of Hungarians, simply wanted to hinder fast enlargement with "Eastern" countries, in spite of their publicly made promises after the collapse of communism. As the enlargement process seemed to take longer than it was supposed to be and Hungary could not join the EU in a smaller elite circle of the best candidates, a new common wisdom statement, rooted in historic experiences and myths about a nation, which was always left alone by the bigger powers, emerged in public: "they are playing fool with us." Old stereotypes, including incorporated Marxists doctrines at school during the communist era about raw economic interests which drive (foreign) countries and are always behind all their political decisions, regained their explanatory strength. Still, this new "Euro-pessimistic" feeling and language in the national discourse was based on no clear ideological assumptions and did not find its "enemy" in "Brussels" as Euro-skeptics always did. Euro-pessimism can be described as a "yes, but" attitude of Hungarians, people living in a relatively small country, which wanted to join the European club of the rich, but its reservations and anxiety have gradually grown when facing its own unknown future under new circumstances.

After Hungary started accession negotiations in March 1998 and following the parliamentary elections right after, the victorious right-wing government introduced a new rhetoric which emphasized the need for defending national interests against the representatives of the EU during the talks. Leading politicians blamed the old member states that they did not have enough courage to tell the truth about the "real timing" of enlargement. The most famous quote from this period was the "bon mot" of then Prime Minister Viktor Orbán: "There is life outside the European Union." An even stronger "outspoken" declaration was the following statement by then President of the ruling party Fidesz, László Kövér, saying, "the European Union had already regretted its mistake to start the enlargement process, just like the dog which had a litter of nine" (quoted by Hegedűs 2001: 243). The new political framing changed the rules of partisan power game. During the next election campaign in 2002, from an opposition position, the Hungarian Socialist Party tried to re-orient itself as the main supporter of Hungarian farmers' demands for more direct payments from the budget of the European Union and criticized the agricultural chapter of the accession treaty agreed upon and "closed" by the incumbent government. All political parties as well as the media started to attack those old member states which were reluctant to open their labor market fearing an influx of workers from new member states and planned to introduce a transition period before providing free movement to them. The general feeling that Hungary was becoming a second class member inside the EU was the new characteristic complaint. This was combined with the claim that Hungary would deserve much more financial support from the richer member states–first of all because of its historical suffering, but also since the Mediterranean countries, after joining the European Community, had received transfers on a significantly higher scale during the eighties-nineties.

"There is no alternative to the European Union"—another fresh common phrase emerged in the public discourse, expressing the unavoidable "fate" of the nation in the eyes of the citizens. By the beginning of the new century, Euro-enthusiasm evaporated and a rather cautious, lukewarm resignation about membership took its place. Remaining the leading politician of Fidesz after losing elections in 2002, Orbán started to talk about a "marriage of inconvenience" when describing the sense of coming accession. After working hard on Hungary's accession, "at the given address, instead of a red carpet, we faced bold and gloomy looking bodyguards, who distributed admission tickets."[7] Fidesz, at this moment, mixed the language of "soft" Euroskepticism, absorbing amorphous protest voices, with "light" pro-European statements, whilst the governing socialist-liberal coalition attacked the major opposition party because of its flip-flop platform. Nevertheless, it was a negative surprise for all the elites in major political parties how fast hard Euro-skeptical gossips spread over in the popular culture when people actually realized that Hungary finally arrived "ante portas." It occurred as an unexpected consequence of an official communication campaign, a centralised mobilization effort before the national referendum on accession to the EU. These "Euro-panic"

---

[7] Orbán, Viktor. *Európa a jövőnk, Magyarország a hazánk* [Europe is Our Future, Hungary is Our Homeland]. Speech at the 16th congress of Fidesz - Hungarian Civic Party, 7 December 2002.

rumours included radical right wing views about the colonization of the nation and popular fears of the prohibition of traditional poppy-seed crêpe by the EU. Other concerns about membership emerged like the fear of price increases and the collapse of Hungarian agriculture in a stronger—and "unfair"—competitive environment.

Although the national referendum which took place on 12 April 2003 brought an 85 percent overwhelming victory for EU supporters, the low, 45 percent turn out was interpreted as a serious failure. In fact, we still do not know how many citizens from the "yes" voters' camp meant an enthusiastic support to the historic change, or these people would have wanted to send an ambivalent Euro-pessimistic "yes, but" message to the elites. Giving a nuanced answer was naturally impossible in such a black and white situation. The lack of any spontaneous carnival-type atmosphere after the positive outcome of the referendum gives a strong support for the second assumption. Perhaps there was no broad ideological dividing line between the pro-EU citizens with reservations, and others staying at home, and even those Hungarians, who decided to express their dominant negative sentiments at the ballots. Self-regret, defiance and inferiority feelings merged in the overall Euro-pessimistic mood (Hegedűs 2005). At least, on the very day of accession, a sort of relief and joy spread over amongst the participants at the celebrations on the streets of Budapest and in the opinion-pieces and comments published in newspapers and magazines. A liberal intellectual, György Konrád, concluded in an article: "As for myself, I do not lack optimism and I think: finally!"[8]

One year after the referendum, Fidesz positioned itself on a more pro-European basis at the first European elections in Hungary following the "Big Bang" enlargement of the European Union with ten new member states on 1 May 2004. During the campaign, the two major parties attacked each other mostly echoing the same simple message: the essence of the fighting was to prove which of them would represent Hungarian interests better in the European Parliament. The overwhelmingly supranational nature of the decision-making processes inside the European Parliament was hardly mentioned in the debates

---

[8] Konrád, György. *Belépőbeszéd* [Entry Speech], *Mozgó Világ*, May 2004, pp. 11–14, www.mozgovilag.hu/2004/05/04%20konrad.htm

(Hegedűs 2005). This was a typical second order election perceived as a revenge of the former national election and a preparation for the next one in 2006. National issues became salient whilst practically no European topics were on the agenda. The situation was somewhat different in the case of the new draft on the European Constitution which was ratified by the Hungarian Parliament in a rapid way in 2004. This time, at least, two issues were raised from the national context and transferred to the European level. The fundamental rights of minorities, meaning national minorities, were suggested by all Hungarian parties to be included into the text and was presented by the government at the intergovernmental conference (partly successfully). The other topic was whether a Christian heritage should be mentioned in the new treaty—this theme was raised by conservative political groups. Still, the Hungarian discourse did not reflect on any other debates about the draft constitution in other member states. When the treaty failed in France and the Netherlands during the ratification process in 2005, and two years later the new Reform Treaty was signed in Lisbon, Hungary behaved like the "best student" and ratified the agreement as the first member state of the EU-27 in 2007.

The attitudes of Hungarian citizens about the European Union started to differentiate at the end of the accession talks and after the 2003 referendum. The change in the views of the electorate reflected the new partisan conflicts on EU matters. Before these debates, ideological concerns did not determine party positions "as far as a clear-cut choice between accepting or rejecting EU membership is concerned" (Bátory 2001). In contrast to this former situation, in 2003, polls showed that right-wing voters supported the project less than the followers of the left-liberal government. Two years later just 47 percent of the people felt that Hungary benefited from EU membership. Although 61 percent of the left wing citizens said "yes" to this question, whilst amongst those who placed themselves on the right side of the political scale this number was only 43 percent (European Commission 2005). Still, the process of crystallization between pro- and anti-Europeans, in contrast to Polish and Czech development, was definitely stopped by Fidesz, the largest right-wing party. Party leader Orbán, for example, emphasized the Christian democratic origin of the integration at the fiftieth anniversary of the European Union in 2007.

Certainly, it was the mass media which provided the main forum for debates between party politicians, experts, NGO leaders and other stakeholders about the accession to the European Union, during the European elections and since then as well. The media has been the major information source of the Hungarians about Europe in general. Just like in the case of all national media in candidate countries and member states, when Hungarian journalists and editors selected the news from the flow of information about EU matters, they used their professional routine which also reflected their own cultural-historical attitudes as well as their partisan-ideological values. The question, who had stronger influence on the construction of a Euro-pessimistic frame; parties, journalists, or the public–in other words: whether the media leads or follows—cannot be answered in a simple way. The gradual shift in coverage on the European Union to a less attractive image, the emergence of numerous negative elements in the rhetoric of public figures and the more ambivalent mood of the people about the historical project were all correlated and occurred simultaneously. From a normative perspective, however, the media had a high sense of responsibility especially in the case of the EU matters, since most Hungarians were ignorant about the subject. The agenda-setting and issue framing abilities of the media gained crucial significance, since Hungarian citizens had no trustworthy reference groups to control and filter information coming from the mass media: "the news media may be more likely to shape perceptions of foreign policy than perceptions of domestic politics" (Norris 2000: 185).

That is why it was so important that although Hungary belonged to the avant-garde of new democracies according to all evaluations and regular reports issued by European institutions, the accession negotiations, especially at the end of the talks, were generally portrayed as a political fight between "us and them" and not as deliberations between "us" and the "future us" in the media. "Rich" member states were often accused because of their "selfishness"[9] and were attacked not to be ready to make more efforts and to pay more in favor of Eastern enlargement. The typical judgment was that "the EU's solidarity towards the Central and Eastern European countries has been decreasing since

---

[9] See for example Aczél, Endre. *Önzés* [Selfishness], *Népszabadság*, 10 May 2001.

the early 1990s when, after the euphoria of the fall of communism, it made generous promises" (quoted by Vidra 2007) Journalists and experts often analyzed Hungary's accession to the EU in mechanical terms of short run comparison of supposed costs and benefits. Values-based analysis was often missing, and the media emphasized again and again that "there will be losers after the accession." Following this logic, even the Schengen Agreement was described as a new financial burden for Hungary whilst the symbolic and practical importance of no border controls, especially for a post-communist country, was often forgotten. Journalists argued that they covered the EU "objectively," hence they wanted to avoid the risk of creating too high expectations in the population. However negative headlines in the papers rather reflected their own Euro-pessimism and the gradual process of banalization of the European story. In order to use an understandable framework, the media introduced the rather humiliating teacher-pupil allegory to point out the naturally unbalanced relationship between an applicant and the long-time members of a club. Then, the "teacher" was also easily deconstructed and criticized for its "double standards," or simply saying that "anyone who keeps exaggerated hopes alive related to the European Union nowadays, pursues illusions," as a first page opinion piece started in *Magyar Nemzet*.[10]

Although institutional and legal adjustment was the most important topic in the media, the content of the chapters at the accession negotiations were usually found too technical and boring by journalists. Except when transition periods were introduced on the labor market of many old member states—better to say, existing measures were not automatically suspended—the media immediately spoke about "restrictions" and did not compare them to a similar agreement reached at the green table that allowed Hungary not to sell agricultural land to "foreigners"—hence, non-Hungarian European citizens—for another seven more years. The question of the future of the Hungarian agricultural sector became a "sacred" topic *per se* in the eyes of the biggest political parties after 1998, at the beginning of accession talks: "How can we avoid the pitfalls? Are we going to be the winners or the losers of accession? We can gain a lot, but probably we may lose even more with it. We may become subordinates to EU countries if we represent our

---

[10] 15 February 2000.

interests badly. One of our aims to achieve is that foreigners would be banned from buying land for 8–10 years,"[11] as a Fidesz expert argued and similar views were represented by socialist politicians. At least in liberal newspapers the criticism of this position also appeared: "The restriction on the sale of agricultural land is a political issue from the beginning full of nationalistic sentiments. Meanwhile the vast majority of experts in all parties represented now in the parliament know exactly that an immediate and complete liberalization would be needed" (all quotes in Vidra 2006: 125–126).

Moralising statements like "we should enter the EU with pride, no need for toadyism" (quoted by Martin 2002), expressed growing inferiority feelings. Negative judgments on European politicians became quite common, like the one on the "hypocrisy" of Günter Verheugen, then Member of the European Commission responsible for enlargement, because of his position on the highly disputed issue how much could be transferred from the EU budget in the form of direct payments to the farmers of new member states. The role of the European Commission during the negotiations was simplified as the agent of the old member states. The concept of an "honest broker" did not appear in the media. In the perception of many journalists, regardless of their political affiliations, the role of the Hungarian media was to "unmask" the unfair methods and practices of politicians and officials representing the old member states and the European institutions as well as to support the national position of the Hungarian governments in their struggle for better political and economic conditions for the country.

According to this sort of "advocacy" journalism, the European Union simply wanted "to push us down." Counter-arguments of the negotiating partners did not appear in the news. "*Népszabadság*, in the last three weeks, placed on its front page twice and wrote an editorial piece on the issue that swill must be heat-treated before feeding to pigs to make it EU-compliant. The editors of the newspaper, sometimes with little irony, sometimes with passionate temper, present this in a negative sense, as if 'they'—the EU—do not allow the pig to eat the good old Hungarian swill, because they want 'our' farmers to work under harder conditions on the single market. As if it were not the solution of the EU which serves better the health of the citizens,

---

11 Béla Glattfelder to *Napi Magyarország*, 28 April 1998.

the protection of the consumers? As if there had been no preparation time for the change and as if the EU had not contributed to its costs?" (Martin 2002). After the Copenhagen summit which completed accession talks in 2002, the liberal economic weekly *HVG* placed on its front page a one euro coin, from which a small part was bitten out, entitled "admission fee." The message was again: the old member states were willing to pay just a small contribution for the enlargement compared to their real capabilities (Hegedűs 2003). As *Magyar Nemzet* elaborated: "[i]n the eyes of the member states the costs of enlargement are too high therefore they bargained with the candidate countries in a very pitiful way."[12] Defiance did neither exclude self-criticism of being an unreliable partner to the EU nor the feeling of backwardness: "The political elite thinks that introducing major reforms can be avoided," *Élet és Irodalom* stated, whilst *Magyar Narancs* argued, that "taking over EU regulations is a hermeneutic problem: we have to apply laws and regulations that were created in a different cultural environment and they seem to be inapplicable in our system... The Hungarian way of making the economy function does not work in the EU" (quoted by Vidra, 2007).

One of the relevant impacts of the Euro-pessimistic coverage of European news—and since most Hungarians have never heard about the concept of positive sum games between partners—was that no signs of solidarity inside the EU could be taken seriously in the Hungarian discourse. Just the opposite: "it is very likely that, at the end of the talks in December, the heads of states or governments, when they fasten on each other in order to close the negotiations, will all leave the ring as losers. They might feel winners at least in contrast to the newcomers."[13] Readers did not learn about the rules and norms of institutional decision-making processes. All sorts of European events, including new reforms and treaties, were seen exclusively from a single perspective, namely whether they brought Hungarian accession closer to its realization. In 1998, foreign minister János Martonyi complained about this narrow approach of the press in an interview,[14] saying "I was a little bit surprised when a part of the Hungarian media interpreted

---

[12] *Magyar Nemzet*, 16 December 2002.
[13] *Népszabadság*, 14 February 2000.
[14] *Magyar Nemzet*, 7 November 1998.

the last summit in Austria as if enlargement had been pushed into the background, although this issue had not been on the agenda at all" (Hegedűs 1999: 10). In other cases "the EU (with a few exceptions) is still considered to be an independent foreign policy item, rather than a horizontal, integral issue" (Gyévai 2002). Better informed, ambitious correspondents from Brussels were not able to change this mentality. Newspapers often gave the impression that the European Union was impotent in decision-making and suffered from harsh conflicts between its member states. At the European summit in December 1998, according to the typical media coverage, "everyone sings his or her own song," France and Germany "returned blow for blow," Chirac "declared his position in an authoritative tone," whilst "Great-Britain stares the other fourteen member states down" (Hegedűs 1999: 8–9).[15]

When an important event was not a real "drama," the Hungarian media did not pay much attention to it: "The press hardly covers the debates about the future of Europe in the Convention in Brussels; any analyses on the long term perspectives of the continent are almost totally unknown for the Hungarian public" (Martin 2002). Meanwhile, although the two big political camps differed in more and more political issues, the EU still had a salvation function before the accession: "The EU will save us from ourselves! However, "ourselves" is understood differently: for the right these are the (ex-communist) socialists, whilst for the left it is rather our political culture with a deeply rooted ideological cleavage between the left and the right that prevents us to reach compromises in national issues" (Vidra 2006: 139).

European reports often appeared in a special section inside newspapers without any link to national issues. Only Hungary's accession helped journalists dealing with EU matters to break out from this "ghetto." This was true even if mentioning the European Union in the press seemed to reach a high level: according to research on the information provided by some newspapers about EU matters. The number of references to the EU was 3.29 per a daily issue in two national newspapers, *Népszabadság* and *Magyar Nemzet*, whilst 1.26 in six regional county papers for half a year in 2000. However, the typical genre was the short news report: 95 percent of the articles belonged to this category. Concerning comments and opinion-pieces, the dominance

---

[15] *Népszabadság*, 12 December 1998.

of positive or neutral coverage about the consequences of Hungary's coming European accession was registered (Terestyéni 2001). Still, the argumentation in favor of the entry often used simplistic common wisdom patterns: "For a small country, the balance is on the side of advantages against the expected disadvantages concerning accession... The EU is not a paradise, but renders huge opportunities for those companies, which are well prepared enough to join the international market" (quoted by Terestyéni 2001).

Moreover, another comparative study found that "[i]n more than 60 percent of the articles, the Hungarian press commented on all three major EU-related events from 1993 onwards in a predominantly negative light, highlighting three major criticisms: (1) the EU's poor performance in managing the Yugoslav crisis, (2) its poor response to economic recession, and (3) an unclear strategy or even a lack of willingness to accept the accession of Eastern European countries." According to this research, "[f]rom the adoption of the Copenhagen criteria in late 1993 onwards, however, and especially after the Luxembourg meeting on enlargement in 1997, the voices critical of the EU have entirely disappeared from the moderate press and remain present only in the press of the extreme right and left" (Szilágyi-Gál 2003: 147–149).

The conclusion drawn from a critical discourse analysis of EU-related issues published in two Hungarian dailies and three weeklies—*Népszabadság, Magyar Nemzet, HVG, Élet és Irodalom, Magyar Narancs*—between 1989 and 2004 was different. Two images of the European Union co-existed with each other in the media. "The negative visions of the EU are focused on two aspects: first, the press wanted to present the EU as a complicated structure (over-bureaucratic, difficult to reform, etc.), second, it was portrayed as an imperative, domineering figure. The positive image was based on the moral, ethical values of the EU" (Vidra 2006: 143). The proportion of the positive image in the analyzed articles was just 25 percent, whilst almost half of the images, 47 percent belonged to the "too complicated" and 28 percent to the "imperative" categories. This research outcome contradicts the "voluntary" mission of those journalists about their vocation, who wanted to "counterbalance" pro-European news in the Hungarian media. The dominance of negative news seems to correlate with the political agenda-setting abilities of the ruling conservative government during the decisive period of accession talks. "Looking at the discursive fields around each topic" represented mostly in the media, "it was first of all the political rhetoric of Fidesz that generated the political and media discourse... The major tendency of the political discourse on the left-side could be defined as a reaction to the dominant position" (Vidra 2006: 150).

After Hungary's accession to the European Union, for first time in the history of Hungarian media, pan-European events became headlines in the mainstream press. This happened because of the institutional-political conflict between the European Commission and the European Parliament. On the day of the "European Government Crisis,"[16] as the then left-liberal *Magyar Hírlap* put it, President-designate of the European Commission "Barroso ordered back his team,"[17] as it was proclaimed by the right-wing *Magyar Nemzet*. The passionate debate on the ultra-conservative views of candidate Commissioner Rocco Buttiglione, whose candidacy was later withdrawn because of the resistance of socialist and liberal MEP-s, sounded familiar to Hungarian domestic ideological struggles. At least, interested citizens finally learned about the significance of the balance of power between European institutions, the role of political groups inside the European Parliament, and the relevance of European values. This positive episode supports the thesis that "European governance needs to make political conflict, both across national and transnational cleavages, more visible" (Meyer 2003: 40). In general, the coverage of the European Union shows a significant improvement in quality—thanks to a spontaneous learning process of both politicians and journalists, and perhaps to training programs organized especially for the latter group by European institutions.

Hungary's entry into the Schengen-zone on 21 December 2007 was finally celebrated without significant cynical voices. Nevertheless, Euro-pessimism, as the dominant framework for European reporting, did not disappear from the Hungarian media after reaching the national objective and Hungary became a member state of the European Union. The right wing *Magyar Nemzet* sniffed at EU membership at the occasion of the first anniversary, citing the views of former President of the Hungarian Academy of Sciences, Ferenc Glatz, who simply

---

[16] *Magyar Hírlap*, 28 October 2004.
[17] *Magyar Nemzet*, 28 October 2004.

proclaimed that Hungary "lost the accession."[18] Clear-cut Euro-skepticism also re-emerged in the same daily. Especially the European Commission was more often under cross-fire: "[t]he adoption of the European Constitution would give even more power to the Commission and more opportunities to take measures, which are not controlled and influenced by the national parliaments and the European Parliament (that is by the European public)."[19] Negative comments on the EU did not become more sophisticated: "The victory of Boris Tadić might wake up Brussels in the very last minute to realize that people in Serbia still have trust in the European Union which is in a serious crisis."[20] Average reporting about the EU still uses the same good old language just like before gaining membership, simply adjusting to the new situation when financial transfers started to arrive at Hungary from the European funds. You can always find reasons for complaining: one of the recent head-lines of *Népszabadság* stated: "EU money does not work well enough."[21]

Meanwhile, the general support to Hungary's EU membership has decreased. In the fall of 2007, 41 percent of Hungarians thought that it was a good thing, whilst the proportion of people with the same view had been much higher, 56 percent four years before. On the other hand, just 18 percent of the respondents had an explicitly negative opinion on this matter. Hungary had a similar position to Austria, heading only Cyprus and the United Kingdom in EU-optimism: 42 percent of its citizens answered "yes" to the question whether the country benefited from membership (European Commission 2007c: 25). Hungarians still had more trust in the European institutions than in their national ones: 60 percent proclaimed trust in the EU, whilst the Hungarian parliament received 21, the political parties 8 percent. Still, Euro-pessimism remained evidently a strong feeling of the Hungarian population: "The interviewees tend to believe that the

---

[18] Csite, András. *Nyomás az EU-ba! Nyomás?* [Let's Join the EU! Let's Join?] *Magyar Nemzet*, 7 May 2005.

[19] Lóránt, Károly. *Bizalmatlanság* [Distrust] *Magyar Nemzet*, 14 May 2005. The author supported the demands of the Euro-skeptical political group in the European Parliament.

[20] Pataky, István. *Belgrád és Brüsszel* [Belgrade and Brussels] *Magyar Nemzet*, 5 February 2008.

[21] 5 March 2008.

insufficient representation of the country is a consequence of its size, as 86% of Hungarians said the biggest countries have the most power in the EU" (European Commission 2007b). What is even more striking is the alienation of the people from the historic enterprise of their country: today, the new commonplace statement sounds like "nothing has changed since our accession." Hungarians seem to concentrate on their hectic domestic political life even more exclusively than five years before. During the European elections in 2009, political parties have practically ignored the European dimension of the contest.

Conclusions

The European public sphere is still under construction. European-wide dialogues between European citizens have to face divergent historical experiences, different connotations of ideas, words and slogans in the member states. Although spontaneous global and European horizontal relations are created by individuals and groups, and the European institutions gradually adjust to the new technological world in their top-down communication, European issues are mostly interpreted and framed in national contexts by national media. The media coverage in the member states about EU matters reflects the historically, politically and psychologically embedded nature of the dominant "meaning" of Europe in each country. Even if there are competing images about the European Union, especially in the case of newcomers, the former communist countries which recently joined the political club of the "West," there are characteristic common symptoms in their public debates which express the ambivalent and suspicious feelings of new European citizens and their national elites. Still, path-dependent attitudes and views on the European project do not determine future development of the integration process and public perceptions about its successes and failures might change in the future.

In Hungary, in a similar way to other post-communist new democracies, Euro-pessimistic views started to dominate the media discourse in accordance with the general decrease of enthusiasm about democratic changes and, later, with the emergence of a polarized partisan competition. The social representations of the European Union remained rather homogenous both in elite and mass perceptions, in spite of a solid differentiation of views reflecting partisan affiliations about EU membership. It was also easier for the media to use old-fashioned stereotypes to portray the EU since the beginning of the accession talks and to make only limited efforts to educate people about the internal political life and decision-making culture of the "moving target."

For the Hungarian media it was quite a complicated task to make EU matters more exciting as "typically elderly male diplomats spoke about not-understandable issues in EU jargon in black suits at press conferences in Brussels" (Sükösd 2003: 76).[22] The shortage of intellectual debates and the lack of clear value-based framework for interpreting EU matters made free way to fuzzy Euro-pessimism in the media. Thus, for most Hungarian citizens, the political world of the EU remained alien in spite of the historical chance and momentum. Instead, they had to rely on past stereotypes from a different age when big powers nearby dictated to Hungary. People threw out new information from their mind that did not fit into their "philosophies," just as Walter Lippmann observed analogue processes in his classic *Public opinion* (Lippmann 1997: 78). Being a relatively new member state of the European Union, Hungarians can finally learn more about common European and national issues from expanding European news–although the usual Euro-pessimistic framework did not disappear after the accession of the country to the European Union.

The differentiation between pro-European and Euro-skeptic political groups and personalities has slightly appeared in the partisan arena. However, it has not become a political cleavage in contrast to the Czech Republic, where "[o]n one hand, many citizens feel well rooted in their Europeanness and voted in high numbers for membership in the EU, still, the country became if not an enfant terrible then at least an "awkward newcomer" to the EU. The main opposing views on European identity (Euro-optimism and Euro-skepticism) can be illustrated and personified by the former President, Mr. Václav Havel, and the current President, Mr. Václav Klaus" (Klicperova-Baker–Košťál (2009: 4). In Hungary, the recent emergence of the extremist, ultra-nationalist party *Jobbik*, which received strong public support both at

---

[22] In fact, it was not a mission impossible to write about European politics in an exciting way for Hungarian readers (see Szlankó, 2007).

the European and national elections in 2009 and 2010, has little direct connection with its (negative) views on European integration.

Content analytical studies can convincingly show a national bias in reporting about the EU in all member states. There are, however, methodological problems that remained unsolved. For example, "[c]an we know whether the shortcomings we find should be seen as specific or just the same, classic problems of political journalism, transferred to a transnational system? If we were seriously trying to consider whether the EU-coverage in national news media reflected some kind of fair priority or attention that is caused by political journalism in general, rather than occurring because of particularities within the EU itself, we would have to contrast our findings with content analysis of other forms of journalism in the same media" (Slaata 2006: 12). Moreover, it is a well-known communication strategy by politicians to create a scapegoat from the EU—or "Brussels"—compensating their own failures or, actually, necessary compromises on European level. It seems to be better not to blame the national media for misinformation about EU matters in an over-generalised manner. Nevertheless, according to a comparative study between 1995–96, in the EU-15 "newspapers usually adopted a Euro-skeptic tone on most issues, although the degree of negative bias remained limited. Out of twenty-five separate issues, the coverage for all but four leaned in a negative direction" (Norris 2000: 196).

The gradually growing knowledge of citizens might challenge the traditional structure of media coverage and its frames about the EU in the near future. Today, "[e]ducation and training for active citizenship is the responsibility of the Member States." Yet, the European Commission "will examine how schools could best provide students with the key competences, and how school communities can help prepare young people to be responsible citizens, in line with fundamental European values" (European Commission 2007: 9). The real breakthrough, however, might occur in consequence of common efforts of national and European elites and through the ongoing process of Europeanization on all levels of the respective societies (Fligstein 2000).

REFERENCES

Alfter, Brigitte (2010) "European Public Sphere." *Watchdog Blog.* April 13, http://blogs.euobserver.com/alfter/tag/european-public-sphere

András, Edit (2004) "Blind spot of the new critical theory. Notes on the theory of self colonization." 18 May, http://www.exindex.hu/index.php?l=en&t=szabadkez&tf=selfcolonization_en.html.

Ash, Timothy Garton (2007) "Europe's true stories." *Prospect*, February, www.prospect-magazine.co.uk/article_details.php?id=8214.

Ash, Timothy Garton (2004) *Free World. Why a crisis of the West reveals the opportunity of our time.* London: Penguin Books.

Bajomi-Lázár, Péter (2003) "Press Freedom in Hungary 1998–2001." In Sükösd, Miklós and Péter Bajomi-Lázár (eds.) *Reinventing Media. Media Policy Reform in East-Central Europe.* Budapest–New York: Central European University Press, CPS Books, 85–114.

Bátory, Ágnes (2001) "Hungarian Party Identities and the Question of European Integration." Sussex European Institute, Working Paper 49, September, www.sussex.ac.uk/sei/documents/wp49.pdf.

Bilčík, Vladimír (2007) "Slovak Republic and the European Union." In Bútora, Martin, Grigorij Mesežnikov and Miroslav Kollár (eds.) *Slovakia 2006. A Global Report on the State of the Society.* Bratislava: Institute for Public Affairs, 327–338.

Bond, Martyn A. (2001) "The UK Media: Influencing Elite and Popular Views on Europe." In Bajomi-Lázár, Péter and István Hegedűs (eds.) *Media and Politics.* Budapest: New Mandate Publishing House, 255–262.

Bozóki, András (1992) "Post-communist transition: political tendencies in Hungary." In Bozóki, András, András Körösényi and George Schopflin: *Post-Communist Transition. Emerging Pluralism in Hungary.* London: Pinter Publishes and New York: St. Martin's Press, 13–29.

Enyedi, Zsolt and Gábor Tóka (2007) "The Only Game in Town: Party Politics in Hungary." In Webb, Paul and Stephen White (eds.) *Political Parties in Transitional Democracies.* Oxford: Oxford University Press, 147–178, www.personal.ceu.hu/departs/personal/Gabor_Toka/Papers/Enyedi-Toka06.pdf.

European Commission (2007a) *Communicating Europe in Partnership*, Brussels, http://ec.europa.eu/commission_barroso/wallstrom/pdf/COM2007_568_en.pdf.

European Commission (2007b) *Eurobarometer No. 68, National Report, Executive Summary Hungary*, http://ec.europa.eu/public_opinion/archives/eb/eb68/eb68_hu_exec.pdf.

European Commission (2007c) *Eurobarometer No. 68, Public Opinion in the European Union, December*, http://ec.europa.eu/public_opinion/archives/eb/eb68/eb68_first_en.pdf.

European Commission (2006) *White Paper on a European Communication Policy*, http://ec.europa.eu/communication_white_paper/doc/white_paper_en.pdf.

European Commission (2005) *Eurobarometer No. 63, Trends Report*, database, spring, Brussels.

Fligstein, Neil (2000) "The Process of Europeanization." *Politique européenne*, April, 25–42.

Fossum, John Erik and Philip Schlesinger (eds.) (2007) *The European Union and the Public Sphere. A communicative space in the making?* London and New York: Routledge.

Frank, Robert (2002) "The Meanings of Europe in French National Discourse: A French Europe or an Europeanized France?" In Malmborg, Mikael af–Bo Stråth (eds.) *The National Meanings of Europe*. Oxford: Berg, 311–326.

Frisch, Julien (2009) *Creating a European Public Sphere: The Hyperlink Story. Watching Europe. 7 July*, http://julienfrisch.blogspot.com/2009/07/creating-european-public-sphere.html.

Gordon, Tamás (2007) *Denials and divisions in Hungary's press, European Voice, 24–30 May*, www.europeanvoice.com/archive/article.asp?id=28126.

Gyévai, Zoltán (2002) *Reporting on the EU: Pan-European and National Approaches*. Presentation at the international conference of the Hungarian Europe Society entitled "The Future of the Enlarged European Union," 29 November, Central European University, Budapest, www.europatarsasag.hu/index.php?option=com_content&task=view&id=205&Itemid=32&lang=en.

Habermas, Jürgen (2001) *So, Why Does Europe Need a Constitution?* European University Institute, Robert Schuman Centre of Advanced Studies, www.iue.it/RSCAS/e-texts/CR200102UK.pdf.

Hague, William (2010) "How the UK's new Tory-led government sees its EU policy." *Europe's World*, summer, www.europesworld.org/NewEnglish/Home_old/Article/tabid/191/ArticleType/articleview/ArticleID/21633/Default.aspx.

Hallin, Daniel C. and Paolo Mancini (2004) *Comparing media systems: three models of media and politics*. Cambridge–New York: Cambridge University Press.

Hegedűs, István (2005) *Party Politics on European Matters and the Divide between Political Elites and Citizens in Hungary*. Presentation at the conference of the European Consortium for Political Research, Budapest Corvinus University, 8–10 September, www.essex.ac.uk/ecpr/events/generalconference/budapest/papers/15/3/hegedus.pdf.

Hegedűs, István (2003) "After the Accession Talks, Facing the Referendum: Hungary and Its Media Joining the European Union." *Central European Political Science Review*, spring, 44–53. Presentation at the Governance, Enlargement and the Media Workshop, European University Institute, Florence, 28 February–1 March 2003.

Hegedűs, István (2001) "Why Do We Like the European Union?" In Bajomi-Lázár, Péter and István Hegedűs (eds.) *Media and Politics*. Budapest: New Mandate Publishing House, 235–244.

Hegedűs, István (1999) "European Ideas - Hungarian Realities." *European Essay* No. 1. London: The Federal Trust, www.fedtrust.co.uk/uploads/Essays/Essay_1.pdf.

Hix, Simon (2009) "Viewpoint: A truly European vote?" *BBC News Europe*, 5 May, http://news.bbc.co.uk/2/hi/europe/8025749.stm.

Hodess, Robin B. (1998) "News Coverage of European Politics: A Comparison of Change in Britain and Germany." In Jopp, Mathias, Andreas Maurer and Heinrich Schneider (eds.) *Europapolitische Grundverständnisse im Wandel*, Bonn: Europa Union Verlag, 449–472.

Huber, Claudia Kristine (2007) "Black Box Brüssel. Journalismus zwischen Affirmation und Kontrolle." 12. *MainzerMedienDisput*, November, www.netzwerkrecherche.de/docs/Studie_Black_Box_Bruessel_2008.pdf.

Jakubowicz, Karol (1996) "Media Legislation as a Mirror of Democracy." *Transition*, 18 October, 17–21.

Jáuregui, Pablo (2002) "'Europeanism' versus 'Africanism.' 'Europe' as Symbol of Modernity and Democratic Renewal in Spain." In Malmborg, Mikael af and Bo Stråth (eds.) *The National Meanings of Europe*. Oxford: Berg, 77–100.

Kende, Péter (1995) "The Trianon Syndrome: Hungarians and Their Neighbors." In Király, K. Béla (ed.) *Lawful Revolution in Hungary, 1989–94*. Highland Lakes, New Jersey: Atlantic Research and Publications, 475–492.

Kevin, Deirdre (2001a) "Debates about Europe in the National News Media." In Bajomi-Lázár, Péter and István Hegedűs (eds.) *Media and Politics*. Budapest: New Mandate Publishing House, 219–234.

Kevin, Deirdre (2001b) "Coverage of the European Parliament Elections of 1999: National public spheres and European Debates." *Javnost - The Public*, Vol. 8, No. 1, 21–38.

Klicperova-Baker, Martina and Jaroslav Košťál (2009) *European Identities in a New Member State: The Case of the Czech Republic and the Paradox of a Euro-skeptical Presidency*, Eurosphere Working Paper Series, No. 21, www.eurosphere.uib.no/knowledgebase/wpsdocs/Eurosphere_Working_Paper_21_Baker_Kostal.pdf.

Kohli, Martin (2000) "The battlegrounds of European identity." *European Societies*, No. 2, 113–137.

Laffan, Brigid and Sonia Mazey (2006) "European integration: the European Union–reaching an equilibrium?" In Richardson, Jeremy (ed.) *European Union. Power and policy-making*. 3rd Edition, Oxford: Routledge, 31–54.

Lippmann, Walter (1997) *Public Opinion*. New York: Free Press Paperbacks [1922].

Løkkegaard, Morten (2010) *Draft report on journalism and new media—creating a public sphere in Europe*. Committee on Culture and Education of the European Parliament, 26 March 2010, www.europarl.europa.eu/sides/getDoc.do?pubRef=-//EP//NONSGML+COMPARL+PE-439.380+01+DOC+PDF+V0//EN&language=EN.

Ludlow, Piers (2002) "Us or Them? The Meaning of Europe in British Political Discourse." In Malmborg, Mikael af-Bo Stråth (eds.) *The National Meanings of Europe*. Oxford: Berg, 101–124.

Machill, Marcell, Markus Beiler and Corinna Fischer (2006) "Europe-Topics in Europe's Media. The Debate about the European Public Sphere: A Meta-Analysis of Media Content Analyses." *European Journal of Communication*, Vol. 21, 57–88.

Malmborg, Mikael af (2002) "The Dual Appeal of Europe in Italy." In Malmborg, Mikael af and Bo Stråth (eds.) *The National Meanings of Europe*. Oxford: Berg, 51–75.

Malmborg, Mikael af and Bo Stråth (eds.) (2002) *The National Meanings of Europe*. Oxford: Berg.

Marcussen, Martin, Thomas Risse, Daniela Engelmann-Martin, Hans Joachim Knopf and Klaus Roscher (1999) "Constructing Europe? The Evolution of French, British and German Nation-State Identities." *Journal of European Public Policy*, 6 (4) Special Issue, 614–633.

Martin, József Péter (2002) "Félünk-e az Európai Uniótól? Az Európai Unió mint hivatkozási alap a hazai közbeszédben" [Are We Afraid of the European Union? The European Union as a Reference Point in the Domestic Public Discourse]. *Figyelő*, 24–31 December. Presentation at the international conference of the Hungarian Europe Society entitled "The Future of the Enlarged European Union," 29 November at the Central European University, Budapest, www.europatarsasag.hu/index.php?option=com_content&task=view&id=80&Itemid=32.

Mesežnikov, Grigorij (2009) "Europessimism, Euroscepticism and Populism in the European Union: Case of Slovakia." Presentation at the international workshop European Elections 2009—Europeanization: Parties, Institutions, Member States organised by the Hungarian Europe Society in the Hungarian Parliament on May 22–23, www.europatarsasag.hu/20070811tol_fajlok_itt/2009juni/Meseznikov_HES_Budapest%20(3).doc.

Meyer, Cristoph O. (2003) "Exploring the European Union's Communication deficit: Old Problems and New Departures." *Central European Political Science Review*, spring, 35–43.

Michnik, Adam (2006) *Harag és szégyen* [Anger and Shame]. Bratislava: Kalligram.

Mihelj, Sabina (2004) "Negotiating European Identity at the Periphery: Media Coverage of Bosnian Refugees and 'Illegal Migration'." In Bondebjerg, Ib–Peter Golding (eds.) *European Culture and the Media. Changing Media–Changing Europe*. Volume I., Bristol: Intellect Books, 165–189.

Molnár, Péter (1999) "Transforming Hungarian Broadcasting." *Media Studies Journal*, Fall, 90–97.

Müller, Jan-Werner (2007) *Constitutional Patriotism*. Princeton and Oxford: Princeton University Press.

Norris, Pippa (2000) *A Virtuous Circle*. Cambridge: Cambridge University Press.

Oberhuber, Florian, Christoph Barenreuter, Michal Krzyzanowski, Heinz Schönbauer and Ruth Wodak (2005) "Debating the Constitution: on the representations of Europe/the EU in the press." *Journal of Language and Politics* 4:2, 227–271, www.ling.lancs.ac.uk/staff/wodak/wodaketal2005.pdf.

Patten, Chris (2004) *The Existential Question–Will Britain Ever "Actually" Join the EU?* Alcuin Lecture, University of Cambridge, January, http://europa. eu.int/comm/external_relations/news/patten/sp04_alcuin.htm.

Peter, Jochen, Holli A. Semetko and Claes H. de Vreese (2003) EU Politics on Television News. A Cross National Comparative Study, *European Union Politics*, Vol. 4, No. 3, 305–327.

Plesu, Andrei (1997) "Towards a European Patriotism: Obstacles as seen from the East." *East European Constitutional Review*, Spring-Summer, 53–55, www.law.nyu.edu/eecr/vol6num2/special/plesu.html.

Rainer, M. János (2002) "Regime Change and the Tradition of 1956." In Bozóki, András (ed.) *The Roundtable Talks of 1989. The Genesis of Hungarian Democracy. Analysis and Documents.* Budapest–New York: Central European University Press, 211–222, www.rev.hu/html/en/studies/transition/roundtable_rainer.htm.

Ruth, Arne (2007) *The press and Europe's public sphere.* 9 May, www.signandsight.com/features/1337.html.

Schild, Joachim (2005) "Ein Sieg der Angst–das gescheiterte französiche Verfassungsreferendum." *integration*, No. 3, 187–200, www.iep-berlin.de/fileadmin/website/09_Publikationen/integration_2005/Schild.pdf.

Schlesinger, Philip (2003) "The Babel of Europe. An Essay on Networks and Communicative Spaces." ARENA Working Paper No. 22, University of Oslo, www.arena.uio.no/publications/wp_03_22.pdf.

Semetko, Holli A., Claes H. de Vreese and Jochen Peter (2000) "Europeanised Politics–Europeanised Media? European Integration and Political Communication." *West European Politics*, October, 121–141.

Sicakkan, Hakan G. (2007) "How to Detect the Presence of a European Public Sphere?" Opening Lecture at the EUROSPHERE Kick-off Conference, University of Bergen, 14 February, Bergen, www.eurosphere.uib. no/activities/conferences/KickOff/How%20to%20Detect%20the%20 Presence%20of%20a%20European%20Public%20Sphere_140207. pdf.

Simecka, Martin M. (2003) "A szlovákok és az EU-csatlakozás" [Slovaks and the Accesion to the EU], *Magyar Lettre Internationale*, Summer, 82, www. c3.hu/scripta/lettre/web/index.htm.

Slaatta, Tore (2006) "Europeanisation and the News Media: Issues and Research Imperatives." *Javnost - The Public*, Vol. 13, No. 1, 5–24, www.javnost-thepublic.org/media/datoteke/13-1-slaata.pdf.

Smith, Julie (2005) "A missed opportunity? New Labour's European Policy 1997–2005." *International Affairs*, Vol. 81, Number 4, July, 703–721.

Statham, Paul and Emily Gray (2005) "Public Debates over Europe in Britain: Exceptional and Conflict-Driven?" *The European Journal of Social Science Research*, Vol. 18:1, March, 61–81, http://ics.leeds.ac.uk/eurpolcom/exhibits/Statham_and_Gray_2005.pdf.

Stråth, Bo and Anna Triandafyllidou (eds.) (2003) *Representations of Europe and the Nation in Current and Prospective Member States: Media, Elites and Civil Society.* Brussels: The European Commission.

Sükösd, Miklós (2003) "Kommunikációs deficit Magyarország európai uniós csatlakozásának médiabemutatásában" [Communication Deficit in the Media Presentation of Hungary's Accession to the European Union]. *Médiakutató*, Winter, 73–83, www.mediakutato.hu/cikk/2003_04_tel/04_kommunikacios_deficit/01.html.

Szilágyi, Zsófia (2002) "The Rising Tide of Euroscepticism." *Transition Online*, 1 March, www.tol.cz/look/TOL/article.tpl?IdLanguage=1&IdPublicati on=4&NrIssue=32&NrSection=19&NrArticle=3735.

Szilágyi-Gál, Mihály (2003) "Press Coverage of the EU and NATO Accession Processes in Hungary and Romania in the late 1990s." In Sükösd, Miklós and Péter Bajomi-Lázár (eds.) *Reinventing Media: Media Policy Reform in East Central Europe*. Budapest–New York: Central European University Press, CPS Books, 137–152.

Szlankó, Bálint (2007) *Az elnök, a képviselő és a diplomata. Történetek az új Európai Unióból* [The President, the MEP and the Diplomat. Stories from the New European Union]. Budapest: Athenaeum–Magyar Narancs.

Terestyéni, Tamás (2001) "Magyarország és az Európai Unió a sajtó tükrében. Egy tartalomelemzéses vizsgálat eredményei" [Hungary and the European Union in the Mirror of the Press. Results of a Content Analysis] *Szociológiai Szemle*, No. 2, 16–34, www.mtapti.hu/mszt/20012/terestye.htm.

Torreblanca, José Ignacio (2001) "Ideas, Preferences and Institutions: Explaining the Europeanization of Spanish Foreign Policy." ARENA Working Papers, 01/26, Univesity of Oslo, www.arena.uio.no/publications/wp01_26.htm.

Törnquist-Plewa, Barbara (2002) "The Complex of an Unwanted Child: The Meanings of Europe in Polish Discourse." In Malmborg, Mikael af and Bo Stråth (eds.) *The National Meanings of Europe*. Oxford: Berg, 215–224.

Trenz, Hans-Jörg (2008) "In search of the European public sphere. Between normative overstretch and empirical disenchantment." Recon Online Working Paper No. 7., May, www.reconproject.eu/main.php/RECON_wp_0807.pdf?fileitem=16662548.

Vidra, Zsuzsanna (2007) "Az Európai Unió képe néhány közép-kelet európai és egy balkáni ország sajtójában" [The Image of the European Union in the Press of Some East-Central European Countries and in One Country on the Balkans]. *Regio*, No. 4, 35–55.

Vidra, Zsuzsanna (2006) "Az EU reprezentációja a magyar médiában a csatlakozási folyamat alatt" [The Representation of the EU in the Hungarian Media During the Accession Process]. In Hegedűs, István (ed.) *A magyarok bemenetele. Tagállamként a bővülő Európai Unióban* [The Marching In of the Hungarians. As a Member State in the Enlarging European Union]. Budapest: Corvinus University of Budapest, Institute for Political Science, Hungarian Center for Democracy Studies Foundation, 115–152.

Wallström, Margot (2005) *Communicating a Europe in stormy waters: Plan D. Speech on the European Voice conference "Simplifying Europe,"* Brussels, 28 June, http://europa.eu/rapid/pressReleasesAction.do?reference=SPEEC H/05/396&format=HTML&aged=0&language=EN&guiLanguage=en.

CHAPTER 4

Pan-European Media: Attempts and Limitations

PETER J. VARGA

Communicating in a Multinational Federation

With institutions patterned on those of federal states on the one hand, and a system of multilevel governance that includes 27 national governments representing peoples who speak 23 official languages on the other, the European Union's avenues for political communication are presented with great challenges, calling into question the success of the European integration project. As integration proceeds, media outlets that serve citizens of Europe at large are expected to emerge and grow, much in the same way that state-wide media outlets did in newly-established countries unified under a single government.

At present, there exist only a few successful media outlets that transcend national boundaries, catering to public audiences that span Europe. In the case of the written press, these audiences are largely specific, not general. Such Europe-wide publications largely serve economic and political elites, in English, the international *lingua franca* of business, trade, academia and diplomacy. These include dailies like the *Financial Times*, the *International Herald Tribune* and *Wall Street Journal Europe*, and the weekly magazine *The Economist*.

Unlike these large Europe-wide outlets, there exist smaller-scale print media established for the purpose of serving a European audience at large. Largely centered in Brussels, where most EU institutions are located, these media—including newsletters, newspapers and websites—are focused on covering EU-related public affairs. They more typically cater to EU functionaries and professionals, businesspeople, international decision-makers, and educational institutions. Importantly, these media appear to have the potential to serve a broader, more general pan-European public. What is the extent of this potential, and what barriers are keeping them from growing to reach audiences as broad as the large, global-international newspapers?

The purpose of this study is to identify the strategies used by print media established for pan-European audiences to report politics and public affairs to the populations of Europe, which are characterized by multinationality, overlapping identities and interests. These strategies overcome specific barriers, identified in this study, which impede the media outlets from: a) reaching their diverse audiences and b) sustaining themselves as viable news businesses.

A total of six media outlets—five based in Brussels and one with major offices there—were examined. These include the weekly newspaper *European Voice*, newsletters Agence Europe (producers of *Bulletin Quotidien Europe*, or *Europe Daily Bulletin*) and Europe Information Service (producers of *Europolitics/Europolitique*), as well as the websites *EU Observer* (euobserver.com), *EurActiv.com*, and *Café Babel* (cafebabel.com). Each was assessed for how it deals with specific barriers to reaching Europe-wide audiences. These include: *language, national identity, European Union political communication deficits*, and *national advertising markets*. Interviews were conducted with editors of media outlets to assess the degree of difficulty that each of the four transnational barriers present to aspiring pan-European outlets, and how to overcome each. These interviews were conducted in Brussels, Belgium, where the media outlets are either based or have local offices that cover Europe-wide affairs.

For purposes of background and comparison, the study includes an overview of four long-established international newspapers as well as two news agencies, Agence France Presse (AFP) and Reuters. The latter two are Europe's oldest international newswire services. Taken to indicate the most successful models of Europe-wide media, this overview allowed some inferences to be made about the possible characteristics of an emerging European public sphere.

Interviews were also conducted with AFP and Reuters' Brussels-based editors; the European Commission's Directorate General Communication, responsible for communicating the activities, objectives and goals of the Commission to the general public; and the European Journalism Centre, and independent organization which trains and briefs journalists in Brussels on how to effectively cover EU affairs.

Emergence of European Public Spheres and Pan-European Media

Unlike previous studies on European print news media, this study investigates the emergence of media that aim to reach a pan-European audience. Past research has centered on investigating whether there exists any evidence of the emergence of a European public sphere in the content of mainstream national media throughout Europe. Such studies seek evidence of "Europeanization": the adoption of common European modes of address. They do not consider transnational print publications sold Europe-wide which are unattached to nationality. Philip Schlesinger's (1999) oft-cited seminal study on the "changing spaces of political communication" in the EU summarizes why: "the growth (of such) transnational media has worked to sustain a restricted elite space rather than to herald generalized access to communication by European publics" (Schlesinger 1999: 263).

This "elite space" comprises economic and political decision-makers, whose work takes them across national borders. To ignore these specialized media, however, is to ignore the reality of multiple, even competing public spheres, which are more likely to be found throughout Europe. The European Union's multilevel structure of governance, which includes national officials (both elected and unelected), EU officials, and national representatives elected to the European Parliament—not to mention the question of local, regional, and national identification by citizens of EU member states—"require us to think in terms of overlapping spheres of publics" (Schlesinger 1999: 270). In this light, the emergence of multiple public spheres (of all-European businesspeople, EU professionals, European academics or artists for instance) is expected to occur first, followed by the emergence of a European public sphere at-large, including other citizens of EU member states.

SPHERES IN EMERGENCE

Machill et al (2006) state that there are two fundamental ways in which a European public sphere can arise: "1. As a pan-European public sphere independent of individual states; or 2. As a European public sphere that emerges as a result of the Europeanization of national public spheres" (Machill et al 2006: 61). The first criterion is demonstrated by pan-European media of the *FT-IHT* variety. The authors pursue the second model as grounds for their study. Even though they concede *FT-IHT* media do have pan-European reach, Machill et al submit that these media are not generalist, and few in number. The authors also highlight the lack of a "uniform European language" as grounds that "the existence of European public sphere are absent" (Machill et al 2006: 62).

In investigating how aspiring and potential pan-European publications report to EU-wide audiences, this study takes Machill et al's first concept as its basis. Such a study has never been undertaken before, presumably because circulation figures of national print media still far outstrip those of pan-European-focused publications. Nevertheless, the relative success of the young Brussels-based pan-European media studied here, most of which were founded from 1995 onward, demonstrates that a market for pan-European readers does exist, and is growing.

BARRIERS TO PAN-EUROPEAN MEDIA
Language and national identity

Language is the immediate, most obvious barrier to the emergence of pan-European media, whether print or broadcast. The European Union officially recognizes 23 languages spoken in its member states. Proceedings in the European Parliament resemble those of a mini-United Nations, where discussions and debates are simultaneously translated into other official languages.

Language is complemented by differences in national identity. Unique reporting traditions, political cultures and histories are central elements of the national identity barrier. These are evident in the results of content-analyses studies of newspapers across Europe, which indicate national differences in framing news events. In their content analysis of a story reported Europe-wide, John Downey and Thomas Koenig (2006) found that "distinctly European framings" are "largely absent." National differences in reporting prevail. Moreover, "ethnicity is seen as largely immutable, and therefore not open to the change of opinion via political and/or communicative persuasion strategies as would be the case if actors were imagined to be part of a Europeanized public sphere" (Downey and Koenig 2006: 184).

Language and nationality present distinct obstacles to pan-European print media in particular. An obvious solution to the language barrier is the establishment of a European *lingua franca*—a Europe-wide language—alongside the various mother tongues. Such is the case for example in India, where English is used as the language of consensus and interchange across the multi-ethnic and multi-lingual federal state (Nariman 1989: 13–14). As is the case worldwide, English is used as the language of communication among European elites, which has worked in favor of the success of publications like the *Financial Times*, the *International Herald Tribune*, the *Wall Street Journal Europe*, or the *Economist*.

Political communication deficit

Reportage of news about institutions and politics that encompass Europe—specifically EU politics—has been confounded by the lack of citizen knowledge and interest in EU institutions and politics. A European public sphere, and with it, pan-European media, cannot be established without the elimination of this obstacle.

Notions of a communication deficit between the EU and citizens of EU-member states, and related perceptions of a democratic deficit in the EU are themselves the subject of a large body of research. Resolving these deficits is seen as being essential to the success of the European integration project. Peter Golding (2006: 13) asserts that "the expectation, or indeed aspiration, that Europe may be the home to an embryonic political culture transcending the national is a necessary dimension to the 'European project'." Yet the emergence of a European public sphere is dependent on citizens' ability, interest in, and willingness to understand the political and decision-making processes of the EU. Recent political science research, drawing on EU and private surveys, shows that citizens lack many of these, as they continue to perceive their national governments as being more important to their lives (see Lord 2004: 40–73 for instance). Ineffective media coverage of the EU is related to this, partly because reporters' attitudes to the EU are similar to those of the general public (Golding 2006: 17–18).

Coverage of the EU following conventional means of political news reporting is infeasible. Political news reporting, as Meyer (2003: 38) states, is commonly based on the criteria of conflict, personalization, drama and relevance—and a number of studies have highlighted that EU governance lacks these elements. Reporters are confronted with the impractical prospect of reporting on "long-dragged out negotiations among civil servants, lobbyists and experts from various settings, which yield compromise solutions with long transition periods and framed in technocratic language" (Meyer 2003: 37–38). Moreover, sources willing to impart information about negotiations that characterize typical EU consensus solutions are elusive. As such, "without the tool of personalization as a short-hand to translate political conflicts into the language of media, Brussels journalists struggle to explain how and why the decision about certain issues is relevant to their readers/audience" (Meyer 2003: 38). Meyer goes so far as to suggest that multinational research cooperation is needed in order to link information and provide coherent reports on the transnational union.

In an article that sums up the theoretical findings of the Adequate Information Management in Europe (AIM) program, Golding (2006) lends further evidence to the impracticality of reporting on the EU in conventional ways. As a consequence, among journalists there exists "a recurrent number of views that are far from enthusiastic about the European ideal, or indeed the EU specifically" (Golding 2006: 17).

Aware of its communication deficits, the EU has undertaken several initiatives in recent years to make its decision and policy-making processes more transparent, and improve communications with the public. To that end, the European Commission recently established a "European Communication Policy," which included the appointment of a Commissioner for Communication and a Directorate General, Communication (Kurpas et al 2006: 2).

Advertising markets

Following the linguistic, cultural and political barriers to pan-European media, there exist national market barriers—which mostly relate to advertising and sales success, and legislation. Political science and communications studies on the emergence of a European public sphere have not highlighted this obstacle. The ability to localize content and cater to each of the various national audiences throughout Europe, as detailed by Chalaby (2002) in his study of broadcast media, appears to be the main determinant to successfully finding and attracting advertisers.

Brussels-based European Media

Said to play host to Europe's, and possibly the world's biggest press corps, Brussels is the workplace of some 1,200 to 1,300 members of the media, according to members of the industry there. In spite of this, Brussels does not register as a capital that hosts the head offices of major media. It does, however, serve as the central location of a collection of smaller-scale written press devoted to the coverage of the EU and Europe-wide public affairs to a European audience.

Examined here as case studies are six Brussels-based public affairs print or Internet publications, selected for their exceptional efforts to offer European news, analysis and opinion for transnational, pan-European audiences. They include: newsletter producers Agence Europe (publishers of daily newsletter *Europe Daily Bulletin*) and Europe Information Service (producer of daily newsletter/newspaper *Europolitics* and French edition *Europolitique*); weekly newspaper *European Voice*, as well as the websites *EU Observer* (euobserver.com), *EurActiv.com*, and *Café Babel*. These outlets have little in common with each other, and hardly consider one another competitors. Figure 1 indicates how readers can access each publication.

With the exception of *Café Babel*, all the selected outlets are staffed by professionals. *Europe Daily Bulletin* is financed strictly by subscriptions, and *Europolitics* largely by subscriptions and a few ads. *European Voice* and *EU Observer* rely primarily on advertising, and *EurActiv.com* primarily on large corporate sponsors.

The sheer variety of these written public affairs media demonstrates that there exist several avenues to reaching audiences throughout Europe. Even though they are very different, the basic limitations and barriers to reaching audiences are the same.

Figure 1. Brussels-based media: Consumer access

Publication	Media type, language, frequency.	Access	Price (2007)	
			Unit	Subscription
European Voice	Weekly newspaper, English, issued Thursdays.	Newsstands; subscription	4.20 Euro	165 Euro/year
Agence Europe: *Bulletin Quotidien Europe*	Daily newsletter: English, French, Italian.	Subscription only	N/A	1,350 Euro/year, via internet. 1,710 Euro/ year, print and internet.
Europe Information Service: *Europolitics*; *Europolitique*	Daily newsletter: French, English.	Subscription only	N/A	1,700 Euro/ year, print and unlimited online access.
EU Observer (euobserver.com)	News website, seven languages, updated twice daily.	Online, free	Free	N/A
EurActiv.com	EU policy portal website, nine languages, daily updates.	Online, free	Free	N/A
Café Babel (cafebabel.com)	Web magazine, daily updates.	Online, free	Free	N/A

(Sources: Publication issues, websites.)

International Media Centered in Europe

PRINT PUBLICATIONS SERVING ECONOMIC ELITES

In any major town or city of Europe, it is possible to find at least one of a handful of long-established print publications circulated throughout the continent. Established in Europe, these outlets grew out of regional markets to reach pan-European markets (and today, global ones) without explicitly targeting all-European audiences. These offer some indication of the existence of a European public sphere of international business, economic and political elites, which meld with a global one. Publications which serve such a sphere include the daily newspapers *Financial Times*, the *International Herald Tribune*, *Wall Street Journal Europe*, and the weekly news magazine *The Economist*.

A simple survey of the key characteristics and circulation figures of each of these print publications, detailed in Figure 2, demonstrates these publications' pan-European reach, and offers some indication of the basic properties that have allowed them to reach readers Europe-wide. All in English, these outlets have circulations that are far surpassed by the biggest national dailies of Europe—however their circulation throughout the continent is unrivalled. As shown in Figure 2, all of these, with the exception of *Wall Street Journal Europe*, have very high circulation shares in Europe relative to other parts of the world.

These media are similar in many respects. They were first established in the world's major capitals and financial centers in the 19th century. All of them, with the possible exception of the *International Herald Tribune (IHT)*, in their beginning catered strictly to a readership of economic elites, who went to the newspapers for information on financial markets, world business, and international news of relevance to these. *IHT*'s readership was in its beginnings focused on a readership of Americans living abroad, not as strictly devoted to finance and economics as were the others, even though its end readership proved to be similar. All are long-established, profitable operations owned by multinational media companies.

Predating the importance of Brussels and the EU, the international papers in effect grew out of important capital cities and world financial centers to reach pan-European levels. It appears that their focus on finance and economics is what allowed them to achieve continental reach with relative ease—particularly since the European integration project has largely centered on economic and trade-related matters. This has allowed them to broaden their roots within Europe. *Wall Street Journal Europe* and *Financial Times Deutschland*'s economic/financial focus, for example, has allowed them to make exceptionally quick inroads to Europe and Germany, respectively.

Even though these newspapers' focus is on financial, economic, and global international news—a certain portion of their content, relating to other matters such as arts, culture and sport do have potential appeal for broader Europe-wide audiences over the long run, hence an at-large European public sphere.

Figure 2. Europe-based international print media

Outlet	Media type	Date and location where established	Central editorial office	Primary readers	Circulation	
					Worldwide (daily or weekly average in year listed)	**Europe** (including % of worldwide circulation)
Financial Times	Daily newspaper	London, 1888	London, UK	Senior business-people; economic and political decision-makers.	432,930 (2007)	124,212 (29%)
Financial Times Deutschland	Daily, in German	February, 2000	Hamburg, Germany			104,000 (in Germany, 2007)
International Herald Tribune	Daily newspaper	Paris, 1887	Paris	General, largely American; international by profession and lifestyle.	242,073 (2006)	140,738 (58%)
The Wall Street Journal Europe	Daily newspaper	Brussels, 1983 (Parent edition: New York, 1889)	European edition: Brussels Central offices: New York	Senior business management and high-income-earners.	2,250,072 (All editions, USA, Asia and Europe, 2005) (USA edition: 2,083,660)	86,539: European edition (3.8%)
The Economist	Weekly news magazine	London, 1843	London	University-educated economic and political decision-makers.	1,197,712 (2006)	396,932 (33.1%)

(Sources: Company websites, factsheets and advertising information packages; independent circulation figures from the Audit Bureau of Circulations (ABC) and the European Business Readership Survey 2006-2007.)

NEWSWIRES

Among the long-established media that serve Europe at large are newswire services, which predate the print publications by decades. These include newswire service Agence France Presse, founded in Paris in 1835, and Reuters, a multimedia news and financial information agency founded in London in 1851. Reuters' origins in fact lie in Brussels and Aachen/Aix-la-Chapelle, where founder Paul Julius Reuter ran a business that bridged a missing telegraph wire link between Paris and Berlin, using carrier pigeons. Stock price information was transmitted via telegraph from Paris to Brussels, from whence Reuter's waiting pigeons delivered it to his office in Aachen. Once received, Reuter sold it to waiting clients who would telegraph the information to Berlin (Taylor 2007).

Since their beginnings as agencies transmitting information throughout Europe, these companies have grown into global wire services. Still, these agencies' European bases have retained the greatest share of their clientele and revenue, which suggests the presence of an at-large European public sphere. Figure 3 briefly summarizes Europe's importance in the operation of these agencies. As shown, Reuters' main source of revenue remains Europe, with miniscule revenue from the Middle East and Africa topping the share off to 53% (Inside Market Data 2006). AFP still counts Europe as its largest single regional source of revenue worldwide. Even though their head offices are located in other major capitals (AFP in France and Reuters in London), their Brussels offices have become the centers from which they cover EU and to an increasing extent Europe-wide affairs.

As a supplier of financial information and data, with a small fraction of its operations devoted to news (a share of about 7%, which nevertheless rivals AFP's entire newswire operation), Reuters has, like its economics and finance-devoted counterparts in print media, benefited from the fact that the European integration project's focus has been on trade and economic matters. "The EU is Europe's biggest financial regulator. So the financial markets are hanging on what the EU decides," noted Reuters' Brussels bureau chief Paul Taylor (2007). Each passing year sees the creation of a set of integration plans to be deliberated among EU officials—and to be reported by his agency.

Figure 3. Europe-based newswire services

Agency	Established	Head office	Market share: Europe/Worldwide	Language of stories reported on in Brussels
Reuters	London, 1851	London	53% for Europe, Middle East and Africa	English, French, German
Agence France-Presse	Paris, 1835	Paris	Europe reported to take up greatest single regional share worldwide.	French, English, German, Spanish

(Sources: Company websites, interviews; Inside Market Data, 2006)

Analysis

OVERVIEW OF CASE STUDIES: PAN-EUROPEAN REACH

Europe's diverse cultures have bred a diversity of media in Brussels, each of which cover the EU and at-large European affairs in slightly different ways, using their own approaches to surmounting barriers of language, national culture, EU communication deficits and advertising to reach their Europe-wide target audience. A quick survey of readership size/circulation and reader location, detailed in Figure 4, nevertheless shows that all media outlets examined here are succeeding at reaching a distinctly pan-European readership. In terms of readership figures and target audience, one media outlet stands out in particular as the most closely measuring up to what could be called a truly independent pan-European publication: news website *EU Observer*.

Taking audience figures and primary readership identities as the criterion for successful reporting of EU public affairs for Europeans, *EurActiv.com*, *Café Babel* and the *European Voice* would have to follow. Newsletters *Europolitics* and *Europe Daily Bulletin*'s limited readership target put them in a distinct category: these report largely to elites, or, according to the theoretical definition, a European public sphere of elite decision-makers. *Café Babel*, in terms of reach and target audience, appears to be a successful example of pan-European media. However its viability as an independent, profitable, professional enterprise has yet to be proven, as it relies on public and private grants for financing and is staffed largely by volunteers, interns and unpaid contributors.

The *European Voice*, the only newspaper of significance devoted to the coverage of EU and European affairs, could also lay claim to being pan-European, were it not for its low circulation levels outside Brussels. The newspaper's paid circulation, moreover, amounts to only about 30 percent, with the rest supplied largely to EU institutions and their members, including EU policy-makers, leaders and civil servants, within Brussels. Nevertheless, the style of the newspaper makes it reader-friendly enough for a general audience that has some knowledge of the EU–leaving room for greater potential beyond Brussels. "We would aim to be a more entertaining read than *Europolitique*," said Deputy Editor Tim King, comparing *European Voice* to the more targeted *Europolitics*. "You don't have to be a specialist to be reading *European Voice*" (King, 2007).

As is the case with most media studied here, the *European Voice* does not consider *Europolitics* nor any of the other media to be competitors. Each outlet appears to have found a stable niche in the Brussels-based European print media market. Their strategies to reaching readers are unique enough to keep them from intruding into each others' audiences, such that audiences are presented with slightly different types of information from each, via different means, and in differing styles. An examination of business models and editorial strategies taken in response to each of the market barriers, detailed in the following sections, demonstrates this.

Figure 4. Brussels-based pan-European media: Readership characteristics

Publica-tion	Estab-lished	Media type	Readership size/ circulation	Primary readership	Reader location 2006
European Voice	Brussels, 1995	Weekly newspaper	Circulation about 15,600 copies per week.	EU officials and those with a vested interest in EU affairs.	83% Belgium 16% Rest of Europe 1% Rest of world
Agence Europe	Brussels, 1953	Daily newsletter, electronic and printed	About 5,000 print copies delivered daily; over 5,000 subscribers to electronic edition.	EU officials; national governments; decision-makers and agencies with a stake in the EU; news media.	40% Brussels 50% Rest of Europe 10% Rest of world (Company estimates)

Publication	Established	Media type	Readership size/ circulation	Primary readership	Reader location 2006
Europolitics/ Europolitique	Brussels, 1972	Daily newsletter/ newspaper	About 10,000 subscribers	EU officials; national governments; businesspeople; educational institutions; news media	47.53% Brussels 43.85% Rest of EU 5.79 % Europe outside EU 2.83 % Rest of world
EU Observer (euobserver.com)	Brussels, 2001	News website, updated twice daily.	25,000 readers (unique visitors) daily, on average.	Varied and general; students and educational institutions form the biggest single group	14.6% Belgium (Brussels) 56.3% Rest of EU 9.1% Europe outside EU 11.7% USA 8.3% Rest of world
EurActiv (euractiv.com)	Brussels, 1999	EU policy web portal	475,000 unique visitors per month.	Management-level professionals; political leaders; educational institutions	21.39% Belgium 40.73% Rest of EU 8.85% USA 1.84% Canada 25% Rest of world, incl. rest of Europe
Café Babel (cafebabel.com)	Paris, 2001	Online magazine	400,000 unique visitors per month, of which 336,000 from Europe	General	84.1% Europe 12.66% Americas (6.35% North Am.) 1.56% Asia 1.12% Africa 0.45% Oceania

(Sources: Company websites, factsheets and advertising information packages; independent circulation figures from the Audit Bureau of Circulations (ABC) and the European Business Readership Survey 2006–2007.)

EUROPE-BASED INTERNATIONAL VS. BRUSSELS-BASED EUROPEAN NEWS MEDIA

Sales and circulation figures show that the Brussels-based publications target European audiences with greater precision than the Europe-based international papers. This is as expected, since the Brussels-based publications are devoted to coverage of Europe and events related to the EU and neighboring countries. The international publications are devoted to global news, and two of these—*Financial Times* (*FT*) and *The Economist*—prove to have worldwide, and not exclusively "pan-European" readerships.

FT and *The Economist* report on events that affect international trade and the global economy, focusing on the world's leading economies. These include the economies of the richest EU member states, the United States and East Asia. Despite their European (London-based) origins and center of operations, *FT* and *The Economist*'s European readerships were not found to be exceptionally higher compared to other parts of the world. As shown in the far-right column of Figure 5, their readership levels in Europe are one-fourth to a third of all copies sold globally. These figures are comparable to prevailing levels in the Americas or Asia.

The *International Herald Tribune* presents a unique case. Unlike the *FT* and the *Economist*, *IHT*'s coverage is more generalist. Coverage is focused on world affairs that are of concern to the U.S. readers. Even though 58% of its circulation is in Europe, content is targeted to an international English-speaking readership that is on the move, currently in Europe. The paper's coverage of news, business, arts and culture appears not to focus any more on Europe than Asia or the Americas, however sports coverage clearly focuses on the United States, with European sporting events given second priority. As such, *IHT* is evidently pan-European in terms of sales and circulation—but not so editorially speaking. Meanwhile, *Wall Street Journal Europe*'s 3.8 percent readership in Europe as a percentage of the paper's overall worldwide readership is so small that it cannot be included in this analysis.

Overall daily readership of the international publications in Europe in absolute terms is greater than that of the Brussels-based media, on the order of five to ten times. However, Brussels-based media are succeeding well at reaching their target audience. Their main challenge is to reach as high a profile as the international ones. All four of the international publications enumerated in Figure 5 have been running for well over a century, while four of the Brussels-based ones are not yet—or scarcely more than a decade old. The management at Agence Europe, the oldest of them, do not even intend to expand their daily news bulletin into a newspaper for the entire general population of Europe (Jéhin, 2007, Ricardi, 2007).

Whether the exclusively Europe-centered publications will be able to increase the size and scale of their publications to the same levels of the internationals depends on their ability to attract general readers and advertisers. The following section examines the strategies undertaken by each of them toward growing to such levels.

Figure 5. Europe-based international vs. Brussels-based European news outlets

	Outlet	Frequency of publication	Circulation or readership in Europe (data for year)	Circulation (readership) in Europe as % of worldwide total
International media	International Herald Tribune	Daily newspaper	140,738 copies daily (2006)	58 %
	Financial Times	Daily newspaper	124,212 copies daily (2007)	29 %
	Wall Street Journal Europe	Daily newspaper	86,539 copies daily (2005)	3.8 %
	The Economist	Weekly news magazine	396,932 copies weekly (2006)	33.1 %
Brussels-based media	EU Observer	News website; updated twice daily	20,000 readers daily (2007)	80 %
	EurActiv	EU policy portal; website updated daily	300,000 readers monthly (2007)	Over 75%
	Café Babel	Online magazine; updated weekly	336,000 readers monthly (2006)	84.1 %
	European Voice	Weekly newspaper	15,600 copies weekly (2006)	99 %
	Europolitics/ Europolitique	Daily news bulletin	10,000 readers by subscription (2007)	97 %
	Agence Europe	Daily news bulletin	5,000 copies delivered daily; 5,000 subscribers to electronic edition (2007)	90 %

(Sources: Company websites, factsheets and advertising information packages; independent circulation figures from the Audit Bureau of Circulations (ABC) and the European Business Readership Survey 2006–2007.)

Strategies to overcoming national barriers

LANGUAGE

In the absence of a recognized *lingua franca*, language limits aspiring pan-European media from reaching readers throughout Europe down to the grassroots. Translation of content for ready reading in several or all European languages is one solution. Of the media examined here, four out of six provide content in two or more official languages of the EU. The oldest agencies of the group, newsletter producers Agence Europe and Europe Information Service (EIS), have always done so. As have two of websites, *Café Babel* and *EurActiv.com*—which offer content in the greatest variety of languages. News website EU Observer and newspaper *European Voice*, on the other hand, report only in English. Reporting in a single language does not appear to have limited nor threatened the success of the latter two outlets. Reporting in multiple languages is perceived among the oldest two outlets as being a necessity, in keeping with the EU's commitment to linguistic diversity, as well as adding value to the publications, and maintaining their readership market reach. For *Café Babel* and *EurActiv.com*, providing content in several languages is in line with these websites' goal of encouraging dialog among readers and contributors, as much as it is to reaching as many European readers as possible.

COMMITMENT TO LINGUISTIC DIVERSITY

Agence Europe has always reported news in three major European Languages—French, English and Italian. EIS has likewise provided its newsletter in two language versions—*Europolitique* in French and *Europolitics* (formerly *European Report*) in English, with plans for a third language edition in Spanish (Lemoine 2007). The editors-in-chief of these long-standing European publications, committed to intimately and meticulously following the EU integration project from its earliest years, admit to the rising importance of the English language throughout Europe, particularly since the accession of Sweden, Finland and Austria in 1995, and the most recent "big bang" accessions of 10 member states in 2004, and two more in 2007. This has translated into a rise in the demand for content in English.

Despite this, Pierre Lemoine, executive publisher and editor-in-chief of EIS's *Europolitique/Europolitics*, said it is important to publish in multiple languages in order to maintain appeal and interest in the publication. "In my opinion, language barriers will always complicate understanding," said Lemoine. In the EU, multilingualism "has been accepted to such an extent that it has been become policy. So we are not ready to change our principal of multilingualism." Moreover, national elites, among the EIS's major clients, "prefer to read in their own national language," Lemoine said, even if they understand English (Lemoine, 2007).

Websites *EurActiv.com* and *Café Babel* follow similar editorial lines on language, to an even greater extent than the older news bulletins. *EurActiv.com*'s main site, produced out of Brussels, features a choice of English, French and German editions containing the same reports. *Café Babel*'s main site also features a choice of identical editions in different languages–with a choice of English, French, Spanish, Italian, German, Catalan, or Polish as well as rich content and blogs in Hungarian, Portuguese, Greek, Bulgarian, Turkish, and Azeri.

EurActiv.com follows up with an added localization strategy to reach more readers in their home countries: the main site has links to partner franchisee sites with their own local content in France, the Czech Republic, Hungary, Poland, Slovakia, Bulgaria and Romania—all in their national languages. "What we're looking for ideally is also for them to adapt content [from the main site] to the local audience," said *EurActiv* managing editor Frédéric Simon. Any article from the main website in Brussels can generate reaction from readers in partner site countries, he added, "whether they are government officials, NGOs or from civil society" (Simon 2007).

Providing content in other languages is particularly important for *Café Babel*, as it is in keeping with the site's founding idea to create a "European public space" where European issues can be discussed. The online magazine, explained the site's Brussels branch president Lorenzo Morselli, aims to provide information "on different societal topics or political issues with a European outlook. So people can see the same issues arise in neighboring countries, and exchange ideas with examples of how the issues have been dealt with" (Morselli 2007). Following that line, added activities of the organization include web forums and conferences to discuss issues with a European perspective.

ENGLISH ONLY

Reporting only in English, the newspaper *European Voice* and website *EU Observer* claim they have not encountered any barriers to reaching their audiences, taking as a given that English is the unofficial *lingua franca* of Europe. Both perceive that most of their readership has English as a second language. "A lot of our readers in the [EU] institutions could be French or German, but they'll have good English, and so will be able to read us" said Tim King, deputy editor for the *European Voice* (King, 2007). Writing for such an audience must be kept simple and straightforward, King admitted, free of cultural references without sacrificing depth and detail in explanation.

EU Observer once considered reporting in other languages, but concluded they did not have the resources to do so. Whether there is a need to do so is a separate question: "We don't know. I don't think we have the need" stated marketing and advertising executive Alexandre Dechaumont. "The audience interested in European affairs normally speaks English," remarked reporter Mark Beunderman (Dechaumont and Beunderman 2007), concurring with King of the *European Voice*.

Recent enlargements of the EU, unprecedented in terms of area and population, have also worked in favor of English usage, according to editors interviewed in this study. The accession of 2004 included nine new languages into the EU, and the accession of 2007 included two more. "We are aware that a lot of our readership will have English as a second language," commented King (2007). "So the *European Voice* has been well-positioned to profit from the fact that enlargement of the European Union has generally meant a further tilt towards English being the dominant language of Brussels."

NATIONAL IDENTITY

"European journalism is still a myth. We write, we broadcast in different traditions. We have different habits," said Guiseppe Zaffuto, director of programs for the European Journalism Centre (EJC) in Brussels, elaborating on local pan-European media (Zaffuto, 2007). The EJC orients and briefs journalists in Brussels about the EU. The program director's illustration of the challenge language and national culture pose to the notion of pan-European journalism is revealing.

"Anglo-Saxon kind of reporting is very much to the point. Facts are separated from opinion," he said. An Italian hailing from Sicily, Zaffuto has worked as an international affairs reporter, and lived in Scandinavia. He went on to illustrate key differences between two (of many) reporting traditions of Europe:

> In the Latin tradition, it's not really like this. Facts and opinion are a little bit mixed. In Italy, Spain, France, Portuguese, Greek maybe–I would say the South European perspective is not really as rigorous as your [Anglo-Saxon] way. Plus I would say that we have a very descriptive style. The example we always make to young European journalism students that come to see us is always–somebody like you would say that somebody died. That's it. One of us would write that in a full river of blood, the person (...) more literally [in a more literary language].
> In my country, if I would write that person died, that means I don't know how to write. Whereas in one of your countries [following Anglo-Saxon traditions] if I would write the Italian way, you would say 'why don't you get to the point?'
> There is no harmonization. We have no harmonization in Europe about journalism. Yet. (Zaffuto 2007)

Zaffuto asserted that pan-European journalism would not appear until such harmonization begins to take root.

Taken literally, Zaffuto's illustration of language and national cultural obstacles is concise. In describing the difference between Anglo-Saxon and Mediterranean/Latin strains of news and public affairs reporting, Zaffuto uses personal pronouns "I" and "you," "my" and "your"–thus indulging, for the sake of explanation, in differentiating the national/regional identities of both himself, as an Italian of the Mediterranean/Latin tradition, and of the interviewer (the resarcher/author of the present chapter) an anglophone Canadian from the French-speaking province of Quebec. Differentiating between one's own nation and other nations is common practice in national media throughout the world. Michael Billig used the term "flagging the homeland daily" characterizing this phenomena (Billig 1995: 91–127).

National reporting traditions affect editorial decisions on writing styles in pan-European publications as well. "There are odd cultural references that you just weed out," explained deputy editor Tim King of *European Voice*. Like most of his colleagues in the editorial department, King hails from the United Kingdom (King 2007). "In an English newspaper background [setting] you might allude to some television program in the 1970s, on the assumption that everyone had grown up on TV in the '70s. Well, you can't do that here." Common pan-European cultural references, if they exist, would be the only ones to include in such papers.

Zaffuto, who has trained and briefed journalists from all over the world in Brussels, claims he has not seen any signs of the emergence of pan-European modes of reporting. The dream of establishing a European newspaper or European television network is of more specific interest to a community "that understands and is interested in European affairs" (Zaffuto 2007). Such a community is to be found in a specific elite sphere of European decision-makers.

Short of serving an educational function, Brussels-based European media will not be sought by readers whose concerns are strictly national, unless an EU issue affects national interests. As such, national identity has the effect of limiting readership to those who perceive the EU as being at least as important to their lives as national affairs. These tend to be younger people who have learned something of the EU in their years of schooling, and/or must do so to improve employment prospects; or political and business management-level decision-makers who have an interest or stake in EU policy-making. The importance of knowledge and interest in the EU is demonstrated in the experiences of employees at the two youngest outlets examined: *Café Babel*, which was founded by university students who lived and studied in EU countries other than their own, as part of the EU-sponsored Erasmus exchange program (Morselli 2007); and the relatively young personnel of *EU Observer*, most of whom attended College of Europe, a university-level institution which has campuses in three EU countries, attended by students from all over Europe (Dechaumont and Beunderman 2007).

COMMUNICATION DEFICITS: TRANSLATING INTO "NORMAL LANGUAGE"

Editors interviewed stated that deficient knowledge of EU institutions among the general population in Europe poses a conventional challenge to reporters—one that is in line with their work as interpreters, whose job it is to make issues understandable to the public. Reporting on national politics is easier than reporting on the intricacies of the EU, which are not well understood by citizens of Europe at large. Making the EU understood constitutes "a sort of first-order journalism challenge," explained *European Voice* deputy editor King, similar to reporting on any other topic whose basics are not understood by the layperson. Journalists' priority is to make all topics in the public interest "understandable to the generalist" (King 2007).

An added challenge of covering the EU, unlike national governments, lies in filtering through particularly vast amounts of information that its institutions generate every day, and rendering its technical language understandable to the public. Reporters with EIS and Agence Europe, who follow the EU institutions on a daily basis, are particularly aware of this. "The EU is machinery that produces news and information every day—it is very effective at this. You get a lot of information which is not really news" explained Sebastien Falletti, foreign affairs and trade reporter with EIS. "[The EU] is also trying to sell their point through the Commission, through the lobbies. So one key challenge is to try to figure out what is news and what isn't" (Falletti 2007).

Falletti, like his fellow reporters at EIS, follows specific issues dealt with in the EU day after day, until key decisions finally break, meriting the production of a story. This experience is unique to the specialized newsletters *Europolitics* and *Europe Daily Bulletin*, which are committed to covering the EU day after day. More generalist media scarcely have the time to do this. General newswire services' experience is particularly telling. EU coverage, according to Agence France Presse's Brussels deputy director Catherine Triomphe, is "definitely more intricate" than covering national governments. "The decision-making process is slower," she explained. "It goes through many phases and compromises which have to be followed closely and deciphered. Because there is a lot of EU jargon used to present the way compromises are gradually being structured, which is difficult for any beginner [reporter] in Brussels" (Triomphe 2007).

In following every step of decision-making, interest in issues often "gets lost in the process", Triomphe said, by readers and reporters alike. Decisions taken by 27 member state governments requires constant compromise, resulting in outcomes that have less impact than anything produced by national or local governments. Such stories make for less interesting news, and are less attractive to reporters, considering the time and constant follow-up required of them.

Troublesome "EU jargon" is a challenge posed to all journalists "especially in legislative processes," noted reporter Beunderman of the *EU Observer*. The challenge, he said, "is to explain that well. We [reporters] are EU experts ourselves. We should always be aware of the need to keep translating it into normal language" (Dechaumont and Beuderman 2007).

Paul Taylor, Brussels' bureau chief for Reuters, asserted the EU is partly to blame for the overuse of unfamiliar jargon. "I think it was deliberate in the sense that, from the outset they wanted to use terminology that did not make it [the EU] sound like a state," he said. "They didn't want it to be thought of as a state." This, he said, is readily evident in debates over the proposed EU constitution (Taylor 2007). A proposed official title of "High representative for the common foreign and security policy" as written in the rejected constitution, for example, would translate quite simply as "EU foreign minister."

Apathy of the general population toward the EU is also part of the communication deficit issue, and the present lack of important, vital stories that have a direct perceived impact on EU-member citizens is perceived by some members of the media as being partly to blame. As director of programs at the European Journalism Centre in Brussels, Giuseppe Zaffuto has seen coverage priorities and reader reaction shift in the last decade. Unlike the mid-1990s, when the European integration project gathered steam with renewed enthusiasm following the end of the cold war and the fall of the Iron Curtain, recent years have seen a decline in interest. Recent big events, such as monetary integration and enlargement to the East, were not unexpected stories. These were largely the product of decisions made in the heady 1990s, Zaffuto remarked. As for the present decade: "I do not see any big priorities that are driving the man in the street towards a better understanding of the institutions," said Zaffuto (2007), "or much more affection towards the Parliament, which is the body that is elected by European citizens."

ADVERTISING MARKETS: IN SEARCH OF A VIABLE BUSINESS
MODEL

Among the six case studies considered, only two rely on conventional
advertising to support themselves. Newsletter agencies Agence Europe
and EIS rely almost exclusively on subscriptions for their revenue.
Website Café Babel still falls short of a professional operation, as it is
relies mostly on public and private grants. Advertising presents a singular puzzle to the remaining three outlets. Their media formats—one
a newspaper, the others web-based, and their aspirations to reaching
a Europe-wide audience that spans at least 27 European states—present important questions to advertisers. Among these three, only the
European Voice and *EU Observer* rely on advertising. EurActiv.com has
established its own unique sponsorship model that, for many, appears
to sacrifice principles of editorial independence. A description of the
business models adopted by the case studies follows.

CONVENTIONAL NEWSPAPERS: THE EUROPEAN VOICE

Even though the newspaper is written for a pan-European audience,
European Voice's readership is made up largely of Brussels-dwelling
expatriates with high incomes. This makes the paper a good place
to advertise local products purchased by affluent customers—such
as flights, banking services, cars, telecom services and luxury goods.
The newspaper easily attracts advertising from lobbying and advocacy groups, and ads for jobs and educational institutions throughout
Europe. Having worked with a number of newspapers throughout his
journalistic career—including *The European*, a failed attempt at a pan-
European English-language weekly newspaper in the 1990s—deputy
editor Tim King is keenly aware of the limitations of advertising with
an aspiring pan-European newspaper, which completely differ from
advertising in conventional local/regional newspapers. "You deny
yourself classified advertising, and you deny yourself property ads—
apart from villas in coastal resorts across Europe," said King (2007).
In terms of property ads, "If you wanted to sell a house in Brussels,
why would you advertise it in a Europe-wide newspaper rather than a
Belgian one?"

National market barriers are not so much the problem, King added: "It's just the physical distance. Restaurants, theater, all that kind

of listings-areas, shops—it doesn't work on a Europe-wide basis." The editor recalled advertising as being a key unresolved puzzle at *The European*, which consistently operated at a loss.

WEB-BASED BUSINESS MODELS: EU OBSERVER AND EURACTIV. COM

Logistical limitations on delivery and circulation limit the reach of newspaper advertising. The Internet, however, with its potentially unlimited reach, appears to present an ideal advertising platform. But practice shows this is far from being the case.

Even though their website is widely read, *EU Observer* has found that a pan-European advertising market does not exist. Genuine pan-European advertising agencies are nowhere to be found, according to marketing and advertising director Alexandre Dechaumont. Even though "all advertising agencies are multinationals" he said, all advertising campaigns they undertake are limited to national markets, with "very few pan-European campaigns" (Dechaumont and Beunderman 2007). Meanwhile, he noted, national ad agencies will not consider the website because it is not judged to have a sufficient "critical mass" within any given state.

Another key limitation to websites is the novelty of online advertising, which has been slow to convince advertisers. "Potential advertisers tend to be very conservative," explained Dechaumont:

[Advertisers] will think they are better off advertising in *European Voice* and paying 3,000 Euros for a weekly ad–I mean like half a page in *European Voice*–than being visible on a website. Even though they might never read the *European Voice* from A to Z, and they might check our website every day. That's something which makes it very hard, for everybody. (Dechaumont and Beunderman 2007)

New methods of advertising are also challenging principles of editorial independence. Integrated content, for instance, which offers links to outside sites that are in some way related to a given story, may sacrifice editorial independence if the content is more promotional than informational. Such new techniques push advertising "to the point where you don't know where the border is between business and advertising," Dechaumont said (Dechaumont and Beunderman 2007).

Calling itself an "EU policy portal" rather than a news site, *Eur-Activ.com* does not rely on conventional advertising. The site's main source of funding derives from corporate sponsors, who provide funding to open "policy sections" on the site. "We wanted to keep the site completely free of charge," explained *EurActiv* managing editor Frédéric Simon. Conventional advertising on the Internet proved to be inadequately developed, "so the sponsorship option was chosen as a founding principle" (Simon 2007). Policy sections cover about 20 major policy issues that concern the EU. Among them are climate change, energy, EU enlargement, financial services, trade and industry, transport, and workers' mobility. "We couldn't cover climate change or energy as deep as we do today without the sponsor funding." Simon explained. "Together with the sponsor, we agree on some dossiers on which we would go a little more in-depth" (Simon 2007).

EurActiv's unique financing model raises questions about editorial independence among editors throughout Brussels. In spite of the fact that *EurActiv* communicates extensive information on the EU and Europe-wide policy issues, its site is packed with links to press releases and position statements which serve more as references, showing little, if any independent interpretation and placement into context. Simon admitted that potential sponsors themselves are often skeptical of the site's editorial independence. "We have to do a lot of explaining," he said, underlining that *EurActiv*'s commitment as a policy portal is to provide fact-based reporting that is free of editorial opinion (Simon 2007). Positions presented by sponsors on the site must also be strictly fact-based, and open to contradictory views and counter-arguments.

Conclusions

Print news media (the written press) established to report to all-European audiences of the European Union must overcome four key barriers to reaching their readers, and sustaining themselves as viable news businesses. A total of six print news media outlets that serve pan-European audiences were selected to identify the strategies used to overcome these obstacles. These barriers, in order of priority, were found in this study to be: national advertising markets; language; national culture; EU political communication deficits.

First, if a business is to survive as an independent enterprise, it must have a viable business model that allows it to sustain itself. This study identifies national advertising markets as the key limiting factor that constrains the success of pan-European news media. This is followed by language, and national identity—both identified as fundamental barriers to the establishment of a European public sphere and associated news media. EU political communication deficits, caused by a lack of education and knowledge of the EU, are identified as a fourth greatest barrier to the success of pan-European print news media. Lack of knowledge about the EU contributes to a lack of interest among readers. Pan-European news media provide information about EU-related events as clearly as possible, taking into account deficiencies in the general population's education about EU policies and processes. This is in fact a first-order challenge of journalism: to inform and shed light on little-understood events that are in the public interest. Strategies used by the six case studies to overcome each of the barriers are varied, and are summarized here.

ADVERTISING MARKETS

Advertising is commonly the largest source of revenue for conventional independent news outlets, and as such, news publications' survival and viability depends on it. Results show that a genuine pan-European advertising market does not exist in the print market. National and local/regional advertising markets prevail. Essential ads that are staples for local newspapers—such as classified and property ads, arts and entertainment ads for instance, do not exist at the European level. Moreover, ad agencies continue to operate on a national/regional basis, tailoring marketing strategies for tastes that are specific from state to state, region to region.

Lacking adequate advertising markets, publications have to rely on other sources of funding. The experience of the publications examined here demonstrates that there exist only two viable alternative sources: subscription revenues—which, when relied upon on their own, create subscription rates prohibitively high for individual subscribers; and financial contributions in the form of endowments, grants or sponsorships.

News agencies Europe Information Service and Agence Europe rely almost completely on subscription revenues. Their buyers are organizations and high-level professionals who rely on accurate day-to-day reporting specializing in EU affairs. Relying on subscription revenues works fine for publications with this specialized readership. Such readers are willing to pay high rates (EIS and Agence Europe charging rates starting at 1,700 Euro a year for print copies in 2007) for information that is essential for their work and livelihood. General readers for whom such information is not essential would not subscribe at such rates.

The advertising question looms large for websites in particular. In addition to the lack of a genuine pan-European market for advertising for the readers' market, advertisers appear to be wary of using the Internet medium. Even though websites have greater potential to reach Europe-wide audiences—due to the increasingly extensive reach of Internet in Europe—advertisers in 2007 remained unconvinced and conservative, sticking to conventional advertising media such as newspapers and magazines (Dechaumont and Beunderman 2007).

Websites *EurActiv.com* and *Café Babel* overcome the advertising barrier by taking on sponsors, and public and private grants. *EurActiv.com*'s sponsorship model has large corporate sponsors—all trans-national—fund the production of dossiers on specific EU-related issues. This model is off-limits to independent news media, as it threatens editorial independence. *EurActiv* defines itself as an "EU policy portal," not a news site, which allows it to keep clear of such issues.

LANGUAGE

Our case studies concur that English is the preferred language in the multinational setting, and is adequate for informing expert readerships of Europe who wish to know more about EU and Europe-wide affairs. Readers seeking news about the EU and Europe-wide affairs tend to understand English well enough to accept this. Offering services in other languages serves more the purpose of providing "added value" to the reader (Lemoine 2007, Jéhin 2007). It could not be concluded with certainty that offering content in multiple languages increases the chances of reaching a Europe-wide audience. Interviews indicated that recent expansions of the EU (particularly from 1995 to 2007)—which now includes 23 official languages–have worked in favor of English as the preferred language of exchange Europe-wide.

NATIONAL IDENTITY

Reporting styles and interest in stories vary by nationality and ethnic identity, according to literature surveys and interviews conducted in this research. No unique pan-European tradition of reporting exists. This barrier works to limit the appeal of pan-European print news media to readers who wish to inform themselves about the EU and Europe-wide affairs exclusively. It can also work to limit the appeal of pan-European reporting overall, as such reporting is characterized as neutral, "simple" and straightforward, without colourful cultural references. Cultural references must be "weeded out" (King 2007) in order for reports to be understandable to European readers at large.

COMMUNICATION DEFICITS

Deficient knowledge of the EU among the general population does not present journalists with an uncommon challenge, as it is a reporter's job to explain any given subject. From the standpoint of journalists, EU communication deficits are best defined by the difficulty posed in covering a trans-national organization that: a) generates vast amounts of information on a daily basis; b) uses jargon that is not understandable to the general public; c) deliberates over exceptionally long periods of time before it produces decisions that are newsworthy. On the latter point, Agence France Presse Brussels bureau chief Catherine Triomphe commented that long deliberation causes interest to get "lost in the process" (Triomphe 2007).

Deficits in education about the EU appear to lay at the root of EU communication barriers. Education is the purview of national governments. Without national education policies that inform future generations on EU history and the basics of EU governance, the written press will be reporting to a public that is *not interested* in the institutions that govern the European Union and the process of European integration. As such, stories on the EU and the integration process will not sell.

Reaching a general Europe-wide audience

Case studies confirm that the Internet, compared to newspapers, is the most effective way to transmit written news information Europe-wide. Newspapers have greater logistical limitations that keep them from spreading their reach across Europe. Of the news media examined, the

EU Observer, despite its small audience, appears to be the most successful genuinely pan-European news outlet in terms of readership. Its readership reach across Europe is the most uniform, without being focused on a single public. The site's number of visitors, 25,000 daily, puts it well ahead of the other outlets. Taking this as a model for the future of pan-European reporting seems feasible. *EU Observer*'s full-time reporters are from all over Europe, functioning in multiple languages but writing in English, normally their second language. Reporters keep informed on stories from other media, largely the common generalist national press, written in their native or other known languages–gleaning these for cues on developing news (Dechaumont and Beunderman 2007). These are easily accessed via Internet, if not in newsprint form. The final product is news with a Europe-wide angle. Websites *EurActiv.com* and *Café Babel*, which produce content in multiple languages, are also very effective at reaching a mass readership throughout Europe, although they are not devoted to news reporting, and largely reliant on sponsors.

Most media examined in the case studies, with the exception of *Café Babel* and *EU Observer*, proved to serve a specific readership that can best be described as a public sphere of government and business decision-making elites, much the same as those elites served by large international print media of the *Financial Times-International Herald Tribune* group. This study concludes that two conditions must come to exist for pan-European media to broaden their appeal beyond this public sphere. First, European integration must become more than a project centered on trade and economic matters. It must broaden to encompass other policy areas covered by national governments. In the first decade of the 21st century, security and foreign policy appear to be the next significant set of policy areas to be devolved from national governments to the EU. As this develops, pan-European media will benefit from their ability to provide more complete coverage of Europe-wide public affairs. Second, European political integration must develop to the extent that readers can identify with key players and public officials in the EU, in the same way that they now identify with key players in their own national governments.

References

Berezin, Mabel and Martin Schain, eds. (2003) *Europe without Borders: Remapping Territory, Citizenship and Identity in a Transnational Age.* Baltimore: Johns Hopkins University Press.

Billig, Michael. (1995) *Banal Nationalism.* London: Sage.

Biltereyst, Daniel. (1992) "Language and culture as ultimate barriers? An analysis of the circulation, consumption and popularity of fiction in small European countries." *European Journal of Communication* 7: 517–540.

Boyer, Dominic and Miklós Sükösd. (2010) "European media and the culture of Europeanness". See in the present volume, pp. 251–275.

Calhoun, Craig. (2003) "The democratic integration of Europe: Interests, identity, and the public sphere." In: *Europe without borders: Re-mapping territory, citizenship and identity in a transnational age.* Eds. M. Berezin and M. Schain. Baltimore, MD: Johns Hopkins University Press, 1–27.

Cederman, Lars-Erik. (2001) "Nationalism and bounded integration: what it would take to construct a European demos." *European Journal of International Relations* 7(2): 139–174.

Chalaby, Jean K. (2002) "Transnational television in Europe: The role of pan-European channels." *European Journal of Communication* 17(2): 183–203.

Commission for the European Communities. (2006) *White Paper on a European Communication Policy.* Brussels.

Dechaumont, Alexandre, Marketing executive, *EU Observer*, and Mark Beunderman, reporter, *EU Observer.* Interview by author, 3 May 2007. Brussels, Belgium. Tape recording and notes.

Downey, John and Thomas Koenig. (2006) "Is there a European public sphere? The Berlusconi-Schulz case." *European Journal of Communication* 21(2): 165–187.

Esser, Frank and Barbara Pfetch, Eds. (2004) *Comparing Political Communication: Theories, Cases, and Challenges.* Cambridge: Cambridge University Press.

Falletti, Sebastien, reporter, *Europolitique/Europolitics.* Interview by author, 8 May 2007. Brussels, Belgium. Tape recording and notes.

Gifreu, Josep. (1996) "Linguistic order and spaces of communication in post-Maastricht Europe." *Media, Culture and Society* 18: 127–139.

Golding, Peter. (2006) "Theoretical issues arising from the research project." In: Adequate Information Management in Europe (AIM) Work Package D6: Theory building, "European identity building/European public sphere" 12–21.

Habermas, Jurgen. (1989 [1962]) *The Structural Transformation of the Public Sphere: An Inquiry into a Category of Bourgeois Society.* Cambridge, MA: MIT Press.

Harcourt, Alison. (2002) "Engineering Europeanization: The role of the European institutions in shaping national media regulation." *Journal of European Public Policy* 9(5): 736–755.

Heikkila, Heikki and Risto Kunelius. (2006) "Journalists imagining the European public sphere: Professional discourses about EU news. Practices in ten countries." *Javnost-The Public* 13(4): 63–80.

Inside Market Data. (2006) *Market Size and Share Analysis*. London: Incisive Media.

Jéhin, Olivier, Deputy editor-in-chief, *Bulletin Quotidien Europe* (Agence Europe). Interview by author, 3 May 2007. Brussels, Belgium. Tape recording and notes.

King, Tim, deputy editor, *European Voice*. Interview by author. 3 May 2007. Brussels, Belgium. Tape recording and notes.

Kurpas, Sebastian, Michael Bruggeman and Christoph Meyer. (2006) "The Commission White Paper on Communication: Mapping a way to the European public sphere." Centre for European Studies Policy Brief No.101: May. Brussels: CEPS.

Lemoine, Pierre, Editor-in-chief, *Europolitique/Europolitics* (Europe Information Service). Interview by author, 2 May 2007. Brussels, Belgium. Tape recording and notes.

Lord, Christopher. (2004) *A Democratic Audit of the European Union*. Basingstone, Hampshire: Pelgrave Macmillan.

Machill, Marcel, Markus Beiler, and Corinna Fischer. (2006) "Europe-Topics in Europe's Media: The Debate about the European Public Sphere: A Meta-Analysis of Media Content Analyses." *European Journal of Communication*. 3(21): 57–88.

Markopouliotis, Giorgios, director, planning and priorities, Directorate General Communications, European Commission. Interview by author, 8 May 2007. Tape recording and notes.

Meyer, Cristoph O. (2003) "Exploring the European Union's communication deficit: Old problems and new departures. *Central European Political Science Review* 4(11): 35–43.

Morely, David and Kevin Robbins. (1995) *Spaces of Identity: Global Media, Electronic Landscapes and Cultural Boundaries*. Routledge: London and New York.

Morselli, Lorenzo, president, Café Babel, Brussels. Interview by author. 10 May 2007. Brussels, Belgium. Tape recording and notes.

Nariman, Fali Sam. (1989) "The Indian constitution: An experiment in unity amid diversity." In: *Forging Unity Out of Diversity: The Approaches of Eight Nations*. Robert A. Goldwin, Art Kaufman, William A. Schambra (eds.) Washington, D.C: American Enterprise Institute, 7–37.

Price, Monroe E. (2002) *Media and sovereignty: The global information revolution and its challenge to state power*. Cambridge, MA: MIT Press.

Price, Monroe E. (1995) *Television: The Public Sphere and National Identity*. Oxford: Clarendon Press.

Ricardi, Lorenzo, director of marketing, Agence Europe. Interview by author. 3 May 2007. Brussels, Belgium. Notes.

Schlesinger, Philip. (1999) "Changing spaces for political communication: The case of the European Union." *Political Communication* 16: 263–279.

Schmitt, Hermann. (2005) "The European Parliament elections of June 2004: Still second-order?" *West European Politics* 38 (3): 650–679.

Simon, Frédéric, managing editor, *EurActiv.com*. Interview by author. 4 May 2007. Brussels, Belgium. Tape recording and notes.

Taylor, Paul, European affairs editor, Reuters, Brussels. Interview by author. 11 May 2007. Brussels, Belgium. Tape recording and notes.

Trenz, Hans-Jorg. (2004) "Media coverage on European governance: Exploring the European public sphere in national quality newspapers." *European Journal of Communication* 19(3): 291–319.

Triomphe, Catherine, deputy bureau chief, Agence France Presse, Brussels. Interview by author. 4 May 2007. Brussels, Belgium. Tape recording and notes.

Valentini, Chiara. (2006) "Constructing public support: EU communication challenges for the process of integration." *Paper for the International Conference 2006 on "Public Spheres and their Boundaries."* University of Tampere, 25–27 May 2006.

Van de Steeg, Marianne. (2002) "Rethinking the conditions for a European public sphere in the European Union." *European Journal of Social Theory* 5(4): 499–519.

Watson, Rory, reporter, *The Times*. Interview by author. 11 May 2007. Brussels, Belgium. Tape recording and notes.

Weiner, Antje and Thomas Diez. (2004) *European Integration Theory*. Oxford: Oxford University Press.

CHAPTER 5

Aiding Integration and Identity: The Unfulfilled Roles and Functions of the Romani Media in Eastern Europe

PETER GROSS AND KATERINA SPASOVSKA

Nationalism and ethnic particularism remain relevant in all the Eastern European countries that have embarked on varied processes of democratization after communism's collapse in 1989, including those that have acceded to European Union (EU) membership.[1] Kupchan's (1995:1) now 13-year-old pronouncement that "In Europe's east, nationalism is in many instances providing a critical source of social cohesion for states in the midst of profound transformation," still rings true today. The conflict between nationalism and the requisites of European integration as it relates to ethnic minorities in the Eastern European nations, particularly the Roma, thus continues to vex the EU and the capitals of the old continent.[2] The Roma have a problem other ethnic groups in the region do not share: their ethnic identity is not yet established.

This chapter examines what roles if any the Romani media play in establishing (a) a Romani identity in Eastern Europe and (b) in helping to integrate the Roma in Eastern European societies. It makes no claim to being anything but a brief introduction to the issue, therefore serving as a starting point for much needed research on a decidedly ignored topic. A brief assessment of the changed (and unchanged) legal, political and cultural atmosphere in Europe vis-à-vis the Roma, and the evolution

---

[1] As of January 2007, Bulgaria, the Czech Republic, Estonia, Hungary, Latvia, Lithuania, Poland, Romania, Slovakia and Slovenia are members of the EU and Albania, Croatia, Macedonia, Montenegro, and Serbia are actively negotiating for membership.

[2] No one knows the exact size of the Roma population. It is estimated there are 5,710,000 Roma throughout Europe, with the bulk of the population, 4,220,000 in Eastern Europe. See Liegeois and Gheorge, 1995; CIA Fact Book 2000.

of Roma communities, one that informs both the possibilities and the pressures brought to integrate the long discriminated against Roma, is discouraging in regard to both issues of Roma identity- building and integration. And, whereas the ethnic media's roles in societies are relatively well established across the globe, neither theory nor praxis dovetails with the Romani media's nature, roles and functions (Ogan, 2001; Cottle, 2000; Cunnigham and Sinclair, 2000; Riggins, 1992; Tio, 1986)

Roma-Directed Policies and Their Failure

The Roma became a transnational or European minority by having "constituted themselves as a minority through their relation to the emerging international structures such as the Organization for Security and Cooperation in Europe [OSCE], the Council of Europe [CE], [and] the European Union [EU]" (Achim, 2004:216). Indeed, in an effort to end the Roma's political marginalization and anti-Roma discrimination, the CE's 1993 Resolution 1203 recognized the Roma's status as a "true European minority."

Since 1993, the EU's legislation, together with that of other European organizations and that of the individual states of Eastern Europe, has endeavored to address the continuing severe problems faced by the Roma: (1) prohibit discrimination against the Roma in employment, social protection and education, housing and access to goods and services, and aid their enfranchisement and development,[3] (2) provide a framework for policies in education, employment and social inclusion, (3) improve the employability of Roma, e.g. through the European Social Fund (ESF),[4] and (4) enhance information and awareness of the

---

[3] See for example the Cologne Declaration of 2001, Part I and II, the 1995 Framework Convention for the Protection of National Minorities; see also the 1992 European Charter for Regional and Minority Languages. For Eastern and Central Europe, see the 2004 Central European Initiative (CEI) Instrument for the Protection of Minority Rights. By Eastern Europe, the authors mean to identify the former communist bloc, with the exception of Eastern Germany and the Soviet Union.

[4] In 2000–2006, the ESF spent 275 million euros on projects specifically targeted at Roma and 1 billion euros on "vulnerable" groups, including the Roma. See Commission of the European Communities (July 2, 2008).

Roma's right to a life free of discrimination and of their contribution to European civilization. Added to these European attempts to legislate anti-discrimination and minority rights, are a host of United Nations declarations and conventions, e.g. the 2005 UNESCO Convention on the Protection and Promotion of the Diversity of Cultural Expressions, the 1992 Declaration on the Rights of Persons Belonging to National or Ethnic, Religious and Linguistic Minorities, the 1966 International Covenant on Civil and Political Rights.

Intentions, of course, cannot always be made operational. Thus, while a laundry list of initiatives introduced in the 1990s continue to be active—including the much-touted Decade of Roma Inclusion 2005–2015,[5] the Roma Education Fund, and the OSCE's Action Plan—not one has yet even come close to meeting its stated goals. The European Commission's (EC) Commission Staff Working Document, "Community Instruments and Policies for Roma Inclusion" (2008:3), reiterates the already well known problems and policies associated with integrating the Roma into the European communities (in employment, education, politics, etc.), end discrimination and marginalization, as well as the challenges faced:

> Though the socio-economic conditions of Roma remain under-researched, it is clear that Roma are particularly exposed to high rates of poverty, unemployment or are largely operating in the informal economy. A recent EU-wide public opinion survey shows that a quarter of Europeans would feel uncomfortable to have a Roma as their neighbor. In some countries half of the respondents take this view. It has been highlighted by research and civil society that anti-Gypsyism is a specific form of racism which is based on (sic) de-legitimization and moral exclusion.

Almost concurrently with the EC's working document's release, the European Roma Summit held in Brussels on Sept. 16, 2008—which brought together representatives of EU member states, those participating in the Decade of Roma Inclusion, the European Parliament, the

---

[5] The initiative is supported by the Open Society Institute (OSI), the World Bank, the EC, CE, CE Development Bank, the UN Development Bank and nine of the Eastern European governments.

European Commission (EC), the French Presidency of the EU, Roma representatives and civil society organizations—called for a "continent-wide drive" to improve the plight of millions of Roma "who face discrimination and poverty" (Associated Press, Sept. 16, 2008). The Roma live "in conditions which are simply not acceptable in the 21st century Europe," said EC President Jose Manuel Barroso.

The reactions to the Summit were rather negative, pointing first to a slew of European-wide and nation-specific policies that have to date brought little change to the situation of the Roma, and second to the failure of the EU to do enough to rectify the appalling human rights and economic reality of this "European minority." Embodying Fukuyama's (2004:115) sentiment about EU policies that "a great deal of …law coming out of Europe consists of what amounts to social policy wish lists that are completely unenforceable," Rajan Zed (Sept. 9, 2008) writes,

> …a comprehensive, uniform, sustainable, cohesive and integrated Europe-wide policy with strategic focus; supported by effective implementation, firm commitment and strong political will is needed to improve the Roma plight. *In the past, policies on paper to tackle Roma discrimination and exclusion had proved very weak to deal with their day-to-day sufferings* (emphasis added).

Added to what surely is a tall order for the Romani media to have to deal with problems of identity building and integration, is an issue that goes to the core of the two problems: despite the policies and pronouncements of governments in the region, their preoccupation remains focused "not on what can be done *for* them, but what can be done *about* them" (Brown, 2001:211). Which "usually means, in truth, what can be done *against* them. If that attitude does not change, the Roma will become Europe's unsolvable problem (emphasis in the original)."

Integration, Ethnic Identity and Roma Mobilization

It is not our intention to delve into the theories and practices of ethnic integration, but we have to understand the notion of "integration" at the most fundamental level in order to gauge what the Romani media might be able to contribute to the process. We propose adopting two of Laitin's (2005:50–51) three models of integration, alone or in combination: [6]

(1) standard integration—A two-way process, whereby "the minority adopts a large range of cultural practices associated with the dominant culture" and members of the dominant culture, "because of the contact that is part of integration...begin to adopt, unevenly and selectively—and often as fads and fashions—some of the cultural practices of the minority;

(2) assimilation—"A form of integration in which the minority adopts virtually all cultural practices of the dominant group in society, and in which adoptions of cultural practices of the minority by members of the dominant group are barely discernible."

Assimilation and integration are hardly unusual processes, under certain conditions, but these conditions are not present in the relationship between the Roma and their cohabiting majority ethnic groups.[7] Ultimately, whether integration of the Roma in Eastern European societies is possible or not, given Kymlicka's (1995) assertion that ethnic minorities often reject adaptation to the majority society for reasons of intrinsic cultural values, heritage and birth, is an unanswered question. What we do know is that the majority of Eastern Europeans seems resistant to the idea of integrating the Roma.

In regard to this resistance, there is an equally if not more salient question that remains unanswered: will the pattern of democratization in Eastern Europe follow the lead of the Western democracies? The question is of utmost relevance, because integration has to do with more than the willingness of an ethnic minority to integrate; it also has to do with the willingness of the majority to accept the integration of the minority. Brown's (2001) above-mentioned, accurate

---

[6] Laitin's third model of integration, Integration into a Common External Framework, is often associated with postcolonial culture and the "dominant group as well as the minority both condition their cultural behavior on some external model, and integrate through a common exposure to this external model" and therefore inapplicable in the case of the Roma.

[7] See for example the work of Schermerhorn (1970); also see Gellner (1964: Chapter 7).

analysis of the flawed approach to the Roma problem by Eastern European governments is a case in point. Fundamentally, that means a commitment to democracy and "an active interest in sustaining it" (Schopflin, 1995:59).[8] "Without such a commitment," writes Schopflin (1995:60), "democracy will become the affair of the elites and thus be vulnerable to popular upsurges of an antidemocratic nature." He warns that the roles of nationhood and nationalism may remain central to the political systems, in which case they will have,

> ...far-reaching implication for the operation of democracy, which presupposes tolerance and compromise as *conditiones sine qua non*. It is important to stress again the distinction between the civil and ethnic dimensions of nationhood in this context and to understand that it is the weakness of the former that has allowed the latter an excessively influential role.

As to identity building, if we accept Smith's (1993:28–29) definition of an ethnic community as a "named human population with a myth of common ancestry, shared historical memories, one or more elements of common culture, a link with a homeland and a sense of solidarity," the Roma could not be considered an "ethnic community." The reasons are unambiguous: Eastern Europe's Roma are divided by language, customs, appearance, religion/rituals and ethnic commonalities. Ultimately, the Roma have little they share in common other than a common Indian ancestry, being discriminated against and exhibiting little solidarity.

Barany (2002:64:80), one of the most astute and knowledgeable students of the contemporary Roma, summarizes some of the problems faced by the Roma in general and, therefore, also in their attempts to mobilize themselves: They (1) have not established an ethnic identity, (2) are short on ethnic solidarity, social capital, highly developed institutions, means of communication, an ideology, a profile, a program, political opportunity, financial resources, symbols and high

---

[8] These newly minted democracies in Eastern Europe remain to be consolidated and continue to denote forms of government rather than conditions of society, as Raymond Aron (1970:9) makes the distinction between unconsolidated and consolidated democracies.

literacy rates, (3) lack a shared language and culture, (4) have very small and disunited leadership cadres.

How then can the Roma create an ethnic "identity"? If Barth (1969) is correct, ethnic groups achieve their own identity as much as this identity is ascribed to them from outside the group. The identity ascribed to the Roma by the dominant (and other non-dominant) populations in the nations of the region is almost uniformly negative, one that more often than not is offered as a justification for discriminating against them ever since, as Angus Fraser (1995) tells us, their unexplained appearance in Europe about ten centuries ago.[9] And the Roma, as already mentioned, have themselves failed to achieve their own identity and there is scant evidence, particularly in the Romani media, that they are working on developing one.

The institutionalization of the Roma's civil and human rights, and the policies to aid this European minority does, theoretically at least, "suggest hope for constructive, local, national and international dialogues in which Roma have a recognized voice" (Bancroft, 2005:31). This also posits the possibility that both ethnic identity creation and integration are part of the dialogue or a result of it. As is often the case in this 21st century, hope for dialogues, socio-political and cultural understanding and integration is tied to the ability of modern mass media to serve as facilitators.

The Romani Media, Ethnic Identity Creation and Integration

In order to mobilize and secure representation at all legislative levels a group must have certain prerequisites: (1) political opportunity, (2) ethnic identity and its formation, (3) leadership, (4) organizational capabilities, (5) a coherent program, (6) financial resources, (7) media, and (8) symbols (Barany, 2005:83–89). The Roma have none of these prerequisites, save perhaps for the political opportunity that the various national and supranational policies, and the general post-communist trend toward (varied forms of) democratization offer them. Romani non-governmental organizations, political parties and a small handful

---

[9] One of the best sources for learning about this discrimination is the European Roma Rights Center in Budapest, Hungary.

of Roma politicians sitting in the region's parliaments, are credible examples of the Roma taking advantage of the newly arisen political opportunities. Despite this, Vermeersch (2001) writes, it is striking that the diversity of Romani interests have "remained absent from the various mainstream political groupings. This can hardly be blamed on fragmentation within the Romani movement."

The focus of our attention here, the Romani media in Eastern Europe, are "still in a nascent state...,"(Galjus, 2006: 139), however. They are, as Ivan Vesely—a Romani media entrepreneur in the Czech Republic; publisher of a slick Romani magazine, Amaro Gendalos, and owner of Radio Rota ("Romany Radio for Everyone")—identifies them as, "pioneers" with unclear roles, functions, import and effects.[10]

Their actual numbers are difficult to pinpoint, because some have short life-spans, others are only sporadically available, new ones quickly appear, and most importantly, there is no central census despite the work of supra-national Romani organizations such as the European Roma Rights Center (ERRC) in Budapest, Hungary.[11] According to the Romani Media Address Book (2006) compiled by the ERRC, there are 47 Roma publications, 21 Radio broadcasts, 13 Radio stations, 14 Television broadcasts, 2 Television stations, and 5 Internet news websites in Eastern Europe. The same year the "Address Book" was released, Gross (2006) calculated that from 1990 to 2005, 58 periodicals, 54 radio and 24 television stations and program, 13 news agencies and 47 websites can be identified as functional at one time or another. The country reports in the South East Europe Media Organization's (SEEMO) 2006 assessment of development in the Romani media sphere (Bauer and Vujovic, 2006) list even more Romani media outlets, without however indicating whether they are operational or not. And, in any case, this data is two years old at the time of this writing and, given the rapid change in the economic support and in the media legislation of the Eastern Europe countries (see below), their evolution was stymied and their numbers appear to be on the decline.

The content of Romani media—mostly entertainment fare, with some news and commentaries, literature and poetry—makes them negligible contributors to Romani public opinion formation, according to

---

[10] Gross interviewed Ivan Vesely in Prague, April 23, 2003.
[11] For an accounting of Romani media see also Bauer and Vujovic (2006).

Galjus (2006:140). The Romani media, particularly the press, "cannot praise itself (sic) for being the best provider, producer, and recorder of the most detailed information about Romani lives," he writes. Television and radio broadcasts offer mostly entertainment fare, and only some informational segments.

The Romani media are published and broadcast in one of the many Romani dialects, in the vernacular, bilingually or multi-lingually, including in English. The use of English as a *lingua franca* in the Romani media is in keeping with a region-wide trend whereby English is percolating upwards through the education system, and downwards from the business and political elite. In the case of the Roma it is decidedly a trickle-down phenomenon. Galjus (2006:135) writes, for example, that ninety percent of Romani magazines "are published in languages other than Romani" (Galjus, 2006:135–36). Romani publications in other than Roma language or dialects are meant to attract "readers from both the majority community and Roma alike." But, Galjus concludes, the degree of euphoria generated by the possibilities of writing in Romani, addressing Roma issues, raising the media profile of the Roma population, and setting up independent broadcasting, has evaporated and left a bitter aftertaste."

In this context, it is difficult to see how the Romani media are preserving and enhancing Roma culture and language, which in any case is not one culture but a string of sub-cultures and languages that are equally varied, given the differing Romani dialects spoken in the many Roma communities. Ethnic identity building is not well served by a Roma media that are "local, and much of their output is in national languages rather than Romany," which makes "their ability to exchange program materials (aside from music)...decidedly limited" (Browne, 2005:51). In short, the Romani media are not platforms for intra-ethnic dialogues that can contribute to ethnic identity building, group organization, or articulating a coherent program.

In most instances, as Galjus (2006:135–36) suggests, the Roma do not appear to even be the intended audience of the Romani media and by all accounts the Romani media are mostly owned and directed by the small strata of Roma elites whose ties to the majority of their ethnic brethren are tenuous at best, being looked upon as "alien" or "different" or "inauthentic" (Pogany, 2004:76–7; Lemon, 2000). It is, therefore, questionable whether this Roma leadership or elite that own some of the media outlets, speak for all Roma. Furthermore, the high rate of illiteracy, the absence of a unitary culture and language, and the endemic poverty among the Roma creates a low level of access to the media.[12] Thus, the Romani press, even if they had well developed distribution networks and access to non-Romani ones, would be consumed by only a small number of Roma and an even smaller number of non-Roma. And Romani broadcasts, by all accounts more successful than the press, are tied to the ability of the Roma to purchase television sets and, in some instances, pay the subscription fees.

Despite a slew of programs to train Romani journalists, the absence of educated and professional journalists among the Roma is a persistent problem for the Romani media. A small handful of Roma journalists end up working for mainstream media and some non-Roma journalists work for Romani media, providing a theoretical argument that there is a modicum of incipient integration happening in the media and, therefore, in society. This may be a very Lilliputian hope for the media and their journalists contributing to integration, despite claims such as that by the Rroma Media Networking Project (2003) that the Romani media have sufficiently evolved as news and information providers, and as a societal institution, that they supply mainstream media with "quality features related to Roma issues" and thus influence the mainstream media's coverage and the non-Roma in "a positive sense." There is no credible evidence for this claim and, in fact, evidence points to a vastly different relationship between the Roma and mainstream media. Andrzej Mirga (in Project on Ethnic Relations, 1996) authoritatively states that, "The Romani media and the non-Romani media are two non-intersecting circles."

If those that argue that "Minorities need (their own) media as agencies of those discussions, which are important for the conception of their collective identity (language, tradition, rites, conventions, and customs" (Bauer, 2006: 8–9) are correct, then both the absence of a well developed Romani media and the inability of the existing outlets to reach their ethnic audience makes them less than relevant in the task of identity building. Furthermore, as Galjus (1999:71) admits,

---

[12] For a good discussion of the issue of language, illiteracy, unitary culture and poverty that affect access to and consumption of media, see Barany (2002), Galjus (1999), Bernath and Messing (1999).

most of the Romani media "have yet to devote enough energy to wider problems…education, employment, culture, language, emancipation in [the] general sense, political participation, social exclusion and discrimination, as well as to positive examples." They also lack "real political and public influence" (Popovic, 1003:27) and they do not seem to have clear identities that, in turn, suggest a role in ethnic identity development.

It is ironic that this very small institution called the Romani media, is also divided politically, adding an element of negativity to what it might contribute to ethnic identity building. In Macedonia, for example, one Romani television station (TV Sutel) was owned by Nezded Mustafa (the station is still run by his family), a politician who is, since the extraordinary elections in 2008, a minister without portfolio; before the election he sided with the opposition. Another television station (BTR TV) is owned by a businessman, Zoran Dimov, who is also doing a balancing act given that his party, another Roma political party and opponent of Mustafa's party, is also part of the government coalition. The work and the very existence of these two stations are very much dependent on the government and on Romani political representatives, and thus obliged to play a role divorced from one that serves to build Romani ethnic identity.

At the very least, the notion that the Romani media are important facilitators of Roma ethnic identity is for the time being treated as highly questionable, despite such proposals as the German-based satellite TELE-Romani European TV program.[13] Some participants at the April 2007 SEEMO Meeting of Editors-in-Chief and Media Executives of Romani and Other Minority Media Representatives made similar proposals for establishing a European satellite to serve a European Romani television. The purpose and viability of such a media outlet remains unclear, given that the majority of Roma in Europe do not have a common Romani language. Because of the issue of language, the establishment of a pan-Romani media outlet may in fact be

---

[13] Macedonian businessman Zoran Dimov made the suggestion for a pan-Romani television station at the SEEMO meeting of editors-in-chief and media executives of Roma and other minority media representatives in April 2007 in Belgrade. He requested 300 million euros for a five-year period (2007–2013) from the EU. The TELE Romani project was never started.

counter productive to ethnic identity building. Husband (2005:468), for example, points out that in a situation like this, characterized by the necessary pragmatics of selecting one or two languages that optimize the potential audience size, there is not only a consequential relative neglect of an internal minority but also the possibility that a dominant language will effectively contribute to the eventual demise of a smaller language group.

Quite aside from any of the real or imagined roles they can carry out, the Romani media's seeming spectacular growth in the 1990s has slowed considerably, due in part to the falling financial support from national governments and Western organizations. The Romani media appear to be less central to the push for greater integration, as exemplified by their exclusion from the budget of the Decade of Roma Inclusion, 2005–2015. At the 2007 SEEMO meeting of Editors-and-Chief and media Executives of Romani and other Minority Media Representatives in South East/Central Europe, Romani editors and owners discussed the declining donations to their media outlets, the tightening of legislation in a number of countries that has them compete for local frequencies and pay the high fees for licenses and compete in the market just as all other media outlets, with no special consideration given them.

Thus, despite the EU's and the Eastern European states' multicultural strategies, inclusive of developing ethnic media, the Romani media are stuck in a kind of developmental no-man's land in which retrenchment rather than progress may be the order of the day. Riggins (1992:8–11) posits five models of ethnic media:

1. The integrationist model—state authorities "assume that subsidizing minority media would not fragment the state but better integrate minorities into national life, because such policies would encourage them to perceive the state as a benevolent institution. At the same time the state would be able to monitor minorities more easily and, if necessary, curtail trends toward political independence. It could also be assumed that through minority media state control would reach those who had not achieved functional bilingualism or fluency in the majority language."

2. The economic model—in a situation in which a particular ethnic group suffers from "economic deprivation and often high rates of illiteracy," which is certainly the case of the Roma, the state "de-

votes considerable resources to multiculturalism, including economic support to ethnic media. The integrationist and economic models are compatible, according to Riggins.

3. The divisive model—the state "can also use ethnicity to maintain or create some levels of tension and rivalry in a country to further its own objective of social control either in the context of colonialism or geopolitical order."

4. The preemptive model—the state establishes "its own minority media to preempt minorities from founding organizations [including media organizations] which would be independent of the state."

5. The proselytism model—"The state or a transnational organization may explicitly attempt to promote values through the mass media and thus devise appropriate means for reaching minority audiences in their own language."

We can pinpoint examples of one or more of Riggins' ethnic media models existing side by side, or a fusion of one or more models, in each Eastern European country. Not one of these models alone or in concert, however, aid ethnic identity building, given the above descriptions of the Romani media, their nature and scant audience among the Roma populations, the relationship between the Roma elites that own media and the Roma communities, and the undefined roles and function that they play.

A perusal of the little information and news found in the Romani press and broadcasts suggests some copying of the mainstream media's formats, reason perhaps for a very tenuous argument that Laitin's (2005) standard integration is taking place. There is no evidence that the mainstream media is taking anything from the Romani media, as already mentioned. What and how much of the cultural practices associated with the dominant culture is adopted by the Roma thanks to the mediation of the Roma media remains to be studied, as does the question of what cultural practices of the minority the dominant majority is adopting. The notion of assimilation also remains to be studied.

Suffice it to say, there is ample evidence that the Romani media do not fit either model of minority media posited by Husband (2001:19): they "neither reflect the dialogue within the ethnic communities nor cultivate the dialogue across the ethnic borders," meaning that to date the Romani media are not aiding integration or the establishment of a Roma ethnic identity. And it is not certain that they are the "key resources in the struggles for visibility, presence, community, influence and symbolic power which (sic) many, if not all, minority groups seek (Silverstone, May 2005)." Consequently, except for their potential symbolic value, their growth defies the customary explanations of the functions, roles, and their effects in a region where, as authoritatively suggested by Tania Gosselin (2003).

As symbols, the Romani media may be contributing to the establishment of one of Barany's elements of mobilization and that in itself, one can argue, shows they exemplify some progress, particularly if we are prepared to accept Silverstone's (May 1, 2005) notion that media should not be seen to determine identity "but contributing to the creation of symbolic community spaces in which identities can be constructed."

The very presence of these symbols, the Romani media, may also contribute to integration simply by the fact that they represent an alternative to the mainstream and to other ethnic media, that is to say they enable the Roma to speak and be heard, albeit in a very limited way, constituting what might be termed participation and recognition (Silverstone, May 1, 2005). It is something of a beginning.

Conclusion

The notion that today's Romani media can successfully deal with the dual assignment of aiding integration and identity building is a chimera; this despite ample evidence that in Eastern Europe, a well-developed and long-lived ethnic media have historically played a key role for ethnic minorities by enhancing their sense of identity, cultural and language specificity, and socio-political presence participation.[14]

Ultimately, the lesson learned in Eastern Europe's post-communist evolutions and the roles that the media have played in them should be taken seriously by those who view the Romani media as

---

[14] The only era in which this the ethnic media were purposefully diverted from their traditional tasks was during the Communist regimes that controlled the region from the 1940s until 1989.

central to the goals of ethnic identity building and integration. That lesson informs us that the roles media play are, first and foremost, indirect and often unwitting, and that economic development, education, and politics are the strings that control the evolution of media and their roles in society or within ethnic communities, particularly in one that is as retarded in its development as a community, as the Roma are.

An even more important lesson to be learned from this brief foray into the world of the Romani media, their roles and effects, is that our knowledge of the subject is limited and, therefore, a definitive analysis of what they can or cannot contribute to Roma identity building and integration in the long run is premature.

REFERENCES

Achim, Viorel (2004). *The Roma in Romanian History*. Budapest–New York: Central European University Press.

Aron, Raymond (1970). *An Essay on Freedom*. Cleveland and NY: The World Publishing Company.

Associated Press (Sept. 16, 2008). "EU criticized at first European Roma summit," in the *International Herald Tribune*. Accessed Sept. 29, 2008. /www.iht.com/articles/ap/2008/09/16/europe/EU-EU-Roma-Summit.php

Bancroft, Angus (2005). *Roma and Gypsy-Travellers in Europe: Modernity, Race, Space and Exclusion*. Aldershot and Burlington, VT: Ashgate.

Barany, Zoltan (2005). "Ethnic Mobilization in the Postcommunist Context: Albanians in Macedonia and the East European Roma." In Zoltan Barany and Robert G. Moser, eds., *Ethnic Politics After Communism*. Ithaca and NY: Cornell University Press, 78–107.

Barany, Zoltan (2002). *The East European Gypsies: Regime Change, Marginality, and Ethnopolitics*. Cambridge, England: Cambridge University Press.

Barth, Fredrik (1969). *Ethnic Groups and Boundaries: The Social Organization*. Little Brown & Co.

Bauer, Thomas A. and Oliver Vujovic (eds.) (2006). *Media and Minorities in South East Europe*. Vienna, Austria: The South East Europe Media Organization – International Press Institute.

Bauer, Thomas A. (2006), "The Villages in Media Landscape. Theoretical Comments Toward Public Care of Diversity of Culture and of Media Competence for Minorities." In Bauer, Thomas A. and Oliver Vujovic (eds.) (2006). *Media and Minorities in South East Europe*. Vienna, Austria: The South East Europe Media Organization – International Press Institute, 1–16.

Brown, J.F. (2001). *The Grooves of Change. Eastern Europe at the Turn of the Millennium.* Durham and London: Duke University Press.

Browne, Donald R. (2005). *Ethnic Minorities, Electronic Media, and the Public Sphere: A Comparative Study.* Cresskill, NJ: Hampton Press.

Commission of the European Communities (2008). "Community Instruments and Policies for Roma Inclusion." Commission Staff Working Document. Brussels, Belgium.

Commission of the European Communities (July 2, 2008). Press Release on the European Commission Report – Community Instruments and Policies for Roma Inclusion. Brussels, Belgium.

Commission of the European Communities (2008). Commission Staff Working Document Accompanying the Communication from the Commission to the European Parliament, the Council, the European Economic and Social Committee and the Committee of the Region. Non-Discrimination and equal opportunities: A renewed commitment. "Community Instruments and Policies for Roma Inclusion." Brussels, Belgium. www.europarl.europa.eu/registre/docs_autres_institutions/commission_europeenne/sec/2008/2279/COM_SEC(2008)2279_EN.pdf

Cottle, Simon (2000). *Ethnic Minorities and the Media.* Berkshire, UK: Open University Press.

Cunnigham, Stuard and John Sinclair, eds. (2000), *Floating Lives: The Media and Asian Diasporas. Negotiating Cultural Identity Through Media.* St. Lucia, Queensland: The University of Queensland Press.

European Roma Rights Center (2006). Romani Media Address Book. A database of existing Romani media and contact information. Accessed January 10, 2007. http://lists.errc.org/databases/media.shtml

Fraser, Angus (1995). *The Gypsies.* Oxford and Cambridge: Blackwell.

Fukuyama, Francis (2004). *State-Building: Governance and World Order in the 21st Century.* Ithaca, NY: Cornell University Press.

Galjus, Orhan (2006). "Roma and Media in South East Europe." In Bauer, Thomas A. and Oliver Vujovic (eds.) (2006). *Media and Minorities in South East Europe.* Vienna, Austria: The South East Europe Media Organization – International Press Institute, 127–156.

Galjus, Orhan (1999). "Stateless: Roma and the Media Today," in *Roma Rights* 4:98–100.

Gellner, Ernest (1964). *Thought and Change.* Chicago: Univeristy of Chicago Press.

Gosselin, Tania (2003). *Minority Media in Hungary and Slovenia: A Comparative Assessment, Actors, Organization, and Resources.* Research Paper. Ljubljana, Slovenia: The Peace Institute.

Gross, Peter (2006). "A Prolegomena to the Study of the Romani Media in Eastern Europe," in *European Journal of Communication*, 2006, Vol. 21 (4): 477–497.

Husband, Charles (2005). "Minority Ethnic Media As Communities Of Practice: Professionalism and Identity Politics in Interaction." *Journal of Ethnic and Migration Studies* Vol. 31, No. 3, 461–479.

Husband, Charles (2001). "Uber den Kampf gegen Rassismus hinaus: Entwurf einer polyethnischen Medienlandschaft." In Brigitta Busch, Brigitte Hipfl, and Kevin Robins (eds.), *Bewegte Identitaten. Medien in trasnkulturellen Kontexten*. Klagenfurt, Germany: Drava, 9–20.

Kupchan, Charles A. (1995). "Introduction: Nationalism Resurgent." In Charles A. Kupchan, ed., *Nationalism and Nationalities in the New Europe*. Ithaca, NY and London: Cornell University Press.

Kymlicka, Will (1995), *Multicultural citizenship. A Liberal Theory of Minority Rights*. Oxford: Claredon Press.

Laitin, David (2005). "Culture Shift in a Postcommunist State." In Zoltan Barany and Robert G. Moser, eds., Ethnic Politics After Communism. Ithaca and London: Cornell University Press.

Lemon, Alaina (2000). *Between Two Fires: Gypsy Performance and Romani Memory From Pushkin to Postsocialism*. Durham, NC and London, England: Duke University Press.

Liegeois, Jean-Pierre and Nicolae Gheorge (1995). *Roman/Gypsies: A European Minority*. London: Minority Rights Group International.

Ogan, Christina (2001) *Communication and Identity in the Diaspora*. Lanham, MD: Lexington Books.

Pogany, Istvan (2004). *The Roma Café: Human Rights and the Plight of the Romani People*. London, England, and Sterling, VA: Pluto Press.

Popovic, Tanja (2003). "The Former Yugoslav Republic of Maceonia." In Ana Karlsreiter, ed., *Media in Multilingual Societies: Freedom and Responsibilities*. Vienna, Austria: OSCE, 21–46.

Project on Ethnic Relations (1992). "The Romanies in Central and Eastern Europe: Illusions and Reality," a conference report, 30 April–2 May, Stupava, Slovakia. Accessed Oct. 10, 2004. www.per-usa.org/rctr_eu.html

Riggins, Stephen Harold (1992), "The Media Imperative: Ethnic Minority Survival in the Age of Mass Communication." In Stephen Harold Riggins, ed., *Ethnic Minority Media. An International Perspective*. Newbery Park, London, New Delhi: Sage.

Rroma Media Networking Project for Central, Eastern and South-Eastern Europe (2003). Accessed July 8, 2004. www.rrommedia.com

Schermerhorn, R.A. (1970). *Comparative Ethnic Relations*. Chicago: University of Chicago Press.

Schopflin, George (1995). "Nationalism and Ethnicity in Europe, East and West." In Charles A. Kupchan, ed., *Nationalism and Nationalities in the New Europe*. Ithaca, NY and London: Cornell University Press, 37–65.

Silverstone, Roger (May 1, 2005). "Editorial introduction: media and minorities in multicultural Europe," in *Journal of Ethnic and Migration Studies*, vol. 31(3): 433–441.

Smith, Anthony D. (1993). *National Identity (Ethnonationalism in Comparative Perspective)*. University of Nevada Press.

Tio, J. Rubio (1986). "Quelques particularites d'Euskal Telebista: Une chaine de television autonome," in *Les moyens d'information en Espagne*. Talence: Presse Universitaire de Bordeaux/Maison des Pays Iberiques.

Vermeersch, Peter (2001), "Advocacy Networks and Romani Politics in Central and Eastern Europe," in *Journal on Ethnopolitics and Minority Issues in Europe*, vol. 2(1) : 1–22.

Zed, Rajan (Sept. 9, 2008). "High-level European Roma Summit at Brussels failed to show concrete results, Hindus assert." Accessed Sept. 26, 2008. www.romea.cz.

Section 2

NATIONAL AND TRANSNATIONAL IDENTITIES

CHAPTER 6

The Media and Nationalism, East and West: A Revision of Existing Debates[1]

Sabina Mihelj

The upsurge of nationalisms and nation-state-building projects across Eastern Europe[2] in the 1990s gave rise to a veritable industry of media monitoring and criticisms of hate speech, as well as numerous insightful case studies. However, apart from a handful of exceptions, the amassed literature available in English[3] has done little in the way of providing theoretically informed comparative analyses, and even less in the way of advancing major theoretical debates on the relationship between nationalism and mass communication. This is partly due to practical obstacles, such as a lack of resources, language barriers, weak research infrastructure, and the relatively recent development of media and communication studies as an autonomous field of scientific inquiry in the region. The other major reason, however, lies in the established theories of nationalism and communication themselves, and in their often indiscriminate application to Eastern European cases.

---

[1] I would like to thank Václav Štětka, Reana Senjković, Veronika Bajt, the editors of this volume, and other members of the COST network *East of West: Setting a New Central and Eastern European Media Research Agenda* for their helpful comments on earlier versions of this chapter. I have also profited from comments provided by the participants of the International Communication Association pre-conference, organized in Budapest in June 2006. All the remaining mistakes are of course mine.
[2] For the purposes of this paper, Eastern Europe is meant to include Albania, Bulgaria, The Czech Republic, Estonia, Hungary, Latvia, Lithuania, Poland, Romania, the Slovak Republic, and all the states formed in the territory of the former Yugoslavia.
[3] Throughout the paper, references to existing research and literature are meant to refer primarily to available literature in English, though some works written in local languages are surveyed as well.

A more cautious approach to nationalism and mass communication in Eastern Europe has much to offer. The specificities of nation-building and cultural diversity in the region, combined with recent experiences of rapid political and economic transformation, should provide a strong incentive for rethinking some of the well-worn theoretical truisms. This chapter aims to make a first tentative step in this direction. It starts by outlining the major drawbacks of classic theories of nationalism and the media, and then turns to an examination of key differences and similarities between nation-building projects and patterns of cultural diversity in Eastern and Western Europe. The final two sections provide a critical revision of existing literature on nationalism and the media in Eastern Europe, and develop recommendations for future research.

Theories of Nationalism and the Media: Major Blanks

Most of the widely quoted works addressing the relationship between the media and nationalism (e.g., Anderson 1983, Gellner 1983, Billig 1995) are drawing primarily on a selection of post-World-War-II experiences in Western Europe and North America, and, to a more limited extent, on post-colonial experiences. Such a selection of cases, particularly when combined with a teleological, West-centric theory of modernization, easily lends itself to the false assumption that by and large, modern national communicative spaces are internally homogenous and their boundaries coincide with state borders. Patterns of mass communication that do not conform to this rule are either overlooked or treated as transitional or aberrant stages of development that should eventually give way to a homogenous national communicative space matching the political unit.

This nation-state-centered approach has haunted media and communication research for almost half a century (Schlesinger 2000). Only after being faced with pervasive phenomena that could not be fitted easily into the nation-state-centered model—such as the rise of satellite and cable television, increased transnational migration and the proliferation of diasporic communication—have media scholars begun to question the classic theoretical framework (e.g., Morley and Robins 1995; Price 2002). Over the past decade, this questioning has led to a denunciation of the nation-state-centered framework, and prompted an exponential growth of research into the media of diaspora, multiculturalism and transnational communication (e.g., Karim 2003; Georgiou 2006). These recent theories acknowledge the mismatch between national communicative spaces and states and are therefore better suited to the analysis of patterns of mass communication and their links with nationhood in Eastern Europe. However, it needs to be noted that these theories normally assume the prior existence of strong nationally minded states and equally strong national communicative spaces coinciding with state borders, and their subsequent decline provoked by globalization. Again, this narrative is not immediately applicable to Eastern Europe, and in fact does not fare too well in several Western European states either.

In Western Europe, departures from ideal-typical national public spheres are most clearly apparent when we take into account long-established multinational and multilingual media systems such as those of Switzerland and Belgium. The Swiss Broadcasting Corporation established its three national stations—French, German and Italian—already in the early 1930s, later adding regular programs in Romansch, with an analogous development taking place in the realm of television from the late 1950s (Erk 2003). Belgian broadcasting history is similarly linguistically diversified, and resulted in separate radio and television services for the three main language communities: Flemish, French and German (Jongen et al. 2005). The narrative premised on a simple progression from the national to the European becomes even more implausible once we turn to the new and aspiring EU members states of Eastern Europe. For all the newly formed nation-states that emerged out of the rumbles of multinational socialist federations, things national were obviously not a matter of the past: instead, the post-Cold-War European integration went hand-in-hand with nation-state building. Furthermore, most of the newly formed states remained ethnically mixed despite recent attempts at national homogenization. Although the recent wave of nation-state building in the region initially included several unambiguous attempts—paraphrasing from Gellner (1983)—to make culture coincide with the state, all states have since abandoned these extreme measures, and have, however begrudgingly, accepted some form of multicultural provisions. This shift is closely related to the fact that this wave of nation-building was faced with parallel processes of institution-building and integration on a supranational, European or global level. Willy-nilly, the prospective EU member states were forced 'to choose between the economic advantages of membership in the EU and legislation designed to protect the language and culture of the majority group' (Johns 2003: 682). Last but not least, the media environment of these recent nation-building efforts has been considerably different from the one accompanying similar historical efforts in Western Europe. Not only has the technological milieu been dramatically different; what is more interesting is that nation-building was happening precisely at a point when the media spaces in the region were subjected to a swift deregulation and re-regulation, transnationalization, commercialization, tabloidization and audience segmentation. The new distribution of powers between the state, the market, and the media is one of the most prominent lines of inquiry in existing scholarship on the media in Eastern Europe (e.g., Splichal 1994; Jakubowicz 2007). Yet curiously, available explorations of the media and nationalism in the region hardly ever consider the implications of this shift for nation-building.

Nations, States and the Media, East and West

Differences between nationalisms in Eastern and Western Europe have long been a topic of scholarly interest and debate. However, these differences have all too often been explained away by referring to the different conceptions of the nation in Eastern and Western Europe. 'Western' nationalism was regarded as predominantly "civic," inclusive, intrinsically peaceful and supportive of democracy, while "eastern" nationalism was seen as predominantly "ethnic," exclusive and inherently more amenable to violence (Kohn 1944; Plamenatz 1973). Yet this is a far too simplistic explanation, and one based on a problematic, value-laden and empirically unsustainable typology of nationalisms. It tends to obscure the violent episodes in the history of Western nations, such as German National Socialism or Italian Fascism (Auer 1995), and the forced assimilation and erasure of sub-national differences (Weber 1976). Also, recent empirical research into popular conceptions of nationality in Eastern and Western Europe showed that the East/West typology does not fit contemporary realities either

(Schulman 2002; Janmaat 2006). Due to that, some authors have suggested to abandon the geographically-bound division of nations altogether and approach civic and ethnic nationalism as ideal types that are to varying extent present in every nation, be it Eastern and Western (Smith 1991). Yet this does not seem to be a solution either (Brubaker 2004), at least as long as we keep assuming that we can distinguish 'elements' of nationhood that are inherently civic and inclusive from those that are indisputably ethnic and exclusive. Language is a case in point, since it was historically used both as an instrument of national assimilation as well as national differentiation and exclusion.

It is obvious, then, that other factors, beyond the conception of nationhood *per se*, need to be taken into account if we are to grasp the different relationships between states, nations and communicative spaces in different parts of Europe. Firstly, and perhaps most obviously, many nation-states in Eastern Europe are fairly recent and, in many cases, rather weak ventures. Even though institutionally supported nation-building long preceded the creation of sovereign nation-states, its resources were poorer than for example in France, Germany or the UK. Even today, the basic infrastructure supporting social integration, e.g. various communication and transport networks, are weaker than in Western Europe, and many states do not exert a firm control over the allocation of frequencies within their borders. Also, these states have been formed in an area criss-crossed by competing interests and expansionist projects of a number of empires, which left the region with a notorious ethnic maze, a range of contested borders and a long-standing tradition of foreign intervention. Some of these particularities of Eastern Europe have led Ernest Gellner (1997) to develop an argument about the different 'time-zones' of Europe, arguing that each of them was characterized by a different timing of the rise of national states and national cultures. East of Italy and Germany, neither national states nor national cultures were readily available when the age of nationalism dawned. Instead, the region was characterized by a complex patchwork of cultural differences, often overlapping with class divisions, which, in his view, was 'a recipe for catastrophe' (ibid.: 54).

Gellner's argument clearly goes further than the simplistic explanations based exclusively on the supposed differences in the conceptions of nationality, and provides important insights into the interaction of nationalist ideas with wider social and political structures.

However, the overall narrative remains overwhelmingly teleological, and premised on a West-centered notion of modernization. This narrative reduces the persistent cultural diversity of modern states, as well as the various historical approaches to cultural diversity that diverge from the nation-state ideal, to mere aberrations that are bound to give way to classic nation-state building. Yet the recent history of European states, and particularly the recent history of states in Eastern Europe, cannot be reduced to a story about the progressive application of the nation-state model. The would-be nation-states established amidst the ruins of the Ottoman, Habsburg and Romanov empires have of course resorted to a variety of strategies that would help them reduce cultural diversity and thereby approximate the ideal of a nation-state by means of forced assimilation, population transfers and ethnic cleansing. Yet several have also, at least for a period, explicitly rejected this ideal, and instead developed alternative approaches to "the national question"— approaches based on the assumption that cultural diversity is an asset to be preserved rather than an obstacle to modernization that should be overcome. This included expressly acknowledging the existence of different nations and/or national minorities within state borders, and implementing legal instruments aimed at securing their cultural reproduction, including instruments affecting the media.[4] Treating all

---

[4] This propensity to reject the model of the homogeneous nation-state was not always driven by strong convictions on the side of Eastern European political elites themselves. With the exception of models of multinationalism developed in socialist and communist states, the main impetus typically came from Western powers, and functioned as a test that Eastern European countries had to pass in order to become members of the European family of states. Ever since the earliest international efforts aimed at safeguarding minority rights in Europe, minority protection obligations had been imposed primarily on the new, newly recognized or newly enlarged states, and in particular on the small and weak states, which were considered to be somewhat backward and illiberal (Inis 1955: 6–7). Given the history of state-formation in Europe, it is of no surprise that these obligations were usually developed by Western European powers, and forced on Eastern European states—without being necessarily upheld in Western Europe itself. This unequal treatment was typically justified by reference to differing levels of civilization and democracy: 'minority legislation has become a yardstick by which to measure Eastern European readiness to rejoin civilisation' (Burgess 1996: 26). The League of Nations' minority rights system, established in the aftermath of World

such cases as aberrations and transitional stages, trying to fit them into an overall narrative of the rise and fall of nation-states—and thereby also national communicative spheres—does not seem to be the right solution.

Obviously, Western Europe is not immune to ethnic diversity. The wave of "peripheral nationalisms" (Keating 1988) that swept through Spain, Britain and France in the 1960s and the 1970s reminded observers that national identity and unity are not as self-evident and uncontested as they expected, and that national integration policies may easily lead to 'nation-destroying' rather than 'nation-building' (Connor 1994 [1972]: 28–66). However, despite the growing awareness of the persistence of ethnic diversity in Western Europe, explicit multiculturalist policies took long to develop. For centuries, Western European powers—which, on the eve of World War II, included Italy and Germany—have seen themselves as democratic and liberal enough to solve ethnic tensions by means of securing individual human rights only, without resorting to collective rights (Preece 1998: 96–98). Until the dramatic reconfiguration of the map of Europe after 1989, minority issues were virtually absent from the mainstream Western European agenda, or were subsumed under the umbrella of universal human rights.

Another thing to note when comparing ethnic diversity and minority protection in Eastern and Western Europe is that until the sudden increase in immigration in the aftermath of de-colonization, ethnic diversity in Western European states was largely containable *within* the borders of the state. For the most part, this diversity amounted to a form of local, regional or proto-national diversity—a remnant or

---

War I, is a particularly clear example of such a balance of powers, obligations and prejudices, requiring minority protection measures to be implemented across Eastern Europe, but exempting Western Europe, including Germany and Italy (Inis 1955: 16–50). In this sense, the current EU minority policies, and particularly the minority requirements which are imposed on prospective new members of the EU, follow a long-established historical pattern: in order to be allowed to enter the European community of states, the prospective members need to accept minority protection measures which are not necessarily in place in the 'old' European states. Or, as Lynn M. Tesser (2003) phrased it: tolerance in Eastern Europe is, yet again, a geopolitical matter, rather than being based on a genuine choice in adopting certain norms and policies.

reactivation of specificities that have not been overcome during nation-building. In the majority of cases, historical Western European minorities—the Catalans in Spain, the Bretons in France, the Welsh and Scottish in the UK etc.—do not stretch across state borders, nor have a putative "motherland" elsewhere. This means that with the exception of countries like Switzerland and Belgium, the coincidence of cultures and state-borders is largely preserved, and that diversity can be described fairly accurately by paying attention exclusively to the interior of each individual media space.

In Eastern Europe, on the other hand, patterns similar to those found in Switzerland or Belgium are the norm rather than an exception. Most historical minorities in the region are not limited to regional/local sub-units of the larger national whole, but instead stretch beyond state borders, and are frequently seen as "belonging" to one of the neighboring states. This creates a particular "triadic nexus" of relations between the "host" state, the putative "motherland" or the kin-state, and the minority (cf. Brubaker 1996: 55–76). This nexus regularly affects also the regulation, funding and institutional organization of mass communication aimed at minority populations (Mihelj 2005). Historically, the triadic nexus has often led to conflict-ridden situations, as the kin-state was trying to intervene into the domestic politics of its neighbor in order to protect the rights of what it saw as "its own" people, or the members of the minority wanted to re-join their kin state. Fears of such foreign interventions and secessionist movements are still very much alive across Eastern Europe, and often surface in the work of media researchers as well, particularly when they address issues of transnational communication (e.g., Kolar-Panov 1997).

The triadic nexus of relations, long known to Eastern European states, has only recently received its approximate counterpart in Western European states. Arguably, the recent immigrant minorities in Western Europe—increasingly dubbed "diasporas" rather than ethnic/national minorities—are, to an important extent, seen in similar terms as the traditional national minorities in Eastern Europe: as extensions of essentially alien national bodies, inherently inclined to be disloyal to their new state. Due to that, recent debates about diasporas and diasporic media in Western European (and more broadly Western) contexts are at least partly relevant to research on minorities and media in Eastern Europe as well.

Beyond the Nation-State-Centered Approach

Existing research on mass communication and nationalism in the region provides little insight into the kind of relationships between states, nations, cultures and the media described in the paragraphs above. Even literature which explicitly deals with cultural diversity—usually in relation to minority media, minority languages and minority access to the media more generally—rarely ventures beyond single-country studies. This automatically results in a neglect of cross-country similarities and thereby also legacies of earlier political arrangements that did not adopt the nation-state model. Researchers of minority media, for example, regularly limit their analysis to minority media aimed at one single minority group in a single state: the Turkish minority media in Bulgaria (Valentovitch 2000), the Russian minority media in Estonia (Jakobson 2002), the Hungarian minority media in Romania (Papp 2005), etc. If a comparative approach is introduced, the focus is likely to be on minority media of one group only, in several states, for example the Romani media across the region (Gross 2006). Comparative analyses looking at both majority and minority media or involving more countries are rare (e.g., Nyíri 2005). A particularly notable exception is David D. Laitin's (1998: 268–299) analysis of the use of different identity terms in Russian-language newspaper articles published in four newly independent states with substantial Russian minorities: Kazakhstan, Estonia, Latvia and Ukraine. Most promising is the situation with existing research into minority media regulation, where considerable advances have been made in comparative research into minority media regulation within the region and beyond (e.g., Klimkiewicz 2003; McGonagle et al. 2003).

A similar pattern can be discerned in the literature examining the media portrayal of various national others. Only rare works examine the portrayal of several national others—ranging from national and religious minorities to "the West"—and/or cover a broader number of countries. Such exceptions include the book on hate speech in the Balkans edited by Mariana Lenkova (1998) and the analysis of daily newspaper reporting on ethnic minorities in a number of Southeast European states (Milivojević 2002). By far the largest is the number of works focussing on media representations of ethnic/national minorities in one country and only exceptionally do authors venture into exploring media stereotypes of groups other than those residing in or in the immediate neighborhood of a particular country. Finally, systematic analyses involving both domestic and foreign media coverage are extremely rare.

Occasionally, the bias of the nation-state-centered framework becomes even more evident, leading researchers to conclude that minority media are inherently dangerous, since they represent a threat to national unity. Such evaluations are often embedded in discussions on the "public sphere" instead of referring to issues of 'culture' and 'identity', yet the basic premises remain more or less the same: minority media are believed to hamper the creation of an all-encompassing national public sphere, and are therefore considered harmful. Jack Snyder's arguments on minority media in Eastern Europe are a case in point: drawing on Todd Gitlin's (1998) arguments on minority media in the USA, he warns that in a deeply divided society, such sphericules may only exacerbate existing fissures. He therefore concludes that "ethnically segmented media markets should be counteracted by the promotion of civic-territorial conceptions of national identity," promoted through an "integrative press" (Snyder 2000: 180).

Dona Kolar-Panov's (1997) work on the media and the multiethnic media sphere in Macedonia follows a similar line of argument. According to her, the activities introduced into the Macedonian media space by the global flow of electronic goods and services allowed minority ethnic audiences to link with what they perceived as their co-nationals world-wide and led to a fragmentation of national audiences along ethnic and life-style lines. She is particularly worried about the effects of commercial ethnic televisions, which, instead of promoting integration into the Macedonian mainstream, see their audiences as "fragments of a neighboring homeland" and encourage them to identify with the neighboring Kosovo, Albania and Serbia instead of Macedonia. A similar set of fears can be discerned in some of the writings on the media in Estonia. Typically, scholars would reflect on the media consumption patterns and conclude that the media consumption of Estonia's Russian-speaking population, which is largely orientated towards Russian TV channels, 'deepens the separation of a large share of the non-Estonians from Estonia's affairs, preventing their integration into Estonian society' (Lauristin and Vihalemm quoted in Vihalemm

T. 1999: 46). As a whole, studies of transnational broadcasting in Eastern Europe therefore share the weaknesses of the literature on satellite television elsewhere in Europe: they evaluate cross-border broadcasting through the prism of national broadcasting, predominantly treating it as a threat to national culture and identity (Chalaby 2005).

However, the consequences of minority media spheres are not necessarily so grim. Both historically and more recently, minority media have often functioned as microcosms of bigger public spheres (Herbst 1995; Cunningham and Sinclair 2001: 28). Although they are expected to be particularizing, this does not doom them from the beginning: "They can involve a rejection of universalism but not necessarily so. In fact the discourse of particularism is far from monolithic. The media that ensure the continued survival of certain groups tend to offer these groups competing visions of their identity. Some are lethal. Some are not." (Dayan 1998: 105) Even in cases when the projections of identity offered by minority media are expressly homogenizing and are trying to establish a clear division between "us," the minority, and "them," the majority, this should not lead us to think that all the members of the minority will necessarily accept such projections as their own. As Asu Aksoy and Kevin Robins (2000) show, Turks in Germany use transnational television from Turkey "to think across cultural spaces" and counter the homogenizing national discourse offered by the program. While the producers may believe that Turkish satellite television keeps Turks in Germany "in touch with their homeland," the viewers were not always eager to accept the claim that Turkey is their true "homeland," and instead situated themselves in relation to, as well as at a distance from, two cultural spaces: the German and the Turkish one.

Furthermore, minority media can often provide a safe space inside which a marginalized minority can search for ways to improve its present situation. This is certainly frequently the case in Eastern Europe, since—as Peter Gross (2006: 490–491) pointed out in response to Jack Snyder's call for a more "integrative press" in post-communist Europe—the media in the region may simply not (yet?) be integrative enough to be able to co-opt minority media. For example, in the case of Macedonia, the very same media consumption patterns painted in such gloomy colours by Kolar-Panov can be interpreted much more optimistically if looked at primarily from the point of view of minority protection rather than country-wide integration. Zoltan Barany's

(2005: 83–89) analysis of ethnic mobilization of Albanians in Macedonia is a case in point. According to him, television broadcasts and newspapers originating in Albania and Kosovo and Albanian-language media within Macedonia have been among the crucial mobilizational prerequisites, and have thus contributed to an improved standard of minority protection in the country. This does not speak against the need for a public sphere cutting across ethnic divisions, yet it does show that minority media are not necessarily an obstacle for the creation of such an integrative public sphere. Quite to the contrary, it demonstrates that minority media are, at least in certain circumstances, themselves contributing to the formation of a more integrative public sphere. While it is true that existing divisions may be deepened and exacerbated if minority media function as self-enclosed ghettos, the very same divisions may also prevent the mainstream media from functioning as truly open, public and integrative forums.

How should we then approach nationalism and mass communication if we are to avoid the bias of the nation-state-centered framework? One solution is offered by those analyses of diasporic communication that focus on the ways in which diasporic audiences challenge the nation-state-centered framework and defy dominant discourses of national identity and belonging (e.g., Aksoy and Robins 2000). Within the realm of Eastern Europe, a closely similar approach, sensitive to the hybrid forms of identity construction, was employed by Maruša Pušnik (2008) in her ethnography-based study into media use and identity-formation among the Slovenian minority in Carinthia which is also among the very few existing studies of nationalism and the media in Eastern Europe that explicitly venture beyond the analysis of media texts and media regulation.

However, this solution can fit only research interested primarily in how the nation-state-centered framework is rejected within the context of reception and everyday life. Yet as both the rise of pan-European satellite channels as well as the history of mass communication in Eastern Europe attest, the nation-state model can be rejected also at the level of media production: media regulation is not necessarily governed by the ideal of conformity between signal transmissions and national borders. As Monroe Price notes, analysis needs to look beyond the state's efforts to protect its own information space and include also efforts by a state to influence the media space or infrastructure outside its own borders, as well as efforts of other large-scale competitors for power who use the regulation of communications "to organize a cartel of imagery and identity among themselves" (2002: 31). In order appropriately to account for various forms of media regulation in expressly multicultural states and multinational federations, however, this model should be diversified further by paying more attention to various competitors for power and markets of loyalties established *below* the level of the state, within particular federal units, regions or legally recognized minorities.

Another fruitful venue is explored by Jean K. Chalaby who argues that transnational broadcasting should not be approached as a deviation from the norm of national broadcasting, but rather examined in its own right. Following this argument, she develops a four-fold typology of cross-border television in Europe, pointing out that each of the types "entertain different relationships with the nation-state, geographical space and culture" (2005: 154). The downside of the approach is that it gives the impression that the principles and solutions adopted by cross-border satellite television have no precedence in history, and that the period before the advent of satellite broadcasting can be appropriately described by using a nation-state-centered framework. At least as far as Eastern Europe is concerned, this assumption is false and it is safe to assume that some approaches to transnational broadcasting discussed by Chalaby—most notably perhaps the "multi-territory channels"—approximate solutions developed in the broadcasting systems established in multinational federations such as the socialist Yugoslavia, Czechoslovakia or the Soviet Union.

Last but not least, moving beyond a nation-state-centered approach should also entail acknowledging the media involvement in the reproduction of supra-national collective attachments and stereotypes in the region. These are not related only to the European Union, but span a much broader horizon and include regional forms of belonging that feed on imperial and socialist legacies. The notions of Central Europe, the Balkan, East and West and Yugoslav brotherhood are all tightly intertwined with individual nation-building projects in the region, and often provide the reference point for newer forms of supranational identification, attached to the EU. Existing literature on the media and nationalism, however, still relatively rarely draws attention to such issues (for exceptions see e.g., Mihelj 2004; Volčič 2007), thereby again conforming to the nation-state-centered perspective.

Towards a Broader Notion of Nationalism

Besides being locked in a nation-state-centered approach, literature on nationalism and mass communication has long remained overwhelmingly centered on the early periods of nation-formation, and on the macro-processes and structural issues fostering the *early* rise and proliferation of national movements and nation-states. Much ink has been spilled identifying the exact balance of continuity and discontinuity between modern nations and pre-modern collectivities (e.g., Smith 1986), and discussing the structural aspects of mass communication that allowed the formation of collective bonds on a large scale (e.g., Anderson 1983; Gellner 1983). In contrast, we know, comparatively speaking, much less about the ebbs and flows of nations and nationalisms *after* their initial rise, and about the micro-politics of nationalist mobilization and de-mobilization in established nations and nation-states. Michael Billig's (1995) study of banal nationalism made a crucial step forward by providing an account of how national attachments are being sustained and reproduced in established states of the West, via a wide array of hardly noticeable routines and categories that permeate the fabric of everyday life, including everyday public communication. Several studies followed, diversifying and complicating Billig's theory by pointing to the multiple layers of sub- and trans-national belonging that are anchored in everyday routines and categories alongside national ones (e.g., Rosie et al. 2004). Others have shown how such mindless nation-maintaining routines and habits enter everyday lives of citizens through a range of communication-related institutions and everyday practices not explored by Billig, for example national currencies, public phones, advertising, and consumption (Foster 2002), as well as the various media of timekeeping such as wristwatches, clocks and calendars (Postill 2006).

The range of literature examining media involvement in everyday, hardly noticeable practices of national identity construction forms a relatively minor part of existing literature on nationalism and the media, yet is growing rapidly and is certainly worth being noted. For example, an increasing amount of works pays attention to the use of deixis (Jakobson 2002), to the gendered nation-making through media coverage of sports events (von der Lippe 2002), and to the construction of national normality through entertainment genres (Luthar

1993). Among rare works that explicitly and predominantly focus on the mediated reproduction of everyday, banal nationalism is Václav Štětka's (2005) study of Czech television news bulletins, which shows how the least visible aspects of news—the amount, length, hierarchy and thematic structure of national and foreign news stories—contribute to the demarcation of the Czech "homeland."

The large majority of existing research, however, remains limited exclusively to most overtly xenophobic and violent forms of nationalism, thereby unwittingly reproducing the stereotype that equates nationalism, and Eastern European nationalism in particular, with heightened emotions and violence. The dominance of the narrow understanding of nationalism in existing studies of media in nationalism in Eastern Europe is most clearly reflected in the choice of research topics. One of the largest bodies of literature addressing the relationships between the media and nationalism in the region focuses on the involvement of the mass media in the gradual formation and escalation of violent conflicts in the region. Predictably, the role of domestic media in the gradual formation and escalation of inter-ethnic conflicts in the former Yugoslavia was most extensively studied. The war-time involvement of domestic media in igniting nationalism in Serbia, Croatia and Bosnia and Herzegovina attracted most attention (e.g., Thompson 1999; Skopljanac Brunner et al. 2000; Žarkov 2007; Kolstø 2009). While most studies have focussed on traditional forms of mass communication, ranging from the press to television, some have also addressed the role of Internet communication (e.g., Bieber 2000). Another recurring topic was the relationship between the media and nationalism in Serbia before the outbreak of violent conflicts, and the gradual formation of nationalist stereotypes (e.g., media-related essays in Popov 2000 [1996]; Slapšak et al. 1997). A substantial number of works also provide an insight into the foreign media's reactions to the Yugoslav wars (e.g., Gow et al. 1996; Kuusisto 1999; Sremac 1999). Finally, the controversial NATO intervention in 1999 has provoked a veritable outpouring of publications, mostly focusing on the foreign media responses to the conflict (e.g., Goff 1999; Hammond and Herman 2000; Ignatieff 2001).

Even when examining the relationship between mass communication and nationalism in peaceful contexts, the vast majority of existing research deals primarily with instances of hate speech and stereotypes of various national others. An important corrective is provided by the handful of articles that focus on the mediated reproduction of national selves rather than the explicitly xenophobic portrayal of national others. These include analyses of web-sites (Senjković and Dukić 2005) and examinations of media reporting on issues such as international sports competitions (e.g., Ilycheva 2005; Barrer 2007), beliefs in historical primacy (Weaver 2005), and integration into international organizations such as the EU (Golubeva 2005) and NATO (Heller and Rényi 2003). These studies draw attention precisely to those instances of "our" nationalism that tend to be seen as unproblematic, benign or even beneficial. Although most of these studies continue to focus on various instances of "hot" nationalism, many of them also discuss less prominent forms of national attachment, and thus help establish a better sense of the multiple ways in which nationalism enters everyday lives of Eastern European citizens.

The adoption of a broader understanding of nationalism has much to offer. For a start, it precludes simplistic explanations that seek the roots of violence in a particular nationalist ideology as such, or assume that Eastern European nationalisms are inherently inclined to violence. Instead, it would encourage raising questions such as: How and under what circumstances is banal nationalism turned into a "hot," violent one, and how do the media contribute to this process? How and under what circumstances is a media war likely to escalate and turn into a real war? How and under which circumstances and with which consequences do wars become perceived as "ethnic" wars? Do these circumstances vary between countries which have different traditions of nation-building, different journalistic culture, different institutional media arrangements? While we have seen some attempts to provide speculative answers to these questions over the past decades, more empirically grounded responses, drawing on a range of case studies involving varying levels of inter-ethnic hatred and violence, started emerging only very recently (Kolstø 2009).

Another field of research that could profit from adopting a broader notion of nationalism is the research on media regulation. This is one of the most developed subfields of research into Eastern European media, and already provides some valuable insights into the relationship between mass communication and nationalism in the region. However, those remain limited largely to explorations of media regulation in relation to minority provisions, minority media and use of minority languages. By contrast, analyses focusing on the broader range of legal provisions that either knowingly or unwittingly foster the mediated construction of national selves are extremely scarce. When discussing the reform of state television in Bulgaria, the Czech Republic, Hungary, Poland and Romania, Alina Mungiu-Pippidi (2003: 50) notes that "all of the broadcasting laws have some general provisions regarding cultural and national identity, as well as programmes destined for national minorities," and mentions examples such as setting quotas for nationally produced programs, supporting particular (supposedly national) values, or banning "country and national defamation." Similar issues have been raised by a number of other works focusing on single countries (Goban-Klas 1997; Milton 1997: 20), yet systematic analyses are virtually absent. The influence of international legislation is rarely considered in this context, and systematic comparisons with Western Europe and other countries are lacking, except when specifically supported by European or other international institutions (e.g., McGonagle et al. 2003). Moreover, little if anything is known about how the particular aspects of media legislation are implemented in practice and what consequences they have for media production and content. The rare cases in which such issues are raised are cases when the non-compliance with legislation becomes an issue of public concern, either nationally or internationally. Typically this happens either when non-governmental organizations are concerned about the non-compliance with legal requirements regarding hate speech or when national governments and politicians feel the national sovereignty and identity are under threat because the quotas for foreign TV programs broadcast on domestic channels have been exceeded. Examples of research prompted by breaches of hate-speech regulation can be found across the region, and particularly often in South-eastern Europe (e.g., Lenkova 1998). Studies arising (partly) in response to breaches of quotas for foreign TV programs can be found in a number works analyzing the Latvian media scene, where several stations catering to the Russian-speaking minority have exceeded the total permitted air-time for programs in non-Latvian languages (e.g., Kruks 2001, McGonagle et al. 2003: 288–294).

And lastly—though this does not exhaust the list of possible research venues—an approach employing a broader notion of nationalism and paying particular attention to its most mundane manifestations could also help us understand the relationship between nationalism, mass communication, and the recent shift from socialist to capitalist economies in the region. It should be quite obvious that media-wise, the post-socialist nation-(re)building in Eastern Europe was not as tightly state-managed as it was traditionally the case in Western Europe. This should have had consequences for the nation-building projects in the region. While the newly formed or newly privatized media may have—and in many cases did—willingly and even enthusiastically fostered the state-led nation-building agenda, many have chose to follow very different, less overtly nationalist strategies of audience-maximization. Even when the media has exploited the nationalist discourse, their agenda may have been very different from the one initially suggested by the political or cultural elites. It is probably sound to start with the assumption that the shift from the state to the market had similar consequences as in Western Europe: it did not lead to a demise of the national, but rather to its metamorphosis. By using the nation as the market, a new kind of relationship was established between the state, the media and the nation (Bourdon 2003: 84–86). Or, to put it differently: commercialization has facilitated the rise of an imagined national community of *consumers*, and let to a marginalization of alternative conceptions of the nation, such as the nation of *citizens* and the nation of *workers*. How exactly this happened in Eastern Europe and what was the role of the various media genres—including not only the news media, but also the popular media genres, tabloids and advertisements—has yet to be established. Among rare studies that addresses some of these issues are Wielslaw Godzic's (2003) study of Polish advertisements and the tensions between the constructions of the viewer/listener as a member of the Polish nation on the one hand and as a consumer on the other hand, and Zala Volčič's (2007) critical examination of links between capitalism and the nostalgia-driven idealisation of socialist Yugoslavia in the post-Yugoslav realm.

Conclusions

Given the peculiarities of its nation-building, as well as its experience with socialism and transition to democracy and economic liberalism, Eastern Europe provides an excellent starting point for any research that aims to move beyond the truisms of classic theories of nationalism

and mass communication. This chapter suggested two broad conceptual and analytical solutions that could prove helpful when developing
such research. The first one is based on a rejection of the nation-state-
centric bias inherent in most of the classic writings on nationalism and
mass communication, but also warns against an uncritical application
of the more recent theories of transnational communication. Instead,
analysis should start by acknowledging a) the involvement of the media
in the reproduction of supra-national collective attachments, not only
those stimulated by EU integration and the rise of satellite broadcasting, but also those drawing on imperial and socialist legacies and earlier
forms of transnational communication in the region, and b) the existence of several overlapping communicative spaces as well as forms of
media regulation that do not conform to the ideal of a national communicative space coinciding with state borders, but instead operate either
below and above the level of a particular state, and entertain different
relationships between states, borders, nations and other collectivities.
The second solution suggested in the chapter entails the adoption of
a broader understanding of nationalism, which includes not only the
most easily discernable, hate-driven or violent forms of nationalism, but
also the more invisible, banal, supposedly benign or "peaceful" forms.
The adoption of such a broader notion of nationalism would preclude
simplistic explanations that seek the roots of violence in a particular nationalist ideology as such, or assume that Eastern European nationalisms are inherently inclined to violence. It could, among other things,
also provide a good starting point for an analysis that seeks to understand the links between nationalism, mass communication, and the recent shift from socialist to capitalist economies in the region.

Comparative research incorporating cases from both Eastern and
Western Europe could allow for a better understanding of how and to
what extent the relationships between the media and nationalism vary
in countries which have different trajectories of nation-state building,
different configurations of national identity, and different historical experiences with ethnic conflicts. Recent conflicts in the region could provide excellent grounds for comparative studies of the role of the mass
media in nationalist mobilization, focusing for example on the precon-
ditions which make the mass media particularly amenable to spreading nationalist prejudices, or social and political contexts which make
the audience more or less resistant to mass mediated propagandistic

messages. The contribution of the mass media to the nation-building efforts of new states in the region is an equally interesting venue for inquiry, especially since these efforts have been conducted in a heavily mediatized context, and were faced with parallel processes of institution-building and integration on a supra-national, European level. Last but not least, a comparative endeavour including cases from both Eastern and Western Europe could help us better understand the relationships between nationalism, the media and European integration. Nationalist media coverage of European affairs can and indeed often does function as an obstacle to European integration. However, numerous cases from the peripheral members of the European Union also suggest that when "Europeanization" becomes a national project—as it was the case across Eastern Europe in the early 1990s—nationalism can have the opposite effect. Whether such an alliance between peripheral nationalisms and Europeanization can last, and what are its consequences for European democracy, is of course a separate issue, and one that will have to be addressed at a different place and time.

REFERENCES

Aksoy, Asu and Kevin Robins (2000) "Thinking Across Spaces: Transnational Television from Turkey." European Journal of Cultural Studies 3, no. 3: 343–365.

Anderson, Benedict (1983) Imagined Communities: Reflections on the Origins and Spread of Nationalism. London and New York: Verso.

Auer, Stefan (1997) "Two Types of Nationalism in Europe?" Russian and Euro-Asian Bulletin 7, issue 12.

Barany, Zoltan (2005) "Ethnic Mobilization in the Postcommunist Context: Albanians in Macedonia and the East European Roma." In Ethnic Politics after Communism. Bárány, Zoltán and Robert G. Moser, eds. Ithaca and London: Cornell University Press, 78–107.

Barrer, Peter (2007) "'Šatan is God!' Re-imagining contemporary Slovak National Identity through Sport." Sport in Society 10, issue 2: 223–238.

Bieber, Florian (2000) "Cyberwar or Sideshow? The Internet and the Balkan Wars." Current History 99, no. 635: 124–128.

Billig, Michael (1995) Banal Nationalism. London, Thousand Oaks and New Delhi: Sage Publications.

Bourdon, Jérôme (2003) "La télévision est-elle un média global? Une perspective historique" (Is television a global medium ? A historical perspective) in Télévision, mémoire et identités nationales. Paris: L'Harmattan, pp. 59–91.

Brubaker, Rogers (1996) Nationalism Reframed, Cambridge: Cambridge University Press.

Burgess, Adam (1996) "National Minority Rights and the 'Civilizing of Eastern Europe'." Contention 5, issue 2: 17–36.

Chalaby, Jean K. (2000) "Deconstructing the Transnational: A Typology of Cross-Border television Channels in Europe." New Media and Society 7, issue 2: 155–175.

Connor, Walker (1972) "Nation-Building or Nation-Destroying." World Politics 24: 319-355.

Cunningham, Stuart and John Sinclair (2001) "Diasporic Media and Public Sphericules" in: Black Marks: Minority Ethnic Audiences and the Media. Ross, Karen and Peter Playdon, eds. Aldershot: Ashgate, pp. 177–193.

Dayan, Daniel (1998) "Particularistic Media and Diasporic Communications", in Media, Ritual and Identity. Liebes, Tamar and James Curran, eds. London and New York: Routledge, p. 103–113.

Erk, Jan (2003) "Swiss Federalism and Congruence." Nationalism and Ethnic Politics 9(2): 50-74.

Foster, Robert J. (2002) Materializing the Nation: Commodities, Consumption, and Media in Papua New Guinea. Bloomington, I.N.: Indiana University Press.

Gellner, Ernest (1983) Nations and Nationalism. Oxford: Basil Blackwell.

Gellner, Ernest (1997) Nationalism. London: Weidenfeld and Nicolson.

Georgiou, Myria (2006) Diaspora, Identity and the Media: Diasporic Transnationalism and Mediated Spatialities, Cresskill, N.J.: Hampton Press.

Gitlin, Todd (1998) "Public Sphere or Public Sphericules?" in Media, Ritual and Identity. Liebes, Tamar and James Curran, eds. London: Routledge, pp. 168–174.

Goban-Klas, Tomasz (1997) "Politics versus the Media in Poland: A Game without Rules" in Post-communism and the Media in Eastern Europe. O'Neill, Patrick, ed. London: Frank Cass, pp. 24–41.

Godzic, Wielslaw (2003) "Advertising Poland: Constructing Identity through Advertisements" in Mapping the Margins: Identity Politics and the Media. Ross, Karen and Deniz Derman, eds. Cresskill, N.J.: Hampton Press, pp. 39–50.

Goff, Peter (1999) The Kosovo News and Propaganda War. Vienna: International Press Institute.

Golubeva, Maria (2005) "EU Accession Debate on the Internet in the Baltic States: 'Own Heterogeneous Messages'?" in The Baltic Media World. Bærug, Richard, ed. Riga.

Gow, James, Richard Paterson and Alison Preston, eds. (1996) Bosnia by Television. London: British Film Institute Publishing.

Gross, Peter (2006) "A Prolegomena to the Study of the Romani Media in Eastern Europe." European Journal of Communication. vol. 21, no. 4: 477–497

Hammond, Philip and Edward S. Herman, eds. (2000) Degraded Capability: The Media and the Kosovo Crisis. London: Pluto.

Heller, Mária and Ágnes Rényi (2003) "Joining NATO: The Analysis of a TV-Debate on Hungary's Alliance with NATO" in NATO, Neutrality and National Identity: The Case of Austria and Hungary. Kovács, András and Ruth Wodak, eds. Cologne: Böhlau Verlag, 305–340.

Herbst, Susan (1995) Politics at the Margin: Historical Studies of Public Expression outside the Mainstream. Cambridge: Cambridge University Press.

Ignatieff, Michael (2001) Virtual War: Kosovo and Beyond. London: Chatto & Windus.

Ilycheva, Maria (2005) "'Faithful until death': Sports Fans and Nationalist Discourse in Bulgarian Internet Forums." Polish Sociological Review 3, issue 151: 251–270.

Inis, Claude (1969 [1955]) National Minorities: An International Problem. Westport, Conn.: Greenwood Press.

Jakobson, Valeria (2002) Role of the Estonian Russian-language Media in the Integration of the Russian-speaking Minority into Estonian Society (Academic Dissertation). Tampere: University of Tampere. Retrieved from http://acta.uta.fi/pdf/951-44-5313-1.pdf, accessed on April 15, 2006.

Jakubowicz, Karol (2007) Rude Awakening: Social and Media Change in Central and Eastern Europe. Creskill, N.J.: Hampton Press.

Johns, Michael (2003) "A Fair Price of Admission? Minority Policies and in and out of the EU." Paper presented at the European Union Studies AssociationBi-Annual Conference, Nashville, T.N., March 2003. Retrieved from http://aei.pitt.edu/6507/, accessed April 15, 2005.

Jongen, François, Dirk Voorhoof and Ann Braeckman (2005) "Media System of Belgium." Project Report for the Study on Co-regulation Measures in the Media Sector, retrieved from http://www.hans-bredow-institut.de/forschung/recht/co-reg/reports/1/Belgium.pdf, 27/05/2007.

Karim, Karim H., ed. (2003) The Media of Disapora. London and New York: Routledge.

Klimkiewicz, Beata (2003) "Giving a Voice: Media Policy for Ethnic and National Minorities in Poland, the Czech Republic and Slovakia" in Reinventing Media: Media Policy Reform in East Central Europe. Sükösd, Miklós and Péter Bajomi-Lázár, eds. Budapest–New York: CEU Press, pp. 155–184.

Kohn, Hans (1944) The Idea of Nationalism: A Study of Its Origins and Background. New York: Macmillan.

Kolar-Panov, Dona (1997) "Crowded Airwaves: Ethnic, National and Transnational Identitties in Macedonian Television." In Programming for People: From Cultural Rights to Cultural Responsibilities. Robins, Kevin, ed. Rome: Radiotelevisione Italiana in association with the European Broadcasting Union, pp. 76–87.

Kolstø, Pål, ed. (2009) Discourse and the Yugoslav Conflicts: Representations of Self and Other. Aldershot: Ashgate.

Kruks, Sergej (2001) "Russian-Language Media: A Foreign Observer?" in Latvijas mediju analīze, Daudzveidība III. Riga: Latvijas universitāte, Sociālo zinātņu fakultātes.

Kuusisto, Riikka (1999). Western Definitions of War in the Gulf and in Bosnia: The Rhetoric Frameworks of the United States, British and French Leaders in Action, Helsinki: Finnish society of Sciences and Letters.

Laitin, David D. (1998) Identity in Formation: The Russian-Speaking Populations in the Near Abroad, London: Cornell University Press.

Lenkova, Mariana, ed. (1998) "Hate Speech" in the Balkans. Athens: ETEPE.

Luthar, Breda (1993) "Identity Management and Popular representational Forms." In National Identity and Europe: Television Revolution. Drummond, Philip, ed. London: British Film Institute, pp. 43–50.

McGonagle, Tarlach, Bethany Davis Noll and Monroe Price, eds. (2003) Minority Language Related Broadcasting and Legislation in the OSCE. OSCE High Commissioner on National Minorities, 2003. Retrieved from http://www.osce.org/hcnm/item_11_13547.html, accessed on April 01, 2006.

Mihelj, Sabina (2004) "Negotiating European Identity at the Periphery: Media Coverage of Bosnian Refugees and 'Illegal Migration'." In Media Cultures in a Changing Europe. Bondebjerg, Ib and Peter Golding, eds Bristol: Intellect Books, pp. 165–189.

Mihelj, Sabrina (2005) "The Mass Media and Nationalizing States in the Post-Yugoslav Space." In Nation-States and Xenophobias: In the Ruins of Ex-Yugoslavia. Pajnik, Mojca and Tonči Kuzmanić, eds. Ljubljana: Peace Institute, pp. 75–98.

Milivojević, Snježana (2002) Slike u ogledalu: Etničke manjine u stampi Jugoistočne Evrope (Mirror images: ethnic minorities in the print media of Southeast Europe). London: Media Diversity Institute.

Milton, Andrew K. (1997) "News Media Reform in Eastern Europe: A Cross-National Comparison." In Post-communism and the Media in Eastern Europe. O'Neill, Patrick, ed. London: Frank Cass.

Morley, David and Kevin Robins (1995) Spaces of Identity: Global Media, Electronic Landscapes and Cultural Boundaries. London: Routledge.

Mungiu-Pippidi, Alina (2003) "From State to Public Service: The Failed Reform of State Television in Central Eastern Europe." In Reinventing Media: Media Policy Reform in East Central Europe. Sükösd, Miklós and Péter Bajomi-Lázár, eds. Budapest–New York: CEU Press, pp. 31–62.

Nyíri, Pál (2005) "Global Modernisers or Local Subalterns: Parallel Perceptions of Chinese Transnationals in Hungary." Journal of Ethnic and Migration Studies 31, issue 4: 659–674.

Papp, Attila Z. (2005) "The Hungarian Press System in Romania during the Nineties – the World of the Operators." Regio – Minorities, Politics, Society 1.

Plamenatz, John (1976) "The Two Types of Nationalism." In Nationalism: The Nature and Evolution of an Idea. Kamenka, Eugene, ed. New York: St. Martin's Press, pp. 22 37.

Popov, Nebojša, ed. (2000 [1996]) Road to War in Serbia: Trauma and Catharsis, translated by Drinka Gojković (Budapest–New York: Central European University Press.

Postill, John (2006) Media and Nation Building: How the Iban Became Malaysian. Oxford: Berghahn.

Price, Monroe E. (2002) Media and Sovereignty: The Global Information Revolution and its Challenge to the State Power. Cambridge, Mass.: MIT Press.

Pušnik, Maruša (2008) "Common history, divided memories : Slovenian and Austrian struggle for the Carinthian past." Anthropological Notebooks 14(1): 49–61.

Rosie, Michael, Pille Petersoo, John MacInnes, Susan Condor and James Kennedy (2004) "Nation Speaking unto Nation: Newspapers and National Identity in the Devolved UK." The Sociological Review 52, issue 4: 437–58.

Schlesinger, Philip (1991) Media, State and Nation. London and New York: Sage Publications.

Schlesinger, Philip (2000) "Nation and communicative space." In Media Power, Professionals and Policy, Tumber, Howard, ed. London and New York: Routledge.

Senjković Reana and Davor Dukić (2005) "Virtual Homeland? Reading the Music on Offer on a Particular Web Page." International Journal of Cultural Studies 8, issue 1: 44-62.

Skopljanac Brunner, Nena, Stjepan Gredelj, Alija Hodžić and Branimir Krištofić eds. (2000) Media and War. Zagreb: Centre for Transition and Civil Society Research; Belgrade: Agency Argument.

Slapšak, Svetlana, Milan Milošević, Radivoj Cvetićanin, Srećko Mihailović, Velimir Ćurgus Kazimir and Stjepan Gredelj, eds. (1997) The War Started at Maksimir. Hate Speech in the Media (Content Analysis of Politika and Borba Newspapers, 1987–1990). Belgrade: Media Center.

Smith, Anthony D. (1991) National Identity. London: Penguin Books.

Splichal, Slavko. Media Beyond Socialism: Theory and Practice in East-Central Europe. Boudler, Colorado: Westview Press, 1994.

Sremac, Danielle S. (1999) War of Words: Washington Tackles the Yugoslav Conflict. Westport, C.T.: Praeger.

Štětka, Václav (2005) Evolution and Transformations of the Nation-Integrative Function of the Mass Media within the Context of Globalisation, Dissertation Thesis. Brno: School of Social Sciences, Masaryk University.

Tesser, Lynn M (2003) "The Geopolitics of Tolerance: Minority Rights under EU Expansion in East-Central Europe." East European Politics and Societies 17, issue 3: 483–532.

Thompson, Mark (1999) Forging War: The Media in Serbia, Croatia and Bosnia-Hercegovina, 2nd expanded edition. Article 19, International Centre against Censorship.

Valentovitch, Igor (2000) Impediments to the Development of Turkish ethnic Minority Media in Bulgaria. Institute for Regional and International Studies, 2000. Retrieved from http://www.iris-bg.org/publications/valentovitch.pdf, accessed April 30, 2006.

Vihalemm, Triin (1999) "Local and Global Orientations of Media Consumption in Estonia, 1993–1998." In Estonian Human Development Report 1999. Oxford University Press. Retrieved from http://www.esis.ee/ist2000/background/other/EstoniaEIA1999.pdf, accessed on April 18, 2006.

Volčič, Zala (2007) "Yugo-Nostalgia: Cultural Memory and the Media in the Former Yugoslavia." Critical Studies in Media Communication 24, issue 1: 21–38.

Žarkov, Dubravka (2007) The Body of War: Media, Ethnicity, and Gender in the Break-Up of Yugoslavia. Durham: Duke University Press.

CHAPTER 7

The Politics of Belonging:
Identity Anxiety in the European Union

FARREL CORCORAN

Questions of identity and its relationship with location, space, time and memory, are crucially important in today's fragmented world of ethnic conflict, guest-worker migration and the widespread displacement of large numbers of people who become refugees, all needing cultural space (as well as, of course, physical and economic space) for forms of ethnic or religious identity previously only gazed upon by host populations in their anthropology museums. In many parts of the world, traditional forms of belonging are in retreat in the face of increasingly rapid rates of social change associated with modernity and with what Hallin and Mancini (2004) refer to as "secularization," that is, the separation of citizens from attachments to religious and ideological "faiths" and the decline of institutions that once structured broad swaths of social life. Global economic and cultural processes erode the significance of local structures that once had the potential to determine the socialization and behaviour of whole populations and the solid and stable identities they could once support: neighborhood communities, churches, trade unions, the nuclear family, the nation state. Where now do people get a secure sense of who they are, their place in society and the times in which they live? Identities are constructed, not in nature, but in specific cultural contexts, where sameness and otherness, belonging and difference are produced and reproduced, and where the markings of us/them are first structured, then policed.

This chapter will reflect on the juxtaposition of national identity with forms of identity that may be taking shape at the European level. There is at present little academic consensus on how to conceptualize the slowly emerging sense of belonging to be found at this complex and difficult border area, situated between national and supranational polities, despite persistent scholarly raiding of a range of disciplines—

history, cultural studies, international relations, political science, sociology, social psychology, media studies, anthropology - for theoretical insights into what kinds of cultural identity might possibly be evolving among citizens of the expanding European Union (EU). The situation is not helped by the interest among some political elites in laying on what Smith calls a "memoryless, artificial culture" (65–66), based on top-down initiatives similar to those typical of some versions of nation building. Seen by some commentators as artificial and contrived, the rhetoric of European identity-construction parallels steps taken in nation states in earlier periods in history to harness the power of the media, shape educational policies, standardize language, and where necessary, use political power to strengthen national consciousness. This can be done by controlling cultural memory to appropriate the past for political purposes, using state funerals, anniversaries of battles, monarchy-related rituals and so on (Corcoran, 2002).

In many ways, the debate about European unity and collective identity is derived from theoretical approaches used in the literature about national consciousness and state formation, so we begin here, in exploring what is meant by identity in ethnic and national contexts. We then examine ways in which this approach has been applied to the question of European identity and the degree to which it may or may not be a good fit. Finally, we explore recent thinking, influenced by postmodern ideas about the demise of nationalism and the urge to find new forms of post-national identity within a global culture of consumer capitalism and the increasing sense of cosmopolitan consciousness associated with it.

National and Religious Identity

The core of the anthropological question of identity is the human propensity of individuals to want to bond with groups of fellow human beings, rather than, like some animal species, to live a lonesome, isolated existence. A peculiar problem arises once the size of the group expands beyond the direct face-to-face capacity of an organic tribal or small, closed village unit, once the transition from "Gemeinschaft" to "Gesellschaft" (Tönnies, 1957) has to be made. Reliance on a dense network of personal relationships based on kinship, robust family ties, strong cultural memory and fixed social roles, is replaced by more formalized and impersonal social relationships, bound together by relatively weak social institutions disconnected from tradition, where individuals depend far less on each other and are much less morally obligated to one another. The members of a unit the size of a nation, even a small one, will never personally know most of their fellow-members, yet they carry around in their daily lives a mental image, however rudimentary, of the larger community to which they belong.

Different types of communities can be distinguished by the way in which they are imagined by their members. As many writers on nationalism have noted, the nation is normally experienced by its members as a deep, horizontal relationship, despite the levels of socio-economic inequality, or gender divisions, or regional tensions, which may actually exist within it. It is not at all uncommon to find that the image of the nation is experienced so coherently and so powerfully by many of its citizens that they are willing to die for it.

Willingness to make the ultimate sacrifice for an imagined community of people one will never personally encounter is not, of course, confined to nations. Since the September 2001 attacks on the US and the initiation of the "war on terror," we have become more aware of the numbers of young people born, and acculturated, in Western Europe, of Pakistani or Moroccan or Palestinian lineage, for instance, who join Islamist organizations. Group bonding activities, initiation rites and visits to the Middle East or Central Asia, encourage new feelings of Muslim patriotism that supersede the feelings of national identity they might be expected to harbour as members of a European nation-state. This new a sense of brotherhood can be so deeply felt that it may lead to the suicide rituals of shaving off all body hair, video recording a personal will and taking the final steps towards martyrdom as a human bomb carrier.

How this new transcontinental, politico-religious consciousness is produced today is poorly understood. However, part of the process may involve a modern version of the ancient form of the pilgrimage, which, as Benedict Anderson has noted (1983: 54), in some sense determines the "outer limits" of the old religious communities of the imagination that are held together by sacred languages—Latin, Arabic, Hindi—through which the great global communities of the past were imagined. Going on pilgrimage, making a long journey between times and places, was always a deeply meaning-creating experience. The significance of the pilgrimage, as a unifying ceremonial passage from one life stage to another, was interpreted to vast numbers of vernacular speakers by the small cohort of bilingual, literate clerics. These could decipher the sacred meaning of the rite of belonging at the center of the pilgrimage. This was an otherwise inexplicable journey of disparate travellers, total strangers to each other, moving in to a religious center from remote and otherwise unrelated localities, meeting around the same monastic refectory table in Rome, or walking clockwise around the Kaaba in Mecca, or dipping in the waters of the Ganges, utterly unable to speak each others' language, but profoundly aware that they have all reached the center of a sacred geography.

Before addressing the Euro-skeptic's rhetorical question "who is going to die for Europe?" it is worth noting that millions have died for various nations (some of them, like pre-Independence Irish soldiers in the British Army in World War I, dying in Flanders for "the rights of small nations," a goal lampooned by their more revolutionary compatriots at-home, plotting rebellion against the same British Army), thinking of themselves to the end as living lives parallel to the lives of groups of other people ("these, but not those") whom they will never meet face-to-face.

This sense of parallelism, or simultaneity, in national consciousness, which has had vast political consequences over the last few centuries, is nicely captured in Benedict Anderson's evocation of the role of the press in shaping the early stages of the evolution of the newspaper-reading, bourgeois, national imagination in many parts of the world. The obsolescence of the newspaper (in terms of the reader's imagination, merely an extreme form of the novel) at the end of the day it is read, prefiguring the in-built obsolescence of modern durables, created an extraordinary mass ceremony: "the almost precisely simultaneous consumption (imagining) of the newspaper-as-fiction ... a substitute for morning prayers ... performed in silent privacy, in the lair of the skull ... each communicant well aware that the ceremony he performs is being replicated simultaneously by thousands (or millions) of others, of whose existence he is confident, yet of whose identity he has not the slightest notion" (1983: 35). In this mass ceremony of nation-formation, the slow, uneven decline of the old pre-modern certainties, driven by the development of increasingly rapid communications, meant that the search was on for a new way to link together in a meaningful manner the dynamic triplet of fraternity, power and collective memory.

Cohesion and Difference

Most approaches to the study of national identity emphasize the importance of a common field of communication, in which particular structures of information and imagery circulate. But many other factors are also in play in the process of national self-definition: inter-marriage preferences and taboos; stereotypes of outsiders and the development of subtle cues for recognizing the Other; the ebb and flow of collective memory and amnesia; symbolic displays acted out on ritual occasions (such as the use of national anthems and flags at sporting events); language revival and maintenance as a marker of difference from other cultures; folkloric performance for tourists and so on.

Of particular importance is collective memory and amnesia (Halbwachs, 1990; Fentress and Wickham, 1992; Connerton, 1989; Middleton and Edwards, 1990; Rowe and Schelling, 1991) and the many ways in which memories are reconstructed, revised and deployed in the production of contemporary culture. We must note, however, Pierre Nora's insistence that we no longer live in a world suffused with memory, where it can be sensed practically everywhere, from religious ritual to culinary practices. Modernity implies in part that we no longer live in real environments of memory, because "the remnants of experience still lived in the warmth of tradition, in the silence of custom, in the repetition of the ancestral, have been displaced under the pressure of fundamentally historical sensibility ... We speak so much of memory because there is so little of it left. The acceleration of history confronts us with the brutal realization of the difference between real memory ... and history, which is how our hopelessly forgetful societies, propelled by change, organize the past" (Nora, 1989: 78)

Central to the shaping of European identity is the way in which difference is constructed, how self/other or us/them categories are marked. How and where is cultural mismatch, or lack of fit, between different cultural systems evoked, understood and given expression in a dominant discourse of identity which sustains a systematized way of talking about difference? Consider how the construction of difference has taken place between what are now considered to be core members of the EU, as outlined by Macdonald (1993). The self-consciously rational Englishman "knows," within a very common discourse of representation, that Frenchmen are emotional and passionate, "excitable, fun-loving and sexy" (228–29). Differences of verbal and body language—the French appear to get very excited with their words and tone, wave their arms about and kiss each other a lot—confirm the distribution of "English" and "French" imagery between the two halves of the us/them boundary in this instance. Macdonald goes on to point out that "one set of cultural practices, when observed or heard through the structures of another, can make its practitioners seem volatile, unpredictable, irrational, inconsistent, capricious, or even dangerous" (1993: 229). The case of Germany is somewhat different, but the process of stereotyping is the same. The force of romanticism in the first half of the 19th century ensured that Germany was allowed, by both Britain and France, a certain degree of musicality, spirituality, mysticism and emotionality. This was to change, however, after the Franco-Prussian war of 1870, when the imagery changed from evoking a nation of "poets and thinkers" to "a mob of barbarous and brutish Huns ... superhuman in efficiency and subhuman in delicacy of feeling" (Macdonald, 1993: 229).

The metaphors in which "the Germans" were constructed drew on an increasingly shared complex of symbolic oppositions, out of which masculinity and femininity were also constructed. So after 1870, Germans were no longer aligned with "feminine" qualities and instead were firmly attributed core "masculine" characteristics. Germans were now seen as "rigid, where the British were spontaneous; supporters of duty, rather than prone to love; prone to display force, rather than sensitivity; brutal, rather than gentle and civil; ruthlessly logical, rather than intuitively able; meticulously professional, rather than muddlingly amateur ... the reign of the German bully had begun" (Macdonald, 1993: 230).

These stereotypes did not remain confined to British drawing-rooms but played a significant role in international relations in Europe, not only within the so-called Westfalian system of nation-states, but also in the emerging EU itself. Images of difference deepened within British national consciousness after the First and Second World Wars, and played a role in European politics as late as the 1990s. The famous

"Riddley affair," involving the Thatcher government, revealed British elite attitudes as well as popular press thinking about Germany's role in the European Community. Nicholas Riddley, a British Cabinet minister, seemed to be speaking for many in England when he conflated German aspirations in the European Community, with post-Cold War German reunification now looming on the horizon, and German aspirations during the Second World War. He likened Chancellor Kohl to Adolph Hitler and suggested that where the Germans had failed militarily, they were now bent on throwing their weight about in the European Community and "winning, through economically dominating displays of their insensitive rationality" (Macdonald, 1993: 230).

Cultural difference is often constructed out of essentialist understandings of "national character" firmly anchored in territory, such as English stereotypes of the French or Germans. In fact it is through the two-way process of defining "others" that people define themselves. (We will see later how some public intellectuals today argue in favor of an emerging European identity that should be constructed in opposition to a post-9/11, post-Iraq American unilateralism.) There is also a sense in which people may have several identities at the same time, linked to several levels of loyalty and felt community roots, any one of which is capable of being activated, depending on the particular social occasion. These identities tend to "nest" one within another. Shore (1993: 37) gives the example of how a man from Northern Ireland might define himself in different social contexts as "from Londonderry," an "Orangeman," "Protestant," "Unionist," "Loyalist" of "Northern Irish." A Catholic from roughly the same area might define herself alternatively as "from Derry," a "Republican," "Fenian," "Nationalist," "Irish" or "Northern Irish." Each apparently minor shift in label conveys messages of considerable political complexity about the speaker's sense of belonging.

A collective identity is thus a complex phenomenon that can shift alongside a whole range of social and economic factors. It can be experienced uniquely by different members of the same group and individuals may even experience tension over the nature of their own identity. This is what O'Brien (1993: 98–117) found in her study of the conflicts of identity among members of a Catalan community in southwest France with a strong regional consciousness, who are at the same time members of the French state bureaucracy. We now turn to look at these facets of identity in the context of anxieties about the politics of belonging in a European sense. These anxieties are often generated by consistently low numbers of people expressing positive sentiments about the EU in Eurobarometer public opinion surveys and the apparent difficulties anticipated by politicians and officials for the emergence of what might be called a European imaginary.

A European Imaginary

The construction of difference and a sense of the Other in Europe, and fears about the role of stereotypes in feeding xenophobia and racism, have been on the agenda of various European institutions for a long time, spurred by debates in the European Parliament from the mid-1980s and the emergence of a common policy on migration. The decision to encourage the internal movement of labor within the EU, heralded in 1992, meant that greater mutual tolerance and understanding among Europe's regions and nation states would be required. There were other reasons, of course, for putting the notion of cultural identity on the agenda, especially what was seen as the need to galvanize popular support and a broad-based political will in favor of economic and political unification. Hugh Seton-Watson in 1985 called this "the need ... for something more exciting than the price of butter ... the need for a European mystique" (quoted in Wintle, 1996: 10).

Enthusiastic politicians, intellectuals and civil servants, moving ahead with unification, would need to reduce the so-called "democratic deficit" and win the support of ordinary citizens for the expansion and deepening of the EU. As early as 1973, the European Council adopted in Copenhagen a "Declaration on European Identity" and a number of official texts on European identity followed. These included Leo Tinderman's "Report on European Unity" in 1976 and the Stuttgart "Solemn Declaration on European Union" in 1983, followed by the Single European Act in 1987.

The Maastricht Treaty of 1992 went further than any of these in setting out the framework for the European Commission's cultural policy. Cultural initiatives should henceforth reinforce the feeling that Europeans share common values and a common cultural heritage, while also contributing to the enrichment of national and regional identities.

The 1984 Green Paper: Television Without Frontiers had already laid out the argument that communication technologies, particularly film and television, can have a decisive impact on cultural identity by maximizing the ability of people to communicate more efficiently across a wide range of subjects with members of their own group. "European unification will only be achieved if Europeans want it. Europeans will only want it if there is such a thing as European identity. A European identity will only develop if Europeans are adequately informed. At present, information via the mass media is controlled at national level" (CEC, 1984:2).

The central assumption here, that a European cultural identity can be created partly by the media, has never been too far from the minds of policy-makers since then. The eleven-nation AIM study of the way EU affairs are reported across European media, for instance, was established to respond to the anxiety that if a truly European public sphere is slow to emerge, the fault must lie with the media (Adequate Information Management in Europe, 2007). The Culture Council planned for May 2007 intends to consider the results of an official consultation on the role of culture in the EU and to shape a new European agenda for culture. President Barroso put the current Commission's case succinctly: "there is a broad consensus on the importance of culture for the project of European integration, European identity and socio-economic cohesion... The future of our union hinges on culture" (Barosso, 2007).

There is substantial scholarly support for the notion that within the framework of nation states, media in different countries have helped create, or reinforce, a sense of national identity out of disparate regional cultures and class divisions, by interacting with pre-existing symbolic resources, such as myths of ethnic origin, markers of distinctness from outsiders, the broad contours of social memory, shared religious, language and educational systems, and so on (Anderson, 1983: Gellner, 1983; Hobsbawm and Ranger, 1983; Blain, Boyle and O'Donnell, 1993). The media contribution relates to the third element in Barth's (1969) list of three key factors that are essential for the crystallization of ethnicity in segments of a large population: a shared common descent (real or fictitious); shared and distinctive socio-cultural characteristics, and a common field of communication.

Shared traditions across Europe are of a different order from those at play in the formation of national identities: Roman law, Judeo-Christian ethics, Renaissance Humanism, Romanticism, the Enlightenment and so forth, the historical trajectory that is sometimes known as the "Plato to NATO" view of Europe. These traditions, however, constitute not so much the notion of "unity in diversity," cherished in official European discourse, as only partially shared cultural backdrops, appropriate to only some parts of Europe, that do not have the same impact on the experience of all Europeans.

Symbolically more powerful forces are perhaps those rooted in the heritage of military conflict in Europe, in the constant awareness of the devastation brought about by centuries of war across the continent, and vast, imperialistic rivalries in the drive to expand into colonies elsewhere on the globe. After all, the actual twentieth century impetus towards a "common Europe" originated in the war-fatigue of the Resistance movement in 1945 and the shocked horror that was the legacy of World War Two. As Schlesinger (1991: 140) points out, this more proximate, but entirely negative memory tends to be left out of official EU discourse, so the difficult task that the EU leadership has set itself is to create an "imagined community" out of what is largely only a geographical space. A strong element of collective memory underpins national consciousness, but shared memory becomes much more problematic when we look for it at a European level.

A Media-Centered View

If we contrast the acknowledged identity-forming work of the media at the level of the nation state with how media function at a European level, and ask if they are beginning to offer more of a Eurocentric, rather than a nation-centered view of the world, then we see that much of the existing policy-oriented discourse about fostering a European imaginary and sense of belonging is infused with a certain amount of wishful thinking. Anderson (1983) stresses the role of news reading and the consumption of mediated political events in the formation of a sense of national identity in different parts of the world of the 19th century. Contemporary print and broadcast media undoubtedly play an important role also in symbolizing politics as a central part of the culture of the nation state, however superficial the detailed awareness of politics that they might actually foster among citizens. But viewed from a European perspective, news media are still very much centered on the nation or the region, and the political news they relay from outside their territory tends to be interpreted and framed fundamentally within a national discourse (Hallin and Mancini, 2004). Press correspondents working in Brussels overwhelmingly report that news about the EU has little chance of moving through editorial gate-keepers in national newsrooms unless it is framed in terms of local relevance, although this tendency is stronger in very market-oriented media than it is among elite newspapers and public service broadcasters (AIM 2007).

The few transnational news media that operate in Europe have a very marginal influence beyond a niche business and political elite: the *Financial Times* and *Wall Street Journal-Europe*, the *International Herald Tribune, BBC World* and *Euronews*. Pan-European television in general increasingly localizes its material to the point of seeking out ethnic and diasporic audiences (Chalaby 2002 and 2005). The mechanisms for producing a unified media output across Europe do not exist. Even in national media, there is abundant evidence of the great difficulty in European journalism in getting beyond the tendency to deploy the most commonly used frame for EU news: its national relevance or interest (Heikkila and Kunelius, 2006: 69–70). The generation of an embryonic, supranational political culture or public sphere that exists beyond the national, would ideally require the dissemination of a European news agenda. This in turn would need to become a significant part of the everyday news-consuming habits of a Europe-wide audience, which would begin to think of its citizenship as transcending the level of the nation-state (Schlesinger, 1999).

Determination to shape cultural identity is seen in Brussels and Strasbourg as a cure for the political and economic ills of Europe, and for all the apparent lack of public interest in the EU revealed in Eurobarometer surveys. However, but this is true only in particular areas of the EU political infrastructure. Communitarian thinking, often associated with the European People's Party, emphasizes that a unified political system can remain stable only if it is anchored, like a nation, in a common history and culture, rooted in a heritage of common movements in religion, philosophy and law. The rhetoric of "unity in diversity," which encapsulates this thinking, originated in the debates around the treaties of the 1970s and 1980s.

Criticism of the communitarian position comes from a realization that the desired forces that might create a strong internal European identity (as distinct from a political cohesion associated with European foreign policy) simply do not support a "Euro-nationalist" view of civic bonding in the future. There is also the problem that millions of non-European immigrants, living in European cities for many decades, cannot recognize any ethnic-religious heritage of "Europeanness" as part of their own cultural identity and would probably not relate at all to the ideology of the European People's Party. Major weaknesses in communitarian thinking also surface in the issues that arise from the question of how Turkey's accession to the EU should be handled and the intense debate (for instance, in the 2007 French presidential election campaign) about where the ultimate frontiers of the EU should be drawn.

Cosmopolitan Memory

There is a different approach to European integration which suggests that anxiety about European identity is misplaced if it sticks to a vision of the slow but inevitable emergence of a European identity that has a strong cultural dimension, arising like a chrysalis out of the collective memories and identities presently bound to nation states. This alternative is the notion of the EU fostering a common civic identity, based on a common political culture, respect for the principles of democracy and the rule of law, with a strong emphasis on universal human rights, a celebration of cultural diversity and enhanced democracy at a local level. Cultural identities and religious beliefs would still be important but would relate more to the private sphere. The liberal ARDE group in the European Parliament, for instance, promotes the idea of a political community based on mutual respect for common, fundamental values and rights, including those of Turks, thus avoiding any "clash of civilizations" in the decision to expand the EU into areas where the religio-cultural heritage is Islamic, rather than Judeo-Christian.

From a republican and political liberal point of view, the slogan "unity in diversity" takes on a new civic and cosmopolitan meaning, based on respect for different cultural practices in different parts of Europe, guided by an emphasis on sharing, not the same cultural identity, but the same civic values which provide the civic bonding and sense of inclusion needed in the expanding democratic polity of the EU.

This, of course, presupposes that a certain kind of European public sphere will emerge in time, one which will support what has come to be known as "constitutional patriotism," a sense of belonging based on common European constitutional principles, supporting popular sovereignty and human rights, developed and applied uniquely in each national culture in the light of its own history and view of its future. This constitutional patriotism, Habermas argues, "can take the place originally occupied by nationalism" (Habermas, 1998: 118). He suggests that the evolution of "constitutional patriotism" will provide the social coherence needed in an enlarged EU based on cosmopolitan identity, its citizens living in a post-national, multi-tiered polity driven more by politico-legal values rather than "deep" cultural identity.

Collective identities are constituted in action, continually reshaped under the influence of both internal social dynamics and external forces, and they also have a strong temporal dimension. The highly complex imaginary process of reconstituting traditions and activating collective memories takes place over time, as members of collectivities socially forget and socially remember. As anthropologist Mary Douglas puts it, "public memory is the storage system for the social order. Thinking about it is as close as we can get to reflecting on the conditions of our thought" (quoted in Schlesinger, 1991: 181).

But cosmopolitan culture has no collective memory comparable with what is at the center of so-called "thick," national cultures. It is frequently linked to the reconstruction of the shared memory of atrocities in 20th century Europe, the two World Wars as well as the Cold War. The Holocaust and Hiroshima are at the root of European supra-national memories that underpin a particular conception of ourselves as part of a global community based on respect for human rights. This kind of cosmopolitan identity, arguably, has been strong enough already, over the last fifteen years, to play a substantial role in shaping both media and public agendas, which some scholars of international relations link to a number of recent humanitarian interventions in countries suffering from conflict, though this linking is also controversial. Sometimes known as the CNN effect, the idea is that the media influence foreign policy by evoking responses in their audiences through concentrated coverage, which in turn applies pressure to governments to act in response to particular conflicts, such as Kurdish Iraq in 1991, Somalia in 1992, Bosnia in 1993, but not Rwanda in 1994 (Robinson, 2000, 2002 and 2005; Shaw, 1996; Gilboa, 2005; Gowing, 1994; Entman, 2004).

One of the problems with promoting a cosmopolitan vision of European identity is that conceptually, it tends to be discussed and promoted not as something that can exist in parallel with the notion of national consciousness, but as something that must stand in opposition to what is a very negative vision of nationalism. Ulrich Beck's (2006) recent work on cosmopolitanism is a case in point. Cosmopolitanism is theorized against a theoretical background that highlights what Beck sees as the contemporary, demonstrative reassertion of national, ethnic and local identities all over the world. This "neo-nationalism" fosters "an aggressive intolerance which is capable of turning on anybody or anything" (Beck, 2006: 4). Cosmopolitan empathy will not so much replace national empathy as "permeate, enhance, transform and colour it," yet he insists that the territorial theory of identity is still "a bloody error, that might be called the prison error of identity" (2006: 7). What is missing from Beck's binary opposition of national (bad) and cosmopolitan (good) identity is an exploration of the possibility that constitutional patriotic identification, like ethnic forms of national identity, is also capable of functioning to legitimize intolerance towards others (Hayward, 2004; Jones, 1999).

Cosmopolitanism and the Range of Nationalisms

To generalize about nationalism as if all varieties are related in some way to the atrocities of Hitler's National Socialism, or Milosovic's Greater Serbia, is to pass over those forms of nationalism that are clearly felt as emancipatory by the majority of citizens that lack the imperative towards territorial expansion. In recognizing the harm that nationalism can do in promoting territorially based forms of consciousness and an ever more retrograde ideology, we must not lose sight of the fact that the set of ideas that connect identities to imaginations of place—roots, boundaries, home—have not always and everywhere been a negative force. Nationalism at the edge of Western Europe is a case in point. There is no doubt that contemporary nationalism in both Ireland and Scotland have as one of their core values the cosmopolitan urge to participate fully in the EU in order to gain local advantage, to enjoy greater levels of political, economic and cultural sovereignty than would be allowed for if they had remained part of the UK. Nationalist and cosmopolitan consciousness coexist peacefully, producing an intensified commitment to the local at several levels of cultural and political life. It is also the case that what is now arguably the most "nationalist" of all political parties in Ireland, working as the political wing of the IRA during several decades of "the Troubles" in Northern Ireland, is also significantly cosmopolitan in its politics. A key part of Sinn Féin's strategy has been to build and maintain international links not just with Irish–Americans, but also with anti-imperialist movements and "people in struggle" in Palestine, South Africa, the Basque country and among indigenous groups in Latin America (Dixon, 2006; Maillot, 2005; Rafter, 2005). Fostering an international dimension among members, and building political support abroad for local political objectives, has become part of the ideology of many national liberation movements in the course of the last century (most notably the Zapatistas in Chiapas, Mexico, who were pioneers in use of the Internet for outreach political purposes).

Advancing the argument for cosmopolitanism as the way forward to build a European identity will make little progress unless it recognizes the different forms of nationalism that have evolved across Europe and the different ways they shape cultural identity. Ichijo and Spohn (2005: 7–8) argue that in a comparative map of European nationalism, one can discern four different paths of nation-state formation: (a) the Western European form of state-led nationalism, as in England, France of Spain, where the formation of states happened before the formation of national identity; (b) the Italian and German experience in the 19th century, where a nationalism became a unifying force acting on smaller, older polities; (c) those places where the process of nation formation resulted in anti-colonial campaigns of separation from overarching empires, as in East and Central Europe (Poland, Czechoslovakia and Hungary) and in Greece and Ireland; and (d) the Eastern European form of empire-contracting nationalism, where nations evolved within traditional empires (Russia/ Soviet Union and Ottoman/Turkey) and transformed the empires into nation-states.

Some of these transformations happened centuries ago, as in Western Europe, where early state-building took place through the agency of centralized educational institutions and the acculturation of ethno-national minorities into the hegemonic nation-state (for instance, Galicia in Spain, or the Occitan region in France). In other parts of Europe, they happened much later. Greater potential for ethno-national conflict can be seen in parts of Central and Eastern Europe, due to the relative lateness of the national transformation process, involving tension-filled, overlapping settlement structures: the hostile national groupings constituting Former Yugoslavia; the beleaguered Hungarian minority in Romania; strained relations tensions between the Baltic states and the central Russian administration; the violent ethno-religious hatreds of the Caucasus.

These transformations may also explain the recent politicizing of extreme forms of xenophobia and racism at the core of the EU's political infrastructure, with the formation for the first time in the Parliament of a far-right coalition, called "Identity, Tradition, Sovereignty." This new force, now given all the privileges of a European parliamentary grouping, is an amalgam of the Greater Romania and the Bulgarian Ataka parties, each with a history within its own borders of hatred for foreigners and ethnic minorities, including Jews, Turks and Roma.

Cosmopolitan Practice

Thus a comparative map of European nationalism reveals quite a wide variation in patterns of nation-building and cultural homogenization, ranging from civic forms to more ethnic forms of nationalism, each emerging across the continent in different historical periods (reference). It is important, therefore, in thinking about forms of democratic cohesion and inclusion in the EU, to distinguish between long-term and short-term structural processes that shape different European collective identities. Country-by-country differences will affect the formation of European cosmopolitan identity in different ways. Cosmopolitan theory is in danger of making the assumption, against those who insist on the continuing primacy of the nation-state in European (and global) affairs, that "nationalism" is a more or less uniform force operating across the different regions of the continent and that there will be a simultaneous decline in national identities over time, as national loyalties are replaced by forms of civic bonding generated by European institutions. The question is whether cosmopolitanism tends to unacceptably override the ethical claims that can be made on behalf of nations and other regional communities of smaller scale that support cohesive human ties to particular groups of people (Jones, 1999). It is undoubtedly true that the globalization of the world economy renders the national sphere incapable of sovereign regulation in many areas of human behaviour. But it is questionable whether the progressivist teleology of cosmopolitanism is correct in writing off nationalism as essentially a negative reaction to "future shock."

In an important sense, cosmopolitanism is yet to come, something awaiting realization, a project whose conceptual content and pragmatic character "are not only as yet unspecified, but must always escape positive and definitive specification, precisely because specifying cosmopolitanism positively and definitely is an uncosmopolitan thing to do" (Breckenridge et al. 2002: 1). Nevertheless, if the concept is to guide thinking about new forms of European identity, it is worthwhile to enquire where we might be able to see already existing examples of cosmopolitan practice. What Beck (2006) calls "banal" cosmopolitanization is obviously seen, for instance, in the transnationalization of law, where national and international legal systems coexist side by side in many areas of European and world politics. It is also seen in the military arena, where security and power depend on international cooperation, as in NATO, where higher command structures have become miniature cosmopolitan societies, in which officers and teams from a range of countries intermingle and cooperate.

But there is also a sense in which the cosmopolitan imaginary is closely linked to the fetishization of liberal individualism, a typical byproduct of consumer capitalism, signified by the icons of singular personhood so prevalent in contemporary popular culture. Breckenridge et al. (2002: 5–6) suggest that the spirit of world citizenship today is best represented, not by ideas, ideals and abstract principles, but by two very different groups of people who cross the media landscape every week in different ways. They include philanthropic individuals—Mother Theresa, George Soros, Ted Turner, Bill Gates, the late Princess Diana and other iconic figures—and those cosmopolitans who are the victims of modernity, "failed by capitalism's upward mobility, and bereft of those comforts and customs of national belonging," that is, refugees, peoples of the diaspora, migrants and exiles, who today concretely represent the spirit of the cosmopolitical community, if such it can be called. Market liberalism and global consumer capitalism play a major role in generating what Beck calls banal cosmopolitanism: "Banal nationalism of the first modernity is being subverted by a banal cosmopolitanization of the second modernity" (Beck, 2002: 85). This subverting is closely connected with mass culture and the forms of consumer capitalism that characterize contemporary societies—displayed in the vast array of exotic foods available in cities, the global range of television programming propagated by multinational media conglomerates, the ubiquitous music and advertising imagery routinely confronting citizens throughout their waking hours. The manufacturing of desires for global brands and products is present to such an extent that the daily rhythm of consumption produces the "side effect cosmopolitanization."

How useful is the idea of cosmopolitanism in thinking about the evolution of the political cohesion of the EU and the future of European identity? Banal cosmopolitanization is certainly well advanced in Europe, though not in an even pattern across all member states of the EU. The ability to travel, and the capacity to consume exotic goods and services, for instance, are far from being evenly distributed. Borders are permeable for many, but remain sealed for the poor, sometimes so desperate to travel that they trust their lives to the ruthless human trafficking industry. Internal migration across the EU is accelerating, especially from poorer to richer regions. But it is doubtful if much of this is producing in low paid workers any of the key facets of what Szerszynski and Urry (2002: 470) refer to as the "cultures of cosmopolitanism": the ability to map one's own society and its culture in terms of a historical and geographical knowledge; the ability to reflect upon and judge aesthetically between different places and societies; the semiotic skills of being able to interpret images of various Others, to see what they are meant to represent, and to know when they are ironic; an openness to other peoples and cultures and a willingness /ability to appreciate some elements of the language/culture of the other. For the diasporic victims of modernity, as Smith (1995:24) points out about cosmopolitanism, "a timeless culture answers to no living needs and conjures no memories. If memory is central to identity, we can discern no global identity-in-the-making, nor aspiration for one, nor any collective amnesia to replace existing deep cultures with a cosmopolitan flat culture. The latter remains a dream confined to some intellectuals. It strikes no cord among the vast mass of peoples divided into their habitual communities of class, gender, religion and culture."

Conclusion

The argument is sometimes made that the USA is the ultimate cosmopolitan nation, the beacon for Europe, since it provides a home for all ethnicities, world cultures and world religion. Beck (2006: 175) correctly argues that the USA is, strictly speaking, a multicultural, rather than a cosmopolitan nation, where commitment to difference extends only as far as is permitted by the commitment to national unity. The American project from the beginning aspired to build a nation pledged to overcoming difference (the "melting pot" metaphor), not a cosmopolitan country that accepts national difference (the "salad bowl"). In his re-evaluation of the imperial Roman version of cosmopolitanism, that can be inferred from the writings of the Stoic philosophers, Pollock (2002: 25–26) reminds us that Romanization was actually indifferent to the cultural diversity of conquered people and often involved "the decapitation of the conquered culture." In the contemporary world, he cautions against accepting the "ugly American" embodiment of cosmopolitanism. Since the re-emergence a decade ago of the neoconservative movement that was to underpin the presidency of George W. Bush, its chief propagandists called for the US to develop a foreign strategy of "benevolent global hegemony" (Kristol and Kagan, 1996). Modern versions of Romanization are commonly expressed in American media content today, indexed to government policy, aimed not only at advancing American interests in the familiar economic and military sense, but also actively promoting American "civilization" and principles of governance abroad. These calls amount to an imperial demand for those who are different "to become like us."

How should Europe react to "ugly American" versions of cosmopolitan thinking? In reacting to the "war on terror" and the current wars in Iraq and Afghanistan, when it is confronted by the naked will to power of the sole military superpower in the world today, Europe is balanced between the reassurances offered by the old order of nation-states and the emerging vision of a cosmopolitan identity still very difficult to define, something awaiting realization. This theme is echoed in the debate initiated in 2003 by Jürgen Habermas and Jacques Derrida on the state of Euro-American relations, and the contributions of several of Europe's leading intellectual figures (among them, Umberto Eco, Fernando Svater, Gianni Vattimo, Péter Esterházy, Timothy Garton Ash, Adam Krzemiński and Karl Otto Hondrich), published in leading daily newspapers across Europe. The aim of the Habermas–Derrida manifesto was to stimulate discussion of Europe's place in the world in the aftermath of the Iraq war and the catastrophic, one-side military decision-making in which the US and Britain had engaged after the Al-Qaida attacks of 2001.

Habermas argued that it is more than ever necessary now to create a Europe that can counterbalance the hegemonic unilateralism of the US. Because of a lack of cohesion in Europe at this stage in its evolution, a "core Europe" (France, Germany, Italy and the Benelux countries) should exert leadership now, as it did in the early years of the European Community, in fashioning a common foreign and security policy for Europe. Any concerns about the emergence of a two-speed Europe would have to yield to the urgency of creating a cohesive European foreign policy as a counter-weight to American power. This debate among European intellectuals places the question of European identity in a new context, as the common consciousness of a shared political fate. However, Habermas admits that an infectious vision of a future Europe "will not emerge from thin air. At present, it can arise only from a disquieting perception of perplexity. But it can well emerge from the difficulties of a situation into which we Europeans have been cast" (Habermas and Derrida, 2005).

We return to the question of what form of identity is worth dying for, Islamist, national or cosmopolitan? What are German or Polish soldiers dying for in Afghanistan or Iraq today, for instance, and is there yet an emotionally engaging cosmopolitan answer that goes beyond what a nationalist frame could offer? If families (and society at large) have some difficulty answering the question in a post-national context, it may be that banal cosmopolitanization is just not enough to ensure the emergence of a satisfying sense of belonging at anything other than a superficial, consumerist level that fetishizes individualism-with-a-world-view.

In a world increasingly de-territorialized by capital flows, global satellite television and mass migration, the nationalist insistence on territorialized imaginations of identity is undoubtedly undergoing change that is as yet only dimly understood. Yet this change is central to the identity anxiety commonly encountered at official levels in the EU, as it propels the search for new forms of civic bonding and transnational citizenship that inspire allegiance and solidarity among strangers. The ideal solution is probably a form of constitutional patriotism, or cosmopolitan nationalism, offering a citizen-identity that serves both the individual's psychological need to belong and the polity's need for allegiance, trust and solidarity, a civic adhesive that would "render tribalism safe" by making people feel like a people, without promoting ethnic intolerance of other people (Hayward, 2004: 7).

A major criticism of constitutional patriotism is that it is too "thin," constantly in need of promotion in order to win popular support. The civic "we" may not be sufficiently moored in citizen's deeply constituted, affective, socio-cultural attachments, where people are capable of being motivated to make significant levels of sacrifice for fellow citizens. Some analysts express doubts about whether the political liberal tradition of human rights, democracy and the rule of law is sufficiently thick to function as the cement of a supranational political community such as the EU, given the persistence of potentially conflicting loyalties connected to ethnically thicker national identities (Kumm, 2005). The answer to this conundrum surely lies in the particular ways in which constitutional identity can enrich and deepen citizens' self-understanding of nationally focused identities in different parts of the EU. It is useful to remember that at an earlier period in European history, there were several pathways to the formation of nation-states. These included cases where collective political entities developed *prior to* a cohesive national identity, where national consciousness did not pre-exist statehood but followed from it, growing out of earlier movements of political empowerment and mobilization among the citizenry. Can the same happen at the supra-national level of the EU? Crucially important in future analysis of this question will be the role played by the press and broadcasting in the mediatization of new forms of European identity.

REFERENCES

Adequate Information Management in Europe (AIM): www.aim-project.net

Anderson, B. (1983) *Imagined Communities*. London: Verso.

Barroso, J.M. (2007) Remarks on Culture. http://ec.europa.eu/culture/eqac/communication/consult en.html

Barth, F. (1969) *Ethnic Groups and Boundaries*. Bergen: Bergen University Press.

Beck, U. (2006) *Cosmopolitan Vision*. Cambridge: Polity Press.

Blain, N., Boyle, R. and O'Donnell, H.(1993) *Sport and National Identity in the European Media*. Leicester: Leicester University Press.

Breckenridge,C., Pollock, S., Bhabha, H., and Chakrabarty, D. (2002) *Cosmopolitanism*. Durham, NC: Duke University Press.

Chalaby J. (2002) "Transnational Television in Europe: the Role of Pan-European Channels." *European Journal of Communication* 17 (2): 183–203.

Chalaby, J. (2005) "Deconstructing the Transnational: a Typology of Cross-Border Television Channels in Europe." *New Media and Society* 7(2): 155–175.

Commission of the European Communities (CEC) (1984) *Television Without Frontiers*. Brussels: European Commission.

Connerton, P. (1989) *How Societies Remember*. Cambridge: Cambridge University Press.

Corcoran, F. (2002) "The Political Instrumentality of Cultural Memory." *Javnost: the Public,* 9 (3): 49–64.

Dixon, P. (2006) Performing the Northern Ireland Peace Process on the World Stage. *Political Science Quarterly* 121 (1): 61–91.

Entman, R. (2004) *Projections of Power: Framing News, Public Opinion and US Foreign Policy*. Chicago: University of Chicago Press.

Fentress, J. and Wickam, C. (1992) *Social Memory*. London: Blackwell.

Gellner, E. (1983) *Nations and Nationalism*. Oxford: Blackwell.

Gilboa, E. (2005) "The CNN Effect: the Search for a Communication Theory of International Relations." *Political Communication* 22(2): 27–44.

Gowing, N. (1994) "Real-time Coverage of Armed Conflicts and Diplomatic Crises." Harvard Working Paper, Shorestein Barone Centre on the Press, Politics and Public Policy, Cambridge MA.

Habermas, J. (1998) *The Inclusion of the Other*. Cambridge: Polity Press.

Habermas, J. and Derrida, J. (2005) "February 15, of What Binds Europeans Together." In D. Levy, M.Pensky and J. Torpey (eds.) *Old Europe, New Europe, Core Europe*. London: Verso.

Halbwachs, M. (1990) *On Collective Memory*. Chicago: Chicago University Press.

Hallin, D. and Mancini, P. (2004) *Comparing Media Systems*. Cambridge: Cambridge University Press.

Hayward, C.R. (2004) "Constitutional Patriotism and its Others." Paper presented to the Annual Meeting of the American Political Science Association, Chicago, September.

Heikkila, H. and Kunelius, R. (2006) "Journalists Imagining the European Public Sphere." *Javnost – the Public.* 13(4): 63–80.

Hobsbawm, E. and Ranger, T. (1983) *The Invention of Tradition.* Cambridge: Cambridge University Press.

Ichijo, A. and Spohn, W. (2005) *Entangled Identities: Nations and Europe.* Aldershot: Ashgate.

Jones, C. (1999) *Global Justice: Defending Cosmopolitanism.* Oxford: Oxford University Press.

Kristol, W. and Kagan, R. (1996) "Toward a Neo-Reaganite Foreign Policy." *Foreign Affairs,* July/August.

Kumm, M. (2005) "The Idea of Constitutional Patriotism and Its Implications for the Role and Structure of European Legal History." *German Law Journal* 6 (2): 319–354.

Macdonald, S. (1993) *Inside European Identities.* Oxford: Berg.

Maillot, A. *New Sinn Fein: Irish Republicanism in the Twenty-first century.* London: Routledge.

Middleton, D. and Edwards, D. (1990) *Collective Remembering.* London: Sage.

Nora, Pierre. (1989) "Between Memory and History." *Representations* 26, 7–25.

O'Brien, O. (1993) "Good to Be French? Conflicts of Identity in North Catalonia." In S. Macdonald (ed.) *Inside European Identities.* Oxford: Berg, 98–170.

Pollock, S. (2002) "Cosmopolitan and Vernacular in History." In C. Breckenridge et al. (eds.) *Cosmopolitanism.* Durham, NC: Duke University Press.

Rafter, K. (2005) *Sinn Fein 1905–2005: In the Shadow of Gunmen.* Dublin: Gill and Macmillan.

Robinson, P. (2000) "World Politics and Media Power: Problems of Research Design." *Media, Culture and Society,* 22(1): 227 232.

Robinson, P. (2002) *The CNN Effect: The Myth of the News, Foreign policy and Intervention.* London: Routledge.

Robinson, P. (2005) "The CNN Effect Revisited." *Critical Studies in Media Communication* 22(4): 344–349.

Rowe, W. and Schelling, V. (1991) *Memory and Modernity: Popular Culture in Latin America.* London: Verso.

Schlesinger, P. (1991) *Media, State and Nation: Political Violence and Collective Identities.* London: Sage.

Schlesinger, P. (1999) "Changing Spaces of Political Communication: the Case of the European Union." *Political Communication* 16(3): 263–279.

Shaw, M. (1996) *Civil Society and Media in Global Crises.* London: St. Martin's Press.

Shore, C. (1993) "Ethnicity as Revolutionary Strategy: Communist Identity Construction in Italy." In S. Macdonald (ed.) *Inside European Identities.* Oxford: Berg, 27–53.

Smith, A.D. (1992) "National Identity and the Idea of European Unity," *International Affairs,* 68 (1): 55–76.

Smith, A. (1995) *Nations and Nationalism in a Global Era.* Cambridge: Polity.

Szerszynski, B. and Urry, J. (2002) "Cultures of Cosmopolitanism." *Sociological Review* 50 (4): 21–36.

Tönnies, F. (1957) *Community and Society.* East Lansing: Michigan State University Press.

Wintle, M. (ed.) (1996) *Cultural Identity in Europe: Perceptions of Divergence and Unity in Past and Present.* Aldershot: Avebury.

CHAPTER 8

European Media and the Culture of Europeanness

DOMINIC BOYER and MIKLÓS SÜKÖSD

Introduction

This chapter offers a discussion of contemporary European media and their cultural impact that may be helpful for considering the contemporary dynamics of the cultural production of Europe and Europeanness more generally. We take as our point of departure how European media cultures remain oddly out of step with dominant trends of supranational economic and political coordination within the European Union. Indeed, with some notable exceptions discussed below, patterns of media production and consumption remain strongly aligned with national linguistic–cultural communities across Europe.

We begin with a brief discussion of the dominant global trends in mass media organization and production since the 1980s, including especially the proliferation of new electronic media technologies and a subsequent trend toward ownership concentration in the media industry, especially in global broadcasting. We next describe the impact of these trends in European media, the most obvious of which has been the saturation of European television broadcasting by North American media content. We then review how the European Union has responded to these trends, beginning with the *Television Without Frontiers* directive of 1989, in the name of making the European audiovisual industry more competitive regionally and globally and of enhancing what is described as "pan-European culture" through new media training, production, and distribution support schemes. Given the framing of our interest, we concentrate especially on those subvention schemes—namely, the Media I, Media II and Media Plus programs (1991–2006) and the Media 2007 program (2007–2013)—that sought to offset a feared Americanization of European media by incentivizing the transnational dissemination of European media content. It is no secret that, while successfully subventing thousands of media projects over the past twenty years, the impact of the Media program series has been limited at best with regard to the two broader goals of fostering industry competitiveness on a European scale and of cultivating pan-European culture. In the final sections of the essay, we analyze the apparent failure of EU audiovisual policy to stimulate a "culture of Europeanness" through media production from a number of different perspectives. This leads us to a further set of conceptual reflections as to how one should interpret the apparent persistent "nationalism" of European media cultures. Returning to questions about the relationship between media, markets, and scales of social consciousness first raised by Benedict Anderson, we look at contemporary trends of elite transnationalism in Europe and suggest that it might be premature to dismiss the historical potential of a culture of Europeanness altogether.

Global Broadcasting and Media Concentration

One thing that must be borne in mind in any discussion of the contemporary state of European media is that mass mediation has undergone profound changes virtually everywhere in the world since the early 1980s.[1] Developments such as the Internet, geostationary satellites, digital transmission, and fiber optic cables have provided the technological basis for satellite and cable television, digital television, new modes of electronic communication (ranging from electronic mail to cellular telephony to blogging) that have made global broadcasting for the first time not only a possibility of mass mediation but a reality in many parts of the world (however unevenly distributed). At the same time, the promise of these new economies of scale and their potential for vertical integration coupled with the large financial investments required to capitalize upon new media technologies led to waves of mergers and acquisitions within the media industry since the 1980s

---

[1] For a general overview of new media developments, see Roger Fidler, *Mediamorphosis: Understanding New Media* (Thousand Oaks: Pine Forge, 1997), and Leah A. Liewrouw and Sonia Livingstone (eds.), *New Media* (London: Sage, 2009).

and 1990s. Globally, major players in the media industry issued calls to governments for deregulation of media ownership laws and policies that had previously served to insulate national media markets from foreign ownership and to regulate the concentration of ownership especially on a cross-platform basis (for example, by limiting the co-ownership of television stations and print media organizations in a single local market). Media corporations claimed that new communication technologies like the Internet and digital broadcasting would guarantee revolutionary media "diversity" regardless of ownership concentration.

These arguments were largely heeded by national governments, usually with little or no public or political debate, leading to legislation like the US 1996 Telecommunications Act that radically liberalized ownership rules and led to further waves of mergers and acquisitions[2] that have in turn generated a handful of media mega-corporations (Time Warner, Disney, News Corporation, Viacom and Bertelsmann) responsible for the vast majority of global broadcasting and for a substantial portion of national broadcasting in places like the United States, Europe, and Australia.[3] Although media ownership concentration is perhaps most visible in the domain of global televisual broadcasting and in the current center of global broadcasting and content production, the United States, it is important to note that ownership concentration has occurred across most media domains (especially in private radio and print media) and within all European national markets to a greater or lesser extent since the 1980s.[4] Moreover, the pro-

---

[2] Sylvia Chan-Olmsted, "Mergers, Acquisitions, and Convergence: The strategic alliances of broadcasting, cable television and telephone services," *Journal of Media Economics* 11:3(1998): 33–46; Stéphanie Peltier, "Mergers and Acquisitions in the Media Industries: Were Failures Really Unforeseeable?" *Journal of Media Economics* 17:4(2004): 261–78.

[3] For critical analyses of these trends see especially Ben H. Bagdikian, *The New Media Monopoly* (Boston: Beacon, 2004); Mara Einstein, "Broadcast Network Television, 1955–2003: The Pursuit of Advertising and the Decline of Diversity," *Journal of Media Economics* 17:2(2004):145–55; Robert W. McChesney, *The Problem of the Media: U.S. Communication Politics in the 21st Century* (New York: Monthly Review, 2004); Eli Noam, "Media Concentration in the United States: Industry trends and regulatory responses," *Communications & Strategies* 24(1996): 11–23.

[4] On media liberalization and concentration trends in Europe specifically, see Peter Humphreys, *Mass Media and Media Policy in Western Europe* (Manches-

portions of private vs. public broadcasting have shifted in favor of private media across Europe. This trend had begun already in the 1980s but was amplified by the political events of 1989. The eventual opening of the media markets of Central and Eastern Europe to western investment from the 1990s tended overwhelmingly to favor the post-1980s media liberalization trend and have exhibited highly-concentrated ownership patterns dominated by the global media interests like News Corporation, Time Warner or Disney, and by Western European media interests like the WAZ group, Axel Springer, Bertelsmann/RTL, Ringier, Bonnier and Burda.

Although mass media transformation and concentration (and concomitant commercialization and Americanization of content and program genres) is truly a global story, it is important to note the variety and importance of local and regional responses to recent trends in media. The penetration of satellite broadcasting to parts of the world never reached by terrestrial broadcasting have often stimulated creative and critical cultural interventions aimed at strengthening local cultural institutions and cultural order against what are predicted to be the solvent effects of global media (as, for example, in the case of Central Australian Aboriginal Media Association).[5]

After a very slow start, public criticism of media concentration has been growing in the United States and Europe as well. A recent report by the Brussels-based, EC-supported European Federation of Journalists, for example, criticizes Europe for its "complacent legislators" and concludes that, "[t]he threats to diversity and plurality in our media have never been greater, and the impact on the range and quality of the work that journalists produce will also be damaging."[6] A second EFJ

---

ter: Manchester University Press, 1996) and Alan B. Albarran and Sylvia M. Chan-Olmsted, *Global Media Economics: Commercialization, Concentration and Integration of World Media Markets* (Ames: Iowa State University Press, 1998), 97–193.

[5] This case has been well-documented by anthropologists of media. See, for example, Faye Ginsburg, "Indigenous Media: Faustian Contract or Global Village?" *Cultural Anthropology* 6:1(1991): 92–112; Faye Ginsburg, "Aboriginal Media and the Australian Imaginary," *Public Culture* 5:3(1993): 557–78; Eric Michaels, *The Aboriginal Invention of Television in Central Australia: 1982–1986* (Canberra: Australian Institute of Aboriginal Studies, 1986).

[6] European Federation of Journalists Report, *European Media Ownership: Threats on the Landscape* (Brussels: EFJ, 2002), 4.

report[7] stressed especially the threat to Central and Eastern European media where media privatization and consolidation have proceeded much more quickly than in Western Europe.[8]As a result of growing concern among professional journalism organizations as well as political debates in the European Parliament, the EC also commissioned a European Media Pluralism Monitor in 2008–09 (the methodology of which is publically available, but was not used yet for systematic data collection).[9]

There are also signs that media reform activism has brought together both conservative and progressive groups in the United States and is gaining in public sympathy, although a concerted political movement away from media liberalization is by no means certain.[10] It may also be the case that now that economies of scale in new media technologies and global broadcasting have been institutionalized that there will be greater opportunities for smaller players as the threshold costs for entering the global market are lowered. This was, we recall, the long-term scenario that was offered by deregulation boosters to legitimate legislation like the 1996 US Telecommunications Act in the first

---

[7] European Federation of Journalists Report, *Eastern Empires: Foreign Ownership in Central and Eastern European Media* (Brussels: EFJ, 2004).

[8] See also Slavko Splichal, *Media beyond Socialism: Theory and Practice in East-Central Europe* (Boulder, CO: Westview Press, 1994) and Colin Sparks, *Communism, Capitalism and the Media* (London: Sage, 1998).

[9] See Valcke, P., R. Picard, M. Sükösd, J Sanders et al., (2009) *Independent Study on Indicators for Media Pluralism in the Member States – Towards a Risk-Based Approach.* Prepared for the European Commission Directorate-General Information Society and Media. KUL: Leuven. http://ec.europa.eu/information_society/media_taskforce/doc/pluralism/pfr_report.pdf and http://ec.europa.eu/information_society/media_taskforce/doc/pluralism/pfr_annex1_userguide.pdf Also available in a book format at Lulu.com: Valcke, P., R. Picard, M. Sükösd, J Sanders et al., (2009) *Indicators for Media Pluralism in the Member States – Towards a Risk-Based Approach* (European Commission): *Volume 1: Final Report,* 179 p. (ISBN 978-1-4452-0769-8), and *Volume 2: User Guide,* 363 p. (ISBN 978-1-4452-2519-7). For a summary, see Valcke, Peggy; Picard, Robert; Sükösd, Miklos; Klimkiewicz, Beata; Petkovic, Brankica; Zotto, Cinzia dal; Kerremans, Robin, "The European Media Pluralism Monitor: Bridging Law, Economics and Media Studies as a First Step towards Risk-Based Regulation in Media Markets" *Journal of Media Law*, 2:1 (2010) 85–113.

[10] See McChesney, *Problem*, 252–297.

place, even though it has failed to come to fruition, and indeed, appears to have had precisely the opposite effect in the most highly deregulated sectors like commercial radio.

Television Without Frontiers and EU audiovisual policy

For our purposes, regarding the media production of Europe and Europeanness, the most salient aspect of media concentration and global broadcasting is how the EU has shaped its own regional response to these trends. This was indeed a matter of positive response rather than proactive engagement. As Alison Harcourt has argued, it was European media companies' "impressive flow of international mergers, acquisitions and cross-national market planning" beginning in the 1980s that "shifted the centre of gravity of media ownership regulation to the European level."[11] The EC itself explains that "[t]he development of satellite broadcasting and the rapid increase of the deficit with the United States in audiovisual trade prompted initiatives on the part of the Community institutions in 1984."[12]

To explain the historical production of this deficit, one must note that, unlike terrestrial broadcasting, satellite broadcasting in Europe were from the beginning commercial and privately-owned rather than public and state-owned media. By capitalizing upon new technological platforms, satellite and (to a far lesser extent than in the US) cable broadcasting also radically expanded the quantity of content (measured in hours of programming) that was available throughout Europe. One of the most successful new businesses of European satellite broadcasters was to provide North American (primarily US) televisual programming to European markets. As new content providers have multiplied, growth has been steady and steadily slanted toward entertainment programming. Between 1994 and 1999, for example, the volume

---

[11] Alison J. Harcourt, "EU Media Ownership Regulation: Conflict over the Definition of Alternatives," *Journal of Common Market Studies* 36:3(1998): 369–389, 372; see also Alison J. Harcourt, *European Institutions and the Regulation of Media Markets* (Manchester: Manchester University Press, 2005); Humphreys, *Mass Media*.

[12] http://ec.europa.eu/avpolicy/index_en.htm

of fiction programming (the largest subcategory of entertainment programming) broadcast by European channels increased from 250,000 hours to 313,000 hours per year.[13] Yet this programming was overwhelmingly dominated by North American content (71% in 1994 and 73% in 1999) while the proportion of European content has continued to drop (from 18% in 1994 to 11% in 1999). Truly, one of the emergent ironies of the past twenty years of European supranationalism has been that transnational cultural content in Europe, such as it is, has come largely in two forms, neither of which sits well with the European self-imagination of politicians and policy-makers in the EU: ubiquitous North American entertainment programming and pornography (perhaps Europe's most internationally successful but least praised cultural industry).[14]

EU audiovisual policy can only be understood against the backdrop of such concerns about the potential Americanization of European culture through its saturation European broadcasting and popular culture. An EC Green Paper titled "Television Without Frontiers," began debate over the reform of the European media industry in 1984 and led eventually to the Council's "Television Without Frontiers" Directive of October 3rd, 1989 (89/552/EEC), hereafter TWF.[15] On the one hand, as in many similar directives, the core objectives were market- and industry-oriented. TWF was designed simply to bring European broadcasting within the common market framework and to reduce barriers to the "free movement of television broadcasting services in the Union." On the other hand, there were clear cultural objectives

---

[13] BIPE, *Final evaluation of the Media II Programme: Final Report for the European Commission*, (Boulogne: BIPE, 2002), 29. [Hereafter: *Media II*]

[14] The industry is poorly documented but estimates suggest total revenues in the billions of Euro and increasing owing to fallout from "culture wars" in the United States that have caused pornographic production to relocate from the United States to places like Bermuda and Europe. Meanwhile, new communications technologies have created huge new markets for adult services. One EC study concluded, for example, that, "of the E252 million spent on content by Western European internet users in 2001, 70% was spent on adult content" (MGAIN Consortium Study, "Mobile Entertainment in Europe: Current State of the Art")

[15] TWF was amended by Council Directive 97/36/EC on June 30th, 1997, revise dand renamed the Audiovisual Media Services Directive (AVMS) in 2007. See http://ec.europa.eu/avpolicy/index_en.htm

informing the new regulatory framework as well. The majority of the directive is devoted to setting standards for advertising, tele-shopping and the protection of minors. In addition, Article 4 states:

> Member States shall ensure where practicable and by appropriate means, that broadcasters reserve for European works, within the meaning of Article 6, a majority proportion of their transmission time, excluding the time appointed to news, sports events, games, advertising and teletext services. This proportion, having regard to the broadcaster's informational, educational, cultural and entertainment responsibilities to its viewing public, should be achieved progressively, on the basis of suitable criteria.

The "where practicable" provision more or less robbed TWF of any binding control over content. However, Article 4 made it clear that stimulating the production and distribution of "European works" in media was considered a key policy objective, one that would (1) generally strengthen the European media industry and help them develop into a global player, (2) reduce the staggering domination of North American media content within European media, and (3) help to cultivate transnational European cultural production between the member states.

One of the more politically contentious dimensions of the TWF directive was that it made no comment on media concentration and suggested no rules concerning cross-ownership of media. Many critics of TWF feared "a repeat at the EU level of national scenarios in which liberalization of media markets, coupled with insufficient national legislation has led to concentration in press or television markets."[16]

Alison Harcourt documented the politics within the EC between the relevant Directorates General concerning potential media ownership regulation and concluded that, "it seems that the Commission's long-term aim could be first to liberalize national media markets with its media ownership proposals, then to follow later with convergence legislation once telecommunications companies have lost market power due to introduced competition and new services have been allowed

---

[16] Harcourt, "EU Media," 375.

to grow."[17]   Indeed, Council resolutions (e.g., Council Resolution of 21 January 2002, 2002/C 32/04; Council Conclusions of 19 December 2002, 2003/C 13/01) have only addressed earlier concerns about media ownership and concentration in the most oblique terms and have instead tended to re-emphasize the importance of broadcasting as a potential growth industry within the EU and as a means of promoting cultural diversity.   The recommendations of the 21 January 2002 resolution center, for example, on media finance issues, and speak in vague terms of studying "the best ways of giving the European audiovisual sector a more important place at [the] world level while respecting cultural diversity." This situation seems unlikely to change in the near future.   Although the TWF directive was revised in 2007 by the EC, none of the focus groups were centered on media ownership/concentration issues, instead focusing on the regulation of content, advertising, and the right to information.[18]

Media I, Media II, Media Plus, and Media 2007

Beyond issuing directives for deregulating the European audiovisual market and encouraging cross-national broadcasting, EU audiovisual policy committed limited, but growing funds to a series of programs that have sought, oriented by the broader goals of TWF, to strengthen the European audiovisual sector through media training, media development and media distribution initiatives. The Council adopted the first of these programs in 1990. From 1990–1995 the Media I program was in force, followed by the Media II program (1996–2000) and the third generation Media Plus program (2001–2006). The annual budgets for the Media program rose fairly substantially in the third cycle. The total budget for Media II was 45 million Euro for training initiatives and 265 million Euro for development and distribution programs[19] but these figures have risen to 59.4 million Euro and to 453.6 million Euro, respectively, for Media Plus. This translates roughly into an increase in average annual budgets from 77.5 million Euro to 102.6

---

[17] Harcourt, "EU Media," 386.
[18] http://ec.europa.eu/avpolicy/index_en.htm
[19] *Media II*, 9.

million Euro from 1995 to 2006. These funds were spread across 14 separate support schemes ranging from support for training of media professionals (TR), to support for the development of audiovisual work submitted by European Independent companies (De1), to support for television broadcasting of European audiovisual works (Di4), to support for cinema distribution (Di7).[20]

The ongoing Media 2007 program (2007–2013) does not support filmmaking itself, but sponsors pre- and postproduction activities in five areas: training (scriptwriting skills; economic and financial management; digital technologies) development (single projects, catalogues, new talent, co-productions, other financing); distribution (distributors, sales agents, broadcasters, cinema exhibitions, digitizing works); promotion (market access, festivals, common events, heritage); and horizontal actions and pilot projects. Media 2007 has a total funding of 755 million Euro for the 2007–2013 period. As the budget breakdown indicates, the distribution of European works enjoys most support to increase screening in the EU states (besides the producing country) and globally: distribution 55%, development 20%, promotion 9%, training 7%, horizontal actions and pilot projects 5% and 4%, respectively.

The increasing budgets for the Media programs signal, in part, fears inside and outside the Council that European media and knowledge industries are falling further behind their global competitors. The European Audiovisual Conference in 1994, for example, identified the "fragmentation of productive structures and markets" as key to "the fragility and the lack of competitiveness of European audiovisual products."[21] With the specter of American media domination ever on the horizon, the Media II program objectives focused on breaking the "vicious cycle of reluctance of distributors and the public for non-national European films."[22]

This emphasis on "non-national European" media content must be highlighted. It underscores the point that whereas national cultural content continues to play quite well to national audiences in European states, the spectrum of transnational cultural content is entirely

---

[20] *Media II*, 8–9.
[21] *Media II*, 10.
[22] *Media II*, 10.

dominated by North America and especially by the United States. Recognition of the weakness of a transnational "culture of Europeanness" in European media is, we would argue, one of the objectives of the Media programs. However, it remained a secondary objective behind industrial policy considerations in EU audiovisual policy more generally. The final evaluation of the Media II program issues a rousing call to arms on the transnational front:

> The production of national European stock programs rapidly grew during the 1990s. This was partly due to the Television Without Frontiers Directive, and the main reason was that European producers were successful in terms of audience. NATIONAL FICTION WON BACK MARKET SHARES ON ALL THE NATIONAL MARKETS.
>
> Can we, however, be satisfied with A JUXTAPOSITION OF NATIONAL SUCCESSES, in a context of stagnation or even DECLINE IN THE TRANSNATIONAL CIRCULATION OF EUROPEAN PROGRAMS?[23]

The expected answer to this rhetorical question is clearly "no" but the brushing aside of recent success stories of European media production at the national level is even more striking. The resurgence of national media cultures is dismissed precisely because this "juxtaposition of national successes" is insufficiently "European" in its character. Here, the value of a principle of supranational Europeanness for EU audiovisual policy becomes clear. The evaluation continues:

> Culturally and politically, the circulation of programs, like that of films, is conditional on the emergence of a pan-European culture, which is itself conditional on the strengthening of a European identity, conscious of itself and of its internal diversities. Economically, the circulation of programs across the continent is essential for the emergence of an industrial sector comprising companies having a critical size and a sufficient level of capitalisation to allow them to be fully independent of the national broadcasters, and to export outside Europe. Over the long term, the cultural and economic objectives strengthen each other.[24]

---

[23] *Media II*, 269.
[24] *Media II*, 270.

Looking at data on the fiction program market in the EU the proximate indices of dissatisfaction become a bit clearer. On the one hand, from 1994 to 1999 (in the period of Media II), the quantity of imported fiction programs from North America has steadily increased from 179,000 hours/year to 228,000 hours/year. At the same time, national productions have fallen from 46,000 hours/yr to 36,000 hours/year. European co-productions have not nearly kept pace, rising from 6,700 hours/yr to only 13,000 hours/year. Indeed, likely the most important statistic from the EC's point of view is that total European fiction programming (national + international) has held more or less steady through the latter half of the 1990s (57,000 in 1994 to 62,000 in 1999) growing at only 1/10th the rate of North American imports.

The overall argument of the Media programs from 1990 to 2006 was clear. To reach a competitive scale in global broadcasting, Europe needs to exist as more than a patchwork of national media cultures. To this end, the Media program evaluation concludes, the efforts of the EU have been insufficient. Despite numerous individual successes (under the television broadcasting scheme alone (Di4), for example, Media II supported 362 production projects to the tune of 39 million Euro), the broader strategic objective of slowing or reversing market trends in the audiovisual industry was not achieved. A self-aware culture of Europeanness is needed to create the basis for a truly transnational European media culture. This was the Media message in a nutshell.

And, yet, one is tempted to ask: does Europe *really* need something more than healthy national media cultures? In whose interests are these policies being undertaken? For the most part, they seem meant to benefit the interests of the European media industry, although European media consumers are consistently also promised access to great media "diversity" and "plurality" (although these terms never move beyond a quantitative gloss of qualitative features and are never defined). Moreover, the policies seem to support the EU since the cultivation of a "pan-European culture" would correlatively strengthen European identification of viewers, the EU's mandate, and legitimize its movement toward greater supranational integration and sovereignty. To this end, EU audiovisual policy appeals to the member states in the rhetoric of a defense against the perceived cultural threat of North American media content. This also explains the focus of the Media programs on television and film production and distribution. If the EU wanted to publicize a true European media success story (beyond pornography of course) it could have focused instead on European news industries, which are far superior to their United States counterparts in both diversity and quality (and these gaps are growing).[25] But news media seem entirely beyond the attention of the EC and they have no place in the Media programs. The focus is instead on the cultural threat of American entertainment programming, or, to be more specific, on the threat that its alternative transnational cultural model poses to the supranational ambitions of the EC.

This is, of course, as other scholars have noted, a delicate game for the EC, one that demands that it steer carefully between its own supranational ambitions and the plurinational expectations of the member states. The production of both pan-European and national media culture could be seen as antidotes to hegemony of American media content. Peter Katzenstein describes how the EC has had to tread carefully in its effort to steer the production of a culture of Europeanness among these two options:

> The Commission's clarion call for Europe's cultural defense was tactically astute: protection against 'foreign cultural predators' was acceptable to national governments, the construction of a collective European cultural identity much less so ... In this sense, the EU's audiovisual policy resembles its cultural policy more generally: it facilitates the 'horizontal' flow of products and information without having an effect on the 'vertical' dimension of content that could create a different collective identity. Because European states guard their cultural sovereignty jealously—more jealously against political initiatives from Brussels than against movies from Hollywood—Europe remains 'plurinational' rather than becoming 'non-national' or 'European.'[26]

---

[25] This trend is much lamented by both media professionals and media scholars in the United States. See, for example, Tom Fenton, *Bad News: The Decline of Reporting, The Business of News, and The Danger to us All* (New York: Regan, 2005) and James T. Hamilton, *All the News That's Fit to Sell: How the Market Transforms Information into News* (Princeton: Princeton University Press, 2004).

[26] In Peter J. Katzenstein, *A World of Regions: Asia and Europe in the American Imperium* (Ithaca: Cornell University Press, 2005), Chapter Five. See also John Borneman and Nick Fowler, "Europeanization," *Annual Review of Anthropology* 26(1997): 486–514.

Katzenstein's analysis is supported by a 2004 report from the EC's DG Education and Culture,[27] which studied the external cooperation patterns within the EU and between member states in the cultural and audiovisual sectors. The study determined that the primary objective of 13 of the 15 core member states studied in external cooperation in these sectors was "to spread national prestige" or "to promote national culture" rather than to strive for international or European cultural objectives (the exceptions were Sweden and the UK).

And, yet, as Media II's call for "pan-European culture" illustrates, vertical expansion in the direction of supranational cultural identity was an explicit (yet secondary) subtext to EU audiovisual policy.

However, in the mid 2000s, toward the end of the Media Plus period, European audiovisual policy experienced a major shift in emphasis, or, at least, rhetoric. In the context of a new iteration of the TWF Directive (now renamed the Audiovisual Media Services Directive [AVMSD] in 2007) and the planning of a fourth generation of the Media program (known as Media 2007 and scheduled to run from 2007–2013) the EC's previous emphasis on stimulating supranational cultural production disappeared entirely from its policy documents. Instead of explicitly seeking to cultivate trans- or non-national European cultural production, EC audiovisual policy stated simply the need to support "cultural diversity." For example, the AVMSD discussion of on-demand services states: "On-demand audiovisual media services have the potential to partially replace television broadcasting. Accordingly, they should, where practicable, promote the production and distribution of European works and thus contribute actively to the promotion of cultural diversity."[28]

And, the Media 2007 program objectives were now listed as:

• to preserve and enhance European cultural diversity and its cinematographic and audiovisual heritage, guarantee accessibility to this for Europeans and promote intercultural dialogue;

---

[27] European Commission DG Education and Culture (Ernst & Young), "Study of external cooperation of the European Union and its Member States in the culture and audiovisual sectors" (June 2004).

[28] (Directive 2010/13/EU of the European Parliament and of the Council of 10 March 2010, § 69).

- to increase the circulation of European audiovisual works inside and outside the European Union;
- to strengthen the competitiveness of the European audiovisual sector in the framework of an open and competitive market.

Whether this shift in emphasis from supranational culture-building to supporting intercultural diversity and dialogue should be viewed as a concession to national political and cultural interests or as a result of internal discussions concerning the limited success of the supranational policies to date remains an open question.

The new policy language is very ambiguous as to what "cultural diversity" actually means, which leaves open the possibility that supranational cultural projects could be supported as well. Nonetheless the EC itself describes the policy shift as a "radical rethink"[29] of priorities. This, in combination with other crises recently sustained by the EU, (e.g., the Constitution crisis, and the more recent European national financial and debt crises), certainly makes one wonder whether the supranational mission of the Media II period is capable of being resuscitated. Some analysts have suggested that the rising significance of economic liberalism in the EU has quelled interest in greater supranational cultural integration, especially after the eastward expansion of the EU in 2004 and 2007.

In the next two sections, we would like to explore some reasons why EU audiovisual policy has failed to generate the culture of Europeanness that it seeks—even before the recent shift from pan-European culture-building to promoting intercultural diversity.

Economic, Political and Technological Reasons of Failure

One set of explanations for the failure (or, at least, the limited success) of the EU's audiovisual policy to stimulate transnational European culture is rather straightforward. The quantity of money that the EC has allocated to media development represents only a miniscule faction of the media production budgets within the European audiovisual industry. To return to figures cited above, the EC did invest 39 million Euro

---

[29] http://ec.europa.eu/information_society/media/overview/2007/index_en.htm

between 1996 and 2000 to support television production in the EU.[30]
But the average level of support was only about 100,000 Euro per
project,[31] which usually represented less than 10% of the total budget
for these projects.[32] At the same time, global (e.g., European and non-
European) investment in these same projects amounted to 572 million
Euro. Even more sobering is the fact that the total income of European
television from 1996 to 2000 was about 250 billion Euro. The 39 million Euro of the Media program thus only represented 0.02% of the
global resources invested into the European television sector during
this period (257).

For the most part, EU audiovisual policy has tried to encourage
greater transnational cultural production by providing funds that in-
centivize transnational co-productions, greater international distribution, subventions for European cinemas willing to show European
films, funds for dubbing, and so on. But, especially on the production front, the sums involved are really too small to make much impact
in the European and global markets. This may be especially true in
terms of providing viable competition to the much better funded North
American media industries, whose sheer size, degree of vertical integration, and control over global distribution systems mean that European
productions stand little chance of competing with them for mass international audiences, inside or outside the EU, at least in terms of the
film and entertainment industry. The limitations of subvention could
be reduced, of course, if the EC were to pursue other policy strategies
besides market incentives.

It would be conceivable, for example, for the EC to develop European satellite and/or cable television broadcasters to produce and
distribute the kind of pan-European cultural programming that it desires. But such an operation would require political support across the

---

[30] *Media II*, 257.

[31] *Media II, 262.*

[32] The overall budgets are also low by comparison to production costs (and
values) in the United States where scripted television programming costs
run about $2 million/episode and where even the more cost-effective (and
thus increasingly popular among managers and owners) newsmagazine and
"reality" TV formats can cost about $400,000/episode; see Mara Einstein,
"The Financial Interest and Syndication Rules and Changes in Program Diversity," *Journal of Media Economics* 17:1(2004): 1–18.

member states to guarantee access to relevant frequencies as well as significant financial backing to build institutional infrastructure (not to mention subventing production, marketing and distribution budgets). This necessary political and financial support, as Katzenstein notes, has never been forthcoming from the member states and seems unlikely to emerge in the near term.[33]

Lastly, the maturation of markets around new digital communications and information technologies has tended globally to subdivide audiences to an unprecedented degree. The era of "national publics" and "national media"—whether real or imagined (see below)—was defined through print media and terrestrial broadcasting, respectively, which are now becoming less important media in many parts of the world. New communications technologies make it easier for media producers, often in the name of luring advertisers, to define and target more specialized audiences. The proliferation of specialty channels on satellite and cable television evinces this trend as does the boom in lifestyle and celebrity publications in print media and, of course, the communicative plurality of the Internet. To talk about a single media industry-wide "trend" toward audience compartmentalization would be seriously misleading though since some domains (like daily newspapers) are, currently, seeking to integrate shrinking audiences while others (like cable and satellite TV) are actively segmenting them. Yet, in the televisual and cinematic sectors of the media industry, market trends would suggest that greater specialization of communication and identification, rather than the cultivation of supranational communitarianism, is the more likely cultural tendency for the near term, especially in the absence of specialty broadcasters that promote broad supranationalism in one way or another.

Cultural and Linguistic Reasons of Failure

This leads us to a second set of considerations of the failure of EU audiovisual policy to date in supporting a culture of Europeanness. One of the most important reasons that "pan-European culture" has so little traction across the member states is that European media cultures

---

[33] Katzenstein, *World*, Chapter Five.

remain strongly national in their characters. What "national" signifies in this context is primarily that media communication is rationalized and organized linguistically by what sociolinguists would call "monoglot standards"[34] or, more simply, "national standard languages." Standard languages cohere "national cultures" through the definition of translocal speech communities and through the experiential enhancement of senses of communicative, cultural intimacy.[35] This is partly an issue of communicative medium, and not just communicative content as, standard languages can subsume foreign cultural content through translational processes. For example, one can watch episodes of "CSI: Crime Scene Investigation" or "Friends" across the EU but outside of Anglophone Europe these episodes will usually be dubbed into the local national language or at least appear with subtitles. Interestingly, this linguistic dimension of media is routinely downplayed by EU audiovisual policy in that it situates the threat of foreign media content, both economic and cultural, in its country of origin. And yet, European citizens have long proved themselves able to "domesticate" foreign media content to national preferences and values. This may also explain why the member states seem ambivalent with regard to the EC's diagnosis of the cultural threat of North American media content.

The connection between media markets and national languages was first discussed at length in Benedict Anderson's classic treatise on modern nationalism, *Imagined Communities*.[36] One of the most interesting and provocative dimensions of Anderson's argument is his portrait of national consciousness as, in essence, a secondary or, in the Marxian sense, "ideological" consequence of the economic and tech-

---

[34] See Michael Silverstein, "Monoglot 'Standard' in America: Standardization and Metaphors of Linguistic Hegemony" In *The Matrix of Language: Contemporary Linguistic Anthropology*, eds D. Brenneis and R. Macaulay (Boulder, CO: Westview Press, 1996), 284–306.

[35] Michael Herzfeld, *Cultural Intimacy: Social Poetics in the Nation-State* (New York: Routledge, 1997); Andrew Shryock, ed, *Off Stage/On Display: Intimacy and Ethnography in the Age of Public Culture* (Stanford: Stanford University Press, 2004); also, Dominic Boyer, *Spirit and System: Media, Intellectuals and the Dialectic in Modern German Culture* (Chicago: University of Chicago Press, 2005).

[36] Benedict Anderson, *Imagined Communities: Reflections on the Origin and Spread of Nationalism*. Revised Edition (London: Verso, 1991).

nological forces of print capitalism. Print capitalism, in its efforts to create and command economies of scale, sought ever larger audiences for its products. In the profoundly heterogeneous cultural and linguistic environment of early modern Europe, this required, Anderson argues, greater rationalization and standardization of communication in order to move printed material at broader scales. In turn, the audiences drawn to new media like newspapers and novels, slowly, recursively, developed a new phenomenology of space and time (which Anderson captures with the term "simultaneity"[37]) that allowed them to imagine meaningful modes of social belonging on a non-immediate, translocal basis. Thus was the imaginary "kinship of the nation" born. The spread of translocal social imagination based upon print-languages gave rise to new projects of political integration in Europe and elsewhere around the "imagined" communities of nations.[38] Although Anderson does not ignore the work of states and class interests in driving the standardization of national languages and national imagination, what is interesting about Anderson's argument is that it is the formal-technical capacities of mass communication rather than the nationalistic content *per se* that he holds responsible for the development of new modes of social consciousness and identification. Although Anderson's critics have rightly pointed to host of teleological and ideological baggage in his model and to the very selective character of his model of language,[39] his central point seems well-taken.

---

[37] Anderson, *Imagined Communities*, 24.

[38] Specifically, Anderson writes, "These print-languages laid the basis for national consciousness in three distinct ways. First and foremost, they created unified fields of exchange and communication below Latin and above the spoken vernaculars ... Second, print-capitalism gave a new fixity to language, which in the long run helped to build that image of antiquity so central to the subjective idea of the nation ... Third, print-capitalism created languages-of-power of a kind different from the older administrative vernaculars;" Anderson, *Imagined Communities*, 44–45.

[39] See, especially, John D. Kelly and Martha Kaplan, *Represented Communities: Fiji and World Decolonization* (Chicago: University of Chicago Press, 2001); Partha Chatterjee, *Nationalist Thought and the Colonial World: A Derivative Discourse?* (Minneapolis: University of Minnesota Press, 1993); Michael Silverstein, "Whorfianism and the Linguistic Imagination of Nationality," in *Regimes of Language*, ed. Paul Kroskrity, (Santa Fe: SAR Press, 2000), 85–138.

To return to the main issue at hand, Anderson's paradigm may explain the failure of "pan-European culture" to undermine national media cultures, and also underscores the historical contingency of this failure. On the one hand, it is no surprise given the essential connection that Anderson posits between standard language and social identification that a pan-European culture industry would find it hard going without a distinctive transnational language to call its own. More to the point, given the fact that nations have little more ontological substance than linguistically-integrated speech communities in Anderson's model, it makes sense that the states who claim these speech communities as the essence of their legitimacy to govern "on behalf" of a national polity would jealously and energetically guard against efforts that threatened more heterogeneous modes of communication and social identification. Indeed, since the institutions of the EU hold no Weberian "monopoly" on the legitimate use of violence with which to discipline member states, it is limited in its operation to the arts of persuasion, moral argument, and technical expertise. In the end, cultural policies must be handled sensitively and argued in terms of their benefits for member states despite the presence of a would-be Trojan horse of pan-European culture.

At the same time, that at least some in the political elite of the EU remain committed to developing a culture of Europeanness despite the failures of the past 25 years of cultural policy should be treated as a significant social fact in its own right. As we explain below, Anderson's paradigm is really double-edged from the perspective of thinking about the culture of Europeanness in the EU. One might recall here that the relationship of capitalism to language to identity that Anderson outlines is meant to be dialectical and historically contingent—indicating that the ecology of social consciousness and identity that contemporary Europeans inhabit now is bound to transform historically as media capitalism itself changes.

Global Media, Elite Transnationalism and the Potentiality of pan-European Culture

Anderson would expect that new regimes of media capitalism would continue their effort to open new and expand old markets and to breakdown linguistic vernaculars that prove inconvenient for establishing new economies of scale. There is no doubt, as we have shown in this chapter, that since the early 1980s media capitalism has become fully globalized and that global broadcasting has become a reality, however uneven, and centered, for the moment, in North America. To extend this argument, it would seem likely that in a historical perspective, global media capitalism would seek to undermine the cultural configurations produced by earlier media regimes, to at least overlay new transnational markets, identities, consciousnesses (as well as new subnational markets and identities[40]) over the modes of nationalism that continue to be valued throughout Europe today. The absence of a standardized transnational language at this historical moment would be an impediment, but not unexpected within Anderson's model. Indeed, it would be precisely the nascent forces of global media—and the new phenomenological scales of simultaneity they would imply—that would push forward the development and eventual institutionalization of supranational modes of communication, identification and consciousness.

Let us add to this scenario a dimension of supranationalism that is rather more obscured in Anderson's paradigm: the special agency of social elites and especially intellectual elites in articulating new modes of social identification and their tendency to generalize their own preferred modes of social belonging and identity as "natural" and "inevitable" for the groups with which they identify.[41] Lomnitz and Boyer have written at length elsewhere of the significance of specialized knowledge-makers, or, "intellectuals," for the articulation and

---

[40] See Dominic Boyer, "Media Markets, Mediating Labors, and the Branding of East German Culture at *Super Illu*," *Social Text* 68:3(2001): 9–33.

[41] See Boyer, *Spirit and System*; Bernhard Giesen, *Intellectuals and the Nation: Collective Identity in a German Axial Age*, Trans. N. Levis and A. Weisz (Cambridge, UK: Cambridge University Press, 1998); Claudio Lomnitz, *Deep Mexico, Silent Mexico: An Anthropology of Nationalism* (Minneapolis: University of Minnesota Press, 2001); Ronald Grigor Suny and Michael D. Kennedy, eds, *Intellectuals and the Articulation of the Nation* (Ann Arbor: University of Michigan Press, 1999); on the social agency of intellectuals more generally, see Alvin Gouldner, *The Future of Intellectuals and the Rise of the New Class* (New York: Seabury Press, 1979) and George Konrád and Ivan Szelényi, *The Intellectuals on the Road to Class Power: A Sociological Study of the Role of the Intelligentsia in Socialism* Trans. A. Arato and R. F. Allen (New York: Harcourt Brace Jovanovich, 1979).

consolidation of new social identities.[42] The point to emphasize here is that the publicization of new modes of social imagination is disproportionately indebted to this elite's own social self-consciousness and "structures of feeling."

At the beginning of the 19th century, for example, there was very little of what one could call distinctively, standardly "German" in the heterogeneous political, economic, and cultural environment of Central Europe.[43] Indeed, it was mostly middle-class intellectuals who envisioned an integrated German fatherland with a national culture modeled upon their own caste values of *Kultur* and *Bildung*.[44] To this end, these social actors vigorously pursued programs of linguistic and cultural standardization, all the while fantasying the eventual development of a *Kulturstaat* (cultural state) that would allow the cultural potentiality of Germanness to realize itself fully. By the end of the 19th century, the cultural, political and economic elites of German-speaking Central Europe had produced something that at least looked like a "nation-state" even though it remained highly vernacularized in many respects and even though it was strongly repudiated by some intellectuals for its counterfeit character.

The moral of this story is that it is worth looking carefully at the self-imagination of social elites, and particularly knowledge-producers or intellectuals, in order to predict the developmental trajectory of modes of social consciousness more broadly. In Europe, we see that at least some social elites are feeling very supranational and not a little global these days,[45] and so it remains a distinct possibility that they will attempt to codify and to advocate a transnational culture of Europeanness modeled upon their own social experience. Indeed, the absence

---

[42] Dominic Boyer and Claudio Lomnitz, "Intellectuals and Nationalism: Anthropological Engagements," *Annual Review of Anthropology* 34(2005): 105–20.

[43] Boyer, *Spirit and System*, 46–98; James Sheehan, "What Is German History? Reflections on the Role of the Nation in German History and Historiography," *Journal of Modern History* 53:March(1981): 1–23.

[44] Giesen, *Intellectuals*, 64, 78.

[45] See, for example, Adrian Favell's "Eurostars and Eurocities: Toward a Sociology of Free Moving Professionals in Western Europe" (Center for Comparative Immigration Studies Working Paper 71, 2003); cf. Borneman and Fowler, "Europeanization."

of a pan-European language might be less of a barrier to such advocacy than at first would seem, since, in linguistic reality, most human beings are not "monoglot" as Anderson argues[46] but rather pluriglossic and able to shift between different linguistic codes and registers as circumstances dictate.[47] For example, across Europe, linguistic competence in English both in elite political, professional, intellectual and educational cultures and in youth culture has already created a potential basis for new life experiences, modes of feeling identities and of socio-political integration. All this would exceed the national-cultural appeals of contemporary European political parties even though these have not, as of yet, been systematically mobilized.

Viewed in the long run, the co-production emphasis of programs like the Media series may be most significant not for their direct, but limited contribution to the flows of media products in Europe, but to their indirect building and coordination of social relations among Europe's intellectual elite, in other words, for their stimulation of European elite transnationalism. Indeed, the imagination and institutionalization of the Media series is *itself* part of the cultural production of transnational Europe, bringing together a variety of elite, expert social actors (politicians, lawyers, policy makers, media professionals, consultants, artists, writers, and so on) into polylogue around problems such as "European media works" and "pan-European culture."

Such settings and collaborative projects are themselves culturally productive, likely more so than the end-products of media content. We see such projects as analogous to the modes of translocal associational life that flourished throughout Europe in the 18th and 19th centuries and that helped to provide an experiential backbone for new modes of social imagination like nationalism.[48] Like many others, we doubt that

---

[46] Anderson, *Imagined Communities*, 38.

[47] Contemporary sociolinguistics has radically unsettled the model of "monoglossia" upon which Anderson's argument relies. See, especially, William F. Hanks, *Language and Communicative Practices* (Boulder: Westview Press, 1996) and Silverstein, "Whorfianism."

[48] Stefan-Ludwig Hoffmann, "Democracy and Associations in the Long Nineteenth Century: Toward a Transnational Perspective." *Journal of Modern History* 75:June(2003): 269–99; also, Boyer, *Spirit and System*; Giesen, *Intellectuals*.

Europe will witness the mobilization let alone the institutionalization of pan-European culture (whatever that would mean) any time soon. Yet we would caution that nascent modes of elite transnationalism in Europe represent a social force that should not be underestimated in its efficacy over time. Of course, whether this force would be more likely to strengthen the historical potentialities of pan-European culture or to weaken them remains an open question.

We see strengthening as a genuine possibility, especially if interregional relations between the United States, Asia, and Europe become more acrimonious over time. Another scenario is that elite transnationalism mostly bypasses Europeanness en route to even broader modes of transnational social identification and affiliation. Although the McLuhanite "global village" is also more fantasy than reality, its alternate transnationalism, as we have suggested in this chapter, seems deeply vexing for the EU as it seeks to stabilize a culture of social identification somewhere between the nation and the global.

CHAPTER 9

Pan-European, National, Regional and Minority Identities in the Eurovision Song Contest

Gonzalo Torres

> "Powerful social chemistry happens when great public events are transmitted live, direct, instantly to television screens in millions of homes" (Landay, 1993)

The Discreet Power of European Entertainment

Media event, intergenerational ritual or clever post-modern joke; an annual forum where nations tell each other about themselves, and themselves about each other; the imagined space where Yugoslavia remains united and the Iron Curtain still stands; a pan-European public election that once crowned a transgendered Israeli; and overall, the mediated contrast between Europe as it aspires to appear, and the one that lurks underneath its institutional patina.

Behold the Eurovision Song Contest.

Over fifty years of uninterrupted broadcasting, combined with estimated audience figures in the several hundreds of millions[1] have afforded the Eurovision Song Contest (ESC) a solid foothold in the European public imagination across generations, national boundaries and social cleavages. Yet at a time when the cultural dimension of the European project is actively sought after, particularly through the means of the audiovisual production-consumption tandem at the

---

[1] Le Guern (2000) puts forth a figure of 400 million viewers on average; this would account for its European audience as well as those watching in non-participant countries where the ESC is publicly broadcast, such as Australia. However, with the increased popularity of live Internet broadcasts, exact viewing figures are hard to ascertain.

core of the MEDIA support program of the European Union, it is somewhat surprising that the ESC has received so little scholarly attention to date. To be sure, it is ostensibly an entertainment program. Formally, it fancies itself as a thoroughly apolitical one. It is genuinely European entertainment program, the kind produced *by* Europe *for* Europe, has a rather lackluster record in bringing about that elusive set of what Bondebjerg and Golding deem the "common experiences and enthusiasms that form the elements of a single culture" (2004). And when the same authors reflect upon European entertainment formats to disappointingly reach the conclusion that "such ritualistic European encounters—in the Eurovision Song Contest, in soccer, in *Jeux Sans Frontieres*—remain bastions of nationalistic stereotypes and presumptions as much as vehicles for cross-national hybridity," they are unquestionably right.

The shortcoming of this line of thought is that it appears to casually dismiss the importance of precisely that kind of unbridled stereotyping and presumption for the formation of collective understandings in general, and those of Europe in particular. At their broadest, stereotype and presumption constitute key elements of collective identity, be it regional, ethnic, national or otherwise. As a rule of thumb, this entails positive presumptions about the in-group, and negative ones about the out-group. This is probably truest in the European sphere that concerns this book. The idea of the European *demos*, reduced by need to its lowest common denominator, is simultaneously that of a somewhat culturally sterile concept of European "citizenship" (and the promise thereof), and a somewhat culturally gravid set of little more than nationalistic stereotypes, presumptions, and cross-national hybridity.

Therein lays the political, cultural and anthropological relevance of such entertainment-based "European encounters," for they mirror and fuel—and are unwilling victims of—both the political success and the inherent contradictions fundamental to the European narrative. Its political success, in the sense that Europe holds its own as an aspirational utopia for nations both within and outside the European Union borders, that ever-shifting mark of "citizenship." Its inherent contradictions, because such citizenship is not built on culture, but in spite of it. The very idea of Europe depends on a complex balancing act of collective perception that micro-manages the relevance of geography, culture and

identity, that appears institutionally blind to these aspects, while relying on subtler mechanisms of acceptable conflict resolution. Albeit wob-
bly at times, the balancing act works; the imagined notion of Europe
stretches from Iceland to Cyprus, even beyond, and slowly expanding.
And it is in these mediated, broadcast 'European encounters' that the
balancing act subtly forges itself in the minds and hearts of the polity.

If European entertainment media content matters, why should the
ESC specifically matter—or more aptly, why do I claim that it matters
so much to merit a chapter of its own? The answer is: it matters by
default. In an ideal European media sphere ripe with information and
entertainment content and means of distribution made *by* and *for* Europe, the relevance of a song contest that stretches back to the 1950s
and seems to inhabit a musical universe of its own would likely be negligible. However, the actual media landscape in which we operate is in
fact rather desolate.

There are of course the pan-European sports competitions, com-
manding very large audiences and providing a much needed space
for managed inter-national conflict. But beyond that, there is nothing
European about them—they are fundamentally universal events, their
rules and rituals belonging to humankind at its broadest and managed
by internationally upheld standards. Moreover, the sort of collective
socialization that occurs on live sport events limits the role of the individual viewer to that of a passive spectator/supporter, with virtually no
voice over the outcome of the event itself. By contrast, the ESC stands
alone (at least so far) as an intrinsically European product, created for
and by Europeans, and incorporating the audience into a complex role
of spectator, supporter and active judge. It is undeniably laden with nationalistic stereotypes, presumptions, and cross-national commingling.
It is, in its own way, Europe's entertainment democracy.

The Eurovision Song Contest: Media Event and European Ritual

The ESC operates under the organizational framework of the European Broadcasting Union (EBU), a conglomerate of national public
broadcasters from Europe and the Mediterranean, set in place in 1950
as a means to enhance technical and cultural cooperation in the then

nascent European television industry. The ESC itself came to existence in 1956, intended as an initiative to promote "peace and harmony in a Europe still recovering from the Second World War" (Tilden, 2003), and inspired by the pan-European commercial success of the annual Italian San Remo Song Contest. The main premise of the contest has remained unaltered for almost sixty years. Each national broadcaster would independently select a song, and then send it to compete against all the others for the maximum amount of points awarded by selected national juries in a live international broadcast. The winning country is subsequently invited to host the following year's event. The initial seven participant countries in 1956[2] have grown over the five decades of the ESC's existence into 39 active participants in 2010—including the two non-traditionally European states of Turkey and Israel, and a number of passive participants where the contest is broadcast but who are not represented by a national entry.

Over the decades, at least three significant changes have been made to the format. First and foremost, since the mid-1990s the traditional national juries have been replaced by direct popular voting through phone- and SMS-voting, effectively altering the role of the audience from passive media consumer to active and sovereign judge.

Second, due to the expansion of participant countries a qualifying round was introduced in 2004, which was subsequently divided into two separate semi-finals for 2008. This meant that competition and conflict amongst nations no longer takes place in order to simply win the contest, but also to *qualify* as a participant in the main broadcast.

And finally, the traditional practice of European public broadcasters to privately appoint their representative has given way to a widespread practice of holding national finals, ESCs in miniature. This further enhanced the role of national audiences as the ultimate decision-makers upon the terms of their national representation.

At a superficial level, of course, the ESC is a song contest and little more. In practice, its resilience and popularity in the face of challenges—such as the privatization and fragmentation of the European audiovisual sphere, as well as the overall declining commercial success of its musical output—can only be truly understood in terms of the ESCs nature as a blend of media event, collective ritual and nationalist rally,

---

[2] Netherlands, Italy, France, Switzerland, Germany, Belgium and Luxembourg.

in which music itself has been largely relegated to the role of a pretext upon which to base the competition.

Dayan and Katz (1992) identify media events as a significant genre of television broadcasting with intrinsic repercussions on the formation and articulation of group/national identities—the major step beyond Benedict Anderson's emphasis on the printed press and its fundamental influence in the creation of 'imagined communities' (1983). The ESC effectively signifies the mobilization of a very large pan-European audience around a localized live event. The contest gathers audiences that are "geographically and socially heterogeneous but who engage in the same activity; [it] conjures up a collective identity, socializes each viewer's singular experience by linking it to that of all other viewers, and creates affective links between them" (Le Guern 2000). The ESC makes it possible for each viewer to belong to a larger community: a pan-European one, "designed to bring together large chunks of national audiences" (idem). Within the framework by Dayan and Katz, the ESC is easily identified as *an interruption of routine*, happening only once a year. Yet at the same time it presents a routine of its own, by which European viewers can expect and count on it to take place invariably every year, invariably in May, invariably on a Saturday evening. It is organized *live* and by a *public body* and is *preplanned, announced and advertised in advance*.

Ultimately, the ESC is a contest-type media event insofar as it frames, miniaturizes and humanizes collective conflict. It is, however, also a European media *ritual*. Couldry (2003) works through Dayan and Katz's framework to emphasize the parallel processes of social representation and social transformation located at a "media center." As we shall see, these parallel processes are truly manifest in the ESC— a ritualistic adherence to that mediated pan-European transformative construct that the ESC actively promotes, operating in conjunction with the nationalistic outbursts inherent in the nature of an event based on contest and competition of songs that actually represent nations. In practical terms, this translates into a procedural framework that reinforces peace, harmony and togetherness, through a carefully calibrated allocation of equal screen-time and voting rights, a structure of common pan-European identity signifiers and the by now familiar cultural and geographical balancing act that constitutes the blueprint for the meta-narrative of a "Europe of the Nations"—the ESC as transformative media ritual.

Under this procedural framework lurks, naturally, something a lot messier; the articulation of *several* Europes coming into conflict. The mere open and mediated manifestation of these various regional cultural spheres (including Northern, Francophone, Balkan, Post-Soviet, Latin regions) that has emerged with vigor in the last decade—thanks to the extensive inclusion of former Communist nations and especially to the introduction of televoting—has begun to expose the institutional *one Europe* as somewhat fictional at best, farcical at worst. This is the main thesis of this chapter; that in the ESC we find the negotiation, and reconciliation, of collective identity expressed in three distinct and overlapping levels: an institutionally promoted, transformative, pan-European one; a manifested and mediated national one; and the unwelcome by-product of the combination of the two in the form of regional collusions.

The ESC and Pan-European Identity: Camelot Revisited

The ESC has presented throughout the years its own form of European public sphere: from its initial core continental group of seven participants, to the inclusion of Israel and Turkey, the welcoming of communist Yugoslavia in the 1960s, the opening up to post-communist Europe in the early 1990s and the current further expansion to the East. It has both reflected and preceded EU expansion, and has been used by nations as a vehicle to "speak" and present themselves to Europe as rightful members of it. Eurovision is, in many respects, pan-Europeanism *par excellence*. Its corporate signifiers, language use, inclusiveness, procedure and ritual make it the mediated, kitsch epitome of the ancient myth of *Camelot*. It is a realm that—like pan-European narrative—"located nowhere in particular, can be anywhere" (Lacy 1986), a roundtable with no head, no leader, and no privileged position. For instance, the early inclusion of Yugoslavia in the ESC in 1961, over thirty years ahead of the rest of Central and Eastern Europe, represented the symbolic granting and accepting of a place at the European (rather the "Eastern block") table, both by the broader European collective and by Yugoslavia itself.

The corporate signifiers of the ESC are designed to reinforce the concept of a common European image not ascribed to any one individual country. The contest's anthem, played in the opening credits of every ESC, is an instantly recognizable (and in true Eurovision fashion, rather "catchy") tune of an early European Christian origin: Marc-Antoine Charpentier's *Prelude to Te Deum*, composed in 1642. Due to its incorporation within the framework of the ESC, the anthem itself was recognized as having attained "iconic status" amongst the European public and became a strong contender for the status of official European anthem (Clark, 1997, 795). This "iconic status" is granted by the fact that a pan-European audience recognizes and reacts to it regardless of national identity or affiliation.

The Eurovision logo, on the other hand, has not remained constant over decades and its collective symbolism is therefore only beginning to take hold. Initially, the design that appeared during the broadcast mirrored what is now the European Union flag (golden stars over navy blue background), but in a clear move to disassociate the two with the incorporation of a substantial (and growing) number of non-EU participants, a new common official logo (a hollow heart, incidentally, to be filled with the colors of the pertinent country's flag) was adopted in 2003. This official logo does not allow for the previous variations that depended on the host country, and promotes a continued and uninterrupted visual identity, regardless of national alignment. The ESC thus possesses audible and visual pan-European signifiers that are both recognizable (highly so, in the case of the anthem) and not country-specific.

Language use at the ESC has also formally promoted pan-Europeanism. During the 1960s and 1970s, the entire show was conducted in a cumbersome combination of English, French and occasional German, with individual national broadcasters providing simultaneous commentary in their national language. This practice has been progressively discontinued, much as the European collective has moved away from the public usage of French and German in intra-European relations in favor of the English language. Nowadays, the ESC is conducted entirely in English regardless of the hosting country, with the exception of a strictly bilingual English-French voting procedure, a ritualized reminder of the former symbolic place that French used to occupy in the European public sphere. When giving out their votes, national spokespeople have the formal chance to opt for either of the two languages—in practice, all but France, Belgium and Andorra have embraced English while voting. This residual usage of French remains part of the symbolic and ritualistic value of the ESC and reflects the somewhat awkward, tacit admission that English is now Europe's *lingua franca*—whilst still nominally upholding the formal value of other European languages.

Similarly, performance languages are significant in terms of highlighting the pan-European construction in the ESC. The contest rules state the principle of "freedom of language," which poses no formal restrictions on the language of the national entries. Singing in English has now become the norm among contestants from across the board (with notable exceptions such as France, Israel or Spain, which have consistently stuck to their national languages—albeit adding English elements in their entries of late). Whatever the underlying reasons for this trend—Anglo-American domination of the international pop music market or deliberate appeal to a common linguistic denominator—the result is that, when Europeans tune in together to listen to each other at the ESC, what they hear is by and large a succession of national entries sung in a de facto common language. The emphasis is thus once again laid on communality of culture rather than national—or regional—difference.

Formal equality of procedure and access at the ESC means that, in form, every participant country receives the same status and consideration inherent in an egalitarian pan-European image (Le Guern 2000). Each entry is allocated the same amount of airtime (a maximum of three minutes). Each country is given the same amount of votes to distribute among the entries, regardless of the size of the national population or of the amount of votes registered within a country. Every national flag is displayed in the same size throughout the voting and at the opening and closing of each national performance. Penalties are in place for any national broadcaster that may not broadcast each and every one of the entries in their entirety and without interruptions, and allow their viewers to vote for each and every entry in equal conditions.[3] Here is once again, the reflection of the narrative of Europe as

---

[3] This formal principle of equality was actually applied and led to Lebanon's withdrawal from what was scheduled to be their first Eurovision appearance in 2005, since "according to Lebanese legislation, Tele Liban is not permitted to broadcast the performance of the Israeli participant, thereby breaching the rules of the Eurovision Song Contest "(*The Scotsman* 2005).

Camelot, the one roundtable in which Malta and San Marino count no less and no more than Russia or Britain. As for strictly political readings of this roundtable, the procedural framework ensure that nothing ostentatiously political (that is, divisive) gets through. Overt political statements in songs are banned by the rules of the contest. As a result of this neutrality of the ESC framework, the composition participants has pitched at various times socialist Yugoslavia together with fascist Portugal, included the autocracy of Belarus, awarded victories to Franco's Spain (twice), pre-Orange Revolution Ukraine and, in 2007, Serbia to whom Europe struggles to relate politically.

Clearly, as far as the ESC is concerned, everyone is welcome to the pan-European narrative. To a large extent the illusion holds healthily, even if—as we shall see later—all is not as it seems under the pan-European surface. The tongue-in-cheek *Eurolympics* of music has delivered in its promise to uphold the myth of One Europe, with little diplomatic quirks of the kind that led Spain, which refused to recognize the State of Israel until the mid-1980s to travel to the 1979 contest hosted in Jerusalem and have its officially appointed jury award the maximum score to the host country, sealing Israel's second consecutive win. Or, just as the Iron Curtain began crumbling in earnest in 1990, choosing as its winner an Italian anthem compelling Europe to "unite" under "a single flag." However, the Zagreb contest of 1990 may have gotten at least part of the *Zeitgeist* terribly wrong; its hostess Helga Vlahović announced for all Europe to hear that "Yugoslavia is very much like an orchestra [...] the string section and the wood section all sit next to each other" (Steyn 2005). But while barely a year later this Yugo-orchestra myth would self-combust for good in real war, the broader European one that does away with borders and walls would begin indeed to forge itself with full force.

All these ritualized procedures, repeated over five continuous decades, is bound to have practical implications on the way that Europe views itself as a collective through the television screen, once every year. The opening up of the contest to the non-traditionally European states of Israel (in 1974) and Turkey (in 1975) entailed that for more than twenty years European viewers in their millions would see, listen to, and compete with both nations in a markedly Euro-centric setting. Viewers are annually faced with two cognitive options: either to acknowledge both states as legitimate European actors, that is, as full members of the round table; or to acknowledge them as distinctly non-European, and therefore understanding their place as illegitimate. The fact that Israel has won the contest thee times (1978, 1979, 1998) and Turkey once (2003) strongly suggests that the general viewers' conceptualization of what legitimately constitutes "Europe" has expanded over time to include the two states, to the extent that Europeans are willing to invest on SMS and phone voting for Israeli and Turkish competitors over other "traditional" European entries in order to grant them victory, and that they consider Jerusalem and Istanbul legitimate hosts for Europe in its entirety when they organize the event the following year.

The incorporation of Turkey and Israel in a common European cultural sphere, implicitly acknowledged with the countries' participation in Eurovision throughout two decades, has been made explicit with their public vote-based victories in 1998 and 2003. What this implies about the ontology of a common European cultural sphere is controversial; the key question is whether Turkey and Israel simply belong, or are *made to* belong. When 69 percent of Israelis now wish to join the European Union (Hansell 2009) and some in the European and Israeli political elites are beginning to show explicit support for the idea (Jerusalem Post, 2008), the question is bound to be asked louder than ever in the near future. It would appear, however, that through the ESC the European public has already given its answer—by phone.

What Will the Neighbors Think? Performing the Nation at Eurovision

Having dealt with the ways in which the ESC has been providing a vehicle through which Europe as a whole views itself, we now turn to the second layer of collective identity articulation that underpins the competition. It must be born in mind that, whilst formally the ESC remains a contest between national public broadcasters represented by a song, in practice it is a competition between *nations*. The on-screen presence of respective national broadcasters' corporate identities is practically null, relegated to the appearance of broadcasters' *idents* when it is time for each country to award its votes. Entries are represented by the visual signifiers of their national flag at the beginning and end of their performance. The international audience present at the venue during the live broadcast waves energetically a sea of national flags. The votes are announced and allocated to countries, not broadcasters or performers (that is, it is the United Kingdom, not the BBC, who is awarded the votes). It is first and foremost a battle of nations.

The ESC has been successful in epitomizing the audiovisual side of *One Europe*, and therefore it should not be surprising that the contest is an arena for nations to establish a dialogue *vis a vis* Europe in terms of their position within it. A country's Eurovision victory comes only every so often—and when it does, Estonia has shown that cost is no object. After becoming the first post-socialist country to win the ESC in 2001, the Estonian government plowed its entire annual tourism budget (26 million US dollars) into hosting the following year's contest in Tallinn (BBC 2004). Clearly, the Estonians thought it was money well spent: "Eurovision is a really big event. The fact that so many people around the world are looking will be very good publicity for Estonia. This is an opportunity to show that we really are a European country," a local person was quoted in the British press (Guha 2002).

Europe is watching, for once it is watching *us*, and there is no desire to disappoint. Empirical examples of this abound; an examination of the contests held in Tallinn in 2002, Riga in 2003, Istanbul in 2004 or Kiev in 2005 show clear uses of broadcast time to promote a thoroughly modern, "European" vision of the hosting nation, with mini-video insertions of modern infrastructure, industry, IT technology and the like in between songs—essentially playing down national idiosyncrasy and highlighting an adherence to a streamlined, modern common European image.

At Eurovision, the nation does not simply talk to Europe—it also talks to *itself*. By framing its own selection of a representative in terms of 'Europe is watching', national dialogue is often established. The topic of conversation is *prima facie* 'what will Europe see when they watch us'; almost automatically follows the real question lurking in the background: 'what are we that we can show'. The Estonian case mentioned above provides an interesting example of this dialogue. Engaged in a specific quest to redefine itself as a Nordic European – rather than post-Soviet- entity (Bruggemann, 2003), in 2002 Estonia selected a Swedish singer with a song in the English language as their entrant in Tallinn. Europe was indeed watching, and what the country chose to show was its new Scandinavian face. Regardless of whether the national broadcaster selects their ESC entry through an open national final with a public vote or through internal appointment, the selection and presentation of national ESC entries has been and continues to be a political issue.

As English becomes the default language of the competition, the mere choice of performing in one's national language also becomes an issue of collective representation. Hence, when in 2006 the notoriously bilingual Norwegian public shunned the entire English-language, middle-of-the-road list of pop songs bidding to be the national entry in favor of the only song performed in Norwegian (a folk-tinted ballad with ethnic musical elements), the public was in fact making a political and cultural choice upon its own outward representation. This was most remarkable as the Norwegian domestic music market is dominated by English-language productions.

This tradition of national self-expression goes well back in time. More often it takes the form of what the nation chooses *not* to appear to be. For instance, in 1968 Franco's public broadcaster chose as its representative a singer-songwriter who, at the eleventh hour, demanded to sing the entry in the minority Catalan language. Francoism, of course, treated Spain as a cultural and linguistic monolith—a political myth that has since largely been discredited. So the government swiftly removed the singer from the competition, replacing him with a last-minute substitute, a female singer from Madrid who towed the official line, sang the song in Spanish and offered the Franco regime somewhat of a diplomatic coup by winning the contest in London. The Catalan language would finally appear in Eurovision when Andorra joined the contest in the 2000s. As far as the ESC is concerned, Spain continues to present its image of monolinguism to date.

Not that this is by any means an isolated incident, a historical anachronism expected of insecure autocracies thirsty for legitimacy. Consider the following recent examples. The Israeli Broadcasting Authority (IBA) selected a Tel Aviv pop group as the national entry to the ESC in 2000, whose song's Hebrew lyrics versed about a bored Kibbutzim Israeli woman who is having a "torrid affair with a Damascus man" (Goldenberg, 2000). The selection turned into a national scandal in the week before the contest, when it became apparent during the dress rehearsals that the group intended to wave Syrian flags during their live performance. Public protests in Israel forced the IBA to contemplate pulling out from that year's ESC, which according to the Eurovision rules would have entailed a financial penalty and possible suspension from participating in future events. As the scandal gathered momentum, the band's manager offered: "The song is about love and peace so we thought it would be a good idea to use Syrian and Israeli flags, because we would like to have peace with Arab countries [...] We represent a new kind of Israeli who wants to be normal and have peace. We want to have fun and not go to war, but the right wing is not happy about that message" (Goldenberg, 2000).

Eventually, the IBA effectively "disowned" the band by allowing it to participate but at their own financial expense, including their lodging in Stockholm, where the contest was being held. The chairman of the IBA publicly stated: "They will compete there, but not on behalf of the IBA or the Israeli people [...] they are representing only themselves" (Goldenberg, 2000). Much as it had two years earlier (in 1998), with the selection and ultimate ESC victory of transgender singer Dana International, Israel engaged in an intense public debate about its national identity and the image it would allow itself to export to the rest of Europe. Whilst the debate in 1998 focused on secularism versus Jewish orthodoxy and morality (Walzer, 2000), on this occasion the controversy voiced was around the perceived affront to the integrity of the nation through the embracing of the flag of an "enemy" country. While the Israeli nation could collectively come to terms with being represented by a transgender singer, the issue of the nation's place within the Arab world and the pervasive narrative of national security proved to be too controversial to be agreed upon.

The case of Serbia and Montenegro in 2006 resulted from the country's withdrawal from that year's ESC. The selection of the national entry took place in a joint live TV event organized by the Serbian and Montenegrin public broadcasters, a contest with an equal number of Serbian and Montenegrin performers and judges—all this with the backdrop of the upcoming referendum on Montenegrin separation from Serbia scheduled for the day after the ESC. When the Montenegrin judges refused to award any votes to any of the Serbian performers, effectively granting victory for a Montenegrin band, the audience in the Belgrade hall began "booing and throwing bottles at the stage" (BBC 2006). The Serbian national broadcaster subsequently refused to accept the result of the national selection. The ensuing scandal across the Federation prompted former Serbian Prime Minister Zoran Živković to state that the commotion had caused "much more excitement last night than the death of Slobodan Milosevic." According to the BBC, "several Montenegrin newspapers [said] the row shows that the federation with Serbia not only fails to work politically or economically, but cannot even function musically"—a view that transcended the boundaries of the national media sphere through the international repercussion of the ESC. Unable to find consensus in a political environment marred by discursive struggles over national identity, Serbia and Montenegro withdrew their participation on the 2006 contest. A day after the European final, Montenegro voted itself out of its federation with Serbia.

Generally speaking, these internal national squabbles do not make it onto the big *One Europe* narrative that constitutes the main ESC Saturday-night broadcast. By then, Europe is presented with the final choice that the nation has made over its 3-minute long representation (or in the case of Serbia and Montenegro in 2006, with nothing at all), and musical bickering is by and large forgotten. Countries may take occasional jabs at each other—in 1982, the year of the Falklands War and Britain's turn to host the contest, Spain abandoned all pretense of political subtlety and sent a tango as its representative. But overall, the event is conducted with remarkable harmony and a sense of togetherness, the musical extension of a happy Europe of the Nations, countries following each other on stage amidst the interventions of the manically smiling host and hostess. At least until the voting begins, and the myth of *One Europe* dissipates in acrimony.

The Europe of the *Europes*: Cultural Regions, Minorities and Voting Blocks

We have already seen how the ESC is an entertainment ritual that reflects and upholds the myth of the European *Camelot* and its round table for all. We have already hinted at the precariousness of this cognitive balancing act in which *One Europe* relies on two tiers of collective identity: national and pan-European. There is little room for anything else—after all, the European project is ultimately the palliative to the horrors that follow when different Europes are allowed to emerge. Ideally, European nations are expected to behave as blindly to geography and culture as the meta-narrative of Europe does. History shows, the narrative says, that a Europe of the Blocs needs to be avoided. That is why when Europe votes, it prefers consensus over majority; and it ultimately pursues audiovisual means to underpin itself, those "unhappy engineers of the European soul," (Bourdon 2007), by virtue of their malleability and geographical reach. The narrative tends to work, as long as it remains in the hands of elite-driven processes. But when given the chance to express it, the people of Europe speak with discordant voices and in favor of what appears to be not one Europe, but several.

A telling anecdote dating back to 1963 serves as an illustration of things to come. That year, during the live broadcast, the Norwegian national jury was asked by the hostess to repeat their casting of votes at the end of the voting round. She seemed not to have heard them well enough, although the available recordings of the contest registered them clearly. Initially, Norway had awarded several points to the Swiss entry, which had gone to win the overall European vote by the end of the tallying. However, after all the countries had cast their votes and Norway was requested to "reconfirm" their choices, and once it was clear that Switzerland had indeed won, the Norwegian jury changed their vote—awarding a lower score than their previous one to Switzerland and a higher one to their neighbor and runner-up Denmark, just enough points to crown Denmark the winner (Kennedy O'Connor, 2005). Apart from the obvious sign of appalling gamesmanship at play there, this is an impressive show of the supranational understandings of Europe in operation; in essence, a country cheating on live television in order to ensure that a neighbor wins.

Forty-odd years on, things have not fundamentally changed. The growing body of academic quantitative analyses of ESC voting patterns—what Gatherer (2006) labels *eurovisiopsephology*, unequivocally shows that, particularly since the mid-1990s, the pan-European voting occurs along the lines of large geo-political blocs that are now capable of influencing the overall outcome of the contest. These regional collusions or voting blocs are not new—as the 1963 anecdote above shows, national juries have long been partial to voting for their neighboring countries—but they have certainly been exacerbated once voting was placed in the hands of the public. Using Gatherer's 2006 study as the most comprehensive and updated, the current blocs stand as follows. There is a "Balkan Bloc'" comprising the six former Yugoslav republics (soon to be joined by Kosovo), plus Turkey, Greece, Cyprus and Romania; what Gatherer labels the "Viking Empire" of the Scandinavian countries plus Finland, Iceland, Estonia, Latvia and Lithuania; the "Pyrenean Axis" of Spain, Andorra and Portugal; and the "Warsaw Pact" countries covered by a common East and Central European cultural sphere.

But if we are talking about different and overlapping cultural spheres, why should this surprise anyone—let alone be considered as something intrinsically negative? Why should it come as a surprise that regions with well-developed political, historical and cultural ties, as well as often mutually understandable national languages, would find their national entries mutually appealing? See for example the case of Serbia and Montenegro in 2004, which joined the contest for the first time (after the breakdown of Yugoslavia) with a sentimental ballad with Balkan folk influences. The song received the maximum scores from the public votes of Croatia, Slovenia and Bosnia-Herzegovina, and the second highest score from the Macedonian vote (whose maximum core went, significantly, to Albania, in clear ethnic alignments). Thanks to this support, Serbia and Montenegro went on to win the contest's semifinal and came second three days later in the final in Kiev. What is most interesting is the fact that Croatians, Bosnians, Slovenes and Macedonians granted unequivocal support to the representative of Serbia in spite of the highly strained political relations and recent history of violence still fresh in the collective memory of ex-Yugoslavians as a whole. They did so out of regional cultural affinities, rallying around a song that stroke an essentially Balkan emotional chord.

Another significant factor highlighted by an analysis of voting patterns is the large amount of public votes awarded by countries with large European immigrant populations to their 'home' nations, i.e., Germany to Turkey, UK to Ireland, Spain to Romania, Scandinavia and Switzerland to the Balkan countries, France to Portugal, etc. Since the establishment of public voting in the mid 1990s, it has become clear that immigrant or national minority populations strongly align themselves with their perceived "homeland." This explains, for instance, that in 2005 the Albanian entry received maximum or near-maximum scores from Macedonia, Greece, Switzerland and Serbia and Montenegro, while being largely ignored by the rest of participants. In other words, when it comes to Eurovision it appears that ethnic Albanians, Turks, Portuguese abroad as well as ethnic Swedes in Finland, or Hungarians in Romania, etc.) vote not as "Europeans" or citizens of their host country, but as ethnic Albanians, Turks, and so on. Combined with the regional collusion voting, this "homeland" voting trend becomes a further expression of the current state of European collective identity: an abstract concept whose existence is flanked by alternative national, regional, and ethnic minority articulations. This is not a suggestion that regional or "homeland" voting patterns are a necessary contradiction with the articulation of a shared European identity. In fact, it can be argued that these trends are constantly negotiated and fluid components of said identity, under which umbrella there is much room for apparent contradiction and multiple identity links. Balkan collusion is one example of this multiplicity of collective identities at play: nationalist representation combines with *Jugonostalgija*, in an accepted pan-European framework.

Once again, if these trends are understandable, where lies the problem, if indeed there is one? The answer relates to the degree to which the ESC has come to be identified as *One Europe* by proxy in the collective European mind.

The Dutch ESC entry of 2005 fared very poorly with the European public vote. The national mass media gave front-page coverage to the failure, alleging the collusion of Central and Eastern European voters as a reason for the poor performance. Three immediate opinion polls reported a "huge advance" of the "no" vote to the European Constitution referendum to be held a week after the contest. *The Times* of London reported: "the country's top pollster found that 71 percent of people think that the fact that substantially more Central and Eastern European than Western European countries have reached the final of Eurovision is an example of how the power within the EU has shifted to the East" (Browne 2003). The Dutch prime minister was reportedly "shocked": "It's the world upside-down that [the Dutch entrant] is being connected to the referendum" (Bakker 2005). As is well known, the European Constitution was subsequently rejected by Dutch voters. This is by no means a suggestion that the ESC was the sole, or even the main, determinant in explaining the Dutch popular decision to refuse the European Constitution. But it serves as an illustration of just how much the ESC has become an arena for European conflict, where the Dutch nation saw its place in Europe reflected as a smack actor losing its political clout to the emerging Central and Eastern European bloc. *The Times* expressed it succinctly: "established half a century ago to bring the people of Europe together through music, the Eurovision Song Contest now seems to blow the European project apart" (Browne 2005).

The ESC may not be the place where musical credibility is at stake, but national and European credibility seem to matter a great deal. Regional collusion shatters the illusion of *One Europe* that the ESC has strove to promote. It has now become somewhat of a tradition that the international audience present at the ESC venue during the broadcast will show their discontent by loudly booing when the inevitable exchange of maximum scores between Greece and Cyprus comes. National commentators such as those in Spain and the United Kingdom routinely express their exasperation with regional voting during their live commentaries, as do subsequent reports in the national mass media which reinforce the victimization identity of "Europe doesn't like us" (see *Eurovision votes "farce" attack,* BBC Online May 16th 2004 for an extensive example (BBC 2004)).

For the ESC as a European ritual, this sort of regional divisiveness has become nothing short of a headache. In 2008, the Austrian public broadcaster ORF announced its decision to withdraw from the contest altogether, citing precisely the kind of geopolitical competition that goes unbridled every year. The ORF's programming director was candid in his analysis of the reasons for the withdrawal: "The Song Contest is clearly a sign of the complicated nature of a united Europe. We've already seen in 2007 that it's not the quality of the song, but the country of origin that determines the decision," he said. "As long as the Song Contest is a political parade ground and not an international entertainment program, ORF has no desire to send more talent out of Austria to a competition where they have no chances" (Holyer 2007). Austria, of course, does not lack neighboring countries in geographic terms—what it lacks is a cultural bloc to back it up with consistent amounts of votes.

Since the 2008 contest that took place in Belgrade, the EBU found a Solomonic solution to the challenge of regionalism. It has divided all the participating countries in two different semi-finals, splitting the "guilty parties" among the two qualifying rounds. This ensures that the pan-European spirit would prevail at least up to the point of selecting which countries will take part in the final. Once there, however, countries did not refrain from overwhelmingly voting along geographic and cultural lines. A more optimal solution appears to have been found with the introduction in 2009 of professional voting juries, taking up 50 percent of the voting in every country. These voting "elites," selected from the music and entertainment industry of the participant countries, appear to have moderated the regional and diaspora voting patterns of the public televote, and have given consecutive victories to Norway and Germany, previous regulars from the bottom of the scorecard.

Conclusion

As it became evident during the research for this paper, an exhaustive analysis of the articulation of collective identity in the Eurovision Song Contest can—and perhaps should—occupy its own volume. This chapter has attempted to outline the fourfold process of collective identity at play in the ESC: pan-European, national, regional and ethnic minority. Even within this chapter's limits, the argument has been made: well beyond its musical content, the ESC is a rich and complex arena for the interplay of collective representation, and it will continue to be so for as long as it remains as popular with viewers as it has become over the past five decades.

In 2010, the show celebrated its 55th hosting, this time in the city of Oslo, Norway. Once again, hundreds of millions of Europeans have staged their public dialogue about their national representation through their local selections, and engaged in interactive viewing and voting, exercising their national, minority, regional and continental identities through it. There are inherent contradictions at play, but then such contradictions are the material of which Europe is made. The Eurovision Song Contest makes for infectious viewing and compulsive political analysis, national pride and—often—embarrassment and "banal" international confrontation. Despite its own identity problems (or perhaps exactly because of them), it remains an intrinsically European classic.

REFERENCE LIST

Bakker, Sietse (2005) *No to Glennis, No to the European Constitution.* On ES-CToday.com, May 25th 2005. Accessible at http://www.esctoday.com/news/read/4608.

BBC (2004) *Eurovision votes 'farce' attack,* BBC Online, May 16th 2004. Accessible at: http://news.bbc.co.uk/2/hi/uk_news/wales/south_east/3719157.stm.

BBC (2006) *Serbia-Montenegro in pop song row.* BBC News Europe, March 14th 2006. Accessible at: http://news.bbc.co.uk/2/hi/europe/4805014.stm.

Bondebjerg, I., and Golding, P. (2006) *European Culture and the Media.* Portland, Ore.: Intellect Books.

Bourdon, Jerome (2007) "Unhappy Engineers of the European Soul–the EBU and the Woes of Pan-European Television." *International Communication Gazette,* Vol. 69, No. 3: 263–280.

Browne, Anthony (2005) *How song contest defeat clouds Dutch euro-vision.* The Times, May 24th 2005. Accessible at http://www.timesonline.co.uk/article/0,,13509-1625029,00.html.

Bruggemann, Karsten (2003) "Leaving the 'Baltic' States and 'Welcome to Estonia': Re-regionalising Estonian Identity." *European Review of History,* Vol. 10, No. 2: 343–360.

Christian, Nicholas (2005) *Null Points as Lebanon Quits Contest.* The Scotsman, March 20th 2005. Accessible at: http://news.scotsman.com/topics.cfm?tid=853&id=299182005.

Clark, Caryl (1997) "Forging identity, Beethoven's 'Ode' as European Anthem." *Critical Inquiry,* Vol. 23, No. 4 (Summer, 1997): 789–807.

Couldry, Nick (2003) *Media Rituals: a Critical Approach.* London: Routledge.

Dayan, Daniel, and Katz, Elihu (1992) *Media Events: the Live Broadcasting of History.* Cambridge: Harvard University Press.

Fenn, Daniel Suleman Omer et al. (2006) *How does Europe make its mind up ? Connections, cliques and compatibility between countries in the Eurovision Song Contest.* Physica A, Oxford University. Accessible at: http://arxiv.org/PS_cache/physics/pdf/0505/0505071.pdf.

Gatherer, Derek (2006) "Comparison of Eurovision Song Contest Simulation with Actual Results Reveals Shifting Patterns of Collusive Voting Alliances." *Journal of Artificial Societies and Social Simulation.* Vol. 9, No. 2.

Goldenberg, Suzanne, (2000) *Outraged Israel Disowns Daring Eurovision Entry.* The Guardian, May 12th, 2000. Accessible at: http://www.guardian.co.uk/international/story/0,3604,219846,00.html.

Hansel, Lars (2009) *Survey regarding the Israeli attitude to the EU and its member states.* Accessible at: http://www.kas.de/proj/home/pub/24/2/dokument_id-16236/index.html.

Holyer, Steve (2007) *Austria Will Not Go to Belgrade.* On EscToday.com, November 20th, 2007. Accessible at: http://www.esctoday.com/news/read/9678.

Kennedy O'Connor, John (2006) *Eurovision Song Contest: The Official Story*; London, Carlton Books.

Landay, J.M. (1993) "Review." *Film Quarterly*, Vol. 46, No. 4 (Summer, 1993): 45–46.

Le Guern, Philippe (2000) "From National Pride to Global Kitsch: the Eurovision Song Contest." *Web Journal of French Media Studies*, Vol. 3, No. 1 (October 2000).

Philips, Roel (2005) *Interview with NOX.* On EscToday.com, April 5th 2005. Accessible at: http://www.esctoday.com/news/read/4165.

Steyn, Mark (2005) Eurovision harmony dies a death. *The Telegraph*, May 24th, 2005.

Tilden, Imogen (2003) *The Eurovision Song Contest.* The Guardian, May 23, 2003. Accessible at: http://arts.guardian.co.uk/features/story/0962463,00.html.

Walzer, Lee (2000) *Between Sodom and Eden: a gay journey through today's changing Israel.* New York: Columbia University Press.

Section 3

EUROPEAN MEDIA POLICY: BOON OR BARRIER TO EUROPEAN INTEGRATION?

CHAPTER 10

European Melting Pots?

European Integration and EU Audiovisual Policy at a Crossroads

KAROL JAKUBOWICZ

Introduction

The European Union and its previous incarnations have always faced a major dilemma of how to provide a more stable and deeply-rooted foundation first for economic, and later, for political integration. The fundamental question at the heart of the European Project has always been: can this top-down, elite-led process make further progress and gain stronger legitimacy without the added impetus of greater unity also in the sphere of social consciousness and culture, which would help make it more of a bottom-up project?

The European Community was, of course, created as "an explicit repudiation of ethnic nationalism—and as a case of possible *exit* from Europe's national past" (Fossum, 2007: 7). However, up until the Maastricht Treaty, the European Community and the nations forming it developed in parallel. According, at least, to one view, things changed radically after the signing of the treaty: "From that moment on the operational assumption was that Europe's progress must mean the weakening of states and the denationalization of their nations" (Manet, 2006). The ideology of governance embedded in the treaty sought to combine strong centralization with possibly equally strong decentralization. The idea was to strengthen the regions and supranational Europe at the expense of the nation-state (Eriksen, 1997).

Indeed, "national identity—that is, identity at the member-state level—has been officially frowned upon since the beginning of the European project" (Fukuyama, 2006a: 13). The Maastricht Treaty appears to have been a product of such an approach.

It is represented, no doubt in a simplified way, in the following matrix of relationships between "European identity" and national identities that seems to have constituted the hidden agenda of the EU approach to the issue for a long time:

Table 1. Matrix of relationships between "European" and national identities (the Maastricht Treaty view)

		"European" identity	
		Strong	**Weak**
	Strong	"Mission impossible"	Low integration capacity
National identity			
	Weak	High integration capacity	Possible disintegration of nation-states and EU

This, we believe and will argue below, has in reality been counterproductive in terms of promoting integration at the EU level.

"European integration" has long been defined as simply the creation and development of European institutions (Mazey, 2001). Different theoretical roots of European integration theory can be found inter alia in federalism, transactionalism, functionalism, neo-functionalism and a state-centered approach, but again this has mainly concerned systems of governance and the political, legal and technical dimensions of integration (Cram, 2001). Of course, yet another approach has been economic, with the focus on creating the Single Market. For a long time, values, belief systems, socio-psychological aspects of community formation, identities (as reflected in the social constructivist approach, claiming that ideas and identities are important in the construction of the EU) did crop up occasionally, but rarely came to the fore in the debate (Cram, 2001). "Civic identity" and post-national "constitutional patriotism" have been posited as a replacement for a culturally-rooted European identity.

Today, there is a new sense of urgency in approaching the issue of "European" and national identity and of European integration. According to Dilsay (2007), "As the European Union becomes more effective, a European identity is now tangible." At the same time, we are seeing shifts in the continent's demographic and geopolitical structures. Already the eastward enlargement of the EU (already completed and planned for the future) is producing a shift in cultural self-understanding. The EU today is "no longer a western enclave centered around the core founding states ... a Europe based on the western heritage of Latin Christendom, the Enlightenment, democracy, and the free-market economy" (Delanty, 2007). The result is a change in the identity of Europe in the direction of a multiple constellation of regions (Western Europe, Central Eastern Europe, Southeastern Europe) with, as Delanty puts it, "different civilizational heritages," though with many common strands. Further upheavals result from intra-European migrations and the influx of immigrants from Africa and Asia, as well as from globalization and the "clash of civilizations," or rather the perceived clash of value systems between Europe and Muslim extremists, resulting in the "war on terror."

All this no doubt adds to this sense of urgency. Rapid and large-scale change usually undermines a sense of individual and national psycho-social and cultural security. As a result, the issue of identity has re-emerged as a subject and focus of debate and policy, at both the EU and national levels.

On the one hand, this has prompted a change of emphasis in EU policy, as a way is sought to promote a greater sense of European unity and greater identification with European values. On the other hand, we are seeing a change of immigration and integration policies at the national level, with "multiculturalism" (where it existed) being replaced by a more determined effort to integrate immigrants into the culture and values of the host country. Yet another European response to this process has been a wave of populism (Krastev, 2006), the electoral success of right-wing parties in many countries, the hardening of attitudes on migration, the politicization of the issue and as a result the imposition of harsh immigration regimes (Statham, Gray, 2005; Inotai, 2007).

Jean Monnet is purported to have said "If we were beginning the European Community all over again, we should begin with culture." According to some sources, however, "Jean Monnet's relatives and collaborators have often protested against the dissemination of this wholly fictitious story about him" (Łukaszewski, 2002: 90). Whether or not he actually said it, Monnet must have known that any focus on culture at the beginning of the European Project would have doomed it to failure: things would never have gone beyond the first meeting.[1]

---

[1] A similar view, expressed by Krzysztof Pomian, a Polish historian living in France, testifies to this: "[European] integration was the work of politicians

Today, we seem almost to have come full circle. In 2002, Romano Prodi, then President of the European Commission, asked the Institute for Human Sciences in Vienna to set up a Spiritual and Cultural Dimension of Europe Reflection Group to assess those values that are particularly relevant to the continuing process of European unification. In its conclusions, published in 2004, the group stated:

> So where are the forces of cohesion for the new political Union to be found if the common interests produced by economic integration are no longer sufficient? We believe that the older forces that animated European unification are no longer sufficiently powerful to provide genuine political cohesion, and that, therefore, *new sources of energy must be looked for and found in Europe's common culture* (Biedenkopf, Geremek, Michalski, 2004: 8. Emphasis added - KJ).

Also in 2004, the Berlin Conference "A Soul for Europe" was held. There, José Manuel Barroso, President of the European Commission, said: "The EU has reached a stage of its history where its cultural dimension can no longer be ignored." During the 2006 Berlin Conference on the same subject, he reaffirmed that view:

> Some people tell me that a President of the European Commission should not speak about culture, an area where the main competence remains at the national and regional level [but] I find it impossible not to talk about something so central to Europe as culture and its meaning for us ... Europe needs culture since culture, without any doubt, contributes to its well-being, its greater welfare and its social cohesion. But, beyond that, Europe needs culture in order to proclaim, at this time of instability, that our values are not negotiable ... culture plays a key role in the "European pact." Culture is the place where

---

representing very different political orientations: socialists, social-democrats, Christian Democrats and liberals. There was no common political or intellectual ground between them, and everyone knew that ... The art of European diplomacy required that that they look for areas of agreement, despite full awareness of the differences between them ... if Spaak [a Belgian socialist] engaged in an ideological debate with Christian Democrats, it would have dragged on until today and the Union would never have been created" (Żakowski: 2006: 4).

creativity most fully expresses itself, and it is a force for innovation and initiative. It is also a vehicle for social integration and hence for social cohesion. Lastly, culture promotes a sense of belonging while paving the way for a plurality of identities ... I do not see anything taboo in the idea that the cultural economy can also contribute to European integration (Barroso, 2006: *passim*).

That, as we show below, has led to a whole program of activities serving to use culture to promote European integration.

This line of thinking is also gaining momentum at the national level, as reflected in the "public philosophies of integration" (Bauböck, 2006). Many countries have changed old citizenship laws based on *ius sanguinis* to those based on *ius solis*, thus potentially opening the door to citizenship for second-generation immigrants. However, they have also introduced linguistic and cultural requirements for citizenship, with a view of drawing the immigrants and minorities into the mainstream.

Our main concern here is the European Union's audiovisual policy. One of its goals has always been to promote the development of European citizenship and the emergence of a "developing European identity" as a way of enhancing European integration. The original impetus behind its development in the 1980s was in fact the hope that EC-regulated transfrontier television could promote the emergence of a common European culture and identity. For a time, that gave rise to an approach that put "[cultural] unity before diversity" (Collins, 1997; see also Machet, 1999; Kaitatzi-Whitlock, 2006). That, however, was quickly rejected in favor of "diversity over unity."

And what is the situation today, following the adoption of the Audiovisual Media Services Directive (AVMSD)? Below, we will look at what this new approach to European and national integration means in practice and whether or not it is reflected in the EU's audiovisual policy.

A Holistic EU Integration Policy: A European "Melting Pot"?

Citizenship of the Union was established by the Maastricht Treaty, which inserted Article 17 into the Treaty establishing the European Community. It specifies that citizenship of the Union shall complement and not replace national citizenship.

The European Commission (2004b: 5) recognizes that citizenship at the European level is a "political construct." Indeed, EU citizenship rights really mean no more than the right to vote for the European Parliament, the freedom of movement within the territory of the Member States and the right to diplomatic protection by EU Member States. In this context, let us not overlook Hoffmann's (2006) view that if European citizenship is not to remain a hollow concept, then what is needed is a rights-based approach to EU citizenship, especially concentrating on communication rights whose exercise by EU citizens could promote deliberative democracy within the EU and thus help deal with the democratic deficit.

This corresponds in a way to the concept of "European civic identity," meaning an identification with a political structure, the set of institutions, rights and rules that preside over the political life of the European community. European civic identity refers to the rights and duties of EU citizens. The substance of an EU identity here lies in its constituent documents, a commitment to the duties and rights of a civic society covering specific aspects of public life, a commitment to the membership of a polity (Inthorn, 2006).

Put another way, civic identity amounts to what is known as "constitutional patriotism," since "European citizenship" is, as we have seen, to be developed on the basis of an area of freedom, justice, security, fairness, tolerance and solidarity, as well as respect for and promotion of fundamental rights. Drawing on Habermas, Fossum (2007: 1) defines "constitutional patriotism" as a mode of attachment wherein citizens are bound together by subscription to democratic values and human rights, rather than through the traditional pre-political ties to which nation states appeal. This type of identity, he adds, is conducive to respect for and accommodation of difference and plurality. It is "thin" in that its substantive content is shaped by, and ultimately made subject to, consistence with a set of constitutionally entrenched procedures.

Constitutional patriotism is a mode of attachment that is based on a particular constellation of "exit" from the organization (understood in a communal and/or territorial sense), "voice" (ability to voice opinions and dissent), and "loyalty." Fossum believes that the form of constitutional patriotism suitable for the European Union is what he calls CP II:

Table 2. A concept of constitutional patriotism for the EU (CP II)

Exit	– High "cosmopolitan openness" for persons and arguments – Provisions for sub-unit (i.e. a member state) exit from the polity, in compliance with democratic norms
Voice	– Rights to ensure individual autonomy – Communication aimed at reaching working agreements – Communication to foster trust in procedures and rights – "Negative voice"
Loyalty	– Ambivalence toward any form of positive allegiance – Systemic endorsement through critique

Source: Fossum, 2007: 8.

This version of the European constitutional patriotism would thus resemble the American identity which was always political in nature and was based on five basic values: equality (understood as equality of opportunity rather than outcome), liberty (or anti-statism), individualism (in the sense that individuals could determine their own social station), populism, and laissez-faire.[2] Because these qualities were both political and civic, they were in theory accessible to all Americans—old and new (Fukuyama, 2006a: 12).

Thus, civic identity or "constitutional patriotism" are proposed as direct opposites of the classic ethno-nationalism.

The problem with that, however, has always been that "ethno-nationalism" or ethnic nationalism has retained an enduring power, and that Europe is "post war [i.e., post World War II – KJ], but not postnational" (Muller, 2008). Europe's national identities "continue to hang around like unwanted ghosts. In each Member State, people still have a strong sense of what it means to be French or Dutch or Italian" (Fukuyama, 2006a: 14). Along the same lines, Eriksen (1997: 255) remarks that "National belonging seems to be a basic foundation

---

[2] In this context, it might be interesting to note another, less formal proposal to develop a "European identity," advanced by Garton Ash (2007). He proposes that it should be based on six shared European goals: freedom, peace, law, prosperity, diversity and solidarity. This identity should not, he says, be developed by the negative stereotyping of an enemy or "Other," nor by myth-making about our own collective past (typical of what Garton Ash calls "Euronationalism"—an attempt to replicate nationalist methods of building political identity at the European level).

of subjective identification to many Western Europeans." For his part, Schöpflin (2007) sees a historic shift in the last fifteen-to-twenty years: the growing belief that too much was being settled in Europe that the state was better at doing. Because of this and other reasons, he says, the impulse to identify with Europe has slackened both at the popular and the elite level: "Thus a re-identification with the nation and, as a result, with the nation-state has returned imperceptibly, though obviously with varying intensity—in time and place, as well in form and content."

Also Fukuyama (2006a: 13) notes that in the period following the Second World War, there has been a strong commitment throughout most of Europe to creating the same kind of tolerant and pluralist political identity that characterizes the United States – in line with the "post-national" ideal promoted by intellectuals like Jürgen Habermas and embodied in the European project. But despite the progress that has been made in forging a strong European Union, European identity—he says—remains something that comes from the head rather than the heart: "While there is thin layer of mobile, cosmopolitan Europeans, few think of themselves as generic Europeans or swell with pride at the playing of the European anthem."

Accordingly, "European nation-building" has not been very successful. The Maastricht Treaty, says Eriksen (1997: 255) aimed explicitly at molding an ever closer community out of the members. The widespread reaction to this proposal was the insistence that "*we* are going to keep our distinctiveness and our national identity, at any cost!"

That and widespread dissatisfaction with the Maastricht Treaty (leading, for a time, to an erosion of public support for the European project; Eichenberg, Dalton, 2007) has led Brussels to forgo its objectives of centralization and homogenization and to return to the goal of unity in diversity: "cultural diversity sustains European unity" (European Commission, 2004a: 5). And rightly so, because also the defeat of the European Constitution in referenda in France and the Netherlands in 2005 can be interpreted as the refusal of core European publics to give up on the idea of the nation-state and sovereignty.

If civic identity is not a sufficient foundation for European integration, it needs to be bolstered with cultural identity, understood to represent a citizen's sense of belonging to a particular group of shared cultural and social practices, ethics, or even ethnicity. Being a European by this definition means belonging to a common European civilization, to a society with many languages and cultures. The concept is linked to the idea of common ancestry, history and destiny of Europeans and the cultural signifiers of European identity (Inthorn, 2006).[3] The need for that is deep-seated: "culture remains an irreducible component of human societies ... The final aspect of the modernization process concerns the area of culture. Everybody wants economic development, and economic development tends to promote democratic political institutions. But at the end of the modernization process, nobody wants cultural uniformity; in fact, issues of cultural identity come back with a vengeance ... We live for the particular shared historical traditions, religious values, and other aspects of shared memory that constitutes the common life" (Fukuyama, 2006).

That is why, as noted by Inthorn (2006) the prospect of Turkey joining the European Union raises in the coverage of the issue in British and German newspapers concerns as regards the cultural consequences of potential Turkish membership. Islam becomes the seemingly natural marker by which Turkish identity is to be understood. References to cultural difference and cultural consequences of Turkish accession to the EU construct a cultural concept of European identity. In news discourse surrounding Turkey's long journey towards EU membership, the cultural concept of European identity becomes a discursive tool to mark the country as the eternal "other" to Europe. When it comes to Turkish EU membership, the European "self" is to be "guarded" against the Muslim "other."

Efforts to create a "People's Europe," by strengthening its social and cultural cohesion and fostering a new "European identity" began

---

[3] One of many inventories of European characteristics can be found in Trandafoiu (2007: 99–100). According to Trandafoiu, they include the uniqueness of European philosophy in the idea of evolution and the spirit of experimentation; doctrines stemming from ancient Greek and Roman cultures and the Christian religion; democracy, liberal public sphere, rationality, sovereignty, law and administration, Christian love and the European social model based on equality and redistribution; the life and structure of the European family; the dominance of industrial employment; the class system and the social fabric; the welfare state and the mass consumer society; the secularization of the egalitarian and individualist universalism that informs our normative self-understanding.

already in the mid-1980s. In recent years, the EU has been attempting to develop a "European identity" that would be distinctively European (rather than global), yet would not negate national and regional
identities:

> Our shared objective should be a Europe that celebrates the cultural
> and national diversity of each Member State, remains attached to na-
> tional identity, yet is also committed to the value of European identity
> and the political will to achieve common goals (European Commis-
> sion, 2004a: 3).

In 2004, the European Commission proposed that the EU should
adopt as one of its main priorities the goal of "making citizenship
work," through

> [the development of] European citizenship, on the basis of an area
> of freedom, justice, security, and respect for and promotion of fun-
> damental rights, and fostering European culture and diversity. Pro-
> moting European culture and diversity contributes to making Euro-
> pean citizenship a reality through encouraging direct involvement of
> European citizens in the integration process, i.e. Youth, Culture, the
> Audiovisual sector and civic participation (European Commission,
> 2004b: 3).

The Commission gave two main reasons for the need to do this: (i) im-
pending enlargement, with the accession of 10 countries in 2004, and
more to follow; and (ii) demographic trends (an aging and shrinking
working-age population), requiring more sustained immigration flows
to fill the needs of the EU labor market. It therefore saw the need for
what it called a "holistic integration policy" (European Commission,
2004b: 5), serving to incorporate the newcomers (the populations of
new Member States, as well as immigrants), placing emphasis on the
shared civic and political values of EU countries (such as freedom, fairness, tolerance and solidarity), as well as on language skills and the
social and cultural environment encompassing shared cultural values.

The European Commission seems to be hoping for a slow, organic process which over the long term will produce something like a
similar result, i.e., for *"a bottom-up development of a European identity*

through the interaction of its citizens" (European Commission, 2004b: 3; emphasis added). Of course, it is to be shared by all inhabitants of Member States, not just the newcomers. It is to be an identity which complements those—national, regional, ethnic, religious—that citizens already have, and is to emerge out of:

> direct, personal experience of what European citizenship and these values mean in practice - be it through participation in dialogue with the institutions, through citizen and youth exchanges, or participation in cross-border projects. Fostering the mobility of citizens, artists, cultural and audiovisual works and events, gives European citizens the possibility of encountering the common elements in their developing European identity (European Commission, 2004b: 2).

As for cultural identity, to be based on shared European cultural values, the main goal of EU action is to contribute to the flourishing of shared European cultural values on the basis of cultural co-operation between artists, cultural operators and cultural institutions, and to the promotion of multilateral European co-operation. Among the objectives are the transnational mobility of people working in the cultural sector; the transnational circulation of works of art (including immaterial works, such as music); and intercultural dialogue.

EU action is to help overcome the obstacles to cross-border exchanges and structures in the European audiovisual industry and fostering youth exchanges, voluntary service and informal learning as well as language learning and training for language-based professionals.

The intention is to surmount barriers to the circulation of works of art or artists, the setting up of networks of museums, opera houses or other cultural institutions, stemming from fragmentation between Member States, or those to whom the circulation of European films and television programs is concerned, resulting from linguistic, cultural and social specificities.

Referring to the European Community policy for the audiovisual sector in the context of the drive to "make European citizenship work," the European Commission (2004b: 13) explains that in addition to promoting a single market for television broadcasting through the "Television Without Frontiers" Directive, the EU has taken measures to promote the European audiovisual industry: "If an enlarging and ever more diverse Union is to flourish, there must be an interaction between the public opinions of its Member States, and an exchange of knowledge across borders on social and cultural matters needs to emerge." Hence the special challenge of overcoming the obstacles that prevent European audiovisual works from circulating outside their own territories and in overcoming the fragmentation of markets.

In 2006, the European Parliament and the Council adopted Decision No 1904/2006/EC establishing for the period 2007 to 2013 the program "Europe for Citizens" to promote active European citizenship. The preamble includes the following rationale for it: "For citizens to give their full support to European integration, greater emphasis should therefore be placed on their common values, history and culture as key elements of their membership in a society founded on the principles of freedom, democracy and respect for human rights, cultural diversity tolerance and solidarity in accordance with the Charter of Fundamental Rights of the European Union." The objectives of the program are as follows:

1. bringing together people from local communities across Europe to share and exchange experiences, opinions and values, to learn from history and to build for the future;
2. fostering action, debate and reflection related to European citizenship and democratic shared values, common history and culture through cooperation within civil society organizations at the European level;
3. bringing Europe closer to its citizens by promoting Europe's values and achievements, while preserving the memory of its past;
4. encouraging interaction between citizens and civil society organizations from all participating countries, contributing to intercultural dialogue and bringing to the fore both Europe's diversity and unity, with particular attention to activities aimed at developing closer ties between citizens from Member States of the European Union as constituted on 30 April 2004 and those from Member States which have acceded since that date.

In 2007, the European Commission launched a "European agenda for culture" (European Commission, 2007a), seeking to achieve three interrelated sets of objectives:

- promotion of cultural diversity and intercultural dialogue;
- promotion of culture as a catalyst for creativity in the framework of the Lisbon Strategy for growth and jobs;
- promotion of culture as a vital element in the Union's international relations.

The European Commission is also returning, though in a changed form, to its hopes from the early 1980s, when responding to the short-lived 1982 "Eurikon" experiment, it said in 1983 that "The Commission feels that the creation of a European television service... is highly desirable. The development of a truly European spirit will therefore become possible in a national audience, who will, of course, retain their full cultural identity" (cited after Machet, 1993: 6). Today, it is concerned that though the written press provides a "remarkable level" of European facts on debated issues, it is really television that is most people's primary source of information, and there EU-related information provided by national audiovisual media takes up less than 10% of the time allocated to national news (European Commission, 2008). Therefore, it is launching a whole array of activities designed to communicate directly to the citizens of Europe via radio (the Euranet network); television (a European television network); satellite television ("Europe by satellite"); expanding the role of the Commission's audiovisual library and its availability to all interested parties; supporting and funding Euronews and its use of more European languages; increasing the Commission's production of audiovisual content and improvement of its distribution via different technological platforms (European Commission, 2008). A separate program of activities concerns the Internet (European Commission, 2007b).

National Melting Pots?

Issues of national and ethnic identity preoccupy many Western Europeans. One case in point are the English, a nation that is suddenly in search of itself as Britain may be heading towards fragmentation (Scruton, 2007). Meanwhile, the Scots, the Welsh and the Irish in Northern Ireland are going through the same process.

This is certainly true also of new Member States from Central and Eastern Europe undergoing post-Communist transformation. Inotai (2007) regards their attachment to the national interest and nationhood as a form of "mental contamination" resulting from "unprocessed history" and lack of awareness that nationalism leads to war. That, however, misses the point, if we agree with Saul (2005) that there has been a reaffirmation of the nation state where one would least expect it, i.e., in the European Union. Taras Kuzio (2002a, 2002b) has identified two strands of post-Communist transformation: post-authoritarian and post-colonial transition. The latter is evident primarily in post-Soviet countries now struggling to build states and nations, in addition to – hopefully – democracy and market economies. Still, these issues are also crucially important in other post-Communist countries, as they rediscover their identities and seek to find their bearings in the process of international integration. They are certainly very cautious about losing their sovereignty and newly recovered national identity.

They are not alone in this. Also "many Western Europeans mobilize for counter-reactions against attempts at the creation of supranational identifications. Like in Eastern Europe, such proposals are met with loud protests and appeals for 'cultural uniqueness,' 'ancient history,' principles of sovereignty and so on" (Eriksen, 1997: 252). Individuals, groups and societies have a vital interest in preserving their way of life and the traits that are central identity components for them and the other members of their cultural group (Gans, 2007). Culture is important for individuals, firstly, because it facilitates autonomy. Autonomy implies a choice between options; and culture provides these options and imbues them with meaning. The individual's sense of identity is more stable and less open to threat when it does not depend on specific achievements, but is instead based on membership in a particular cultural group. Finally, since people's cultural identity is the basis of their personal identity, their self esteem is dependent upon the degree to which their culture and their cultural group are recognized and valued by others (Hammer, 2007).

Issues of national and cultural identity are also clearly evident in national immigration and integration policies. Especially striking is a departure from the old policy of multiculturalism, as practiced in the United Kingdom and the Netherlands, for example. In the Dutch case, this was defined as "socioeconomic integration [of migrants]... while retaining the original cultural identity" (Veenman, 2006).

Multiculturalism was intended to produce a "salad bowl"—a healthy mixture of contrasts (Ascherson, 2004). However, it has in fact led in the United Kingdom to the "ghettoization" of immigrant communities (in part because of lack of equal economic opportunity) and consequently, because of rising tensions and other factors, to "voluntary apartheid" and "separate development" of increasingly numerous ethnic groups (Goldston, 2005). In the Netherlands, the policy of multiculturalism was perceived e.g., by the Dutch society "as the downgrading of its own core values in the name of accommodating immigrants" (Schöpflin, 2007). In both countries and elsewhere, it was Muslim communities that proved particularly resistant to integration (Statham, Koopmans, 2004; for a discussion of *tankesuktan,* "Swede[s] of Arabic descent, proud of [their] Muslim background, and actively engaging in resisting the assimilative forces within Swedish society," see Lacatus, 2007). Similar processes can be observed also in other European countries. They have given rise to a defense of the national identity, perceived as bound up with sovereignty and as a barrier to the erosion of core national values.

Fukuyama (2006a) has noted that the policy of multiculturalism pursued by some European countries has served as a framework for the coexistence of separate cultures and for a corporatist organization of society into separate communities, rather than as a transitional mechanism for integrating newcomers into the dominant culture. The result was the emergence of identity politics, with all the social strains and conflicts this implies, including the ghettoization of minority communities. Immigration and asylum have become contentious political issues. Such arguments quickly develop into emotive and highly sensitive debates about the ethnic and racial identity of the national community, which in many cases leads to national identity being seen as under a "cultural" threat from immigration. National publics and politicians who already see national identity and sovereignty as under challenge from the combined forces of European integration and globalization have found a convenient outlet for expressing these grievances in a reassertion of the national community as united against these newcomers. As a consequence, immigration and asylum conflicts have increasingly come to focus on the perceived and real ethnic differences between the native population and migrants (Statham, Gray, 2005).

For this reason, Fukuyama argues that the old multicultural model needs to be replaced by more energetic efforts to integrate non-Western populations into a common liberal culture: "The civilization of the European Enlightenment, of which contemporary liberal democracy is the heir, cannot be culturally neutral, since liberal societies have their own values regarding the equal worth and dignity of individuals. Cultures that do not accept these basic premises do not deserve equal protection in a modern liberal democracy" (Fukuyama, 2006a: 15).

Veenman (2006) supports this view, noting in the Dutch context that integration policies should not be one-sided, but should incorporate both socioeconomic and cultural dimensions. He adds that social integration is usually operationalized with two interrelated dimensions: behavior and attitude or orientation. Behavior includes formal participation (involvement in society's core institutions such as education, labor market, housing, and the political system; as well as informal participation (interethnic contact, particularly with native citizens). For its part, orientation encompasses social distance (i.e. the appraisal/ evaluation of interethnic contacts) and cultural orientation (the acceptance of the dominant value system in the receiving country, including individualism, authority, secularization, women's position in society, etc.). Formal participation in education and in the labor market can be described as socioeconomic integration, while the combination of informal participation, social distance and cultural orientation indicates cultural integration.

This approach is reflected in official immigration and asylum policy in the Netherlands. The 2007 coalition agreement of the Dutch government had this to say on social cohesion and integration:

Peaceful coexistence, public spiritedness, shared mores and values and solidarity are characteristics that enable a national community to make the most of opportunities and maintain its resilience in an open, international society. Achieving social cohesion requires permanent commitment to fostering a climate of security, responsibility and participation, and social integration is a prerequisite for that. Integration is not merely a question of individuals finding their place in society … For integration to succeed we need to be able to comprehend, understand and live with each other. Knowledge of the Dutch language, society, common values and history is essential to social integration and participation. Anyone who wishes to live in the Netherlands needs to go through the civic integration process. Those who complete the process have earned the right to consider themselves accepted by society. *The civic integration requirements under the new law must be bolstered by a substantial civic integration programme and a compulsory test* (Coalition agreement ..., 2007: 27. Emphasis added—KJ).[4]

A similar development has taken place in the United Kingdom, especially following the terrorist attacks of July 2007. Testimony to this is the furious reaction to the suggestion of the Archbishop of Canterbury that sharia law be given limited recognition in relation to the Muslim community. The government swiftly rebutted this proposal, insisting that British law would be based on British values (Butt, 2008; Woodward, Butt, 2008). That reaction sprang from the British government's policy orientation on integration, designed to replace multiculturalism with inclusion and cultural integration.

A document setting out the British Government's "vision and proposals for constitutional renewal" and submitted to Parliament in July 2007, provides for the development of "a British statement of values ... that will set out the ideals and principles that bind us together as a nation," giving "people a better sense of their British identity in a globalised world." The document deals at length with citizenship and national identity, noting that while each individual possesses multiple identities, in addition "there is a national identity that we can all hold

---

[4] Similar tests are mandatory in the United States, where in 2007 the government introduced new questions into the civics test (first developed in 1986) that immigrants have to pass to become naturalized American citizens. Immigration officials said they sought to move away from civics trivia to emphasize basic concepts about the structure of government and American history and geography. In contrast to the old test, which some immigrants could pass without any study, the officials said the new one is intended to force even highly educated applicants to do reviewing. Several historians said the new questions successfully incorporated more ideas about the workings of American democracy and better touched upon the diversity of the groups—including women, American Indians and African-Americans—who have influenced the country's history (Preston, 2007).

in common: the overarching factor—British citizenship—that brings the nation together" (Secretary of State for Justice and Lord Chancellor, 2007: 53). This should be valued and meaningful for recent arrivals looking to become British, as well as to those who have the right to permanent residence in the UK, says the document.

The British Government has already improved a considerable range of measures aimed at raising the profile and meaning of citizenship, introducing language and Knowledge of Life tests for new applicants and starting the highly successful citizenship ceremonies which are organized in Town Halls across the country. Local authorities are to be helped to create positive strategies for building cohesive communities where rights and responsibilities are clearly understood and protected and where positive relations between new arrivals and long-term residents are supported.

All this is to create a common bond between all types of citizens in the UK, whether born in the country or naturalized. The document argues, therefore, that it is important that there is more widespread agreement and understanding around the nature of the rights and responsibilities that come with citizenship, as this will help build a sense of shared identity and social cohesion: "It is important to be clearer about what it means to be British, what it means to be part of British society and, crucially, to be resolute in making the point that what comes with that is *a set of values which have not just to be shared but also accepted ... A British citizen, fully playing a part in British society, must act in accordance with these values*" (Secretary of State for Justice and Lord Chancellor, 2007: *passim*. Emphasis added—KJ).

In these two countries, and in many other European ones,

> Citizenship is no longer attached to ethnic identity and descent, but neither is it accepted as an individual entitlement and a tool for integrating societies of heterogeneous origin. Instead, citizenship becomes a reward for those who do not pose a threat to the wider society because they have sufficient income, can communicate in the dominant language, identify with the history of their host society, and subscribe to its public values (Bauböck, 2006).

All this suggests a turn towards a "melting pot" philosophy of integration, at least to some extent. Naturally the impact of such a policy, affecting only new immigrants, can only be limited, but the change of direction is very telling.

There are also those who try to strike a happy medium, arguing that it is wrong to "think of multiculturalism as antithetical to, rather than as a reformer of, national identity" (Modood, 2007). They argue that it does not make sense to encourage strong multicultural or minority identities and weak common or national identities; strong multicultural identities are a good thing—they are not intrinsically divisive, reactionary or subversive—but they need the complement of a framework of vibrant, dynamic, national narratives and the ceremonies and rituals which give expression to a national identity. After all, goes the argument, where multiculturalism has worked and been accepted as a state project (Canada, Australia and Malaysia, for example) it has been integral to a nation-building project (to creating Canadians, Australians and Malaysians).

It is not certain whether in the inflamed political climate of Europe today, such views have a chance of being heard.

National and "European" Identities on a Collision Course?

It appears from the foregoing analysis that the EU might be torn apart by two contradictory processes: the enhancement of both the common European identity and, at the same time, of national identities.

This may be confirmed by the debate on the Lisbon Treaty, replacing the rejected Constitutional Treaty. At British and Dutch instigation, the reform treaty stipulates that the EU is to lose its symbols, such as the flag, the anthem and "Europe day." As noted by Schneeberger (2006: 1), "With symbols, the European Union wants to give itself a face and foster a European identity among its citizens." Hence the action of these two "anti-integrationist member-states," as Schöpflin (2007) calls them. They "recognised that the symbols would enhance the relationship of the citizens of Europe with the EU [...] these states did not want to take the risk of finding out whether establishing a stronger political relationship between the EU and the putative European demos would weaken the cohesiveness of the nation-state."

This could be seen as confirming Bondebjerg's (2006: 8) view that as a consequence of globalization and Europeanization, the tendencies towards cosmopolitan visions in culture and politics are met with strong nationalistic and traditionalistic counter attacks. He sees "a contradictory development, with deep European integration of more than 50% of all important political and cultural areas, and at the same time deep sceptical attitudes and ideological separation from the EU-project."

A resurgence of nationalism is apparent in many countries. Halliday (2004) states:

> Around the world, the constraints of law and general moral decency that once restrained nationalism seem to have been eroded. In Israel, the public mood has shifted further towards aggressive action; across Europe, advocates of immigration and multiculturalism are under attack; in many former Soviet republics and in eastern Europe, nationalist demagogues hold sway; in Japan, a revived rhetoric of national assertiveness is taking hold.

For his part, Saul (2005) has proclaimed "The Collapse of Globalism and the Reinvention of the World," including the return of "19th-century nationalism." He points out that at the end of the 20th century "nationalism and nation states were stronger than at the beginning of the process of globalization," and also, as noted, in the European Union.

In view of this, the "European identity" project needs to be very careful about the way it relates to national identity. How can the two be reconciled? Is it possible to create "Europe" as "a continent of peoples, separate but interwoven" (Saul, 2005: 279)—not only politically, but also culturally?

National identity has always been socially constructed; it revolves around history, symbols, heroes, and the stories that a community tells about itself (Fukuyama, 2006a). Smith (1991: 179) defines a "collective cultural identity" as those feelings and values with respect to a sense of continuity, shared memories and a sense of common destiny of a given unit of population which has had common experiences and cultural attributes.

A national cultural identity (as distinct from an ethnic, group or e.g. territorial cultural identity) can be understood as—roughly speaking—the historically produced sum total of traits and characteristics typical of the culture of a given nation, shared by a majority of its members and underlying their sense of distinctiveness from other nations. It is sustained by dual action: one of inclusion which provides a boundary around "us," and one of exclusion which distinguishes "us" from "them."

Kivikuru (1990) makes several distinctions between cultural and national identity. Cultural identity, she says, means a social potential for cultural self-expression; national identity gives a base for self-understanding. It should be approached more in terms of symbol and value axes. National identity, she believes, is by definition more institutionalized and power-oriented, since it leans more towards societal institutions. National identity stands for cohesion and order; it is a gatekeeper, a selection mechanism exercising critical control over cultural influences and the interaction of societies.

Theoretically, therefore, a strong, vital and powerful national identity might indeed be a barrier to the parallel existence of a "European" identity. It could perform its role as a "selection mechanism," and exercise control over the interaction between societies of Member States, and between them and "Europe" and its "identity," in such a way as to prevent acceptance of a "European identity."

We have seen that this is exactly what has happened so far. There is little that is "post-national" in the attachment of the societies of Member States to their national identities.

However, Schlesinger (1991) notes that collective identities are constituted in action and as continually reconstituted in line with both an internal dynamic and external balances of forces. One should be aware of the temporal dimension through which the complex process of reconstituting traditions and activating collective memories occurs. Also Ang (1990: 252) makes the point that:

> what counts as part of a national identity is often a site of intense struggle between a plurality of cultural groupings and interests inside a nation and therefore national identity is, just like popular identities in Latin America and elsewhere, fundamentally a dynamic, conflictive, unstable and impure phenomenon.

A similar view is expressed by Kivikuru (1990) who describes cultural identity as a mixture of cultural similarities and contrasts, disorganized and almost chaotic, a multitude of cultural layers: dominant cultures, countercultures, subcultures and their combinations.

Theoretically, therefore, there could be room in individual, collective, national, regional and "European" identities for a variety of elements, representing all these levels of identity formation and articulation. Promotion of "European identity" need not necessarily lead to obliteration of the fundamental core of national or ethnic identity.

Saul (2005) distinguishes two types of nationalism: negative nationalism (one that is "dependent on fear and anger") and "positive nationalism" ("tied to self-confidence and openness and a concept of the public good"). He describes "positive nationalism," perhaps a little idealistically, as follows:

> It is a relief in the positive tension of uncertainty and the central importance of choice ... Citizens feel comfortable with this complexity because they are anchored into a fundamental view of themselves and *others* as part of a civic commitment ... The world is filled with nation-states that have a great deal of unfinished business. The question is ... how to ensure that this new nationalist era is citizen based, focused on the national common good and on developing binding treeaties in a range of areas at the international level ... If people who do not know each other well, perhaps because they come from different cultures, serve the welfare of their fellow citizen, they may well discover how similar their values are ... this would be the process of positive nationalism (Saul, 2005: *passim*)

This could potentially be the element of national identity promoted by the EU for the purpose of providing a foundation for integration and development of a "European identity."

Guido Martinotti and Sonia Stefanizzi (cited in Hurrelmann, 2006) distinguish four types of citizen orientations in the European multi-level system:

- "integrated" (positive orientations towards both the EU and one's Member State),
- "nation-statist" (negative orientation towards the EU, positive orientation towards one's Member State),

- "innovative/escapist" (positive orientation towards the EU, negative orientation towards one's Member State, based on the conviction that the nation-state is an anachronistic form of social organization)
- and "alienated" (negative orientations towards both the EU and one's Member State).

Of these four, the "integrated" orientation is no doubt more advantageous in terms of the "European identity" project.

Hurrelmann (2006) looks at legitimacy relationships between the EU and nation states and proposes the following classification (table 3):

Table 3. Types of Legitimacy Relationships between EU and Nation-State

		Assessment of the nation-state as	
		Legitimate	**Illegitimate**
Assessment of the EU as ...	**Legitimate**	Positive-sum relation-ship (resulting in "integrative" citizen orientation)	Zero-sum relationship (resulting in "innovative/escapist" citizen orientation)
	Illegitimate	Zero-sum relationship (resulting in "nation-statist" citizen orientation)	Negative-sum rela-tionship (resulting in "alienated" citizen orientation)

Source: Hurrelmann, 2006: 4.

As we have seen, the Maastricht Treaty posited, at least to some extent, the "innovative/escapist citizen orientation." That, however, has been rejected both by individuals and by Member States. What is needed, therefore, is acceptance of the "integrative" citizen orientation, expressed in the idea of a "double allegiance" of Europeans to the EU and their respective Member State. In terms of legitimacy relationships, this means that the EU contributes to the Member States' legitimacy by helping them to achieve social and economic goals, while the Member States prop up the legitimacy of the EU by making available national loyalties as a source of EU support. In terms of identity articulation, this means acceptance of both the national and the "European" identity.

Is there no contradiction here? Not really. Participation in a process of integration requires a sense of security in one's individual, ethnic and national identity, as a foundation for the ability to engage with other peoples and nations with confidence and on a basis of equality. This is confirmed by the different approach of "big" and "small" countries to international integration schemes. Many "small" countries or nations have an acute sense, often based on historical experience, of the fragility and vulnerability of their existence and identity, and are therefore more determined to protect them (for a general discussion of the position of small Member States in the EU, see Sepos, 2007). In consequence, they often resist more advanced forms of integration which they perceive as a possible threat to themselves. By contrast, the "big" countries are usually secure in their culture and identity, confident that integration will not undermine their sense of themselves. Their sense of security naturally also derives from the fact that due to their size and potential, they are not likely to be on the short end of the stick in any form of international endeavor they engage in.

Thus, promotion of international cooperation and integration may require boosting the sense of security of participating societies, especially the smaller ones, and enhancing their integration capacity, meaning, paradoxically, strengthening their national identity. This point is eloquently made by Muller (2008):

> One could argue that Europe has been so harmonious since World War II not because of the failure of ethnic nationalism but because of its success, which removed some of the greatest sources of conflict both within and between countries. The fact that ethnic and state boundaries now largely coincide has meant that there are fewer disputes over borders or expatriate communities, leading to the most stable territorial configuration in European history.
>
> These ethnically homogeneous polities have displayed a great deal of internal solidarity ... Several decades of life in consolidated, ethnically homogeneous states may even have worked to sap ethnonationalism's own emotional power. *Many Europeans are now prepared, and even eager, to participate in transnational frameworks such as the EU, in part because their perceived need for collective self-determination has largely been satisfied* (Emphasis added—KJ).

Returning to Figure 1, we can see that the EU's preferred type of relationships between national and European identities (weak and strong respectively) corresponds to what Hurrelmann calls the "innovative/

escapist citizen orientation" (the upper right quadrant in Table 3). Given that it has proved ineffective, a different approach should be sought: something corresponding to the "integrative citizen orientation." This is represented by the upper left quadrant in Table 4.

Table 4. Matrix of desirable relationships between "European" and national identities

	European identity	
	Strong	**Weak**
Strong, secure	High integration capacity	Low integration capacity
National identity		
Weak, or potentially threatened	Resistance to integration	Possible disinte- gration of nation-states and EU

Hurrelmann (2006) also considers three logics of mutually reinforcing legitimacy assessments of the EU and its Member States: those of analogy, complementarity, and derivation:

- Under the logic of analogy, the legitimacy of EU institutions is justified by pointing out that EU institutions conform to the same principles that underlie the legitimacy of the Member States. In most cases, this argument implicitly presupposes that these principles themselves are appropriate, that they are adequately met in the Member States, and that they can be applied to the EU as well;
- The logic of complementarity justifies the legitimacy of the EU by pointing to the systematic differences between European and national institutions, arguing that their specific capacities supplement each other in an effective way;
- The logic of derivation treats one level as normatively superior to the other. In the European context, most arguments grant this privilege to the nation-state. The legitimacy of the EU is then grounded in the fact that it can be controlled by its Member States, and is thus no more than an instrument of their policy making.

This approach can usefully be applied to the issue of identity and we would argue that all three logical constructions enter into the picture to some extent in determining relations between national and "European" identities:

- "Analogy," because this is a question of *shared* European values, both civic and cultural, so there must be fundamental congruence between national and "European" identity in these regards;
- "Complementarity," because they complement each other and neither can replace the other;
- "Derivation," because national identity is clearly perceived by EU citizens as more important and "European identity" can be accepted if it is recognized as analogous and complementary with it.[5] Nevertheless, derivation can work both ways. National identity is far from being in demise, Delanty (2007) points out, but rather than look for a European level of identity over and beyond national identities or see the latter as resisting a top-down supranational European identity, attention should be focused on the mixed or hybrid nature of national identities, which have been transformed in numerous ways by Europeanization. For this reason, the logic of Europeanization has tended towards the Europeanization of national identities rather than the demise of national identity. This is evident in many spheres: in communication, lifestyles, and the many areas in which the EU has gained legal competences, such as education and citizenship.

This would confirm our thesis about the application of the logics of analogy, complementarity and derivation in relations between national and "European" identities.

---

[5] Garton Ash (2007) recognizes that "Europeanness remains a secondary, cooler identity," and admits that it will never generate the kind of fiery allegiances that were characteristic of the pre-1914 nation state, nor does it "need or even want that kind of emotional fire."

European Audiovisual Policy and Audiovisual Media Services Directive: Killing Two Birds with One Stone?

It can be surmised from the foregoing that the issue of "European" and national identities is a minefield, and that accordingly any EU strategy actively to promote both kinds of identity requires a very careful balancing act.

One test of its ability to do that has been the adoption of the Audiovisual Media Services Directive in 2007, replacing the Television Without Frontiers Directive. Below we will consider aspects of this process against the background of the EU's more general audiovisual policy.

As already noted, in the years 1981–1984, as the Community's media policy began to be developed, it was hoped that media (and television in particular) would be the means by which a European identity and citizenship could be forged. However, by 1984/5, that cultural approach to broadcasting was abandoned and the view became that the audiovisual sector was of fundamental importance in completing the internal market and in creating a European common market in production and distribution which could challenge the United States (or *le defi americain*) in economies of scale. Hence the Commission's Green Paper of 1984 on the establishment of a common market in broadcasting, dedicated to promoting these objectives (see Goldberg, Prosser, Verhulst, 1998; Machet, 1999; Ward, 2002).

This economic focus derived primarily from the fact that it was only with the Maastricht Treaty that the EC gained legal competence to deal with cultural matters. By then, however, the market-based approach to the media had been firmly established and took "precedence over less well established areas such as cultural policy" (Harrison, Woods, 2001: 478). David Ward argues that the EU media policy is "a highly sophisticated regulatory framework that is driven by certain needs. These of course are economic, but they are also cultural and political, and underpinned by certain democratic values" (Ward, 2002: ix). It has, he adds, provided for the maintenance of democratic media within the terms of the EC Treaty and fully accepted the right of Member States to support instruments for the democratic needs of society. That is a somewhat isolated view, however (see Jakubowicz, 2007). Kaitatzi-Whitlock (1996: 455) has commented that the EU's "media policy" is in fact an "industrial policy," arguing based on the example of abortive debates on EU-wide regulation of media concentration that it is impossible to fit "the political and cultural issue of [media] pluralism on to the economistic Procrustean bed of the Single European Market."

The European Commission's (1999) communication on audiovisual policy in the digital age stressed that the European Community's particular competence, also in the media field, concerns the freedom to provide services and support for the industry. Promotion of cultural and linguistic diversity was mentioned, but as one of many issues.

Today, with a new emphasis on culture, things should be different. However, that does not really seem to be the case. Another Commission policy document, dealing with the EU's regulatory audiovisual policy (European Commission, 2003), mentions the following areas where policy objectives should be pursued: competition; media pluralism; copyright; electronic communications networks and services and information society services; accessibility for people with disabilities to television; consumer protection; laws applicable to non-contractual obligations; trade policy; promotion of cultural diversity in external relations; right to information; promotion of production, chronology; commercial communications; protection of minors and public order; right of reply. Again, although some of these policy objectives have cultural ramifications, no specific focus on cultural and identity issues can be seen.[6]

---

[6] Kaitatzi-Whitlock (2006) has pointed out that because of the "deculturation" and depoliticization of audiovisual policy, the revision process of the Television Without Frontiers directive was deliberately dissociated from the "Plan-D for Democracy, Dialogue and Debate" project to reinvigorate European democracy and assist the emergence of a European public sphere, by allowing citizens to actively participate in the decision-making process and gain ownership of the European project (see European Commision, 2005b). The same is true of efforts in the field of promoting integration and "European" identity formation. By a quirk of EU organization, the "cultural" goals in this field were at the time of writing the domain of the Directorate General for Communication, working under the authority of the Vice President (Margot Wallström), with a mission to inform the media and citizens of the activities of the Commission and to communicate the objectives and goals of its policies and actions. Meanwhile, audiovisual policy was at the time of writing the province of Directorate General for Information Society and Media, under

The media's contribution to identity formation consists primarily in the fact that "media contents ... reflect and express the culture of the society in which they operate ... Second, the media should encourage cultural creativity and originality and promote the production of cultural contents ... cultures should not be perceived as static. A culture should not be regarded as a museum of particular traditions. Instead, a dynamic conception of culture is desirable, whereby culture is seen as changing and evolving, as the outcome of a process of examination and debate amongst members of the cultural group" (Hammer, 2007: 7–8).

Accordingly, the greatest contribution of the EU's audiovisual policy could be to ensure that the program industry is well developed and that an appropriate level of cultural participation through the media is possible. Of course, given the "European vs. national" dilemma, the question immediately becomes: which culture should be reflected in the media, and if both, then can EU policy decide what proportions should apply?

Of course, as noted by Humphreys (2005), EU media policies do impact—directly or indirectly—on the cultural role of the media. EU policies regarding the regulation of the European audiovisual market determine the increasingly commercial international context within which national cultural policies for broadcasting and public service broadcasters operate. The EU's stance in world trade talks bears positively on the Member States' ability to protect and promote cultural production and ultimately even on the long-term future of public service broadcasting. EU policies regarding the convergence of broadcasting, IT and telecoms, under the impact of digital technologies, provide another important constraint. Above all, EU competition policy places a question mark over the future funding basis of public service channels. Incidentally, given the cultural obligations of public ser-

---

Commissioner Viviane Reding. Accordingly, the view that "Unless Europeans are able to watch stories, dramas, documentaries and other works that reflect the reality of their own lives and histories, as well as those of their neighbors, they will cease to recognise and understand them fully" (European Commission, 2004b: 13) has been formulated by DG Communication and not by DG Information Society and Media, and is part of "communication policy" and not of "audiovisual policy."

vice broadcasting (Jakubowicz, 2006), this does not bode well for the preservation of national cultures and cultural identities.

EU policies in this field serve two kinds of EU integration, in policy, legal and regulatory terms. One is "negative" integration, i.e., the transfer of regulatory capacity to the EU, resulting in unilateral action and regulation by the Commission, or the European Court of Justice. The other is "positive integration," i.e., regulatory harmonization at the national level. "Negative integration" is usually deregulatory in nature, serving to promote competition and liberalization of market. A prime example are the ECJ rulings in the 1974 Sacchi case and the 1980 Debauve cases, defining television programs as a service, and thus opening the door to subordinating television to the EC's Single Market, deregulatory policies and to the principles of the freedom to provide services and movement of capital. "Positive integration" is generally re-regulatory (and often culturally protectionist) in nature, serving to provide common "market correcting" measures. Table 5 illustrates these divisions in the area of audiovisual policy.

Table 5. National and EU capacity for media regulation

EU regulatory capacity: high	
• Single audiovisual market (negative integration) • Convergence: regulating "electronic communications" (negative integration) • Competition policy with a "Community dimension" (negative integration)	• GATT/WTO negotiations (shared competence between EC and Member States) • Competition policy as concerns public service broadcasting (EC policy strongly affected by Member State determination to preserve PSB)
National capacity: Low	**National capacity: high**
• Anti-concentration rules and cross-media ownership (failed EU positive integration) • Broadcasting content regulation/ international commercial broadcasters	• National audiovisual production support schemes • Broadcasting content regulation/ Public service broadcasting
European regulatory capacity: low	

Adapted from: Humphreys, 2005.

This table can help map the conflicting cultural trends. Where EU regulatory capacity is predominant, the effect is deregulation and market liberalization, usually to the detriment of the ability of Member States to safeguard the cultural role of their audiovisual media, primarily television. Where national regulatory capacity is high, the Member States' ability to preserve their culture is enhanced, sometimes to the point of subverting EU measures designed to promote European cultural integration. The EU audiovisual policy, as well as the TWF and AVMSD directives, are the results of a compromise between economic liberalism and cultural protectionism (thus respectively weakening or designed to strengthen national identity). The moot question concerns the relative importance of each of these two contradictory tendencies in that compromise.

EU negative integration in the audiovisual field was achieved during the 1980s by a process that culminated in the enactment of the 1989 Television Without Frontiers (TWF) Directive, creating the legal framework for a single European audiovisual market. The rationale behind this directive was the conviction that EU-wide liberalization was required in order to create for European companies the economies of scale and scope associated with a large internal market that, it was hoped, would boost the international competitiveness of the European audiovisual industry *vis a vis* the USA. The ambition to achieve global competitiveness has had far-reaching effects on EU policies as they related to the audiovisual sector.

TWF opened up the European TV market by mandating the free reception and establishment of broadcasting services from other Member States subject to the observation of fairly liberal minimum content and advertising regulations that were harmonized at the EU level by the Directive. The European Court of Justice has continued to play a direct role, ruling on a number of occasions against "protectionist" Member States for failing to comply with the liberalizing requirements of the Directive, concentrating on market liberalization (e.g., cross-border broadcasting). On the other hand, it tended to ignore TWF provisions relating to public interest goals (e.g., restriction of advertising time, content quotas) and sometimes overriding them (e.g., protection of minors). This has eroded the national capacity to regulate media markets and created a situation of regulatory arbitrage in Europe.

The main thrust of the 1989 TWF directive was clearly de-regulatory, removing national legal and regulatory barriers to the single European audiovisual market. That facilitated, and was actually intended to lead to, the expansion of Europe's largest media concerns. Another consequence was the internationalization and transnationalization of television programming in Member States (Sepstrup, 1989). With the advent of satellite and cable television that would have happened anyway, but the directive virtually deprived those national governments that may have wanted to do it, of any ability to influence or slow down the process.

In her wide-ranging critique of the EU audiovisual policy, Kaitatzi-Whitlock (2006: 7–8) has actually gone much further, claiming the EU's audiovisual policy has not only been indifferent to culture, but in fact destructive of it, both at the Community and national levels. It has, she says, effected a double shift, involving "first a displacement of the field of communications, from the national to the supra-national level, and secondly, its transfer from the control of political forces to commercial forces. Ultimate control was thus relegated to the automatic pilot of the self-regulating market: competition." Referring specifically to the Green Paper which foreshadowed the adoption of the Television Without Frontiers Directive (European Commission, 1984) and to the directive itself, she says that in adopting the policies behind the two documents,

> Member state governments were asked to make unconditional concessions: (a) of sovereignty, (b) of cultural self-determination and (c) of policy prerogatives on framing the political sphere. Conversely, the opponents, in this tug of war, free-marketeers of global capital, received their gains without any commitments to Europe's political integration. As a corollary, the normally superordinate objectives of the national communications and cultural orders soon became subordinate or even open to doubt altogether.

The result, she says, is that as an area of EU policy the "democratic political-cultural arena" of the media has been commodified, according to Kaitatzi-Whitlock, and largely deprived of any political or cultural content. Equally, there has been commercialization and commodification of television and the erosion of the Member States' ability to defend their audiovisual markets and their cultures.

Another area of negative integration in the audiovisual field is competition law and policy. Ironically, competition concerns appear to be the only reason for the EU's and especially the European Commission's interest in public service broadcasting. No element of active EU audiovisual policy is oriented to promoting public service broadcasting, but the EU has had to develop its *acquis* on the role of PSB in response to a large number of complaints from the private sector about alleged distortion of the media market and thus violation of EU legislation serving to promote competition. This, they claimed, resulted from what they regard as unfair benefits enjoyed by public service broadcasters, most notably their use of public funding to enter new media markets that could be left to the private sector (e.g., 24-hour news services, children's channels) and also - in many cases - their drawing supplementary funding from advertising. Against its natural, market-oriented instincts (see Jakubowicz, 2004), the European Commission (which would probably agree with commercial broadcasters and their political supporters that in the multi-channel era public-service broadcasting should be confined to areas of clear market failure, restricting themselves to providing what the market fails to deliver) has usually ruled in favor of PSB (Ward, 2002). Under pressure from Member States, it has developed an approach to the application of State-aid rules to PSB (European Commission, 2001) that makes it possible to retain comprehensive "European-style" public service broadcasting. Though doubts remain (Mortensen, 2005, 2006), the European Commission is coming round to accept that PSB organizations can fully employ new digital technologies and distribution platforms to modernize and adjust to the requirements of the digital age, turning them into public service *media*, rather than simply broadcasters. Thus, depending on policy at the national level, public service media will continue to be able to perform its cultural role in the future. It was also at a Member State suggestion that the Audiovisual Media Services Directive includes a recital which reads: "The Resolution concerning public service broadcasting reaffirmed that the fulfilment of the public service broadcasting's mission must continue to benefit from technological progress. *The co-existence of private and public audiovisual media service providers is a feature which distinguishes the European audiovisual media market*" (emphasis added—K.J.)

In other competition decisions on mergers, acquisitions and joint ventures, the European Commission has sought to promote "European champions" (such as the RTL group/Bertelsmann, Telefonica, and Vivendi) and pan-European market mergers rather than individual market concentrations (Ward 2002: 94), on the tacit assumption that if it is impossible to protect the European audiovisual market in terms of ownership by legal or administrative means, then there is need to grow such "champions," capable of defending their natural markets by being able effectively to compete with media giants from elsewhere.

That also determined the EU's approach to media ownership and pluralism. Claiming lack of an explicit legal basis in the Treaty, the European Commission abandoned in the late 1990s efforts to introduce media-specific anti-concentration rules designed to safeguard pluralism, or at least to harmonize media ownership regulations in Member States. The real reason, however, was its inability to overcome the determined resistance of influential Member States (notably Germany) and of powerful vested interests in the media field. Again under pressure from Member States and the European Parliament, the European Commission returned to the question of media pluralism (European Commission, 2007c), but this time the outcome is not to be legislation, only the development of media pluralism indicators for use by Member States wanting to assess the level of media pluralism in their markets. This must be regarded as more of a smokescreen operation than anything else, and its practical effect in terms of preventing or reversing excessive media concentration, especially at the European level, is likely to be negligible at best.

As we said earlier, the EU audiovisual policy is a compromise between contrasting tendencies. For both economic and cultural reasons, the EU has sought in WTO and GATS negotiations to safeguard the ability of Member States to protect their audiovisual markets. Faced with the US insistence on open audiovisual markets, the EU tried at first to obtain during the Uruguay Round of these trade negotiations recognition of a "cultural exception" from the general trend to liberalize trade relations, or of "cultural specificity," to obtain in the end a cultural "carve-out:"

> What the Community obtained as a result of the Uruguay Round is ... the freedom to act, which is essential in order to maintain and develop national and Community policies in the audiovisual sector. This freedom of action is at the heart of the negotiating mandate which was adopted by the Council for the Seattle ministerial conference and is still valid for the Doha conference (Reding, 2001).

The extent of the application of basic GATS principles is fixed by each Member's "schedule of specific commitments." Only the services mentioned and described in these schedules are subject to the application of these disciplines. These schedules lay down the level of liberalization offered by each Member in each service area. Ultimately, no EU state made any commitment during that round to liberalize market access or guarantee equal treatment between foreign and domestic companies ("national treatment") in the audiovisual field. The EU as a whole, a total of 33 most-favored nation (MFN) exemptions specifically mentioning the audiovisual sector were introduced, with an additional 8 MFN exemptions applying to all service sectors which would potentially include audiovisual services.

That step, while very important, must of course be complemented by action at the EU and national levels to promote the media's contribution to identity formation. As indicated above, this refers primarily to media contents and their ability to reflect national or "European" culture.

At the EU level, measures serving this goal include the successive versions of the MEDIA program. In addition to its very modest funding, however, the program does not fund actual production of films or television programming, only training, development, distribution and promotion (though the first MEDIA program did provide support for production). A proposal to establish a special mixed private/public loan guarantee fund for European film-makers was blocked altogether. Its impact on the actual contents of what is shown in cinemas and on television must therefore be limited.

The EU is also promoting production and use of content for interactive and online media (see European Commission, 2007d; Screen Digest Ltd., CMS Hasche Sigle, Goldmedia Gmbh, Rightscom Ltd., 2006) and these efforts, while needed and welcome, cannot have but limited impact.

Another well-known case of EU intervention in favor of the cultural role of the media is, of course, the European television quotas, first introduced by the TWF directive. Article 4 of TWF stated that a majority of broadcasting time (not counting news, sports, games, advertising and teletext) should be reserved for European works and Article 5 specified that broadcasters should reserve at least 10 per cent of their programming budget or transmission time for European works created by the independent production sector. According to the most recent report on the implementation of these provisions (European Commission, 2006; see also Cristina, Hungerbühler, Morici, Prario (2008), the EU-average transmission time reserved for European works by all covered channels in all Member States was 65.18% in 2003 and 63.32% in 2004 representing a 1.86 point decrease over the reference period, and a fall of 3.63 points over four consecutive years (2001–2004). The EU-average proportion reserved for European works by independent producers (independent productions) broadcast by all covered channels in all Member States was 31.39% in 2003 and 31.50% in 2004, representing a 0.11 point increase over the reference period, but a considerable decrease of 6.25 points in four years (2001–2004). While the general trend is downward, the averages still exceed the limit by a high margin, especially as concerns independent productions.

This effort to promote the European culture and identity, while successful on its own terms, is running into two obstacles: greater preference for American content rather than non-domestic European content, and a clear preference for domestic over non-domestic European content. Concerning the first question, as Bondebjerg (2006) explains, the purpose of EU action is to Europeanize cultural institutions, the culture of symbolic and aesthetic forms of communication and the culture of everyday life. It is no secret, he adds, that this endeavor has met with heavy resistance, deriving primarily from the sheer existence of heavy national, cultural traditions and institutions making real transnational European collaboration difficult:

> The consistent pattern over many years in both areas of media fictions is thus that we seem to identify with our own national fiction, that American fiction is trans-nationally extremely popular and that the fiction from other European nations very rarely reach prime time and big audiences - with British fictions as the occasional exception ... the European film and TV imaginary is clearly divided into the national and the American. This is the imaginary mediated world that holds us together, whereas the European as a dominant imaginary is roughly non-existent outside the art cinema distribution and consumption system ... The lack of a very strong link between the products and everyday culture dominating each of the European nations and the European tradition as such makes it hard to reach a pan-European

audience. European audiences are in fact more national and American that they are European (Bondebjerg, 2006: *passim*).

On the second question, there is abundant evidence that a program of promoting the circulation of European works, with all the implications for European culture and identity that this was meant to produce, is being hijacked by Member States in order to promote their own cultures and identities. A study on the impact of EU measures found that "Member States have taken advantage of their freedom to pursue national cultural objectives by applying additional requirements on broadcasters such as specific language requirements and investment in regional production. These may, however, have acted as barriers to cross-border trade, thus possibly inhibiting cultural exchanges among Member States. While the hours of non-domestic European works (that is works made in another European country) have grown, there has not been a significant shift in the tastes and viewing habits of Europeans towards the development of a more pan-European cultural identity" (David Graham and Associates Limited, 2005: 17–18). The study confirmed Bondebjerg's view that there is a greater appetite for US programming among European audiences than for programs produced in other Member States. European production has a national cultural appeal which does not travel well. In the period covered by the study, the share of qualifying transmission time devoted to works made in another European country ("non-domestic European works") increased from 10.9 per cent in 1993 to 13.9 per cent in 1999; it fell to 12.3 per cent in 2002.

The process of drafting the AVMS directive provided another opportunity to consider the way EU audiovisual regulation could help the cause of European integration and/or "European" and national identity formation.

A number of provisions bear on these issues. They are:

- European and independent production quotas;
- Provisions on major events and short reports;
- Jurisdiction issues.

We will consider them in turn. As concerns the European and independent production quotas, it became clear early on in the process that they would be retained in the new directive. In its Issues Paper on this subject (European Commission, 2005a), prepared to focus the debate on the revision of the directive, the European Commission noted the use (or perhaps abuse) of European quota provisions to promote primarily national works, and mentioned proposals to encourage the circulation of "European works of non-domestic origin," or to create incentives to broadcast "non-national European works" (e.g. by doubling the weighing for the transmission of non-national European works with regard to fulfilling the quota of Article 4, though this would be incompatible with EU treaties). During one of the focus groups which discussed this issue, the European Commission returned to the question of splitting the European quota into a "domestic" and "non-domestic" part, to ensure the presence of at least a set quota of works from other European countries in the television program services of Member States, but the proposal did not find favor with the national experts present. Articles 4 and 5 were thus incorporated into the new directive without any change.

On the other hand, the new directive does strike a blow for (hopefully) European integration by extending the European quota to non-linear services. Under Article 3i, Member States must "ensure that on-demand audiovisual media services provided by media service providers under their jurisdiction promote, where practicable and by appropriate means, the production of and access to European works." As possible forms of such promotion, the directive mentions "financial contribution made by such services to the production and rights acquisition of European works or to the share and/or prominence of European works in the catalogue of programmes offered by the on-demand audiovisual media service."

As with the European quotas for linear services, Member States are to report to the Commission (though not every two years, as with the quotas for linear services, but every four years) on the implementation of this provision. Thus, in 2011, these reports, as well as an independent study to be commissioned by the European Commission, we will have a first indication of what contribution the actual mode of implementation of this provision makes to the promotion of either "European" or national identities.

The new directive also retains the old article 3a (now 3j) which states that Member States "may take measures in accordance with Community law to ensure that broadcasters under its jurisdiction do not broadcast on an exclusive basis events which are regarded by that Member State as being of major importance for society in such a way as to deprive a substantial proportion of the public in that Member State of the possibility of following such events by live coverage or deferred coverage on free television." These are mainly sports events involving national teams, and their emotional impact on national integration and identity is considerable. Even though relatively few Member States have actually taken advantage of this possibility (Austria, Belgium, Finland, France, Germany, Ireland, Italy, United Kingdom[7]), it does offer a chance to ensure that major events will be available on television to everyone, giving the nation a chance to unite at times of sporting triumphs (or defeats).

Here, too, the new directive has gone further than the old one. Under Article 3k, Member States are now under an additional obligation to "ensure that for the purpose of short news reports, any broadcaster established in the Community has access on a fair, reasonable and non-discriminatory basis to events of high interest to the public which are transmitted on an exclusive basis by a broadcaster under their jurisdiction." Such short extracts are to be used solely for general news programs and may be used in on-demand audiovisual media services only if the same program is offered on a deferred basis by the same media service provider. Of course, such short extracts (e.g., showing goals scored by the national football team or any other memorable elements of "events of high interest" cannot match full-length transmissions of sports or other events in terms of their power to unite a large part of the nation behind the national flag, or a popular sportsman or other national figure. Nevertheless, they may permit brief moments of pride or emotion, and by the same token of identification both with the nation's "flag-bearer" and with all other compatriots experiencing similar emotions, and thus may add to the pool of shared experience that serves integration at the national level.

An important element of the directive revision debate was the question of jurisdiction. This issue has dogged the entire process of the preparation, implementation and revision of the TWF directive (see Nikoltchev, 2002; 2006), as many Member States found it hard

---

[7] Denmark originally introduced measures under Article 3a of the TWF directive in 1999, but then revoked them as of January 1, 2002.

to accept that under the "country of origin" principle enshrined in Article 2 of the directive, they had no control over transfrontier television services originating in another country, but targeting audiences in those Member States. One of their main concerns was that under Article 3 they were permitted to introduce more detailed or stricter rules in the areas covered by this Directive, and thus for example introduce culturally-specific provisions in their broadcasting legislation (e.g. a prohibition on advertising in children's programming, as in Sweden). Under the directive, however, these provisions would apply only to broadcasters established in the particular Member States, but not to those established in other Member States, yet targeting the audience in the country where such more detailed or stricter rules apply. These provisions have given rise to "jurisdiction shopping," "delocalization" or "relocation," as broadcasters have become established in countries with a more favorable legal framework in order to broadcast (usually via satellite) program services to countries with more restrictive rules.

In short, the question of jurisdiction, as ultimately raised in the directive revision debate by at first 11 and then 13 countries can better be understood as a question of a balance between European and national audiovisual policy, indeed, to some extent, as a question of sovereignty. Those EU Member States wished that more respect be accorded to their own policies, and that they would not have to renounce the ability to shape, at least to some extent, the television offer available to their citizens.

At an Education, Youth and Culture Council meeting on 13 May, 2005, the delegations of Belgium, Austria, Czech Republic, Estonia, Ireland, Latvia, Lithuania, the Netherlands, Poland, Slovenia and Sweden submitted under "Other business" a note on this subject, referring to several occasions when "several Member States voiced their concerns regarding their inability to regulate broadcast services that are primarily targeted at their countries (that is to say, broadcast services that primarily target a Member State, but derive from a broadcaster established in another Member State, are not subject to regulation by the target-country)." They asked the Commission to specifically address the issue outlined above, either by establishing a specific study group, by tasking a reconvened Focus Group or by any other means and, to report to the Council on the outcome of its proceedings. In an "Additional Commentary," they said they fully recognized the importance of the "country of origin" principle upon which the Directive is built, but said that since broadcasting was "an important feature of the cultural landscape," and that "given the impact of broadcasting, its indispensable role in the social, democratic and cultural life of our societies and the importance of preserving cultural diversity, one cannot regard broadcasting as a solely economic activity or service. Indeed the promotion of cultural and linguistic diversity is one of the key principles underpinning the Directive." On this basis, they urged the Commission "to identify ways in which the legitimate concerns voiced here can be addressed" (Council of the European Union, 2005).

Then, in December 2005, Denmark—acting on behalf of the "Gang of 13," as the group (now numbering 13 countries) became informally known—sent a letter[8] to Commissioner Reding, outlining ideas how "important national rules can still be applied to broadcasting services that target our Member States" in an environment where broadcasters have the freedom to be based in any Member State.

In an accompanying note on "Application of National Rules to Broadcasting Services," Denmark made it clear that "The revised Television Without Frontiers Directive should ensure that each 'broadcasting service' (television channel) is subject to only one set of national rules and that the national rules applying are those of the Member State that is primarily targeted by the broadcasting service." To this end, it proposed that emphasis of the revised directive should no longer be on applying rules to "broadcasters" and instead focus on applying rules to "broadcasting services," so that different rules could apply, depending on the circumstances, to different services transmitted by one and the same broadcaster. Accordingly, "broadcasting services available in only one Member State would be subject to the national rules of that Member State," regardless of where those services came from. The note pointed out that "there is also some concern that the concept of a 'level playing field' is being eroded; the current Directive allows Member States to adopt stricter rules for cultural reasons. However, when broadcasters relocate to a lighter regulated Member State it forces all Member States – for economic reasons – to apply the lightest rules, totally undermining the concept of culturally-driven stricter rules."

---

[8] That informal letter has not, to the author's knowledge, been published.

These were quite revolutionary ideas by EU standards and they met with fairly robust response by the European Commission, arguing that the "country of establishment" principle and freedom to provide services (e.g., such as television program services) were among the cornerstones of the European Union and could not be modified.

Following prolonged negotiations, a compromise was reached, detailed in recitals 32-34 and 66 of the preamble to the directive, as well as in article 3. The main solution proposed in the directive is cooperation among Member States and their regulatory authorities in case of circumvention by a broadcaster established in a country of more detailed or stricter rules in force in another Member State, based on the case law of the European Court of Justice (Case C-212/97 Centros v. Erhvervs-og Selskabsstyrelsen; Case C-33/74 Van Binsbergen v. Bestuur van de Bedrijfsvereniging; Case C-23/93 TV 10 SA v. Commissariaat voor de Media, paragraph 21). This could apply specifically to situations when "more than one Member State is concerned" when a broadcaster is licensed (meaning the broadcaster is licensed in one country, but addresses the program service to another country). In such situations, "it is desirable that contacts between the respective bodies take place before such licences are granted." In other words, the licensing authority could presumably ask a regulatory authority in the country where the program service is to be received whether the broadcaster is not choosing to become established in another Member State in order to avoid being subject to more detailed or restrictive regulations in the receiving State and potentially take a decision on the license in the light of such knowledge. Detailed procedures regarding such situations are laid down in Article 3. Upon request of the regulatory authority in the receiving State, the regulatory authority in the transmitting State may decide to request the broadcaster to comply with the stricter rules of the receiving State, but such a request cannot be binding. If this fails to produce the desired result, the receiving State may take other measures against the broadcaster (under Article 2 and 2a), but under strict supervision from the European Commission must ensure that such measures are compatible with Community law.

In short, the new directive has gone further than the old one to recognize the issue of deliberate circumvention of culturally-driven stricter rules applied in the receiving State, and has given it some tools to react in such situations. Symbolically, this change is important, but the practical effect of these new provisions remain to be tested.

All in all, however, in all the cases discussed above (extension of European quotas to non-linear services, provisions on short reports and on jurisdiction issues) the outcome may be favourable to the preservation of national culture and identity (especially if providers of non-linear services behave like broadcasters and use the "European" quota to promote mainly domestic works).

Conclusion

A variety of forces at the global, but also national level, have led to a fundamental change of integration policy in the European Union and in Member States with a clear emphasis on integration around common cultural and axiological systems. In both cases, therefore, there is a renewed emphasis on identity—European at the EU level, and national at the Member State level. This means a departure from the concepts of "civic identity" or "constitutional patriotism" which have been proposed as unifying forces in a supposedly "post-national" European Union where, in fact, both nationalism and populism are on the rise. In some Member States, that has meant a policy change from supporting multiculturalism to promoting national cultures and values as means of anchoring migrants in the host country.

In the European Union, strong national identity has long been perceived as an obstacle to European integration. The new emphasis and recourse to "European culture" and identity as the unifying force of the European Union potentially puts it on a collision course with Member States and their newly assertive stance on national culture, values and identity. This need not be the case, as strong and secure national identities can in fact be conducive to integration at the supranational level. Nationalism can, at least in theory, be either "negative" or "positive" and in the latter case may help international integration. What is needed is an "integrated" citizen orientation, positive towards both the EU and one's Member State. The official policy of the EU does not appear, however, sufficiently to have recognized this fact.

In part because of this, the audiovisual policy of the EU is primarily economically-driven and is not diversified and sophisticated enough to respond to the complexities of these conflicting currents, all the more so that it is separate from the European Commission's "communication policy" which appears to be more attuned to these needs.

The revision of the TWF directive has handed a number of (primarily symbolic) victories to Member States and their ability to use media policy to achieve cultural goals. The practical impact of this in terms of national integration is bound to be limited, however.

REFERENCES

Ang, Ieng (1990) "Culture and Communication: Towards an Ethnographic Critique of Media Consumption in the Transnational Media System." *European Journal of Communication*, 5(2–3): 237–260.

Ascherson, Neil (2004) *From multiculturalism to where?* http://www.opendemocracy. net/arts-multiculturalism/article_2052.jsp.

Barroso, José Manuel (2006) Speech at the Berlin Conference "A Soul for Europe," 17–19 November 2006, http://europa.eu/rapid/pressReleasesAction.do?reference =SPEECH/06/706&format=PDF&aged=1&language= EN&guiLanguage=en.

Bauböck, R. (2006) "Who are the citizens of Europe?" *Eurozine*, http://www. eurozine.com/articles/2006-12-23-baubock-en.html#.

Besio, Cristina, Ruth Hungerbühler, Luca Morici, Benedetta Prario (2008) "The Implementation of the Quota Requirements of the Directive 'Television Without Frontiers'." The Broadcasters' Perspective. *International Communication Gazette*, 70(2): 175–191.

Biedenkopf, Kurt, Bronislaw Geremek and Krzysztof Michalski (2004) *Concluding Remarks: What holds Europe together?* The Spiritual and Cultural Dimension of Europe Reflection Group. Vienna and Brussels: Institute for Human Sciences, The European Commission, http://www.iwm.at/publ/ rep-fin.pdf.

Bondebjerg, I. (2006) The European Imaginary. Media Fictions, Democracy and Cultural Identities. Paper presented during an international conference "Media, Democracy and European Culture." University of Copenhagen, October 4–6.

Butt, Riazat (2008) "Uproar as archbishop says sharia law inevitable in UK." *The Guardian*, February 8, http://www.guardian.co.uk/ print/0,,332426404-103602,00.html.

Coalition agreement between the parliamentary parties of the Christian Democratic Alliance, Labour Party and Christian Union (2007) The Hague: Ministry of General Affairs, http://www.government.nl/Government/Coalition_agreement.

Collins, R. (1997) "Unity in Diversity? The European Single Market in Broadcasting and the Audiovisual 1982–1994." In S. Stavridis, E. Mossalios, R.

Morgan, and H. Machin (Eds.) *New Challenges to the European Union: Policies and Policy-Making.* Aldershot: Dartmouth Publishing Co., 329–358.

Collins, R. (2006) *Misrecognitions: positive and negative freedom in EU media policy and regulation, from Television without Frontiers to the Audiovisual Media Services Directive.* Paper presented during an international conference "Media, Democracy and European Culture." University of Copenhagen, October 4–6.

Council of the European Union (2005) Statement on the review of the "Television Without Frontiers" Directive (Council Directive 97/36/EC of 19th June, 1997 amending Council Directive 89/552/EEC), 8806/05. Brussels, European Union.

Cram, Laura (2001) "Integration theory and the study of the European policy process: towards a synthesis of approaches." In Jeremy Richardson (ed.) European Union. *Power and policy-making.* London and New York: Routledge, 51–74.

David Graham and Associates Limited (2005) *Impact Study of Measures (Community and National) Concerning the Promotion of Distribution and Production of TV Programmes Provided for Under Article 25(a) of the TV Without Frontiers Directive.* Final Report, http://ec.europa.eu/avpolicy/docs/library/studies/finalised/4-5/27_03_finalrep.pdf.

Delanty, Gerard (2007) "Peripheries and borders in a post-western Europe." *Eurozine.* http://www.eurozine.com/articles/2007-08-29-delanty-en.html.

Dilday, KA (2007) Defenders of the nation. Opendemocracy, http://www.opendemocracy.net/ article/globalisation/global_village/defender_of_the_nation.

Dissanayake, W. (2006) "Globalization and the Experience of Culture: The Resilience of Nationhood." In N. Gentz, S. Kramer (eds.) *Globalization, Cultural Identities, and Media Representations.* New York: State University of New York Press.

Eichenberg, Richard C., Russell J. Dalton (2007) "Post-Maastricht Blues: The Transformation of Citizen Support for European Integration, 1973–2004." *Acta Politica* 42: 128–152.

Eriksen, Thomas H. (1997). "In search of Brussels: Creolizatoin, Insularity and Identity Dilemmas in Post-National Europe." In J. P. Burgess (ed.) *Cultural Politics and Political Culture in Postmodern Europe.* Amsterdam: Rodopi.

European Commission (1984) *Television Without Frontiers. Green Paper on the Establishment of the Common Market For Broadcasting, Especially by Satellite and Cable.* COM(84) 300 final. Brussels, EEC.

European Commission (1999) *Principles and Guidelines for the Community's Audiovisual Policy in the Digital Age,* COM (1999) 657. Brussels: European Union.

European Commission (2001) "Communication from the Commission on the application of State aid rules to public service broadcasting." *Official Journal of the European Communities,* C 320: 5–11. Brussels: European Union.

European Commission (2003) *The Future of European Regulatory Audiovisual Policy*. COM(2003) 784 final. Brussels: European Union.

European Commission (2004a) *Building our Common Future. Policy challenges and Budgetary means of the Enlarged Union 2007-2013*. COM(2004) 101 final/2. Brussels: European Union.

European Commission (2004b) *Making Citizenship Work: fostering European culture and diversity through programmes for Youth, Culture, Audiovisual and Civic Participation*. COM(2004) 154 final. Brussels: European Union

European Commission (2005a) Cultural Diversity and the Promotion of European and Independent Audiovisual Production. Issues Paper for the Liverpool Audiovisual Conference. Brussels: European Union, http://ec.europa.eu/avpolicy/docs/reg/modernisation/ issue_papers/ispa_cultdiv_en.pdf.

European Commission (2005b) *The Commission's contribution to the period of reflection and beyond: Plan-D for Democracy, Dialogue and Debate*, COM(2005) 494 final. Brussels: European Union.

European Commission (2006) *Seventh communication on the application of Articles 4 and 5 of Directive 89/552/EEC "Television without Frontiers," as amended by Directive 97/36/EC, for the period 2003–2004*. COM(2006) 459 final. Brussels: European Union.

European Commission (2007a) *A European agenda for culture in a globalizing world. COM(2007) 242 final*. Brussels: European Union.

European Commission (2007b) *Communicating about Europe via the Internet. Engaging the citizens. SEC (2007)1742*. Brussels, European Union.

European Commission (2007c) *Media pluralism in the Member States of the European Union. Commission Staff Working Document. SEC(2007) 32*. Brussels: European Union.

European Commission (2007d) *Creative Content Online in the Single Market. COM(2007) 836 final*. Brussels, European Union.

European Commission (2008) *Communicating Europe through audiovisual media. SEC(2008)506/2*. Brussels: European Union.

Fossum, J. E. (2007) *Constitutional patriotism: Canada and the European Union*. RECON Online Working Paper 2007/04, www.reconproject.eu/projectweb/portalproject/ RECONonlineWorkingPapers.html.

Fukuyama, F. (2006a) "Identity, Immigration & Democracy." *Journal of Democracy*, 17(2): 5–20.

Fukuyama, F., (2006b) *After the "end of history."* http://www.opendemocracy.net/ democracy-fukuyama/revisited_3496.jsp.

Gans, Chaim (2007) *Individuals' Interest in the Preservation of their Culture. Law & Ethics of Human Rights: 1(1), Article 2*, http://www.bepress.com/lehr/vol1/iss1/art2

Garton Ash, T. (2007) "Europe"s true stories." *Prospect Magazine*, Issue 131, February, http://www.prospect-magazine.co.uk/article_details.php?id=8214.

Goldberg, David, Prosser, Tony, Stefaan Verhulst (1998). *EC Media Law and Policy*. London, New York: Addison Wesley Longman Limited.

Goldston, J. A. (2005) "Multiculturaism is not the culprit." *International Herald Tribune* August 30.

Halliday, F. (2004) *The crisis of universalism: America and radical Islam after 9/11.* http://www.opendemocracy.net/debates/article-3-77-2092.jsp.

Hammer, Yoav (2007) "Multiculturalism and the Mass Media. Law & Ethics of Human Rights." *The Berkeley Electronic Press.* Vol. 1, Issue 1, Article 6, http://www.bepress.com/lehr/vol1/iss1/art6.

Harrison, J., and Woods L.M. (2001) "Defining European Public Service Broadcasting." *European Journal of Communication* 16(4): 477–504.

Hoffmann, J. (2006) *Re-conceptualizing Legitimacy: The role of Communication Rights for the Democratization of the European Union.* Paper presented during an international conference "Media, Democracy and European Culture." University of Copenhagen, October 4–6Humphreys, Peter (2005) *The EU and Audiovisual Regulation: An Agency for De-regulation or Re-regulation - A Research Agenda.* ESRC project: "Globalization, regulatory competition and audiovisual regulation in 5 countries." http://regulation.upf.edu/ecpr-05-papers/phumphreys.pdf.

Hurrelmann, A. (2006) *Multi-Level Legitimacy: Conceptualizing Legitimacy Relationships between the EU and National Democracies.* TranState Working Papers, 41. Bremen: Universität Bremen.

Inotai, A. (2007) "Economic patriotism fuels populism and demagogy." *Euractiv,* http://www.euractiv.com/en/enlargement/economic-patriotism-fuels-populism-demagogy/article-165646.

Inthorn, S. (2006) "What Does It Mean to Be an EU Citizen? How News Media Construct Civic and Cultural Concepts of Europe." *Westminster Papers in Communication and Culture.* London: University of Westminster, Vol. 3(3): 71–90.

Jakubowicz, Karol (2004) "A Square Peg in a Round Hole: The EU's policy on Public Service Broadcasting." In I. Bondebjerg, P. Golding (Eds.) *European Culture and the Media.* Bristol: Intellect Books, 277–302.

Jakubowicz, Karol (2006) "If not us, then who? Public service broadcasting and culture in the 21st century." In Christian Nissen (Ed.) *Making A Difference. Public Service Broadcasting in the European Media Landscape.* Eastleigh: John Libbey Publishing, 35–50.

Jakubowicz, Karol (2007) *Rude Awakening: Social And Media Change in Central and Eastern Europe.* Cresskill, N.J.: Hampton Press, Inc.

Kaitatzi-Whitlock, S. (2006) *Why the Political Economy of the Media Is at the Root of the European Democratic Deficit.* Paper presented during an International Conference on "Media Democracy and European Culture." University of Copenhagen, October 4–6.

Kivikuru, U. (1990) *Tinned Novelties or Creative Culture? A Study on the Role of Mass Communication in Peripheral Nations.* Helsinki: University of Helsinki.

Krastev, Ivan (2006) *The new Europe: respectable populism, clockwork liberalism.* http://www.opendemocracy.net/democracy-europe_constitution/new_europe_3376.jsp.

Kuzio, T. (2002a) *National Identity and Democratic Transition In Post-Soviet Ukraine And Belarus: A Theoretical And Comparative Perspective* (Part 1). RFE/RL East European Perspectives, 4(15), 24 July, www.rferl.org/eepreport.

Kuzio, T. (2002b) *Is Nationalism Always a Bad Thing? National Identity and Democratic Transition in Post-Soviet Ukraine and Belarus.* http://www.taraskuzio.net/lectures/ columbia_nationalism.pdf.

Lacatus, Corina (2007) "What is a blatte? Migration and ethnic identity in contemporary Sweden." *Journal of Arab and Muslim Media Research*, 1(1): 79–92.

Łukaszewski, Jerzy (2002) *Cel: Europa. Dziewięć esejów o budowniczych jedności europejskiej.* Warsaw: Noir sur Blanc.

Machet, E. (1999) *A Decade of EU Broadcasting Regulation. The Directive "Television Without Frontiers.* Mediafact. Düsseldorf: European Institute for the Media.

Manet, P. (2006) "Kryzys Europy, kryzys narodów, rozmawiał Maciej Nowicki." *Europa*, No. 139, 2.

Mazey, Sonia (2001) "European integration. Unfinished journey, or journey without end?" In Jeremy Richardson (ed.) *European Union. Power and policy-making.* London and New York: Routledge, 27–50.

Modood, T. (2007) *Multiculturalism citizenship and national identity.* http://www.opendemocracy.net/faith-europe_islam/multiculturalism_4627.jsp#.

Mortensen, Frands (2005) *EU and State Aid to Public Service Broadcasting 1992–2005.* MS.

Mortensen, Frands (2006) *New media as part of the public service task? The EU Commission's interpretation of Article 86(2).* Paper presented during an international conference on "Media, Democracy and European Culture," Copenhagen, October, 4–6.

Muller, Jerry Z. (2008) "Us and Them. The Enduring Power of Ethnic Nationalism." *Foreign Affairs* , March/April, http://www.foreignaffairs.org/20080301faessay87203/jerry-z-muller/us-and-them.html.

Nikoltchev, Susanne (2002) (ed.) *Jurisdiction over Broadcasters in Europe. Report on a Round-table Discussion and Selection of Background Materials. IRIS Special.* Strasbourg: European Audiovisual Observatory.

Nikoltchev, Susanne (2006) (ed.) *Audiovisual Media Services without Frontiers. Implementing the Rules. IRIS Special.* Strasbourg: European Audiovisual Observatory.

Preston, Julia (2007) "New Test Asks: What Does 'American' Mean?" *The New York Times*, September 28, http://www.nytimes.com/2007/09/28/washington/28citizen.html?scp=1&sq=New%20Test%20Asks&st=cse.

Reding, Vivian (2001) *Position by Mrs Reding on cultural policy and WTO in the framework of the 58 Mostra Internationale D'arte Cinematographica. DG DEAC C.1/XT D(2001).* Brussels: European Commission.

Saul, John Ralston (2005) *The Collapse of Globalism and the Reinvention of the World.* London: Atlantic Books.

Schlesinger, Philip (1991) "Media, the Political Order and National Identity." *Media, Culture and Society,* 13(3): 297–308.

Screen Digest Ltd, CMS Hasche Sigle, Goldmedia Gmbh, Rightscom Ltd (2006) *Interactive content and convergence: Implications for the information society.* A Study for the European Commission (DG Information Society and Media). London: Screen Digest.

Schneeberger, A. I. (2006*) Europe in the Picture: The Usage of EU Symbols and News Coverage on National Television.* Paper presented during an International conference on "Media, Democracy and European Culture." University of Copenhagen, October 4–6.

Schöpflin, G. (2007) *European Union: after the reform treaty.* http://www.opendemocracy.net/democracy_power/future_europe/after_reform.

Scruton, R. (2007) *England: an identity in question.* http://www.opendemocracy.net/globalization-kingdom/england_identity_4578.jsp.

Secretary of State for Justice and Lord Chancellor (2007) *The Governance of Britain,* http://www.official-documents.gov.uk/document/cm71/7170/7170.pdf.

Sepos, Angelos (2005) *Differentiated Integration in the EU: The Position of Small Member States. EUI Working Paper RSCAS No. 2005/17.* Florence: European University Institute, http://www.eui.eu/RSCAS/WP-Texts/05_17.pdf.

Sepstrup, Preben (1989) "Implications of Current Developments in West European Broadcasting." *Media, Culture and Society* 11(1): 29–54.

Smith, A. (1991) "Towards a Global Culture?" In M. Featherstone (ed.) *Global Culture: Nationalism, Globalization and Modernity.* London: Sage Publications.

Statham, Paul, Emily Gray (2005) *The Politics of Immigration and Asylum Policy in Western Europe.* Briefing Paper. Working Paper Series. Issue 12/05 Centre for European Political Communications. Leeds: University of Leeds.

Statham, Paul, Ruud Koopmans (2004) *Problems of Cohesion? Multiculturalism and Migrants' Claims-Making for Group Demands in Britain and the Netherlands.* Working Paper Series, Issue 7/04, Centre For European Political Communications. Leeds: University of Leeds.

The Governance of Britain. Presented to Parliament by the Secretary of State for Justice and Lord Chancellor by Command of Her Majesty, July 2007, http://www.official-documents. gov.uk/document/cm71/7170/7170.pdf.

Trandafoiu, Ruxandra (2006) "The Whole Greater than the Sum of Its Parts: An Investigation into the Existence of European Identity, Its Unity and Its Divisions." *Westminster Papers in Communication and Culture,* Vol. 3(3): 91–108.

Veenman, Justus (2006) *Integrating Migrants in the Netherlands: The Role of Education, Employment, and the Media.* Lecture delivered in the International Seminar for Experts "Integrating Migrants In Europe," Cicero Foundation, Paris, 15–16 June, http://www.cicerofoundation.org/lectures/58Lecture_Justus_Veenman_June_2006.pdf.

Ward, David (2002). *The European Union. Democratic Deficit and the Public Sphere. An Evaluation of EU Media Policy.* Amsterdam: IOS Press.

Woodward, Will, Riazat Butt (2008) "Laying down the law: ministers cool on archbishop's sharia suggestion." *The Guardian*, February 8, http://www.guardian.co.uk/uk/2008/feb/08/politics.religion/print.

Żakowski, Jacek (2006) "Nikt nie rodzi się Europejczykiem. Rozmowa z prof. Krzysztofem Pomianem." In Jacek Żakowski, *Koniec.* Warszawa: Sic!, 219–246.

CHAPTER 11

Which Frontiers for EU Media Policy?

An assessment in the context of the European project

Monica Arino[1]

Introduction

The project of European integration was initially conceived as a strategic security project based on economic trade. More than fifty years have passed since the signing of the Treaty of Paris in 1951, establishing the European Coal and Steel Community. Today, nobody would dispute that the idea of European integration has evolved to encompass much wider political and social ambitions. Although the ideal of European *economic* integration continues to drive the regulatory activity of the European Commission, increasing emphasis is also placed on initiatives towards a socially responsive Europe, resulting in intense debates on the degree of necessary *political* integration. And yet, several Treaties and enlargement waves after, the European Union continues to be, in many ways, a plurality of entities and players without a unitary outlook. The now twenty-seven Member States are divided between those who wish to increase the level of integration and expand the range of action of the community's policies, and those that are willing to cooperate only on certain issues, favouring a "two-speed" process. Following the negative responses from France and the Netherlands to the referendum on the so-called "EU Constitution," the European Member States decided to move forward with a much less ambitious Treaty, which has ostensibly purged identity symbols such as the European anthem or the flag.

---

[1] Monica Arino works as a Senior Manager for European Policy in Ofcom's international team. Any views expressed in this chapter are those of the author and are neither endorsed nor do they necessarily reflect Ofcom's policy position on any of the issues discussed.

There remain concerns about what is in many camps perceived as an inexorable trend towards concentration of power in Brussels, especially when this takes place in areas that are beyond the EU's remit of competencies. Moreover, there continues to be a perception that "Europe" is remote and unresponsive and that its institutions are distant from national citizenry, creating difficulties in the acceptance of EU policies and enhancing concerns about the lack of democratic legitimacy of its processes. This notwithstanding, and even if it could be argued that the European project has seen better days, its legislative and institutional machinery seems, for better or worse, in many ways unstoppable. The presence and power of the EU has continued to grow steadily, if unevenly, and it could be argued that in a more numerous Union and in an increasingly globalized geo-political context, there will be an increasing need for European countries to seek coordination (and thus direction) at a regional level.

This chapter explores the tensions between national and EU agendas in one particular area: audiovisual media. As is well known, the audiovisual media is primarily a national issue, being often described as a matter of "culture," for which the Member States remain exclusively competent. However, insofar as the provision of audiovisual media constitutes a commercial service, the EU must ensure that there are no barriers to cross-border exchanges of audiovisual material.

In the pursuit of this objective EU activity in the media sector has been significant, often extending beyond what one would have described as strictly of an internal market nature. In effect, the EU has developed its own media policy, distinct from, and at times compromising, that of individual Member States. The chapter considers the goals, both stated and implicit, of EU media policy, as enshrined in legislative measures such as the Television without Frontiers Directive, its review completed in 2007 and related soft law measures. All of these have, as its core objective, the creation of a transnational content market and the development of "pan-European operators." The question that underlies the analysis is that of whether or not these measures are aimed to, or *de facto* do, positively contribute to European integration, understood not only as an economic or legal process, but also as a socio-cultural phenomenon of greater approximation and understanding of the national traditions, beliefs and practices of the different members of the EU, and the development of a distinct and supranational "European culture."

It is argued that the EU track's record in this respect seems rather negative, insofar as it is possible to measure, and that the failure to develop a truly European identity and culture might partly have to do with the objectives that the EU has set for itself in this area. This raises questions regarding the extent to which the current balance of competences between the EU and the Member States in the media sector truly reflects the reality of day-to-day policy making. Further, if we accept that there is a fundamental link between the media, societal integration and democratic processes, should we also be making the case for a greater EU role in media policy as a necessary condition for the success of the European project?

Media Policy and the European Project

A key resolution of the Treaty of Maastrich (1992) was the establishment of a common European citizenship, as the basis to pursue social and economic progress deepening "solidarity between the peoples of Europe, while respecting their history, their culture and their traditions," within a single institutional framework based on the principle of subsidiarity. The aim was to turn "a rather vague idea of Europe into a well-defined political institution that will, in time, acquire a culture and an identity" (Guibernau, 2001:24).

The relationship between European identity and progress in European integration had already been underlined in 1975 by the former Belgian Prime Minister Leo Tindemans who, in a landmark report on European integration, criticized the contradiction between economic integration and political fragmentation and argued that "Europe cannot proceed to a greater degree of political integration without the underlying structure of a unifying European identity" (cited in Banus, 2002:159). A similar thought was also expressed by Jean Monnet, when later in his life he is attributed to have said that, were Europeans to do it all again, we should begin with culture.

Today, it is generally accepted that the completion of the European project critically depends on agreement on issues which go beyond the mere economic integration, namely issues of identity and culture and how they affect, or are affected by the process of European integration. Importantly, the focus on European culture and identity has not only an internal dimension, but the aim is to reaffirm it in dialogue with third countries and international organizations, as required by Article 151.3 of the Treaty.[2] Accordingly, the European Community has elaborated an ambitious development policy, which includes a cultural component with certain regions of the world, particularly the African, Caribbean and Pacific (ACP) region and the Mediterranean. Furthermore, cultural diversity has become one of the major issues of international debates within the Council of Europe, the United Nations or the World Trade Organisation (the infamous "cultural exception").

Such progressive affirmation of EU cultural diversity at an international level is a response to growing concerns of loss of cultural specificities and local heritage in a context of market globalization. The promotion of an intercultural dialogue is also perceived as crucial for the maintenance of peace, security and stability at a global level.

This ambitious program, however, appears to contradict the perceptions of European citizens regarding the Union's priorities. According to the First Results of the Standard Eurobarometer 2007, and although overall support for EU membership is at its highest for over a decade and the EU is trusted more than the national governments and parliaments (except for the UK, Germany, Sweden and Finland), citizens do not consider that cultural policy would contribute to strengthen the EU in the future, and when asked which aspects should the European Union emphasize they opted for the fight against crime (36%), environmental (33%), immigration (33%), energy (27%) and social issues (26%), with cultural policy accounting for only (6%), two points below the 2006 results.

Related, there has been a growing recognition that the EU must bring itself closer to citizens. It is against this backdrop that in the July 2005 report on Intra-EU Communications Strategy, Commissioner Margot Wallström stated that "this Commission has made communication one of the strategic objectives for its term in office' and, most encouragingly from a public diplomacy perspective, that 'communication is more than information: it establishes a relationship and initiates a dialogue with European citizens, it listens carefully and it connects to

---

[2] "The Community and the Member States shall foster co-operation with third countries and the competent international organizations in the sphere of culture, in particular the Council of Europe."

people. It is not a neutral exercise devoid of value, it is an essential part of the political process."[3]

Unsurprisingly, the media are at the center of this strategy, being primary responsible for establishing such communication. It is widely accepted that the media fulfill important social and political functions, contributing to the enhancement of national integration (or national "identity"), ensuring that individuals feel part of and responsible for their society. The media affect how we perceive the world and directly influence the sociological and cultural attitudes of citizens towards their own communities and towards others. In this line, the media also contribute to the creation of standards of literacy, taste and knowledge, facilitating the expression and the promotion of cultural diversity within a territory. There is also a fundamental democratic role of the media, being the principal mechanism through which political information is provided, and the most influential means of public opinion formation that directly affects political and democratic processes (Cook 1998, Mazzoleni and Schulz, 1999). Linked to this is the decisive contribution of the media to the creation of a socially inclusive "public sphere" distinct from the State and understood as a realm of social life where the exchange of information and views on questions of common concern takes place and where public opinions can be formed.

These cultural and political aspects inevitably shape media policy at the national level and are equally present at the EU level. As stated by William Hahn: "Information is a decisive, perhaps the most decisive factor in European unification [...] European unification will only be achieved if Europeans want it. Europeans will only want it if there is such a thing as European identity. A European identity will only develop if Europeans are adequately informed. At present, information via the mass media is controlled at national level. If European unification is to be encouraged, Europe must penetrate the media" (quoted by Whiddington, 2000:175).

In this spirit, joint projects such as Euronews, the five-language news channel, and *Arte*, the European cultural affairs channel, together with transnational specialist programs were conceived with the purpose to make the European dimension in our daily lives

---

[3] http://www.europa.eu.int/comm/dgs/press_communication/pdf/communication_com_en.pdf

easily comprehensible. Similarly, the removal of barriers to cross-border broadcasting through the Television without Frontiers Directive was seen not only as an inherently internal market measure, but, perhaps more importantly, as a means to foster cultural exchanges, promoting greater awareness and understanding of the diversity of European culture, for example through the encouragement of Europe-wide broadcasts of major European events.

As critically put by Schlesinger (2001:103), this logic 'has had an enduring impact on subsequent thinking and debate. First of all, it assumes, simplistically, that there is a strong, unilinear and homogenizing causal connection between media consumption and collective identity formation. Next, the national level of media production and distribution is seen as an obstacle to be transcended in the interests of forging "Europeaness." And finally, the desired shaping of a new cultural identity is linked to the transnational distribution of information, that is, to the formation of a European public sphere.

The Tildeman's report, although "politely received [was] left to gather dust on Community shelves" (Andrew and Gordievsky 1993:140). Attention to European identity, and the associated need to develop a "European culture" to provide a more human dimension to the integration project, have been marginal and never at the core of the European integration process, coming to the forefront of debate only at times when a major crisis has called for solutions aiming to (re)connect the people to the European project. Successive waves of integration and the debacle of the European Constitutional process have recently made Tildemans' remarks as salient and topical as ever, prompting, once again, the need for the EU to bring itself closer to the citizens, for them at least to tolerate, if not accept, increasing integration and wider membership.

The Development of a Distinct EU Media Policy

Media and communications have traditionally been a matter for national laws, intrinsically linked with national cultural and public interest concerns. European television and radio stations are normally national in coverage and in audience, primarily for linguistic reasons. In addition, the national scope of intellectual property rights has perpetuated the exercise of national distribution policies by rights own-ers. At present, Member States have the exclusive competence for li-censing, spectrum planning, all aspects of media pluralism, and the definition of the public service remit.

Before considering to what extent EU media policy contributes to European integration, we need to establish what are the basis, powers and limits of EU intervention in this sector and whether or not one can in effect talk about EU media policy as a discipline in its own right. This is not straightforward since the Treaty of the European Union does not unmistakably establish a conclusive list of competences. Rather, it promotes a large number of different, often inter-related and broadly framed objectives that are not always easily reconcilable.[4]

Even if Article 3 recognizes that Community activities extend to "the contribution to the flowering of the cultures of the Member States," Article 151 qualifies such an extraordinarily broad statement by limiting Community action in the audiovisual sphere to "support-ing and supplementing" (para 2) whilst explicitly excluding any har-monization of the laws and regulations of the Member States (para 5). Crucially, however, Article 151 also attributes certain powers of action to the Community requiring it to take cultural aspects into account in its action, and in particular to respect and to promote the diversity of cultures. This wording has been described as "rather vague and, at best, aspirational" (Barendt and Hitchens, 2000:167), and seems more as a reminder of the Community of Member States' sovereignty in this field. Thus, in many respects the Union's role would appear to be lim-ited to that of a coordinator.

However, this needs to be balanced with the significant preroga-tives enjoyed by the European Institutions, and particularly the Euro-pean Commission, to intervene in the audiovisual sector as a result of internal market competences. As is well known, by 1974, the Euro-pean Court of Justice had already established in the *Sacchi* case that

---

[4] These are set out in Article 2 of the EC Treaty and include "sustainable de-velopment of economic activities, a high level of employment and of social protection, equality between men and women, sustainable and non inflation-ary growth, a high degree of competitiveness and convergence of economic performance, a high level of protection and improvement of the quality of the environment, the raising of the standard of living and quality of life, and eco-nomic and social cohesion and solidarity among Member States."

broadcasting, to the extent that it had an economic or commercial function, qualified "by its nature" as a service, coming within the ambit of the Treaty.[5] Thus, the Community can legitimately intervene as long as the purpose is to remove transnational restrictions to harmonize audiovisual legislation and ensure fair competition.

As a result of this apparently strict distribution of competences, and the restricted economic aims, one would expect relatively limited EU activity in this area, beyond the removal of barriers to trade and the monitoring of the observance of the relevant legislative provisions in this area, namely, the Television without Frontiers Directive. Yet, as any observer would attest, this is certainly not the case. Over the last 20 years, European policy initiatives have steadily increased in number and expanded to cover a wide range of issues, effectively limiting the capacity of Member States to frame their national cultural and media policies. There is a large body of literature which analyses the various ways in which EU sector specific regulation in related areas (e.g., electronic communications markets) as well as EU competition policy has directly influenced the regulation of media markets and the development of media policy at the national level (Harcourt 2005, Levy, 1999, Hills and Michalis, 2000, Ward, 2002). In particular, Harcourt (2005) has detailed how the EU institutions have effectively driven a media policy of regulatory convergence at the national level. This influence goes beyond what one would characterize as a competence for harmonization or monitoring and justifies a separate analysis of EU media regulation as a field of its own.

In addition, on-going processes of liberalization, globalization and technological convergence have bolstered the impact of European legislation and other combined and complementary actions on national developments of media markets. Collins and Murroni (1996:188) refer to this phenomenon as the "erosion of national communications sovereignty through technological change." Indeed, the amount of

---

[5] Case 155/73, *Italy v Sacchi* [1974] ECR 409 para.6. See also para.427, in which the Court states that 'the transmission of television signals, including those in the nature of advertisements, comes, as such, within the rules of the Treaty relating to services' while 'trade in material, sound recordings, films, apparatus and other products used for the diffusion of television signals are subject to the rules relating to the freedom of movement for goods'.

regulations that directly or indirectly affect the audiovisual media has increased substantially in a digitally convergent environment. A number of factors have contributed to this trend.

Firstly, the EU competence in related areas has allowed the European institutions to exercise their powers in a number of informal ways. The connections between audiovisual policies and other EU policies have been used to leverage power into the media. For example, by promoting of the liberalization of the telecommunications sector, the Commission gradually expanded policy-making into the broadcasting field. Digital broadcasting was partly regarded as another technical service to be transmitted over new digital highways. Broadcasting networks have thus been regulated along with associated technical facilities such as Electronic Programme Guides or Application Programme Interfaces, upon which the provision of audiovisual services depends, and that lie at the frontier between content and carriage. Other examples include competition policy, and particularly state aid policy in the field of broadcasting, intellectual property policies, the information society agenda, telecommunications policies (notably the e-Commerce Directive[6] and the "Electronic Communications" package[7]), and policies on consumer protection.[8]

Secondly, in areas without a clear competence, Community legislators have exploited soft law instruments such as guidelines, recommendations or Green Papers and have designed extensive proposals (or attempted to do so) with the aim of achieving equivalent national legislation. For example, the Commission has expanded the Community's competence for the media sector by proposing a series of communications on the transition from analogue to digital, with the aim

---

[6] Directive 2000/31/EC of the European Parliament and of the Council of 8 June 2000 on certain legal aspects of information society services, in particular electronic commerce, in the Internal Market (*E-commerce Directive*) O.J. [2000] L 178/16.

[7] See, in particular: Directive 2002/21/EC of the European Parliament and of the Council of 7 March 2002 on a common regulatory framework for electronic communications networks and services (*Framework Directive*), O.J. [2002] L 108/33.

[8] This phenomenon has been described as "cultivated spillover," with the Commission systematically linking different issues through studies and/or reports, or adopting policy measures that rendered other measures necessary or desirable (Natalicchi, 2001).

to accelerate switchover (the Commission has set the indicative target date of 2012). Although the management of spectrum remains a treasured national issue, there is certainly a need for regional coordination and the EU has a useful role to play in this respect. However, the Commission's rhetoric inevitably leaps further, linking the realization of benefits at the national level (increased efficiency in spectrum use, improved quality of picture and greater choice) to the development of cross-border and pan-European services for which "part of any spectrum dividend should be made available,"[9] even if it remains unclear what these services are and on what grounds the Commission is promoting them so keenly.

Thirdly, the diminished capability of national authorities to deal with cross-national and cross-sectoral developments has led to calls for European action. For instance, the Commission has praised the benefits of convergence trends between the telecommunications, broadcasting and ICT sectors in terms of employment, consumer choice and cultural diversity while, at the same time, has warned about the risks of being surpassed by Europe's major global competitors. Using "carrot and stick" tactics, it has again conditioned the realization of national economic benefits to co-ordination at the regional level. In the 1997 Green Paper on Convergence, the Commission noted that: "the pace and scope of change, if not co-ordinated at a European level, could risk creating significant new barriers between Member States and slowing the transition to the Information Society."[10] The Commission thus attributed itself a major and central role in the delivery of convergence (a multi-dimensional dynamic and still undefined notion), and its associated benefits, introducing major regulatory reforms in the areas of content, spectrum, networks and digital rights. This was set out in the wider context of the i2010 initiative, which defined the overall strategic framework for the creation of a single European information space and

---

[9] European Commission: Communication from the Commission to the Council, the European Parliament, the European Economic and Social Committee and the Committee of the Regions on accelerating the transition from analogue to digital broadcasting, Brussels, COM(2005) 204 final, 3.

[10] European Commission: Green Paper on the regulatory implications of convergence between the telecommunications, media and information technology sectors: towards and Information Society approach. (*The Convergence Green Paper*), COM (1997) 623, at 34.

the achievement of an all-inclusive and democratic society where all information, media and communications services would become easily accessible to all citizens.[11]

The development of a distinct and often wide-reaching EU media policy is thus the result not only of the desire to deepen cross-border trade of broadcasting and other communications services, but of the wider strategic goal of creating an "integrated" or "connected" Europe. However, it is clear that such a goal is far from realized, presaging everlasting follow-up work in the area of media and communications policy. Critically, these are not one-off interventions ending with the eventual publication of a Communication or a Recommendation, but on-going initiatives, which result in a boost of the Commission's own role and influence in this area. The exact boundaries of EU media policy, however, remain porous and its objectives undefined, or worse, ill-defined. It could be argued that the EU policy is, in this as in other areas, simply, pragmatically and inevitably the result of what is, in essence, a moving and living target: the European project itself.

The Impact of EU Media Policy on European Integration

What is the relevance (if any) and potential contribution of specific EU media policy initiatives to European cultural integration? The major EU instrument in this respect was the Television without Frontiers Directive (TVWF), which was first adopted in 1989. The Directive coordinates national regulations in a number of fields relating to the provision of broadcasting services. These include establishment criteria, advertising, sponsorship, tele-shopping, protection of minors, public order, right of reply, and the promotion of European programs. Member States are required to ensure that broadcasters under their jurisdiction comply with the minimum program standards set out in the Directive,

---

[11] See Communication from the Commission of 1 June 2005 to the Council, the European Parliament, the European Economic and Social Committee and the Committee of the Regions - "i2010—A European Information Society for growth and employment" [COM (2005) 234 final, June] http://www.ec.europa.eu/information_society/activities/internationalrel/docs/wsis/com02062005_en.pdf.

although they can also impose additional (stricter) domestic requirements, as most Member States do. The TVWF Directive has recently been reviewed, to update it and modernize it in the light of technological and market developments, and re-christened the "Audiovisual Media Services" (AVMS) Directive. This new title reflects the extension of the scope of the rules to cover video on-demand services irrespective of the technology used to deliver them, or the platform through which they are accessed. After two years of intense negotiations, the new rules were adopted in December 2007, with two years envisaged for transposition into national law within the Member States.

In recognition of the fact that users exercise greater choice and control over on-demand offers, the Directive distinguishes between linear and non-linear services, and applies different regulatory requirements: linear services are defined as analogous to television broadcasting, with scheduled content "pushed" by the broadcaster to the viewer, while non-linear services are "pulled" by the viewer. The Directive applies a higher tier of regulatory controls to linear services, similar to the ones currently applied to television broadcasting, albeit with some modest liberalization of advertising restrictions (for example the removal of the requirement that twenty minutes elapse between advertising breaks) and product placement, which can now be permitted in certain genres (e.g., cinematographic films and series made for television) and under certain conditions (e.g., signalling requirements and no undue prominence). On-demand services, on the other hand, are subject to lower levels of regulation, primarily designed to provide protections for minors against content which could seriously cause harm (i.e., adult and extremely violent content), prohibit content which incites hatred on the basis of sex, religion, race and nationality, promote the production and distribution of European works, encourage greater access to services by people with disabilities, and ensure that the content meets minimum qualitative advertising rules (e.g., general prohibition of tobacco advertising and restrictions on advertising of alcohol to minors). The Directive establishes only minimum requirements, but Member States can go further and adopt stricter rules in accordance with their national interests and culture (which most have done in the area of broadcasting).

Even if the Directive is based on a "services" rationale rather than a "cultural" one (where harmonization continues to be firmly excluded under article 151 of the EC Treaty), some provisions indirectly pursue wider cultural goals with the objective to "create a closer union amongst people."[12] As the following sections will illustrate, this is the case with Articles 4 and 5 on the promotion of European and independent productions, and Article 3a on events of major importance to society.

THE PROMOTION OF EUROPEAN AND INDEPENDENT WORKS

Film and television productions are seen as extremely important instruments for the dissemination of culture and identity. Articles 4 and 5 of the TVWF call on the Member States to ensure where practicable and by appropriate means, that broadcasters within their jurisdiction reserve the majority of their transmission time for European works, and at least 10% of their broadcasting time or programming budget to European works, particularly recent ones, created by producers who are independent from broadcasters. This excludes time devoted to news, sports events, games, advertising and tele-shopping services. Article 6 paragraph 4 spells out that productions which are not "European works" but are made in the framework of bilateral co-production agreements concluded between Member States and third countries will be treated as European works provided that the Community co-producers supply a majority share of the production costs and the production is not controlled by the producer from the third country.

Even though these regulations refer primarily to television programs, the expectation was that they would have a positive impact on the production of European audiovisual works, in particular on feature films. The Directive also aimed at the construction of a European identity in opposition to what was perceived to be a culturally invasive "other." Thus, the goal was twofold. Firstly, to strengthen the competitiveness of the European audiovisual industry; and, secondly, by doing so, to promote cultural diversity and heritage in Europe, assuming that as long as the audiovisual industry was strong, cultural diversity would follow.

On the basis of reports forwarded by the Member States, the European Commission reports every two years on the application of these provisions in the Member States. In its Seventh Report on the

---

[12] See Recital 1 of the "Television without Frontiers Directive" (1989).

application of Articles 4 and 5 of the Television without Frontiers Directive[13] covering the 2003–2004 period, the Commission highlighted how Europe's television broadcasters on average devoted over 60% of their programming time to European works and over 30% to works by independent European producers. The Commission reported that the EU-average transmission time reserved for European works by all covered channels in all Member States was 65.18% in 2003 and 63.32% in 2004, representing a 1.86 point decrease over the reference period. However, when considered against the results of previous reporting periods, the average proportion for European works was 66.95% in 2001 and 66.10% in 2002 in the EU-15, which effectively amounts to a fall of 3.63 points over four consecutive years (2001–2004). The Commission attributes this fall to two factors. Firstly, the fact that the report for the first time included figures from the 10 Member States that joined the Union in 2004 whose broadcasters and regulators have had little experience in implementing these measures and reporting on their application. Secondly, the Commission has included data on all channels concerned, regardless of their importance in terms of audience share (secondary channels with less than 3% share were previously not included). This change in the Commission's measurement is regrettable. If the goal is to encourage viewing and by extension production of EU works, it would seem reasonable to link more directly viewing figures with program expenditure in the overall assessment, and focus on those channels that command the largest audiences.

As far as independent, European works the EU-average proportion reserved for European works by independent producers (independent productions) broadcast by all covered channels in all Member States was 31.39% in 2003 and 31.50% in 2004, representing a 0.11 point increase over the reference period. Again, however, if compared with the previous reference periods (37.51% in 1999, 40.47% in 2000, 37.75% in 2001 and 34.03% in 2002), there was a considerable decrease of 6.25 points in four years (2001–2004) and an equally large decrease

---

[13] Communication from the Commission to the European Parliament, the Council, the European Economic and Social Committee and the Committee of the Regions - Seventh communication on the application of Articles 4 and 5 of Directive 89/552/EEC "Television without Frontiers," as amended by Directive 97/36/EC, for the period 2003–2004, COM/2006/0459.

(6.01 points) over six consecutive years (1999–2004). Thus, it could be said that the overall medium-term trend was downwards, painting a relatively gloomy future picture.

Unsurprisingly, many of the small specialist channels are generally unable to meet the Directive's requirements and, indeed, in the case of small broadcasters or start-ups, the burden of compliance may be very onerous. However, the fact that many of the small and niche channels do not (and probably will never) reach the quotas in Articles 4 and 5 should not obscure the fact that this explosion of channels has provided many more opportunities for independent and European production than existed before.

THE MEDIA PROGRAM

The objective set out in Articles 4 and 5 of the Television without Frontiers Directive of promoting the transmission of European programs and independent films through quota mechanisms was to be empty of meaning if there were not enough local productions to fill them. This is how specific programs to boost European content such as the *MEDIA I* and *MEDIA II*, the *Eurimages Fund* or the *eContent* multi-annual program have become a key component of EU audiovisual policy. Its purpose is to provide financial support to expand Europe's output of quality films and TV programs and to make the local industry more competitive internationally. A major goal is to counter the European audiovisual industry trade deficit with the US industry which is estimated to be in the range of 6 to 7 billion Euros every year.

The Council under the chairmanship of France formally established *MEDIA* programs in 1990.[14] They are jointly run by the DG Information Society and the Media and the Education, Audiodivual and Culture Executive Agency and deal with (i) training of professionals, (ii) the development of production projects (feature films, television drama, documentaries, animation and new media) as well as companies; (iii) the distribution of cinematographic works and audiovisual programs; (iv) the promotion of cinematographic works and

---

[14] The initiative was based on a modest program which the Commission had earlier established using its own resources in 1988 as MEDIA 92. The Council of Ministers' endorsement strengthened the program which was renamed MEDIA 95.

audiovisual programs and (v) the support for cinematographic festivals. It is divided into two sub-programs: *MEDIA Plus* and *MEDIA Training*. The *MEDIA Plus* program entered into force in January 2001 and was equipped with a budget of 513 million Euro. About 60% of the funds are destined to support the European cinemas network which has 570 cinemas in more than 60 countries. The *MEDIA training* activities, on the other hand, focus on advanced training in areas like economic, financial and commercial management, screenplay writing, and multimedia technologies and benefit from a budget of 59.4 million Euro. In July 2004, the European Commission proposed continuing these sub-programs under the title Media 2007, to run from 2007–2013, with a budget of just over one billion euro.

THE RELATIVE IMPACT OF THE QUOTA PROVISIONS

The so-called "quota provisions" remain a highly contentious measure. The "where practicable" clause reveals the deep divides between the Member States at the time of the negotiations. The provisions have been described as effectively resulting in a highly protectionist system of quotas intended to boost the European production industry against foreign competition, and in particular to challenge the screen dominance of the United States (Katsirea, 2003). Indeed, the combination of industrial policy (European competitiveness) and cultural policy (the protection of Europe's audiovisual heritage) goals appears to have little to do with the removal of barriers to cross-border trade.

Whether the Directive has had any significant impact on the development of a European culture or identity, and whether Articles 4 and 5 in particular have contributed positively to the process of European integration is also far from clear. It has been argued that, because the European requirement may be fulfilled by a Member States' own national product, the quotas neither contribute to intra-European understanding nor develop a European collaboration (Harrison and Woods, 2000). There continues to be limited demand for cross-border media and even in areas which are international in nature programs are for the most part presented and interpreted by audiences according to a predominantly domestic perspective. National productions continue to be most popular amongst audiences, to the detriment of not only American productions but also productions from other European countries, while entertainment formats are not simply imported, but adapted to suit local tastes (Liebes and Livingstone 1998). There remains a concern about the impact of foreign films or television programs on the national public which results in enhanced efforts for the preservation of national "culture," understood as the 'embodiment of some distinctive collective configuration of values, beliefs and practices' (Schlesinger, 2001: 99).

In the area of news reporting, arguably the most critical in shaping citizens attitudes towards Europe, editorial decisions favored the presentation of national television news, versus news from other European countries, while the printed media showed almost no capacity to travel across borders, despite increased foreign ownership (McQuail, 2001). Furthermore, although there is evidence of a link between positive European media coverage of EU affairs and support for European integration (de Vreese and Boomgaarden, 2006), empirical research continues to be limited regarding the reporting of "Europe" as a distinct subject, disputing the existence of a genuinely European public sphere, something which is perceived as a necessary condition for any further political integration.[15]

In effect, there is an inherent tension within the cultural goals of the Directive. On the one hand, there is the largely implicit goal to build a European cultural identity through the increased exposure to content from other European countries; on the other hand, the Directive, and European media policy in general, is geared towards the recognition and protection, through the media, of the diversity that characterizes the national cultures, in the spirit of the broader European theme of "Unity in Diversity," resulting in the reaffirmation of national identities. Sometimes the two may be in conflict as where, for example, national regulations relating to program production in indigenous languages act as a barrier to intra-Community trade in program production.

Somehow unexpectedly, the issue of quotas did not feature prominently in the latest review discussions, with only Germany openly questioning their existence. The Commission did not propose any changes to the quota provisions for linear services. There was general agreement

---

[15] Some studies point out to the overall extremely small proportion of EU topics in the national media, with EU players featuring in only minor roles (Machill et al., 2006).

in the consultation process and in discussions on the Commission's Issues Paper on "Cultural Diversity and the Promotion of European and Independent Audiovisual Production" of July 2005 that while it was accepted that the current quota provisions had a relatively positive effect with regard to the defense of the European audiovisual production sector, such rules were not appropriate for on-demand services and could risk hindering the development of these services. The proposals did, nonetheless, introduce a requirement for Member States to promote access to European works on non-linear services and an obligation on Member States to report to the Commission on progress in this respect.

Both the Council and the European Parliament supported the Commission's proposals but went further and introduced a list of examples of how such promotion could take place, including the financial contribution made by such services to the production and rights acquisition of European works or a share and/or prominence of European works in the catalogue of programs proposed by the service. In this way, European institutions have sent a political signal of the importance still attached to the promotion and support for European content. However, the likelihood that this provision will have any direct impact on the production and distribution of European content is feeble, to say the least.

THE LEGISLATION ON "MAJOR EVENTS"

Another interesting example of the pursuit of public interest goals through the TVWF initiative is the so-called "major events legislation." In 1996, Rupert Murdoch almost acquired the European rights to broadcast the Olympic Games for the period 2000–2008. Two years later, his German colleague Leo Kirch was more successful in bidding for the rights for the next two World Cup soccer finals in 2002 and 2006, taking them away from the EBU (Solberg, 2002). These episodes alarmed commercial and public free-to-air broadcasters across Europe. The European Parliament lobbied vigorously in favor of making certain sporting events accessible to all citizens on free-to-air, rather than on pay television. The competition controversy over the first *Eurovision* decision[16] had made reliance on a joint bidding system for broadcasting rights uncertain while European digital pay-TV operators seemed to be on their way to monopolize property rights to major events (and

---

[16] Commission decision *EBU/Eurovision System* [1993] OJ L 179/23.

particularly sports events). There was a general feeling that access to certain content should be ensured and that generic competition law was not the right instrument to deal with media specific policy concerns.

The first review of the Television without Frontiers Directive in 1997 offered a good opportunity to address the issue, and Article 3(a) was introduced. It allows Member States to draw a list of national or non-national events that they consider to be of "major importance to society," which should be available for free live or through deferred transmission, even if pay television stations have bought the exclusive rights. Although these measures might impede the free flow of services from and to other EU countries, they are accepted insofar as they seek to ensure that a substantial proportion of the population of the Member State is not deprived of viewing these events.

Each country may draw a list of national or international protected events and notify this to the Commission who will verify their compatibility with Community law within three months.[17] A consolidated list of measures taken by the Member States is published on an annual basis.[18] Naturally, the lists vary from country to country depending on national traditions and preferences, but in most countries these lists primarily refer to sports events (particularly 'football').[19] Although Article 3(a) does not mention sports explicitly, Recital 18 of the Directive refers to the Olympic Games, the World Cup and the European football championships as examples of these events.

The introduction of provisions on the access of the public to events of major importance is relatively new to the concept of

---

[17] This is a procedural rather than a substantial check, as the Commission examines issues of transparency, effective and due notification, proportionality, but not at the content itself.

[18] At the time of writing, only Italy, Germany, the UK, Austria and Ireland had implemented measures while France and Belgium have submitted drafts. See http://europa.eu.int/comm/avpolicy/regul/twf/3bis/implement_en.htm.

[19] For instance, Germany includes The summer and winter Olympic games; all European Championship and World Cup matches involving the German national football team and the final of any European football club competition (Champions League, *UEFA* Cup) involving a German Club. In Italy, all events but one (the Italian music festival of San Remo) are sports-related. In addition to football events, Austria has included the World Alpine skiing championship, the Vienna Philharmonic Orchestra's New Year concert and The Vienna Opera Ball.

media regulation, and has been seen as the most important innovation brought about by the revision of 1997 (Drijber, 1999).[20] The legislation aims to strike a delicate balance between the industry's entrepreneurial interest in marketing high profile sports and other events through exclusive subscription channels, with integration and cultural benefits flowing from the wide coverage of major sports and the individual's special interest in receiving information on these events (Grünwald, 2003).

Underlying this provision are some economic-related rationales. The possibility that, by obtaining access to key content, a firm could acquire a dominant position in the market for certain forms of content and would be both able and willing to use that dominant position to restrict competition in the downstream infrastructure. However, a second and much more powerful set of arguments relate to the social function attributed to sports. In this light, the public should not be forced to pay more to view sports that are part of their cultural environment.[21] The EU Member States have formally recognized the "social significance of sport, in particular its role in forging identity and bringing people together."[22] This understanding was further developed in a Declaration on the specific characteristics of sport and its social function in Europe adopted in Nice.[23] Televised sports do not share all of the above social benefits, nevertheless they are a fundamental part of the wider social phenomenon. It has also been suggested that televised sports constitute a means of promoting national discourses and sentiments (Barker, 1999).

The potential of sports as a means of encouraging national integration and celebrating identity is likely to be reduced if only a minority

---

[20] Yet, the idea should not be viewed as an EU innovation. The UK had a similar provision in the 1990 Broadcasting Act and in France the *Conseil supérieur de l'audiovisuel* had already agreed a list of nonexclusive events with *Canal Plus* (Art.18 of the *cahier de charges* of Canal Plus).

[21] This argument requires that the sport and the event actually enjoy a widespread recognition by the general public. If this assumption is not satisfied, the legitimacy of a listed event is questionable.

[22] Declaration 29, Annexed to the Treaty of Amsterdam.

[23] The Declaration is available at: http://europa.eu.int/comm/sport/doc/ecom/decl_nice_2000_en.pdf See also: Resolution of the European Parliament on the role of the European Union in the field of sport, 1997 OJ C 200/252 and European Commission: Report to the European Council with a view to safeguarding current sports structures and maintaining the social function of sport within the Community framework COM (1999) 644 final (*The Helsinki Report on Sport*).

of the people have access to the channels broadcasting a specific event. Some sporting events reflect common identity and are indeed of such national importance that broad free access should be given to them (Wachtmeister, 1998). The TWVF adopts this "cultural" line, recognizing the importance of access to information on any event that could constitute "great common experiences" of shared social and cultural values.

In effect, the EU intervention can be seen as a response to the fear that top sporting events would migrate (or be siphoned off) to subscription television, and hence, inaccessible to the great majority of the population (Hoehn and Lancefield, 2003). Thus, in truth, this piece of legislation had protectionist cultural aims, rather than economic aims (Carter, 2001). There is an underlying intention in Article 3(a) to protect national broadcasting companies that might otherwise be prevented from broadcasting certain events. Some argue that this is justified based on the fact that national broadcasting companies have public service responsibilities which make them less profit-driven and less profitable than they would otherwise be and, for that reason, they cannot afford to outbid big commercial broadcasting companies (Temple Lang, 1998). Even if major events legislation remains controversial, and if it appears to be increasingly difficult to justify on public interest grounds, it has remain untouched in the current revision, being an example where cultural and social objectives have prevailed over market imperatives.

Concluding Remarks

The idea of a 'European identity' is closely connected to the idea of furthering European integration and strengthening the EU in an increasingly globalized geopolitical context. The Treaty of Rome does not specifically acknowledge the political and cultural dimensions of the media. When combined with the principle of subsidiarity, this absence seemingly leaves little margin of manoeuvre at the EU level in the field of media, which has always been perceived as an intrinsically national matter.

As a result, the "stated aims" of the European Union's media policy have been presented in essence as economic: ensure the free movement of services and promote the development of a large European media market, especially in the audiovisual sector, that could compete in scale with the US. The reality, however, is not as simple. As this chapter illustrates, despite the fact that the scope for supra national action in the audiovisual sector is relatively small, the European institutions have effectively played a significant role in developing a "European media policy," which unstated objective is the enhancement, through the media, of European identity and citizenship as a key element of the European integration project and the democratic foundations of the Union. We have seen how EU action, directly through regulation, but also indirectly through positive aid measures such as subsidies for EU productions, has been substantial. However, it is generally difficult to assess whether this has had any impact, for better or worse, on European integration. At times, the effect of a particular measure has actually been quite contrary to its intended purpose. The speculation around the contribution that satellite broadcasting could make to the development of a European cultural identity has not materialized in practice. We have seen, for example, how while "European quotas" were meant to promote trans-border movement of European television works, they resulted in the promotion of domestic programming. There is indeed little evidence that the system of quotas has contributed to a greater understanding of, or interest in, different European cultures, and much less to the development of a distinct "pan-European" cultural identity.

This notwithstanding, we can expect cultural matters (in the widest sense) to continue to play an important role in the Community's audiovisual policy. The fact that debates about the revision of the Television without Frontiers Directive concentrated on the issue of its scope or the problem of circumvention of stricter national domestic rules should not obscure the fact that the promotion of European works, including in the on-demand environment, remains an important objective of EU media policy.

In addition, initiatives in related policy areas have effectively allowed for the expansion of the EC sphere of action in the cultural realm, reinforcing the creation of a supranational legal framework. In practice, Community law has gradually restricted the capacity of Member States to regulate their media and has encouraged the convergence of national media policies across Europe. The wide-ranging use of Article 151 shows that cultural diversity has become an important aspect of the EU integration process and part of the EU language (Donders,

2003). The leading role of the European Commission not only in shaping national audiovisual and cultural policies but also in developing a 'European' media policy of its own must be accredited.

The distribution of competences over the media still remains unclear and highly controversial. Some prominent authors are markedly against the use of what they view as Community's essentially technocratic decision making processes to achieve political goals which belong to the national realm (Levy, 1999). This is a legitimate concern. At times, the distribution of competences in the media arena appears rather as a power struggle of the Member States to avoid interference by the Community, than as a constructive coordination. These tensions are unlikely to disappear in the near future, and it can be argued that the European integration project benefits from them, as well as from the interaction between the various levels of governance in this area. Indeed, EU action in the sphere of media has had an overall positive effect. However, there is a danger that the drive to develop a pan-European culture and a pan-European identity might conflict with, or even fundamentally compromise, the diversity within the individual national cultures, thereby undermining the competence of national governments in this field. All in all, the centrality of socio-political considerations in the EU media policy agenda raises questions about the desirable frontiers of EU media policy. Whether the current balance is sustainable in the long run remains to be seen.

REFERENCES

Andrew, Christopher and Gordievsky, Oleg (1993) *Comrade Kryuchkov's Instructions: Top Secret Files on KGB Foreign Operations 1975–1985*, Stanford University Press, Palo Alto.

Banus, Enrique (2002) "Cultural Policy in the EU and the European Identity." In Farrell, Mary, Fella, Stefano and Newman, Michael (eds.) *European Integration in the Twenty First Century: Unity in Diversity?*, Sage, London, 158–184.

Barendt, Eric and Hitchens, Lesley (2000) *Media Law: Cases and Materials*, Longman, London.

Barker, Colin (1999) *Television, Globalisation and Cultural Identities*, Open University Press, Buckingham.

Carter, E. J. (2001) "Market definition in the broadcasting sector." 24 *World Competition* 1, 92–124.

Collins, Richard and Murroni, Cristina (1996) *New Media, New Policies: Media and Communications Strategy for the Future*, Polity Press, Cambridge.

Donders, Yvonne (2003) "The Protection of Cultural Rights in Europe: None of the EU's business?" 10 *Maastricht Journal of European and Comparative Law* 2, 117–147.

Drijber, Berend J. (1999) "The revised Television Without Frontiers Directive: Is it fit for the next century?" 36 *Common Market Law Review* 1, 87–122.

Grünwald, Andreas (2003) *Possible options for the review of the European Convention on Transfrontier Television*, Council of Europe Report, April.

Guibernau, Montserrat (ed). (2001) *Governing European Diversity*, Sage, London.

Harcourt, Alison (2005) *The European Union and the regulation of media markets*, Manchester University Press, Manchester.

Harrison, Jackie and Woods, Lorna (2000) "European Citizenship: Can Audiovisual Policy Make a Difference?" 38 *Journal of Common Market Studies* 3, 471–495.

Hills, Jill and Michalis, Maria (2000) "Restructuring Regulation: Technological Convergence and European Telecommunications and Broadcasting Markets." 7 *Review of International Political Economy* 3, 434–464.

Katsirea, Irini (2003) "Why the European broadcasting quota should be abolished." 28 *European Law Review* 2, 190–209.

Levy, David A. (1999) *Europe's digital revolution. Broadcasting regulation, the EU and the nation State*, Routledge, London.

Liebes, Tamar and Livingstone, Sonia (1998) "European Soap Operas: The Diversification of a Genre." 13 *European Journal of Communication* 2, 147–180.

Machill, Marcell and Beiler, Markus et al. (2006) "Europe-Topics in Europe's Media: the Debate about the European Public Sphere. A Meta Analysis of Media Content Analyses." 21 *European Journal of Communication* 1, 57–88.

McQuail, Dennis (2001) "The Media in Europe." In Guibernau, Montserrat (ed), *Governing European Diversity*, Sage, London, 195–259.

Schlesinger, Philip (2001) "Tensions in the Construction of European Media Policies." In Morris N., Waisbord S. (eds), *Media and Globalisation. Why the State matters*, Rowman and Littlefield, Maryland, 95–117.

Solberg, Harry A. (2002) "Cultural Prescription—The European Commission's Listed Events Regulation—Over Reaction?" 5 *Culture, Sport, Society* 2, 1–28.

Vreese de, Claes H and Boomgaarden, Hajo G. (2006) "Media Effects on Public Opinion about the Enlargement of the European Union." 44 *Journal of Common Market Studies* 2, 419–36.

Ward, David (2002) *The European Union Democratic Deficit and the Public Sphere. An evaluation of media policy*, IOS Press, Amsterdam.

Whiddington, Charles (2000) "European Union." In de Avillez Pereira, Miguel (ed.) *Antitrust and New Media*, Kluwer Law International, The Hague, 173–200.

CHAPTER 12

The Clash and Resonance: Media Pluralism in European Regulatory Policies[1]

BEATA KLIMKIEWICZ

> Only where things can be seen by many in a variety of aspects without changing their identity, so that those who are gathered around them know they see sameness in utter diversity, can worldly reality truly and reliably appear.
>
> Hannah Arendt[2]

Introduction

Media pluralism has been widely used in European media policies as a valuable normative concept rather than a category for regular measurement and monitoring. It has mostly generated a consensus over its merits and importance for the democratic processes and identity formation at the European level. These processes are closely related to media exposure of distinctive opinions on European matters, as well as values and cultural representations that influence them. Indeed, various studies show that the news media matters in shaping public opinion about European integration, but mainly when their users are exposed to a *considerable level* of news coverage with a consistent evaluative direction.[3] It was also observed that highly knowledgeable media

---

[1] This is a revised version of the text published first in *Press Freedom and Pluralism in Europe: Concepts and Conditions* ed. by A, Czepek, M. Hellwig and Ewa Nowak (2009), Bristol: Intellect.

[2] Arendt, H. (1958), *The Human Condition*, Chicago: The University of Chicago Press, 57.

[3] de Vreese, C. H.; Boomgaarden, H. G. (2006) "Media Effects on Public Opinion about the Enlargement of the European Union." *Journal of Communication and Media Studies*, Vol. 44, No. 2, 419–436.

users are more likely to support the idea of advanced European integration. At the same time they are also more likely to reflect and think critically about the democratic nature of EU institutions.[4] Media pluralism contributes to richness of European public opinion and identity formation, yet its complexity has a propensity toward ambiguity. Its interpretational variety, the manifold character, constitutive vagueness and ever-changing circumstances provide for a wide range of ways in which the concept is being used in the formulation of policy objectives and rationales, as well as in policy implementation.

This contribution aims at a conceptual analysis of media pluralism as it has been used and operationalized in European media policies. Three aspects will be observed in this respect: vocabulary used, methods of reasoning, and development of a policy process itself. The chapter argues that problematization of media pluralism stems from different standards of rationality (cutting across geopolitical divisions), and that it implies an ambivalent policy-makingand ambiguous language in which policy process is negotiated.[5] Despite this conflict of rationalities, media pluralism has stimulated policy resonance, especially at an institutional and participatory level.

Definitions and Approaches in Media Policy

CONCEPTUAL INTERPRETATIONS

The context and scale of media pluralism, as well as its relations and interdependencies with the political system and larger society, define the way and discourse through which the term itself is conceptualized and operationalized as a policy rationale. Media pluralism is approached at a number of layers through which complexity of the media manifests itself. These include: a macro level of media systems (media

---

[4] Karp, J.A.; Banducci, S. A. and Bowler, S. (2003) "To Know it is to Love it. Satisfaction with Democracy in the European Union." *Comparative Political Studies*, Vol. 36, No. 2, 271–292. See also: Inglehart, R. (1990), Karp, J.A.; Banducci, S. A. and Bowler, S. (2003).

[5] A close relationship between ambiguity of language and ambivalence of political conduct was distinguished and conceptualized by Michael Oakeshott (1996) *The Politics of Faith and the Politics of Scepticism*, New Haven and London: Yale University Press.

ownership and service structures, entry costs and conditions), a meso level of media institutions (media performance, professional practices, user access and the way the user interacts with the content and services), and a micro level of media content. Media pluralism is also being interpreted through conceptual dichotomies or alternatives such as external/internal, proportional/open, organized/spontaneous, polarized/moderate, evaluative/descriptive or reactive/interactive/proactive. The table below illustrates this conceptual framework:

Table 1: Comparison of conceptual dichotomies and alternatives of media pluralism

EXTERNAL	* plurality of independent and autonomous media outlets and providers, *multiple centers of ownership, production, performance and distribution control	ORGAN-IZED	*media pluralism is organized in a segmented structure of media outlets and providers representing different social groups, cultural communities and political orientations, *a strong link to institutions representing these groups and interests
INTERNAL	*diversity of media contents, services and sources reflecting and generating a broad variety of opinions, views, representations and values of a social, ethical, political and cultural nature	SPONTA-NEOUS	*media system is structured more spontaneously, *media representation of various interests and values is individualized
PROPOR-TIONAL (REPRE-SENTATI-VE)	*media pluralism proportionally reflects existing population's preferences; political, geographical and cultural (including ethnic, linguistic and religious) differentiation of a society;	POLAR-IZED	*media are identified with ideologically opposed tendencies; distinct cultural, ethnic, religious traditions (ethnic, cultural, religious cleavages are deep), *advocacy and commentary-oriented journalism
OPEN	*media pluralism equally or openly reflects population's preferences; political, geographical and cultural differentiation of a society	MODER-ATE	*ideological distance represented by the various media is narrow, tendencies toward the center are stronger, *cultural, ethnic, linguistic differences are not projected into the media structure

DESCRIP-TIVE	*describes media pluralism conceptual and factual features, indicators, aspects	REACTIVE	*media pluralism is evoked by diversity of opinions, political views, identity choices, cultural representations among users through media performance, services, content, structural aspects
EVALUA-TIVE	*evaluates descriptively identified features	INTERAC-TIVE	*media pluralism results from a variety of interactions between media users and providers
		PROAC-TIVE	*media pluralism generates and actively shapes diversity of opinions, political views, identity choices, cultural representations among users through media performance, services, content, structural aspects

Sources: own research, MM-CM, 1994; McQuail, 1992; Van Cuilenburg and Van der Wurff, 2000; Kekes, 1996; Hallin and Mancini 2004.

In the context of media policy, an operational definition of media pluralism has most notoriously developed around the axis of external/ internal dimension. In one of most comprehensive ways this axis has been elaborated by the Council of Europe and its advisory committees (later successively used and modified by other European institutions). The Activity Report of the Committee of Experts on Media Concentration and Pluralism (MM-CM) conceives pluralism as *"internal in nature, with a wide range of social, political and cultural values, opinions, information and interests finding expression within one media organisation, or external in nature, through a number of such organisations, each expressing a particular point of view."*[6]

---

[6] MM-CM, Council of Europe's Committee of Experts on Media Concentrations and Pluralism (1994) *The Activity Report of the Committee of Experts on Media Concentrations and Pluralism*, submitted to the 4th European Ministerial Conference on Mass Media Policy. Prague, 7–8 December 1994. See also: Jakubowicz, K. (2006) *Media Pluralism and Concentration: Searching for a Productive Research and Policy Agenda (in the light of the Council of Europe Experience)*, paper presented at the Working Group 3 meeting of COST Action A30, Budapest, 22–23 September 2006.

The frequently drawn distinction between *external* "plurality of autonomous and independent media" and *internal* "diversity of media contents available to the public" seen from the media supply point of view, revealed a problematic relationship between the two dimensions. Namely, the research has not so far conclusively proved that this relationship is casual and direct. A strong link between plurality of ownership and diversity of content cannot be in practice easily demonstrated. Although some researchers sustain that extensive media concentration leads to promotion of corporate values and political preferences of media owners and advertisers in media contents,[7] others convincingly argue that a direct link between media concentration and content diversity cannot be identified in quantitative terms.[8] Most commentators also agree that media pluralism is a multidimensional issue and should not be confined to mere plurality of ownership and diversity of content. Let us begin to approach the term from a slightly different angle.

THE POTENTIAL OF MEDIA PLURALISM

The traditional concept of media pluralism is being challenged by the changing media ecology and societal transformation resulting from the impact of the digital revolution, convergence and multiplicity of media platforms, services and providers. In this new context media pluralism presents a POTENTIAL full usage and exploitation of which depends on individual users, their ability to read (also critically and against the production routines) the "media script," to generate their own messages, and ways of distribution and interaction with the media services. The potential of media pluralism can be conceived through its "building blocks" and the capacities these blocks are able to mobilize. Thus it is to be thought as a *condition conducive to* the balance between multiple centers of media control, compensation of multiple sources of information, competition between various opinions and views, socialization through numerous forms of media access and participation, recognition and representation of multiple values and choice between diverse forms of interaction.

---

[7] Bagdikian, B. (2000) *The Media Monopoly*, 6th edition, Beacon Press
[8] Ward, D. (2006) *Final Report on the study commissioned by the MC-S-MD "The Assessment of content diversity in newspapers and television in teh context of increasing trends towards concentration of media markets,"* MC-S-MD (2006) 001, Strasbourg: Council of Europe.

Table 2: Potential of Media Pluralism: Key Aspects and Capacities

"BUILDING BLOCKS"	CAPACITIES
MULTIPLE CENTRES OF MEDIA CONTROL	BALANCE SHARED CONTROL
MULTIPLE SOURCES	COMPLEMENTARITY COMPENSATION
MULTIPLE OPINIONS AND VIEWS	COMPETITION (DISCURSIVE, NOT INSTRUMENTAL)
MULTIPLE ACCESS AND PARTICIPATION	SOCIALISATION
MULTIPLE VALUES	RECOGNITION AND REPRESENTATION (NOT FRAGMENTATION)
MULTIPLE FORMS OF INTERACTION	CHOICE

An important capacity of the media pluralism potential is a balance between multiple centers of media control. These are not necessarily identical with the ownership structures, although the latter definitely play the most influential role as it comes to the development of media networks (usually very centralised due to complex technological conditions and investment needed). The centers of control vary in the extent to which they balance ownership and provider control with journalistic and content producer autonomy and independence, and more generally, with regulatory constraints. Subscription systems handled by digital providers are often criticised for the exclusive use of proprietary technical solutions and the lack of service interoperability, resulting in the increased control exercised both over subscribers and producers.[9] It is therefore relevant in this context to what degree multiple competing centers of media production, performance and delivery "control mutu-

---

[9] Nissen, Ch. S. (2006) *Public Service Media in the Information Society,* the Report prepared by the Group of Specialists on PSB in the Information Society (MC-S-PSB), Strasbourg: Media Division, Directorate General of Human Rights, Council of Europe.

ally themselves" and whether there is a broad respect for this limited or shared media control.

The compensation of multiple sources is linked to a "communicating vessels effect," a media user is able to activate. Media pluralism potential may be used more effectively, if a media user at a disadvantage with respect to one source of information may compensate for this lack by exploiting his access to a different source. In an era of source-recycling, when content from the same sources is re-packaged and used across the full range of media platforms and distributed by different divisions of the same conglomerate, clear identification and recognition of the sources is of crucial significance. The competition between multiple opinions and views is another key capacity of the media pluralism potential. Proliferation of the content on new platforms does not in itself guarantee pluralism. Freedom of choice is an essential possibility, which can be exercised if the choice is made between different options. It is also important *how* this choice is made. Jadwiga Staniszkis warns that competition between different opinions and views should be discursive in its nature to raise the quality of a public discussion. Competition which resembles the stock exchange where diversity becomes instrumental and rational arguments could not be developed due to technocratic procedures or journalistic routines, leads to meaningless diversity.[10]

Multiple access to, and participation in, an exchange of media images, words, and representations defines a process of socialization and shapes models of behaviour. Media use is woven into the fabric of everyday life, the media substitute for social activities and change the character of social institutions.[11] Thus, as such, the potential of media pluralism depends on the quality of socialization accompanied and strengthened by media literacy skills, such as a competence to distribute ideas in different media formats, an ability critically to read media contents and oppose, when necessary, biased and harmful media representations. Media pluralism is also often described through the capacity of recognition and representation of multiple, often conflict-

---

[10] Staniszkis, J. (2006) "Pluralizm i władza" [w] *Dziennik/Europa – Tygodnik Idei*, No. 42, 21. 10. 2006, 8–9.

[11] Schulz, W.: (2004) "Reconstructing mediatization as an analytical concept," [in] *European Journal of Communication*, Vol. 19(1).

ing values. Yet this polarised media projection of values can reinforce existing prejudices, widen the gap between different communities, or contribute to a fragmented society, in which individuals interact primarily with those in the same identity community, and are exposed mostly to those opinions with which they already agree.[12] Thus, the potential of media pluralism may be effectively used if the representation and recognition of multiple values does not lead to fragmentation and ghettoization.

Finally, the full exploitation of the media pluralism potential depends on choice between multiple forms of interactions with the media. The fact that media users may increasingly control the way how and when they interact with media services stimulates diversity. The users are free to decide what will be the proportion between attention they want to pay to passive (push) or interactive (pull) media use, what are the issues they want to scrutinise and contribute to interactively, and what contents they prefer to receive passively. Yet, an interactive future is certain to produce new types of scarcity (of talent), monopoly (bottlenecks controlled by private suppliers) and new forms of exclusion (low level of media literacy) that can only be tackled with purposeful and positive intervention to remedy information and media access asymmetry.[13] Moreover, interactive services are still not universal. Elderly people and poorer communities are much less likely to have Internet access, interactive and mobile TV and so find it harder to access more diverse content.[14]

Media pluralism comes into being through relations and context in which it is involved. It is also conditionally linked to the public sphere and articulation of issues of common concern, which may be under-

---

[12] Hoynes, W.(2002) "Why media mergers matter" [in] *openDemocracy*, 16.01.2002, http://www.opendemocracy.net/debates/article-8-24-47.jsp., accessed on 13 October 2006.

[13] See e.g., Graham, A. and Davies, G. (1997) *Broadcasting, Society and Policy in the Multimedia Age*, Lutton: John Libbey; Freedman, D. (2005) "Promoting Diversity and Pluralism in Contemporary Communication Policies in United States and the United Kingdom." *International Journal of Media Management*, Vol. 7, No. ½, 16–23; Collins, R. and Murroni, C. (1996) *New Media, New Policies*. Cambridge: Polity.

[14] Publishing Market Watch: Final Report (2005) A study commissioned by DG Enterprise to Turku School of Economics and Business Administration and Rightscom, 27 January, 2005, 117.

stood in pluralistic terms. In media policy, the relevance of the concept itself is marked by its potential. In other words, it is important how the potential of media pluralism is seen to be activated and how connections between its "building blocks" and capacities are to be stimulated in policy language, way of reasoning and development of a policy process itself.

INCLUSIVE AND AUTONOMOUS APPROACH

In media policy thinking, media pluralism is regarded in the broader social and political context - as a contribution deliberative democracy or as a fundamental condition for a democratic public sphere.[15] Such diversity being primarily about variety of views, opinions, attitudes of a political, religious, ethical nature, serves as a founding rationale for defenders of more proactive positive measures. Yet pluralism is also seen in industrial and economic terms - as increasing freedom of choice for the consumer, freedom of operation for the industry, right to self-regulation and institutional autonomy; in other words, in opposition to interventionist public regulation.

The two perspectives on the conceptualization of media pluralism for the purpose of media policy can be examined through the role of functional differentiation.[16] In the first, *inclusive* approach, the media (to contribute to appropriate functioning of a democratic system) are not seen as fully differentiated from other spheres of social life (politics, culture, civil society) and social bodies (political groups, the state, interest groups). The media, as central institutions of the pub-

---

[15] Habermas, J.(1995), *The Structural Transformation of the Public Sphere. An Inquiry into a Category of Bourgeois Society*, Cambridge, Mass: The MIT Press; Habermas, J. (1996), *Between Facts and Norms: Contributions to a Discursive Theory of Law and Democracy*, Cambridge, Mass: The MIT Press; McQuail, D. (1992), *Media Performance: Mass Communication and the Public Interest*, London: Sage Publications; Cavallin, J. (2000), "Public Policy Uses of Diversity Measures." In J. van Cuilenburg i R. van der Wurff (ed.) *Media and Open Societies: Cultural, Economic and Policy Foundations for Media Openness and Diversity in East and West*, Amsterdam: Het Spinhuis, 105–170.

[16] See: Luhmann, N. (2000), *The Reality of the Mass Media*, Stanford: Stanford University Press; Alexander, J. C. (1981), "The Mass News Media in Systemic, Historical and Comparative Perspective." In E. Katz and T. Szecskö (eds.), *Mass Media and Social Change*, Beverly Hills: Sage Publications, 17–51.

lic sphere, are expected to identify and politically expose problems (a warning function), but also to thematise them and furnish them with possible solutions (a problematizing function). Although their capacity to solve these problems seems limited, it is to be utilised to oversee the further treatment of problematic areas by the actors of a political system.[17] Thus, the inclusive option asserts that the media are institutionally connected to social and political organizations, such as political parties, interests groups, churches and cultural organizations. Media pluralism is to be best structured and achieved at the level of a media system as a whole, through the existence of a range of media outlets or organizations reflecting the points of view of different groups or cultural representations rooted in different traditions of a society. Such a system characterised by a dominant presence of external (and organized) pluralism will obviously be considered to have a high level of political and cultural parallelism (the extent to which a media system reflects the major political, cultural division in society).[18] Advocacy status of civic, cultural, religious, alternative or politically-oriented, media can also suggest that they will use alternative portrayals which may differ from the canons of professional journalism.[19]

The *autonomous* approach assumes that the media are in a process of becoming autonomous systems and networks due to functional differentiation. Thus, the media are being functionally differentiated from other systems within a society and their institutional relations with the state, political groups, cultural and social organizations are significantly dispersed.[20] Differentiation does not mean that the media system is detached from the sphere of politics and other arenas of social life. Media networks and their applications increasingly organize and shape relations between the different actors of a political and social system. As a

---

[17] Habermas, J. (1996), *Between Facts and Norms: Contributions to a Discoursive Theory of Law and Democracy*, Cambridge, Mass: The MIT Press, 359.

[18] Hallin, D. C., Mancini, P. (2004), *Comparing Media Systems: Three Models of Media and Politics*, Cambridge: Cambridge University Press, 28.

[19] Dahlgren, P. (1995), *Television and the Public Sphere: Citizenship, Democracy and the Media*, London: Sage Publications, 156–159.

[20] Luhmann, N. (2000), *The Reality of the Mass Media*, Stanford: Stanford University Press; Hallin, D. C., Mancini, P. (2004), *Comparing Media Systems: Three Models of Media and Politics*, Cambridge: Cambridge University Press.

result, these relations can be interpreted both as political and as relations of information and communication.[21] The autonomous approach can also be characterised by the growth of professional norms, self regulation and the degree of universalism in national civil cultures.[22] The trend towards differentiation is to a large extent driven by economic factors and commercialization. Media pluralism could be best manifested through the dominance of internal pluralism—achieved within each individual media outlet or organization. A system characterised by a dominant role of internal pluralism will have a low level of political and cultural parallelism and particular media outlets will aim at maintaining universal provision, neutrality and at focusing on the experience and perspective of the "common" citizen.[23] The question is whether with growing media autonomy (autonomy from a political system but not economic forces), other cultural and social fields will not lose their own autonomy as they are increasingly influenced and "colonised" by the mass media.[24]

The normative frameworks and grounds for policy options described above are rooted in different standards of rationality rather than interests. Jadwiga Staniszkis points out that "rationality" refers to the way of reasoning which is logical and correct in a light of given rationales and method of reality problematization. Hence, different or even conflicting choices of two parties using different rationales, may be perfectly rational, given the different logic and way of reality conceptualization. The conflict of interests on the other hand refers to a situation in which different parties function within a framework of the same rationales but propose different choices or solutions.[25] Inclusive

---

[21] Van Dijk, J. (2006) *The Network Society: Social Aspects of New Media*, London: Sage Publications.

[22] Hallin, D. C., Mancini, P. (2004), *Comparing Media Systems: Three Models of Media and Politics*, Cambridge: Cambridge University Press, 79.

[23] Ibid.

[24] See: Habermas, J. (1996), *Between Facts and Norms: Contributions to a Discursive Theory of Law and Democracy*, Cambridge, Mass: The MIT Press; Bourdieu, P. (1998), *On Television*, New York: The New Press; Meyer, T. (2002) *Media Democracy: How the Media Colonize Politics*, Cambridge: Polity.

[25] Staniszkis, J. (2004), *Władza globalizacji*, Warszawa: Wydawnictwo Naukowe "Scholar," 19.

and autonomous approaches to media pluralism conceptualization draw, to a certain extent, upon main conflicting lines between European institutions and pressure groups as regards regulatory initiatives on media pluralism.

Competitive Globalization: European Commission

CULTURAL DIVERSITY AND COMPETITIVENESS

The European Commission's approach towards media diversity has been governed by the logic of *competitive globalisation*—"media diversity" is important insofar as it contributes to competitiveness of European ideas, cultures, languages—and most crucially—media and communication industries as a whole, on the global scene. This strategy shares many common characteristics with the belief in autonomy of "differentiated" media systems and lacking reasons for instruments stimulating external pluralism. One of the symptomatic features is also an acceptance of internal pluralism measures, where they can strengthen competitiveness. Media pluralism has been mentioned explicitly in the AVMS Directive as one of particular rationales along with freedom of information and diversity of opinions (all linked to democracy) that justifies the application of specific rules to audiovisual media services.[26] Also, the recital 28 of the AVMS Directive asserts that "pluralism of information should be a fundamental principle of the European Union."[27] At the same time, media pluralism has been discoursively connected with "a strong, competitive and integrated European audiovisual industry."[28]

---

[26] European Parliament and the Council (2007) *Directive 2007/65/EC of the European Parliament and the Council of 11 December 2007 amending Council Directive 89/552/EEC on the coordination of certain provisions laid down by law, regulation or administrative action in Member States concerning the pursuit of television broadcasting activities (Audiovisual Media Services Without Frontiers Directive)*, O.J. 18.12. 2007 L 332/ 27–45. (http://ec.europa.eu/avpolicy/reg/avms/index_en.htm; retrieved 27.01.2008), Para. 3, p. 27.

[27] Ibid., Para. 28, p. 30.

[28] Ibid.

Some aspects of media diversity have been defined and used to protect a common European media space against US imports and to support European dominant media players. The concept of 'cultural diversity' has served as an argument for state aid to the film and audiovisual industries as well as a support for measures concerning European works and requirement of independent production during the drafting and enactment of the AVMS Directive.[29] In its issues paper on cultural diversity, the Commission called for creation of incentives increasing the distribution of European co-productions: *"Positive likely impacts in cultural terms might be a deeper understanding of Europe's cultural diversity and richness and a wider acceptance of the European integration process."*[30] In this sense, the promotion of European works, co-productions and works made by independent producers has been increasingly perceived and interpreted as an essential contribution to nurturing cultural diversity both within and outside Europe, as a pertinent way of correcting proportions between media representations of cultures on a global scale.

The relational perspective strengthens the view on cultural diversity as a key value shared by all Europeans, that needs to be constantly reaffirmed in subsequent media regulatory designs. In this process, cultural diversity contributes to fostering a European awareness and a feeling of collective belonging, intrinsically and conditionally linked to the progress of the Union.[31] It is interesting to observe how the once highly contentious European quota issue has transformed in the alchemy of media policy making and implementation into a widely accepted media policy instrument. Different approaches to cultural diversity and some criticism on implementation and monitoring functions, have not harmed a gradual consensus that the rules on the promotion of Eu-

---

[29] *"National aid to the film and audiovisual industries is one of the chief means of ensuring cultural diversity,"* Council Resolution on National Aid to the Film and Audiovisual Industries, 12.02.2001, O.J., 2001, C 73, s. 3. See also: See: European Commission (2005) *Impact Assessment – Draft Audiovisual Media Services Directive*, COM (2005) 646 final.

[30] European Commission (2005), *Issues Paper for the Liverpool Audiovisual Conference: Cultural Diversity and the Promotion of European and Independent Audiovisual Production*, Brussels: DG Information Society and Media, 4.

[31] More on this perspective see the report of Department for Culture, Media and Sport (2005) *Liverpool Audiovisual Conference: Between Culture and Commerce*, 20–22 September.

ropean and independent production have provided a stable and flexible framework for the protection of cultural diversity (seen of course from the perspective of European culture). Herein, 'cultural diversity' has conceptually functioned as a European cultural projection: it has been the conscious effort by media policy makers and industry to place recognizable images and representations of European culture (through diverse cultural expressions) in the global public sphere.[32]

Yet, the extension of the AVMS Directive's scope to non-linear audiovisual media services brings far less agreement, although it can be perfectly justified from the position of European *cultural competitiveness* in the global context. A potential of non-linear audiovisual services to replace linear services, upholds, in a view of the Commission, regulatory commitment to promotion and distribution of European works—and thus promotion of cultural diversity—on non-linear services. The AVMS Directive stipulates that on-demand media service providers promote production of and access to European works,[33] financially contribute to the production and acquisition of rights in European works, puts forward a minimum share of European works in video on demand catalogues or the attractive presentation of European works in electronic program guides.[34] Due to the risk of bypassing these regula-

---

[32] More on cultural projection see: Merelman, R.M. (1995) *Representing Black Culture: Racial Conflict and Cultural Politics in the United States*, New York: Routledge.

[33] *Directive 2007/65/EC of the European Parliament and the Council of 11 December 2007 amending Council Directive 89/552/EEC on the coordination of certain provisions laid down by law, regulation or administrative action in Member States concerning the pursuit of television broadcasting activities (Audiovisual Media Services Without Frontiers Directive)*, O.J. 18.12. 2007 L 332/ 27–45. (http://ec.europa. eu/avpolicy/reg/avms/index_en.htm; retrieved 27.01.2008), Article 3i, p. 42.

[34] Most of these added by the European Parliament during the drafting process of AVMS *Directive. European Parliament and the Council (2007) Directive 2007/65/EC of the European Parliament and the Council of 11 December 2007 amending Council Directive 89/552/EEC on the coordination of certain provisions laid down by law, regulation or administrative action in Member States concerning the pursuit of television broadcasting activities (Audiovisual Media Services Without Frontiers Directive)*, O.J. 18.12. 2007 L 332/ 27–45. (http://ec.europa.eu/ avpolicy/reg/avms/index_en.htm; retrieved 27.01.2008), para. 48. Compare with: European Parliament (2006) *Draft Report on the proposal for a directive of the European Parliament and the Council amending Council Directive 89/552/ EEC, Committee on Culture and Education, 2005/0260 (COD)*, 1.8.2006, Amendment 26, Recital 35.

tory requirements by companies set up outside the EU, the weight of cultural diversity promotion carries a more symbolic rather than pragmatic significance and might be, in the future, related more closely to public media services than non-linear services generally.

PLURALISM AS AN "ADDED" VALUE?

During the 90s, "media pluralism" has been conceptualized by the Commission merely through anti-concentration and media ownership policies (in fact, stimulating external pluralism). Attempts to introduce such media pluralism regulation have been discreetly pushed down by the Commission to the competence of Member States, equally reluctant to limit mergers of dominant national players. Thus, (external, structural) media pluralism was not seen as a value to be generated through EU media policy instruments, but rather as an "added value" to be addressed by other European (Council of Europe) or national institutions.

In 1992, at the request of the European Parliament, the European Commission published a Green Paper: *Pluralism and Media Concentration in the Internal Market*. Its main purpose was to assess the need for Community action on the question of concentration in the media (television, radio, press) and to evaluate different approaches of involved parties[35] line of and the Commission concluded that an initiative on media ownership might prove necessary.[36]

A second round of consultations resulted in a discussion paper prepared by DG Internal Market, proposing a possible 1996 draft directive on media pluralism. In the course of discussions, the document's focus was modified from 'Concentrations and Pluralism' to 'Media Ownership' in the Internal Market. Gillian Doyle points out that this signalled a move to deflect the focus from pluralism (where the Commission's competence would be uncertain) towards removing

---

[35] Commission of the European Communities (1992), *Pluralism and Media Concentration in the Internal Market: An Assessment of the Need for Community Action*, Commission Green Paper, COM (92) 480 final, Brussels, 23.12.1992.

[36] Commission of the European Communities (1994) *Follow-up to the Consultation Process relating to the Green Paper on "Pluralism and Media Concentration in the Internal Market – an Assessment of the Need for Community Action,"* COM (94) 353 final, Brussels, 5.10.1994. p. 6.

obstacles to the Internal Market.[37] Even with such significant modifications and flexibility, the initiative was rejected. Underscoring the difficulty to propose any kind of rules harmonizations between the EU Member States on media pluralism, the Commission has withdrawn from this policy area emphasising the importance of added value of additional European actions. [38]

The failure in this case stemmed not only from profound tensions between contradictory policy agendas of the involved parties. In the regulatory debate the concepts of media pluralism and media ownership elided, although they are obviously not identical. "Media pluralism" served as a conceptual shell used most often in reference to anti-concentration measures and media ownership. This limitation goes even further than confining media pluralism to external media pluralism, as it excludes a number of important structural aspects. One of them is for instance the form of financing. Diversity of media owners will not bring much difference in terms of content if these media are all financed by advertising. There is historical evidence that advertising is, in fact, a limited source—it is growing at about the same rate as the over-all economy. Thus, if policy seeks media to serve as an engine for creating new economic opportunities and jobs, it should focus on the development of media not supported by advertising.[39] Another important aspect are mutual relations and interdependencies between media structures and the larger society. This does imply also diverse ways of interacting with media as the way of interaction ultimately changes the vectors of media pluralism (pull, not push) and modes through which the media operates in a larger system.

Publication of the EP report on media pluralism following the EP's *Resolution on the risks of violation, in the EU and especially in Italy, of freedom of expression and information* (2004)[40] and drafting of AVMS Direc-

---

[37] Doyle, G. (2002), *Media Ownership. The Economics and Politics of Convergence and Concentration in the UK and European Media*, London: Sage Publications, 164.

[38] European Commission (2005), *Issues Paper for the Liverpool Audiovisual Conference: Media Pluralism – What should be the European Union's role?* Brussels: DG Information Society and Media.

[39] Galbi, D. (2001) *Communications Policy, Media Development and Convergence.* Federal Communication Commission.

[40] Resolution on the risks of violation, in the EU and especially in Italy, of freedom of expression and information, O.J. 2004, C 104 E.

tive provided a new opportunity for addressing the issue. *"The issue of media concentration is back on the political agenda,"* wrote Aidan White, Secretary General of the European Federation of Journalists in the EFJ report *Media Power in Europe: The Big Picture of Ownership.*[41] The report once again links media concentration with media pluralism concluding that pluralism is not an issue to be left to local politicians, but it is a European issue that requires a European response. "The European response" to repeated claims of the European Parliament and interest groups, however, took on a slightly different direction. This was certainly a result of coping with heterogeneous interests represented by a diversity of organizations, but more importantly following the logic of the autonomous approach, in which all policies affecting the media are to be tested against the editorial freedom and the economy of the media industry.[42]

In a series of meetings with the publishing industry,[43] it became apparent that the industry representatives clearly aim at the prevention of any new legislation at the European level to regulate media concentration and pluralism,[44] and demand recognition of a publisher's competitive position in a process of drafting policies aimed at other media market players (such as AVMS Directive).[45] Publishing indus-

---

[41] European Federation of Journalists (2006) *Media Power in Europe: The Big Picture of Ownership,* http://www.ifj.org/pdfs/EFJownership2005.pdf, accessed on October 10 2006.

[42] DG Information Society and the Media (2006) *Task Force for Co-ordination of Media Affairs,* http://europa.eu.int/information_society/media_taskforce/index_en.htm, accessed on 15 October 2006, see also: Commission for European Communities (2005) *Commission Staff Working Paper: Strengthening Competitiveness of the EU Publishing Sector, The Role of Media Policy,* SEC(2005) 1287, Brussels, 7.10.2005.

[43] These included: European Publishers' Forum 2005 (annual meeting), December 6th, Brussels, Editors-in-Chief meeting with Information Society and the Media Commissioncr Viviane Reding, Brussels, 23 September 2005 and the second meeting on 23 October 2006.

[44] See: European Publishers Council (2005) *Memorandum on Pluralism and Media Concentration addressed to the Members of the European Parliament's Intergroup on the Press, Communication and Freedom,* http://www.epceurope.org/issues/MemorandumPluralismMediaConcentration.shtml, accessed on October 20 2006.

[45] European Publisher's Forum (2005) *21ˢᵗ Century Publishing in Europe "Promoting Knowledge, Information and Diversity": Calls for Action,* Brussels December 6th, 2005, http://europa.eu.int/information_society/media_taskforce/doc/publishing/calls_for_action.pdf, accessed on October 20 2006.

try has also unanimously reminded the Commission that there has not been and there should continue to be no competence for the EU to intervene in matters of media pluralism, other than its current rules on competition and merger regulation.[46] The Commission's approach concerning competitiveness of the EU Publishing Sector has plainly demonstrated that this is the key perspective the media policy is being "filtered through." A Staff Working Paper on *Strengthening Competitiveness of the EU Publishing Sector* recognizes that the productivity of the publishing and printing industries in the EU is higher than in the US, however this sector is seen to be under strong economic pressure, due to the increasing digitization of content, changing consumer patterns and modes of distribution. Publishers have not yet been able to build the business models necessary to exploit on-line distribution; their online publications are frequently cross-subsidised by print revenues.[47] Thus, media policy should support sustainable competitiveness, bringing together the economic, environmental and social (high rates of employment) objectives of the European Union, in order "to enhance pluralism and culture at the European level."[48]

The audiovisual industry has raised equally strong arguments. Regulatory priorities were addressed directly by James Murdoch, CEO, British Sky Broadcasting during the Liverpool Audiovisual conference:

> Nobody can seriously say that there is a problem with plurality when there are hundreds of TV news channels, millions of news websites and weblogs, and—perhaps—more importantly the ability for citizens to access information in an unmediated way direct from its original source. (...) I fully accept that big companies in any industry will come under intense scrutiny and have to show that they are compet-

---

[46] ENPA (2005) *ENPA Response to the Commission Issues Paper on Media Pluralism – What Should Be the European Union's Role?*, http://ec.europa.eu/comm/avpolicy/docs/reg/modernisation/issue_papers/contributions/ip6-enpa.pdf, accessed on October 10, 2006.

[47] Commission of the European Communities (2005) *Commission Staff Working Paper: Strengthening the Competitiveness of the EU Publishing Sector, The Role of Media Policy*, SEC (2005) 1287, Brussels 7.10.2005.

[48] Ibidem, 30.

ing fairly, but I do hope that the old argument of equating bigness with a lack of plurality is consigned to the old world.[49]

This reasoning—rooted in a *competitive globalization approach*—presented one of the main lines developed in the Issues Paper *Media Pluralism—What should be the European Union's Role?*, prepared for the discussion on the new AVMS Directive during the European Audiovisual Conference in Liverpool:

> A balance between the safeguard of media pluralism in Europe and the possibilities for European companies to compete globally is crucial if we want a European presence at the global 'top table' in the communications and media sector, especially in view of trade deficit of around $8bn p.a. with the U.S.[50]

Karol Jakubowicz emphasizes that the only explanation for issuing the document which shows, in fact, no intention to deal with media pluralism, could be that the European Commission was trying to demonstrate to the European Parliament that it had made a strong commitment to take up the issue.[51]

Yet, the "added" value approach to media pluralism has not only reactive, but also proactive potential in the multi-level EU media policy-making. Following the logic of *competitive globalization*, Commission policy activities and discourses benefit from the adding of the 'value of media pluralism' to strengthen the Commission's bargaining position vis-à-vis external actors (both industry representatives and various interest groups). A good example can be the adding of the "value of media pluralism" to the project of the new AVMS Directive, promoted through the three major measures which contribute to media plural-

---

[49] Murdoch, J. (2005) Speech to the 2005 European Audiovisual Conference, 21 September 2005.

[50] European Commission, DG Information Society and the Media (2005) *Issues Paper for the Liverpool Audiovisual Conference: Media Pluralism – What should be the European Union's role?* 5.

[51] Jakubowicz, K. (2006) *Revision of the European Convention on Transfrontier Television in the Context of International Media Policy Evolution*, paper presented during the meeting of Working Group 3 of COST Action A30, Budapest, 22–23 September 2006, 5.

ism: an obligation for Member States to guarantee the independence of national regulatory authorities, the right of broadcasters to receive 'short reporting' and promotion of European works and content from independent European producers.[52]

On January 16, 2007 the Commission published a staff working document *Media Pluralism in the Member States of the European Union*, indicating further steps in a policy process regarding this matter.[53] The document sustained a familiar argument against submitting a Community initiative on pluralism at present, but it emphasized a necessity to closely monitor the situation. The monitoring process was designed to involve an independent study on media pluralism indicators (published in 2009) and a Communication from the Commission concerning these indicators. Thus, "concrete" indicators of assessing media pluralism present a crucial methodological category used for developing a more sophisticated risk-based monitoring mechanism, including such areas as:

– policies and legal instruments that support pluralism in MS,
– the range of media available to citizens in different MS,
– supply side indicators on the economics of the media.[54]

The *Independent Study on Indicators for Media Pluralism in the Member States—Towards a Risk-Based Approach* has developed a monitoring mechanism to detect and assess risks for media pluralism in a particular country.[55] The study recognizes media pluralism as a broadly

---

[52] European Commission, DG Information Society and the Media (2005) Why and how Europe seeks pluralism in audiovisual media, http://europa. eu.int/information_society/services/doc_temp/tvwf-sht5_en.pdf, accessed on 10 September, 2006.

[53] Commission of the European Communities (2007) Commission Staff Working Document: *Media Pluralism in the Member States of the European Union*, SEC (2007) 32, Brussels, 16 January.

[54] Ibid. 17–18.

[55] K.U. Leuven et al. (2009) Independent Study on Indicators for Media Pluralism in the Member States—Towards a Risk-Based Approach. Prepared for the European Commission Directorate-General Information Society and Media. KUL: Leuven. Available at: (http://ec.europa.eu/information_society/ media_taskforce/doc/pluralism/pfr_report.pdf; retrieved.29.11. 2009). The Independent Study is also available in a book form via Lulu.com: P Valcke,

defined concept and highly complex phenomenon. It represents a diagnostic tool—Media Pluralism Monitor—that does not offer ready-to-use remedies for particular Member States, or at the EU level. Proposing a highly robust scheme of empirical assessment of various dimensions of media pluralism (political, cultural, geographical, type and genres, ownership and control) the study aims, in the first place, to collect empirical data according to analytical risk-based framework. The interpretation of these data and a subsequent choice of regulatory action would depend on a Member State's "risk appetite" or "risk tolerance," *"that being the amount of risk that one is willing to take in pursuit of value."*[56] If a Member State prefers to accept a higher level of risk, it can favor minimal regulation. On the other hand, if a Member State will exhibit a lower risk tolerance, it can employ more pro-active media pluralism regulation. The study certainly provides a step forward to break down with the policy deadlock, but its highly flexible and robust structure (including comprehensive User Guide) resulting from integration of diverging standpoints renders it difficult to predict its applicability. Moreover, the monitoring itself is not likely to bring a significant qualitative change in current EU media policy-making guided by the rationality of competitive globalization, presents rather a potential base (the Member States or Commission may or may not use) for more substantial policy change depending on a critical mass of information needed for an initiation of new solutions. The Commission's idea to monitor conditions of media pluralism in the EU Member States however resonates with European Parliament's and Council of Europe's priorities concerning policy on media pluralism, at the same time, this resonance also generates gains in autonomy vis-à-vis media industry and interest groups.

R Picard, M Sükösd, J Sanders et al., Indicators for Media Pluralism in the Member States – Towards a Risk-Based Approach (European Commission, 2009): Volume 1: Final Report, 179 p. (ISBN 978-1-4452-0769-8), and Volume 2: User Guide, 363 p. (ISBN 978-1-4452-2519-7). For an academic summary, see Peggy Valcke, Robert Picard, Miklos Sükösd, Beata Klimkiewicz, Brankica Petkovic, Cinzia dal Zotto, Robin Kerremans. (2010, forthcoming). The European Media Pluralism Monitor: Bridging Law, Economics and Media Studies as a First Step Towards Risk-Based Regulation in Media Markets. The Journal of Media Law, Vol. 2, Issue 1.

[56] K.U. Leuven et al. (2009), 6.

INTERNAL PLURALISM: RESERVED FOR PSM?

Internal pluralism regulation usually refers to the legal obligation of media providers to render for pluralism within their contents and services. This kind of regulation has been historically central, although not exclusive, to the model of public service media (PSM). The Protocol on the system of public broadcasting appended to the EC Treaty by the Treaty of Amsterdam links public service broadcasting with the democratic, social and cultural needs of each society and with the requirement to protect media pluralism.[57] Werner Rumphorst points out that this relation to media pluralism is very specific and "internal" in its nature. It may be plausibly argued that any media outlet, even the most polemical one, contributes to media pluralism. But the PSM are singled out from the external plurality of other media outlets in their normative task to ensure impartial, comprehensive and quality information contributing to the formation of a well informed citizenship.[58] Thus, the public status of PSM justifies intervention in broadcaster's programming autonomy in the interests of media pluralism and cultural diversity. This is well transposed to programming obligations of PSM in most European countries which frequently require a transmission of a specific proportion of culture-related programs, promotion of local culture and works, and often broadcasting of programs representing all the regions in a given country.[59] Moreover, internal pluralism is reflected the PSM's normative attempt, as Karol Jakubowicz puts it, to meet an audience's needs as "complete human beings," offering a full range of services generating different collective identities (citizens; members of different social groups, communities, minorities and cultures; consumers and users of information, education, advice and entertainment).[60]

---

[57] Protocol on the System of Public Broadcasting in the Member States, 2. 10. 1997, O.J. 1997, C 340, 109.

[58] Rumphorst, W. (2006) *The Requirements for the Independence of Public Service Television*, paper presented at the EBU-MTV conference "From Secret Service to Public Service," 3 November 2006.

[59] Ader, T. (2006) "Cultural and Regional Remits in Broadcasting" [in] *IRIS Plus Legal Observations of the European Audiovisual Observatory*, No. 8, 7.

[60] Jakubowicz, K. (2006) *Public Service Broadcasting: The Beginning of the End, or a New Beginning?* presentation at the EBU-MTV conference "From Secret Service to Public Service," 3 November 2006.

The Protocol allows the Member States to finance PSM on the ground of these democratic, social and cultural needs, but the ways in which they are interpreted and understood are marked by a profound ambiguity. Complaints which have been brought since the beginning of 90s by private broadcasters of an unfair competitive regime giving privileges to PSM, provide compelling evidence of growing tension between the wish to permit PSM to realize fully their mission (and thus provide for internal pluralism within their services) and the general rules of European competition and state aid policy. Media industry consortia have repeatedly emphasized a growing discrepancy between the mission statements and the actual activities of Europe's PSM,[61] and distortion of markets (due to collecting advertising revenues in addition to state aid) in excess of what is acceptable to private operators to be able to effectively compete with PSM.[62] The fact that PSM are the third most subsidised "industry" in Europe, adversely affects, in a view of the private stakeholders, the whole media market in Europe including the press and Internet publishing, not only private TV and radio broadcasters.[63]

In its assessment of public financing for PSB in the past, the Commission examined whether public financing applies to measures that are essential for fulfilment and continuation of a public service mission on the basis of Article 86 (2) EC. The Commission approved such a financing in the case of public broadcasting channels "Kinderkanal" and "Phoenix" in Germany,[64] the financing of a 24-hour news television channel with a license fee in the United

[61] ACT, AER, EPC (2004) *Safeguarding the Future of the European Audiovisual Market: A White Paper on the Financing and Regulation of Publicly Funded Broadcasters.*

[62] European Publisher's Forum (2005) *21st Century Publishing in Europe "Promoting Knowledge, Information and Diversity": Calls for Action*, Brussels December 6th, 2005, http://europa.eu.int/information_society/media_taskforce/doc/publishing/calls_for_action.pdf, accessed on October 20 2006.

[63] See: European Publishers Council (2005) *Memorandum on Pluralism and Media Concentration addressed to the Members of the European Parliament's Intergroup on the Press, Communication and Freedom*, http://www.epceurope.org/issues/MemorandumPluralismMediaConcentration.shtml, accessed on October 20 2006.

[64] State Aid – Germany, NN 70/98, O.J. 1999, C 238, 3.

Kingdom,[65] the public financing of the 9 BBC digital television channels (BBC's digital curriculum)[66] and the financing of the creation of
an international news channel in French.[67] The Commission however
raised objections in the case of public financing of the Danish public broadcaster TV2. On the one hand, the Commission accepted the
broadly defined public service broadcasting remit under which TV2
ensured internal pluralism of its services providing a mix of programs
on culture, sport, entertainment and news on several television channels. On the other hand, the Commission found that TV2 had been
overcompensated by State funding and that the State compensation
was not proportionate to the net cost TV2 had to bear in fulfilling its
public service mission.[68] Thus, within the framework of the EU competition policy, having a crucial impact on the EU media policy generally, an internal pluralism remit is being tested and discussed through
the logic of economic competition, one of the crucial components of a
competitive globalization approach.

The tension between PSB and private operators is becoming intense not only because PSM institutions fail to distinguish sharply
enough between an internal pluralism remit and commercial activities, but also because of a discussion on the role of PSM in the digital
era. The central point here revolves around the legitimacy of new non-
linear services to be offered by PSM organizations and the controversial idea to confine PSM remit to traditional linear broadcasting. In its
Communication on the application of State aid rules to public service
broadcasting the Commission states that

> the public service remit might include certain services that are not
> 'programmes' in the traditional sense, such as on-line information ser-
> vices, to the extent that (...) they are addressing the same democratic,
> social and cultural needs of the society in question.[69]

---

[65] State Aid – United Kingdom, NN 88/98, O.J. 2000, C 78, 6.

[66] State Aid – United Kingdom, N 631/01, O.J. 2003, C 23, 6.

[67] State Aid – France, N 54/2005, C 2005 1479 final of 7 June 2005.

[68] Commission Decision of 19 May 2004, C(2004) 1814 final, of 19 May
2004.

[69] European Commission (2001) *Communication from the Commission on the application of State aid rules to public service broadcasting*, 2001/C 320/4, 8. Emphasis added–B.K.

Former Commissioner Reding reaffirmed this position, stating that PSM are free to develop activities other than traditional broadcasting and make available socially valuable content on other platforms, however the scope and financing of such activities should be clearly defined by the Member States.[70] Public service media see their involvement in new media platforms and services, such as online content services, as necessary to safeguard media pluralism and fulfill fundamental European policy objectives in the digital environment, such as social cohesion, cultural diversity and public information services.[71] Moreover, the legacy of PSM commitment to internal pluralism is being linked to the paradoxes of new digital environment and operations: mere quantity of platforms, channels, thematically fragmented services does not automatically bring more media pluralism and diversity. New private platform providers increasingly control the revenue streams of program makers and multiple publishing of a single product economically privileges programming schemes that can be traded in many countries and localised more easily in multiple versions, thus reducing cultural specificity and profound diversity.

Yet some of recent interpretational attempts of the Commission support an assumption that in a multichannel media environment (catering to both specialist and universal interests and tastes), PSM does not necessarily have to provide internal pluralism through a whole range of non-linear services, but rather focus predominantly on traditional linear or related services in fulfilling their mission. Verena Wiedemann points out that DG Competition in its letter to the German Government considered on-line services of the public service media permissible only if "closely linked" to the traditional broadcasting services. Moreover, contents made available by PSM on mobile platforms should be inadmissible *per se* in a view of DG Competition.[72] In other words, mobile

---

[70] Reding, V. (2006) *The Role of Public Service Broadcasters in a Vibrant and Pluralist Digital Media Landscape*, speech at the joint EBU-MTV's conference "From Secret Service to Public Service," Budapest, 3 November 2006, http://ec.europa.eu/comm/commission_barroso/reding/docs/speeches/ebu_mtv_20061103.pdf, accessed on 20 November, 2006.

[71] EBU (2006) *EBU Comments to the EC Commission's public consultation paper on Content Online in the Single Market*, DAJ/HR/jmc, 23.10.2006.

[72] Wiedemann, V. (2005) *Legislating and regulating for pluralism*, paper presented at the European Parliament's Seminar on *Pluralism not Concentration: an EU Media Policy*, 7 April 2005, Brussels.

platform services are apparently regarded by the Commission as being outside an area that can be considered as "services of general interest."[73]

It might be to early to assess this regulatory direction, but some Commission declarations reflect a policy of trying to limit public financing of PSM to the *strict minimum* and call for a comprehensive reform of state aid rules in light of the Lisbon strategy. Closing the existing procedures under EC Treaty state aid rules (Article 88 (1)) and following changes made to the financing of public broadcasters in France, Italy and Spain, the Commission concluded: "*Financing of public broadcasters should not exceed the strict minimum necessary to ensure the proper execution of the public service mission, should not unduly benefit commercial activities (cross-subsidies) and should be transparent.*"[74] A key concept emerging from the debate on state aid rules reform in the context of the Lisbon Strategy is "market failure," seen as a situation where the market does not lead to an economically efficient outcome. One of the areas where markets do not achieve economic efficiency is public goods. These are beneficial for a society, but are not normally provided by the market, given that it is difficult or impossible to exclude anyone from using the goods. The Commission recognizes *some* types of public broadcasting to be such a case.[75]

The Commission has certainly not questioned media pluralism as a rationale justifying the special status (and thus also financing from state aid) PSM enjoy within the national context of Members States. It seems that some online services can be accepted by the Commission to meet democratic, social and cultural needs and to protect media pluralism in MS societies. Yet this "national dimension" of EU media policy making is being increasingly tested through the logic of economic competition and counterbalanced with the globally oriented competitive approach. The economic and pro-competitive course of action with regard to state aid policy will not only aim to reduce the general level of

---

[73] Nissen, Ch. S. (2006) *Public Service Media in the Information Society*, Report prepared by the Council of Europe's Group of Specialists on PSB in the Information Society (MC-S-PSB), 27.

[74] European Commission (2005), *State aid: Commission closes inquires into French, Italian and Spanish public broadcasters following commitments to amend funding systems*, IP/05/458, 20.04.2005.

[75] Commission of the European Communities (2005) *State Aid Action Plan: Less and Better Targeted State Aid: A Road Map for State Aid Reform 2005 – 2009*, COM (2005) 107 final. Brussels, 7.06.2005, 7. Emphasis added–B.K.

state aid, but it will require it to justify any support, also for the purpose of providing internal pluralism within the services of PSM, by way of market failure. The rationality of *competitive globalization* confines internal pluralism measures to the question of competition, state aid rules and curtailment of the PSM remit, should PSM fail to be more explicity recognized in a transnational context (as institutions fostering well-informed pan-European citizenship) and the new digital environment.

A Catalyser of Well-Informed Citizenship: European Parliament and Council of Europe

EUROPEAN PARLIAMENT

Unlike the Commission, other European institutions (mainly the European Parliament and the Council of Europe), interest groups and professional institutions (International Federation of Journalists) have repeatedly highlighted the importance of media pluralism for the democratic nature of a European media landscape and expressed the need to formulate a common regulatory approach at the EU level. This is seen as indispensable in order to accommodate growing tensions between:

- processes of media concentration and citizens' rights to receive information from diverse and independent sources;
- PSM status and EU competition and state aid policy;
- structural media diversity and high costs of market entry;
- unequal representation of minorities and pressure from advertisers in favor of mainstream audiences;
- journalistic autonomy and political influences.

Despite its weak legislative powers, the European Parliament has more frequently initiated Community media policy than has the Commission or the Council.[76] In particular, the Parliament has pressed for ac-

---

[76] Verhulst, S. and Goldberg, D. (1998), "European Media Policy: Complexity and Comprehensiveness." In L. d'Haenens and F. Saeys (eds.) *Media Dynamics and Regulatory Concern in the Digital Age*. Berlin: Quintessenz Verlags GmbH, 17–49.

tion to pursue policies protecting media pluralism. Throughout 1990s, it adopted an impressive number of reports developed into resolutions addressing various facets of media pluralism. Originally, concrete and policy-shaped discussions on the issue revolved around a series of party-specific initiated documents and motions for resolutions. Katharine Sarikakis emphasizes that despite internal and ideological differences, the European Parliament did not find it difficult to reach consensus on two major issues: the definition of the problem itself and the action needed in terms of policy.[77]

Although some MEPs highlighted positive aspects of media concentration, the conviction was broadly shared that unlimited media concentration might endanger the independence and freedom of journalists and thus also, the right of citizens to access information from diverse and transparent sources. The formation of the conception of media pluralism has been gradual and has come into shape in the course of subsequent documents and discussions. Its conceptual framing was rooted in normative democratic expectations, while the causal and direct relation between media concentration and diversity of opinion was perceived as an eventual hindrance to democratic performance. This reading of the emerging notion of media pluralism is embedded in the *Resolution on Media Takeovers and Mergers* (1990)[78] referring to many 'worrying examples' of concentrations which could readily be observed in national and transnational European media landscapes.

Proposals to implement *comprehensive* media pluralism regulation at the EU level were formulated in the *Resolution on Media Concentration and Diversity of Opinions* (1992).[79] The Parliament called on the Commission to submit a proposal for a Directive harmonizing national restrictions on media concentration enabling the Community to intervene in the act of concentration which endangers pluralism on a European scale. Secondly, the Parliament proposed the creation of a European Media Council with an advisory function to: monitor the

---

[77] Sarikakis, K. (2004) *Powers in Media Policy: The Challenge of the European Parliament*, Oxford: Peter Lang.

[78] Resolution on Media Takeovers and Mergers, O.J. C 68, 19.3. 1990, 137.

[79] Resolution on Media Concentration and Diversity of Opinions, O.J. C 284, 2. 11. 1992, 44.

developments of the European media landscape (and also in a global context), ensure transparency of media ownership and provide the Commission with reports, recommendations and proposals concerning media developments and policy in Europe. Finally, the Parliament called for actions improving journalistic independence and freedom. The proposals included drafting a framework Directive safeguarding journalistic and editorial independence in all media and approval of a European Media Code setting basic standards of professional ethics.[80]

Further EP's resolutions such as the *Resolution on the Commission Green Paper "Pluralism and Media Concentration in the Internal Market"* (1993),[81] *Resolution on concentration of the media and pluralism* (1994)[82] and *Resolution on Pluralism and Media Concentration* (1995)[83] accompanied the debate on the Commission's Green Paper "Pluralism and the Media Concentration in the Internal Market" (1992) and its Follow-up (1994), and reaffirmed the position arguing for comprehensive regulatory measures. After the double rejection of the draft directive by the College of Commissioners, parliamentarians themselves admitted that media pluralism is "without doubt the biggest failure of the EP."[84] Media pluralism regulatory initiatives did not prove successful in the 90s, even though the Parliament has renewed efforts to address the issue.

Still in the following years, media pluralism has remained on EP's media policy agenda. In 2004 the EP adopted the *Resolution on the risks of violation, in the EU and especially in Italy, of freedom of expression and information* (2004).[85] Examining the situation in selected Mem-

---

[80] Ibid. See also: Resolution on the Commission Green Paper "Pluralism and Media Concentration in the Internal Market," O.J. 1994, C 44, 14.2. 1994, 177.

[81] Resolution on the Commission Green Paper "Pluralism and Media Concentration in the Internal Market," O.J. C 44, 14.2. 1994, 177.

[82] Resolution on concentration of the media and pluralism, O.J. 1994, C 323, 21.11. 1994, 157.

[83] Resolution on Pluralism and Media Concentration, O.J. C 166, 3.7. 1995, 133.

[84] Sarikakis, K. (2004) *Powers in Media Policy: The Challenge of the European Parliament*, Oxford: Peter Lang, 132.

[85] Resolution on the risks of violation, in the EU and especially in Italy, of freedom of expression and information, O.J. C 104 E, 30.4. 2004, p. 1026. The Resolution was followed by the publication of *Final report of the study on*

ber States and focusing on Italy in particular, the resolution proposes that the Commission review the existing powers and the monitoring of public broadcasting to adopt pertinent measures ensuring the protection of media pluralism. European Parliament stressed in the resolution that free and pluralist media reinforce the principle of democracy on which Union is founded. This is closely linked to the conception of EU citizenship - citizens have the right to stand and vote in municipal and European elections in a Member State of which they are not a national. Hence, the European Union has a political, moral and legal obligation to ensure within its fields of competence that the rights of EU citizens to free and pluralist media are respected.[86]

According to the European Parliament, other pragmatic reasons justify minimum EU conditions to be respected by Member States to ensure an adequate level of media pluralism. One of them is the lack of recourse of the Community courts by individuals in the case of an absence of pluralism in the media.[87] This direction of reasoning clearly demonstrates that media pluralism is seen by the European Parliament as a fundamental value of the European Union sustaining and reinforcing its democratic ideals. As recognition of this value facilitates democratic participation of its citizens, it should, in the words of the EP, affect the institutional practice of the European Union and its Member States.[88]

COUNCIL OF EUROPE

A commitment to democratic participation has resulted in numerous policy initiatives developed in order to set up common media pluralism standards within the framework of the Council of Europe. One of the fundamental incentives in this respect, has been a positive action approach, with regard to Article10 ECHR. In this sense, Article 10 has functioned not only as a guarantee against interventions by states in the field of freedom of expression and freedom of the media, but it has

---

"the information of the citizen in the EU: obligations for the media and the Institutions concerning the citizen's right to be fully and objectively informed," prepared by the European Institute for the Media on behalf of the European Parliament, 31 August, 2004.

[86] Ibid., 1027.
[87] Ibid., 1027.
[88] Ibid.

also encouraged a positive action approach to ensure citizen's right to be fully and impartially informed, and to receive the information from diverse and independent sources.[89]

This approach has been supported by a significant volume of resolutions, recommendations and declarations adopted by the Parliamentary Assembly and by the Committee of Ministers, many of which stressed the importance of the active implementation of Article 10 ECHR for the appropriate development of media pluralism and access to a diversity of information sources. Most of these documents are not legally binding, but they do set a number of principles and strategies suggested to Member States for further implementation. The table below illustrates the thematic spectrum and the level of complexity reflected in numerous measures designed to protect media pluralism. A chronological ordering of these documents shows how closely CoE's objectives in this matter, were linked to given historical circumstances and developments, such as democratization of media systems in Central and Eastern Europe. A sustained democratic commitment prompted both the Committee and the Assembly repeatedly to call Member States' attention to the need to adopt recommended measures protecting various aspects of media pluralism and ultimately to break through the implementation stalemate.

Table 3: Media pluralism related resolutions, recommendations and declarations adopted by the Parliamentary Assembly and by the Committee of Ministers of the Council of Europe

COMMITTEE OF MINISTERS	PARLIAMENTARY ASSEMBLY
2007 – Declaration on protecting the role of the media in democracy in the context of media concentration *alerts member states to the risk of misuse of the power of the media in a situation of strong concentration of the media and new communication services, and its potential consequences for political pluralism and for democratic processes	

---

[89] Voorhoof, D. (1998) "Guaranteeing the Freedom and Independence of the Media" [in] *Media and democracy*, Strasbourg: Council of Europe Publishing, 35–57.

COMMITTEE OF MINISTERS	PARLIAMENTARY ASSEMBLY
*2007 – *Recommendation Rec (2007) 3 on the remit of public service media in the information society* *recognizes the continued full legitimacy and specific objectives of public service media in the information society	
*2007 – *Recommendation Rec (2007)2 on media pluralism and diversity of media content* *reaffirms that media pluralism and diversity of media content are essential for the functioning of a democratic society and are the corollaries of the fundamental right of freedom of expression and information as guaranteed by Article 10 ECHR *stresses the need to revise this issue in the context of new technological developments	
*2006 - *Declaration on the guarantee of the independence of public service broadcasting in the member states* *reaffirms the vital role of PSB as an essential element of pluralist communication and of social cohesion which seeks to promote, in particular, respect for human rights, cultural diversity and political pluralism	*2004 – *Recommendation 1641 (2004) on public service broadcasting* *recognizes that PSB offers a variety of programs and services catering for the needs of all groups in society and recommends the Committee of Ministers to adopt a new major policy document on PSB
*2006 – *Recommendation Rec(2006)3 on the UNESCO Convention on the protection and promotion of the diversity of cultural expressions* *recommends that member states ratify, accept, approve or accede UNESCO Convention	
*2003 – *Recommendation Rec (2003) 9 on measures to promote the democratic and social contribution of digital broadcasting* *recalls that the existence of a wide variety of independent and autonomous media, permitting the reflection of diversity of ideas and opinions is important for democratic societies	*2003 – *Recommendation 1589 (2003) on freedom of expression in the media* *asserts that media concentration is a serious problem across the continent and asks the Committee of Ministers to urge all European states to ensure the plurality of the media market through appropriate anti-concentration measures
*2000 – *Recommendation No. R (2000) 23 on the independence and functions of regulatory authorities for the broadcasting sector* *recognizes importance of genuine independence of the regulatory authorities for the broadcasting sector	

COMMITTEE OF MINISTERS	PARLIAMENTARY ASSEMBLY
2000 – Declaration on cultural diversity *recalls the commitments of MS to defend and promote media freedoms and media pluralism as a basic precondition for cultural exchange	*2001 – Recommendation 1506 (2001) on freedom of expression and information in the media in Europe* *highlights that pluralist and independent media system is essential for democratic development, and that the current market restructuring might lead to further concentration restricting media pluralism
1999 – Recommendation No. R (99) 1 on measures to promote media pluralism *stresses the importance for individuals to have access to pluralistic media content and recommends the States to promote political and cultural pluralism by developing their media policy in line with Article 10 ECHR	*1999 – Recommendation 1407 (1999) on media and democratic culture* *states that sheer quantity of information does not by itself provide variety and quality, and recognizes the problem of the delicate relationship between freedom of expression and the citizen's right to objective, undistorted information
1996 – Recommendation No. R (96) 10 on the guarantee of the independence of public service broadcasting *reaffirms the vital role of PSB as an essential factor of pluralistic communication	*1991 – Recommendation 1147 (1991) on parliamentary responsibility for the democratic reform of broadcasting* *recommends national parliaments to revise broadcasting regulation to ensure pluralism at least at the level of the overall media landscape
1994 – Recommendation No. R (94) 13 on measures to promote media transparency *recalls that media pluralism and diversity are essential for the functioning of a democratic society and recommends that the governments promote media transparency	*1975 – Recommendation 747 (1975) on media concentrations* *draws up a model statute to secure internal freedom of the press and sets up criteria for an establishment of CoE's information center on mergers and business failures in the press sector.
1982 - Declaration on freedom of expression and information *supports the existence of a wide variety of independent and autonomous media reflecting diversity of ideas and opinions	
1974 - Resolution (74) 43 on press concentrations *recommends certain measures of public aid to the press	

Already in the 1970s, the Committee of Ministers and Parliamentary Assembly recognized a risk affecting the diversity of the press landscape due to a wave of major mergers and business failures in the press sector. Many daily newspapers had ceased publishing or were bought up by rival papers. The Committee of Ministers reacted to this devel-

opment with Resolution (74) 43 to help endangered newspapers and
the Parliamentary Assembly adopted Recommendation 747 (1975) on
the internal freedom of the press.[90] In 1981, the Committee of Ministers set up the Steering Committee on the Mass Media (CDMM),
which has created a succession of subordinate bodies to deal with the
issue of media concentration and pluralism.[91]

The first of them, a Committee of Experts on media concentrations and pluralism (MM-CM) was established in late 1991 to conduct
an in-depth examination of media concentrations phenomena with the
help of a network of national correspondents. One of the important
questions addressed by empirical research, tested a necessity of implementation of harmonized measures at the European level in order to
rectify negative effects of concentrations on political and cultural pluralism. Fundamental differences of opinions within the Committee of
Experts rendered impossible to support such a harmonization. Instead,
the Committee observed that the trend towards ever-larger media units
has made it increasingly difficult to trace ownership and information
sources. Finally MM-CM drew up guidelines designed to promote
transparency in the media, which the Committee of Ministers adopted
as Recommendation No. R (94) 13 on Measures to Promote Media
Transparency. The lack of consensus concerning direct influence of
media concentration on pluralism has not impeded further CoE's commitment regarding these issues, but required to redress them in a more
complex setting. A work of the Group of Specialists on Media Pluralism (MM-S-PL) established in 1999, has been symptomatic in this respect. The Group elaborated a text adopted by the Committee of Ministers as Recommendation No. R (99) 1 on Measures to Promote Media Pluralism. In this document, media pluralism is conceived as a catalyst of democratic participation and well-informed citizenship, which
manifests in three principal normative aspects: individuals should have

[90] Möwes, B. (2000) *Fifty Years of Media Policy in the Council of Europe: A Review*, 6th European Ministerial Conference on Mass Media Policy Cracow
(Poland), 15–16 June 2000, MCM (2000) 003.
[91] Jakubowicz, K. (2006) *Media Pluralism and Concentration: Searching for a
Productive Research and Policy Agenda (in the light of Council of Europe experience)*, paper presented during the meeting of Working Group 3 of COST
Action A30, Budapest, 22–23 September 2006.

access to pluralistic media content; the media should enable different groups and interests in society—including minorities—to express themselves; and democracy should be enhanced and consolidated by the existence of a multiplicity of autonomous and independent media outlets at the national, regional and local levels.[92] The main findings of the MM-S-PL in the course of its mandate were summarised in the *Report on Media Pluralism in the Digital Environment*.[93] The document did not propose any immediate regulatory action, but identified issues that demand a response from Members States, especially in the context of a rapidly changing digital environment.[94] A wider media diversity perspective has been at the center of focus of the subsequent Advisory Panel on Media Diversity (AP-MD), set up in 2001, and reflected in two Panel's reports *Media Diversity in Europe*[95] and *Transnational Media Concentrations in Europe*.[96] The Group of Specialists on Media Diversity (MC-S-MD), continuing the work of the Panel, concentrated on the ongoing assessment and monitoring of conditions affecting cultural diversity and media pluralism, especially in the context of digital environment and democratic performance.

New technological developments and implementation difficulties urged the Council of Europe to revise instruments proposed in the already existing recommendations. On 31 January 2007 the Committee of Ministers of the CoE adopted three new documents referring to media pluralism: Recommendation Rec (2007) 2 on Media Pluralism and Diversity of Media Content, Recommendation Rec (2007) 3 on the Remit of Public Service Media in the Information Society and the Declaration on Protecting the Role of the Media in Democracy in the Context of

---

[92] Council of Europe (1999) *Recommendation No. R (99) 1 of the Committee of Ministers to Member States on Measures to promote Media Pluralism*.

[93] Council of Europe (2000) *Report on Media Pluralism in the Digital Environment*, adopted by the Steering Committee on the Mass Media in October 2000, Strasbourg, CDMM (2000) pde.

[94] The report reflects in part results of the study on *Pluralism in the multi-channel market: suggestions for regulatory scrutiny* prepared on behalf of MM-S-PL to explore the means by which media pluralism can be maintained or even strengthened in the digital future.

[95] Council of Europe (2002) *Media Diversity in Europe*, Report prepared by the AP-MD, H/ APMD (2003)001.

[96] Council of Europe (2004) *Transnational Media Concentrations in Europe*, Report prepared by the AP-MD, AP-MD (2004)7.

Media Concentration. In Recommendation Rec (2007) 2 on Media Pluralism and Diversity of Media Content, the three basic dimensions of media pluralism are re-formulated, especially with regard to a positive interpretation of Article 10 and the role of media transparency in well-informed policy making, and critical media analysis by citizens.[97] The Recommendation links requirements concerning freedom of expression with media pluralism: demands of the Article 10 of ECHR can be fully satisfied only if citizens are given the possibility to form their own opinion from diverse sources of information.[98] Transparency of media ownership is seen as an important precondition for well-informed decisions and analysis by regulatory authorities and the public.[99]

This brief account of ways in which media pluralism is exposed in documents of the European Parliament and Council of Europe leads to the common ground. In the case of both institutions, the logic of setting up media pluralism standards involves harmonizing or balancing the forces of globalization (outside the EU) with a stimulation of democratic participation, well-informed and more pro-active citizenry (inside the EU). This citizenry is not to be nationally, but rather transnationally defined to articulate and cope with common issues now emerging across national boundaries. Despite the fact that both institutions are involved in policy formulation processes and have a representative set of societal interests, the difficulties are marked in the implementation and transposition stage. This is related not only to ensuring that all member states adopt agreed upon standards but also that they support transposing these standards into harmonized rules and measures, both at the European and national levels.

The Question of a Structural Asymmetry

These different (and in many aspects conflicting) ways of media pluralism problematization have led to "see-saw" efforts to introduce and abandon media pluralism regulatory measures at the European level.

---

[97] Council of Europe (2007) *Recommendation Rec(2007)2 of the Committee of Ministers to member states on media pluralism and diversity of media content.*
[98] Ibid.
[99] Ibid.

The problem however does not only seem to be rooted in a structural asymmetry of EU policies that led to easier achievement of deregulatory harmonization than to pro-active regulatory integration. Pointing to structural asymmetry of EU governance, Fritz Scharpf argues that "negative integration" refers to the removal of barriers or other obstacles to free and undistorted competition. "Positive integration" on the other hand concerns reconstitution of an economic system of regulation through market-correcting measures.[100]

This regulatory asymmetry has been emphasized by other scholars when analysing EU or European media policies. Alison Harcourt has stressed this deregulatory bias in reference to pro-market oriented nature of EU media policies.[101] Shallini Venturelli focused on legislative clarification positive information rights as political rights and a dominance of negative free-speech rights, showing that deregulatory media policies have stood in contrast with supporting and more interventionist mechanisms such as a European quota.[102] Dennis McQuail and Jan van Cuilenburg saw normative grounds for deregulatory asymmetry in a new communications policy paradigm. The new paradigm results from such developments as technological and economic convergence, merging the branches of computing, communications and content (publishing). The emerging policy paradigm for media and communications is mainly driven by an economic and technological logic. This media policy shift legitimizes retreat from regulation where it interferes with market development or technological objectives and it gives more priority to economic and technological over social-cultural and political welfare when priorities have to be set.[103] Many scholars found a dominance of "asymmetric" EU's approach to communication, which reflects polity's construction closer to neoliberalism than to the European social wel-

---

[100] Scharpf, F. (1999) *Governing in Europe: Effective and Democratic?*, Oxford: Oxford University Press, 45.

[101] Harcourt, A. (2004) *The European Union and the Regulation of Media Markets*, Manchester: Manchester University Press.

[102] Venturelli, S. (1998) *Liberalizing the European Media: Politics, Regulation and the Public Sphere*, Oxford: Clarendon Press.

[103] Van Cuilenburg, J. and McQuail, D. (2003) 'Media Policy Paradigm Shifts: Towards a New Communications Policy Paradigm', *European Journal of Communication*, 18 (2), 181–207.

fare model.[104] (Harcourt, 2005; Harrison and Woods, 2007; Sarikakis, 2008). In another vein, Peter Humphreys has argued that EU's competencies in the audiovisual field remain limited.[105] Varied dimensions of audiovisual policies generate more differentiated responses: for example, with regard to its external audiovisual policy (such as promotion of European works), the EU has certainly not been deregulatory.[106]

The structural asymmetry in European media policies is not exclusively rooted in a dichotomy between deregulatory and pro-active measures or a dichotomy between economic and political/cultural objectives. Both pro-market and market correcting measures may be used for the same rationale as is the case of *competitive globalization*. Namely 'this objective' guides the European Commission's policies on media pluralism/diversity (as it is understood and incorporated in media policy language) in both deregulatory (reluctance towards harmonizing "media pluralism" anti-concentration measures) and market-correcting directions (protection of cultural diversity through European quota, European co-productions and production by independent producers).

The dividing line comes rather from two different ways of perceiving and conceptualizing media systems in the context of larger societies or political environments. In other words, a policy on media pluralism is rooted in two different standards of rationality: one seeing the media as increasingly politically autonomous and differentiated, playing a central role in a process of competitive globalization; the second perceiving the media as a part of deliberative, democratic system. The first option is constructed in the (external) global context, especially vis-à-vis challenges of global economic competition, cultural and linguistic imperialism, technological convergence. The second approach refers

---

[104] Harcourt, A. (2004) *The European Union and the Regulation*; Harrison, J. and Woods, L. (2007) *European Broadcasting Law and Policy*. Cambridge: Cambridge University Press; Sarikakis, K. (2008) "Communication and Cultural Policies Research in Europe: A Review of Recent Scholarship." in *Communication and Cultural Policies in Europe* (eds.) Fernández Alonso, I. and de Moragas i Spà, M. Universitat Autònoma de Barcelona: Barcelona.

[105] Humphreys, P. (2008) "The Principal Axes of the European Union's Audiovisual Policy." In *Communication and Cultural Policies in Europe* (eds.) Fernández Alonso, I. and de Moragas i Spà, M. Universitat Autònoma de Barcelona: Barcelona.

[106] Ibid.

to the (internal) European political and civic space recognized mainly through the concept of European citizenship. In the case of the former, policy debates are most decisively influenced by the media industry— seen as a main and autonomous subject of possible regulation. In the sense of the latter, the crucial role in the debate is played by civic and non-governmental organizations, political parties, media expert institutions, and journalists.

In the conceptual framework of competitive globalization, media pluralism is divided into other partial categories to be dealt with in different policy areas ("cultural diversity" through audiovisual policy measures, 'media pluralism' through ownership and competition rules, "internal pluralism" through general policy towards PSM and state aid rules). In the framework of democratic participation and well-informed citizenship, media pluralism is conceived in complex terms and it is to be addressed in one common regulatory model. Some might argue that there is a contradiction between positing one common normative model for safeguarding media pluralism, as media pluralism in itself implies diversity of media types, organizations, ways of operation and interaction with audience. This is namely the argument used by non-linear service providers striving for no or minimal regulation on grounds that different audiences have different expectations, therefore the same rules cannot be imposed on all media.[107]

It is also interesting to see whether media pluralism is recognized as a value in both models of rationality. Undoubtedly, media pluralism is a value the democratic participation and well-informed citizenship are founded on, at the same time, it is the objective the process of democratic participation is striving for. On the other hand, within the model of competitive globalization, media pluralism functions as an added value to be generated by 'other' institutions through "different" objectives. One common theme for both approaches is a search for a new media policy paradigm in existing schemes. As regards the latter, the 'new' paradigm is to certain extent modelled on other policy fields, therefore gradual reduction of media specific measures is one of its most characteristic features. In the case of the former, it is not merely a plea for reconstruction of the "old" public service media policy para-

---

[107] Williams, G. (2005) *"What is the Television Without Frontiers Directive?,"* [in] Free Press, No 148, September/October.

digm, but rather an attempt at redefinition in a new transnational political constellation and digital environment.

Table 4: Models of rationality, within which media pluralism is being used as a media policy conception and objective

	COMPETITIVE GLOBALIZATION	DEMOCRATIC PARTICIPATION
MEDIA	AUTONOMOUS increasingly autonomous and differentiated system	INCLUSIVE part of deliberative democratic system
CONTEXT	EXTERNAL global economic competition, cultural and linguistic imperialism, technological convergence	INTERNAL European political and civic space, European citizenship
MAIN COMMENTATORS	media industry	civic and non-governmental organizations, political parties, media expert institutions, journalistic environment
REGULATORY FRAMEWORK	FRAGMENTED 'cultural diversity' - audiovisual policy measures, 'media pluralism' - ownership and competition rules, 'internal pluralism' - general policy towards PSB and state aid rules	COMPLEX
VALUE ORIENTATION	ADDED VALUE	CORE VALUE AND OBJECTIVE
MEDIA POLICY PARADIGM	REDUCTION of media specific measures	REDEFINITION of 'old' public service media policy paradigm in a new transnational political constellation and digital environment
INSTITUTIONAL FRAMEWORK	European Commission	European Parliament Council of Europe

At the same time it should be recognized that a "clash of rationalities" has been a process, in which opposing approaches have not been confined "to their own ghettos." There has been a growing resonance of media pluralism as a salient and autonomous issue, that needs to be observed, measured against the risks and fully used if potentially available.

Conclusions

Let us return to the initial question: Is the clash of rationalities leading nowhere? The clash effects may be both negative and productive: both standards of rationality—competitive globalization and democratic participation—provide at once limits and impetus for European media policy concerning media pluralism. The tensions between the two poles confer on media policy language its ambiguity (media pluralism conceptualized through autonomous and inclusive approach) and media policy activities its ambivalence (fragmented regulatory actions, or soft measures, such as monitoring, and a complex framework for enforcing common, harmonized standards at the European level). Both ambiguity and ambivalence stimulate an opportunity of internal change. The clash between the two standards of rationality on the one hand brings the risk of policy stagnation, but on the other hand brings a potential for the reform that would not be possible in a unified structure.

The policy concerning media pluralism has been seen as one of the biggest failures of EU institutions (both the Commission and Parliament). Despite the increasing need for harmonized European rules on media pluralism, the EU still lacks the formal powers (especially if member states' interests strongly diverge) and the institutional capacities necessary to enforce the compliance with the rules and their transposition in the member states. The most important regulatory instrument continues to be competition law, which, while strong and intrusive, is limited in scope and is a poor substitute for other regulatory powers and capacities.[108] Council of Europe' continuous efforts to repeatedly address the need of common standards on media pluralism, have not so far brought a legally binding outcome.

Yet the clash of rationalities through which the issue of media pluralism is being conceptualized, provides an alternative route of harmonization, especially through defining the limits of both standards. One such a limit is confining media pluralism to the issue of media

---

[108] Grande, E. and Eberlein, B. (2005) "Beyond delegation: transnational regulatory regimes and the EU regulatory state." *Journal of European Public Policy*, Vol. 12 (1) 89–112.

concentration or a structural, external dimension, often equated with media ownership. The relevance of the concept of media pluralism in media policy is increasingly marked by its potential and modes of activation. Its traditional and static framing is being challenged by the ongoing identification, whose sense depends on mutual relations and interdependencies. Thus, the potential of media pluralism is conditionally linked to capacities that can be mobilized through its "building blocks," such as multiple centers of media control, sources of information, etc. At the same time, its full usage is increasingly determined by individuals, their ability critically to read the media contents, to generate their own messages, modes of delivery and ways of interaction.

These new interpretational dimensions challenge centers of gravity in media policy-making. The idea to regulate media pluralism at the structural level (prevention of concentration through anti-concentration rules, imposing diversity on media actors) is being replaced by resonance of soft and indirect regulatory levers, such as monitoring, transparency, promotion of media literacy. Through information exchange and networking, both EU institutions and the Council of Europe, develop harmonized strategies focusing predominantly on information and competence (e.g., a support for media literacy). An individualised and interactive character of media use amplifies a possibility better to safeguard media pluralism through supporting citizens and interest groups with a special knowledge enabling them better to establish their relations with the mainstream media, to get their messages heard, cultural expressions represented and opinions addressed. In this sense, it's more important to teach media users to fish than to provide them with a fishing rod.

The fact that media pluralism is rationalised in different ways, and that there is a tension between them, does not decrease its potential and a chance for vital policy-making. The important question is, however, whether "policy bridges" are built between divergent practices rooted in different approaches, and whether they, in consequence, activate media pluralism potential. This multirationality and multifunctionality of the media policy process itself creates a complicated, multilayered setting that in certain circumstances brings a harmonized solution and strengthens European institutions vis-à-vis external actors. An instructive example would be promotion of cultural diversity (European works, independent productions and co-productions) as a key value shared by all Europeans, and a regulatory rationale that needs to be constantly reaffirmed in subsequent media regulatory designs. On the other hand, European institutions have not established a harmonized approach enabling them to redefine PSM's role in transnational democratic constellations (as institutions nurturing well-informed *pan-European* citizenship) and new digital environment.

Finally, the clash of rationalities, resulting in ambiguity of policy language and ambivalence of policy action, changes the patterns of democratic legitimacy. Accompanied by institutional interdependencies and functional convergence, European media policy-making creates a high complexity and at the same time, structural gaps in democratic control. This participation-limiting legitimacy stands in contrast to a trust-demanding social and public policy system in Europe.[109] The sophistication and complexity of policy process demands that Europeans must be prepared to trust unknown solutions.

REFERENCES

Ader, T. (2006) "Cultural and Regional Remits in Broadcasting." *IRIS Plus Legal Observations of the European Audiovisual Observatory*, No. 8.

Alexander, J. C. (1981) "The Mass News Media in Systemic, Historical and Comparative Perspective." In E. Katz and T. Szecskö (eds.), *Mass Media and Social Change*, Beverly Hills: Sage Publications, 17–51.

Arendt, H. (1958), *The Human Condition*, Chicago: The University of Chicago Press.

Bagdikian, B. (2000) *The Media Monopoly*, 6th edition, Beacon Press.

Bourdieu, P. (1998), *On Television*, New York: The New Press.

Cavallin, J. (2000) "Public Policy Uses of Diversity Measures." In J. van Cuilenburg and R. van der Wurff (eds.) *Media and Open Societies: Cultural, Economic and Policy Foundations for Media Openness and Diversity in East and West*, Amsterdam: Het Spinhuis, 105–170.

Commission of the European Communities (2007) Commission Staff Working Document: *Media Pluralism in the Member States of the European Union*, SEC (2007) 32, Brussels, 16 January.

Collins, R. and Murroni, C. (1996) *New Media, New Policies*. Cambridge: Polity.

---

[109] Merelman, R.M. (2003) *Pluralism at Yale: The Culture and Political Science in America*, Wisconsin: The University of Wisconsin Press, 286–287.

Dahlgren, P. (1995), *Television and the Public Sphere: Citizenship, Democracy and the Media*, London: Sage Publications.

Doyle, G. (2002), *Media Ownership. The Economics and Politics of Convergence and Concentration in the UK and European Media*, London: Sage Publications.

Freedman, D. (2005) "Promoting Diversity and Pluralism in Contemporary Communication Policies in United States and the United Kingdom." *International Journal of Media Management*, Vol. 7, No. ½, 16–23.

Giddens, A. (1991) *The Consequences of Modernity*, Stanford: Stanford University Press.

Graham, A. and Davies, G. (1997), *Broadcasting, Society and Policy in the Multimedia Age*, Lutton: John Libbey.

Grande, E. (2001) *Institutions and Interests: Interest Groups in the European System of Multi-Level Governance*, Working Paper No. 1/2001.

Grande, E. and Eberlein, B. (2005) "Beyond delegation: transnational regulatory regimes and the EU regulatory state." *Journal of European Public Policy*, Vol 12 (1), 89–112.

Habermas, J.(1995), *The Structural Transformation of the Public Sphere. An Inquiry into a Category of Bourgeois Society*, Cambridge, Mass: The MIT Press.

Habermas, J. (1996), *Between Facts and Norms: Contributions to a Discursive Theory of Law and Democracy*, Cambridge, Mass: The MIT Press.

Hallin, D. C., Mancini, P. (2004), *Comparing Media Systems: Three Models of Media and Politics*, Cambridge: Cambridge University Press.

Harcourt, A. (2004) *The European Union and the Regulation of Media Markets*, Manchester: Manchester University Press.

Harrison, J. and Woods, L. (2007) *European Broadcasting Law and Policy*. Cambridge: Cambridge University Press.

Humphreys, P. (2008) "The Principal Axes of the European Union's Audiovisual Policy." In *Communication and Cultural Policies in Europe* (eds.) Fernández Alonso, I. and de Moragas i Spà, M. Universitat Autònoma de Barcelona: Barcelona.

Inglehart, R. (1990) *Culture Shift in Advanced Industrial Societies*, Princeton: Princeton University Press.

Jakubowicz, K. (2004) "Ideas in Our Heads: Introduction of PSB as Part of Media System Change in Central and Eastern Europe." *European Journal of Communication* 19 (1), 53–74.

Jakubowicz, K. (2006) *Media Pluralism and Concentration: Searching for a Productive Research and Policy Agenda (in the light of the Council of Europe Experience)*, paper presented at the Working Group 3 meeting of COST Action A30, Budapest, 22–23 September 2006.

Jakubowicz, K. (2006) *Revision of the European Convention on Transfrontier Television in the Context of International Media Policy Evolution*, paper presented during the meeting of Working Group 3 of COST Action A30, Budapest, 22–23 September 2006.

Karp, J.A.; Banducci, S. A. and Bowler, S. (2003) "To Know it is to Love it. Satisfaction with Democracy in the European Union." *Comparative Political Studies*, Vol. 36, No. 2, 271–292.

Kekes, J. (1996) *The Morality of Pluralism*, University of Princeton Press.

K.U. Leuven et al. (2009) *Independent Study on Indicators for Media Pluralism in the Member States—Towards a Risk-Based Approach*. Prepared for the European Commission Directorate-General Information Society and Media. KUL: Leuven.

Luhmann, N. (2000) *The Reality of the Mass Media*, Stanford: Stanford University Press.

McQuail, D. (1992) *Media Performance: Mass Communication and the Public Interest*, London: Sage Publications.

Merelman, R.M. (1995) *Representing Black Culture: Racial Conflict and Cultural Politics in the United States*, New York: Routledge.

Merelman, R.M. (2003) *Pluralism at Yale: The Culture of Political Science in America*, Wisconsin: Wisconsin University Press.

Meyer, T. (2002), *Media Democracy: How the Media Colonize Politics*, Cambridge: Polity.

MM-CM, Council of Europe's Committee of Experts on Media Concentrations and Pluralism (1994) *The Activity Report of the Committee of Experts on Media Concentrations and Pluralism*, submitted to the 4th European Ministerial Conference on Mass Media Policy. Prague, 7–8 December 1994.

Möwes, B. (2000) *Fifty Years of Media Policy in the Council of Europe: A Review*, 6th European Ministerial Conference on Mass Media Policy Cracow (Poland), 15–16 June 2000, MCM (2000) 003.

Nissen, Ch. S. (2006) *Public Service Media in the Information Society,* the Report prepared by the Group of Specialists on PSB in the Information Society (MC-S-PSB), Strasbourg: Media Division, Directorate General of Human Rights, Council of Europe.

Oakeshott, M. (1996) *The Politics of Faith & the Politics of Scepticism*, New Haven and London: Yale University Press.

Petković, B. (ed.) (2004) *Media Ownership and its Impact on Media Independence and Pluralism*. Ljubljana: Peace Institute.

Sarikakis, K. (2004) *Powers in Media Policy: The Challenge of the European Parliament*, Oxford: Peter Lang.

Sarikakis, K. (2008) "Communication and Cultural Policies Research in Europe: A Review of Recent Scholarship." In *Communication and Cultural Policies in Europe* (eds.) Fernández Alonso, I. and de Moragas i Spà, M. Universitat Autònoma de Barcelona: Barcelona.

Scharpf, F. (1999) *Governing in Europe: Effective and Democratic?*, Oxford: Oxford University Press.

Schulz, W.: (2004) "Reconstructing mediatization as an analytical concept." *European Journal of Communication*, Vol. 19(1).

Staniszkis, J. (2004), *Władza globalizacji*, Warszawa: Wydawnictwo Naukowe "Scholar."

Staniszkis, J. (2006) "Pluralizm i władza." *Dziennik/Europa – Tygodnik Idei*, No. 42, 21. 10. 2006, 8–9.

Valcke, P., R. Picard, M. Sükösd, J Sanders et al., (2009) *Indicators for Media Pluralism in the Member States—Towards a Risk-Based Approach* (European

Commission): *Volume 1: Final Report,* 179 p. (ISBN 978-1-4452-0769-8), and *Volume 2: User Guide,* 363 p. (ISBN 978-1-4452-2519-7). Lulu.com.

Valcke, P., R. Picard, M. Sükösd, B. Klimkiewicz, B. Petkovic, C. dal Zotto, R. Kerremans. (2010, forthcoming). "The European Media Pluralism Monitor: Bridging Law, Economics and Media Studies as a First Step Towards Risk-Based Regulation in Media Markets." *The Journal of Media Law,* Vol. 2, Issue 1.

Van Cuilenburg, J. and McQuail, D. (2003) "Media Policy Paradigm Shifts: Towards a New Communications Policy Paradigm." *European Journal of Communication,* 18 (2), 181–207.

Van Cuilenburg, J. and R. van der Wurff (eds.) (2000) *Media and Open Societies: Cultural,Economic and Policy Foundations for Media Openness and Diversity in East and West.* Amsterdam: Het Spinhuis.

Van Dijk, J. (2006) *The Network Society: Social Aspects of New Media,* London: Sage Publications.

Venturelli, S. (1998) *Liberalizing the European Media: Politics, Regulation and the Public Sphere,* Oxford: Clarendon Press.

Verhulst, S. and Goldberg, D. (1998), "European Media Policy: Complexity and Comprehensiveness." L. d'Haenens and F. Saeys (eds.) *Media Dynamics and Regulatory Concern in the Digital Age.* Berlin: Quintessenz Verlags GmbH, 17–49.

Voorhoof, D. (1998) "Guaranteeing the Freedom and Independence of the Media." *Media and democracy,* Strasbourg: Council of Europe Publishing, 35–57.

de Vreese, C.H; Boomgaarden, H.G. (2006) "Media Effects on Public Opinion about the Enlargement of the European Union." *Journal of Common Market Studies* Vol. 44, No. 2, 419–436.

Ward, D. (2002) *The European Union Democratic Deficit and the Public Sphere: An Evaluation of EU Media Policy.* Amsterdam: IOS Press.

Ward, D. (2006) *Final Report on the study commissioned by the MC-S-MD "The Assessment of content diversity in newspapers and television in the context of increasing trends towards concentration of media markets,"* MC-S-MD (2006) 001, Strasbourg: Council of Europe.

Westphal, Dietrich (2002) "Media Pluralism and European Regulation." *European Business Law Review,* 13 (5), 459–487.

Wiedemann, V. (2005) *Legislating and regulating for pluralism,* paper presented at the European Parliament's Seminar on *Pluralism not Concentration: an EU Media Policy,* 7 April 2005, Brussels.

Williams, G. (2005) "What is the Television Without Frontiers Directive?" *Free Press,* No 148, September/October.

CHAPTER 13

Digital Television and the Search for Content

PETROS IOSIFIDIS

Introduction

Digital Television (DTV) offers the potential to overcome some of the limitations of analogue television, such as spectrum scarcity and picture interference. The availability of bandwidth allows viewers access to hundreds of channels, each aiming at specific market segments and each catering to specific interests. For some (Gilder, 1992; Negroponte, 1995) digital networks will bring about vast opportunities for specialised production and distribution, which will eventually mean the end of dominance of centralised broadcasting systems. DTV also comes with the promise to lower entry costs for new broadcasters, thus allowing the entry of new, small and talented broadcasters, with fresh ideas, that will contribute to innovation, more choice and diversity. For these reasons the European Commission (EC) promotes DTV adoption[1] and has published two Communications to accelerate digital switchover as a main driver for DTV take-up (EC, 2003; EC, 2005; Iosifidis, 2006).

This study argues that digitalisation has led to more channels, increasingly interactive and personalised services, but the switchover to digital broadcasting has only marginally benefited the public in terms of access, choice and programming diversity. Free-to-air digital content is a late phenomenon and notwithstanding some notable exceptions

---

[1] EC's support for DTV is implemented through several instruments. For example, eEurope acknowledges and encourages the role of DTV in a multi-platform approach to the Information Society. The policy is expected to provide widespread access to advanced communication and information services for all EU citizens. eEurope required Member States to publish their switchover plans by the end of 2003. The new regulatory framework for electronic communications also promotes the roll-out of DTV networks.

(i.e., the UK) it has yet to make an impact on European citizens. As European media markets expand and more and more channels are available, there is consequently a massive increase in demand for programming, but this programming is dominated by foreign, often American, output.

In turn, the penetration of European markets by American content inhibits European culture and denies European citizens their entitlement to a collective identity. The prevalence of domestic output in the new digital offerings is another factor inhibiting the creation of a "European public sphere." Thus the Television without Frontier's (TWF) (now Audiovisual Media Services) objective to influence the flow of European programming among Member States so as to motivate the emergence of a common culture could be flawed. Evidence suggests that the digital media have not enabled a borderless media flow and thus have not led to a strong sense of cultural belonging across Europe, not least because of the national character of the television market and the prevalence of foreign, notably US output. Market segmentation and audience fragmentation, two of the main characteristics of the digital age, reinforce the argument that social cohesion may be at stake.

In terms of structure, the first part of the article presents an overview of current developments of DTV across the EU. Emphasis is paid to the process of digital switchover and the role of digital terrestrial television (DTT) as the main drivers for encouraging digital take-up. Part two examines the programming of the new digital channels launched by established terrestrial broadcasters, including public broadcasters, in selective EU Member States (France, the UK and Spain) and discusses whether the new digital services can contribute to programming diversity. The concluding part considers whether EU policy in the area of digitalisation is mainly industrial and economic or whether it involves a cultural element too and as such promotes European integration and contributes to the creation of a common European identity.

Digital Switchover and the Development of DTV

Digital switchover (the progressive migration of households, from analogue-only reception to digital reception) has in recent years been put high on the agenda of both national and European regulators. The role of DTT, in particular, was underscored in the e-Europe 2005 action plan as one of the three main access platforms to the information society, together with UMTS and fixed broadband access. According to the e-Europe action plan, all Member States were required to disclose their national strategies for the switchover from analogue to digital terrestrial television by the end of 2003. In June 2005 the European Commission published a Communication "on accelerating the transition from analogue to digital broadcasting" which urged EU Member States to bring forward the likely date of analogue switch-off and called for a coordinated approach to making freed-up spectrum available across the EU. The EC suggested the year 2012 as a possible target for the completion of switchover (EC, 2005). This Communication builds on the 2003 Communication "on the transition from analogue to digital broadcasting" (from digital "switchover" to analogue "switch-off"), which set the benefits of switching over to digital broadcasting and initiated the debate on EU policy orientations on the amount and future uses of spectrum potentially released at the switch-off of analogue terrestrial television transmission (EC, 2003).

DTT has already been introduced in most of the countries of the EU, while some others are still in the planning stage. The dates for the analogue switch-off that have been set by national governments vary greatly, depending among others upon penetration of digital services, the infrastructure and public awareness of the process to switchover (see Iosifidis, 2005; Iosifidis, 2006). Table 1 shows that most EU Member States have stated their intention to switch-off the analogue frequency sometime between 2010 and 2012. The Netherlands, Finland and Sweden were among the first EU Member States to switch-off analogue terrestrial television at a national level. However, with the successful completion of the first switchover process in August 2003 Berlin/Brandenburg has played a pioneering role in Europe and beyond. But taken as a whole, Germany is not expected to turn-off the analogue transmissions before 2010. At the other end of the scale, national governments which have not committed to a prompt fixed date for analogue switch-off include some of the Southern European countries as well as some of the new members which joined the EU in 2004 and 2007 (see Table 1).

Table 1: DTT roll out and switch-off dates of analogue terrestrial TV in selected EU countries and Norway (2009)

COUNTRY	DTT ROLL OUT	SWITCH-OFF DATE
Austria	2006	2009
Belgium (Flanders)	2005	2012
Britain	available since 1998	2008-12
Denmark	31 March 2006	1 November 2009
Finland	available since 2001	31 August 2007
France	31 March 2005	2011
Germany	2002	2009 (Berlin/Postdam region switched in 2003)
Greece	March 2006	2012
Hungary	2007	31 December 2012
Ireland	2008	2012
Italy	available since 2003	31 December 2012 (Cagliari switched 1 March 2007)
Lithuania	2006 in Vilnius	2012
Luxembourg	April 2006	September 2006
Netherlands	since 2003 in Amsterdam	11 December 2006
Poland	no decision yet	2015
Portugal	2009	2010
Slovakia	2006	2012
Slovenia	2009	2012
Spain	available since 2000	3 April 2010
Sweden	available since 1999	5 October 2007
Norway	N/A	2009

Source: Author's analysis based on the MAVISE database (available at http://mavise.obs.coe.int) developed by the European Audiovisual Observatory.

Table 2 shows that most of the countries with advanced levels of DTV penetration have also set early dates for analogue switch-off. Finland

and Sweden for example, which were committed to making the switchover to digital in 2007, had in 2007–08 a DTV penetration of above 50 per cent. Norway, with a 2009 switch-off date, also ended 2008 with more than half of its households accessing DTV. Exceptions to this are Britain, arguably the most advanced European country with a DTV adoption well above the European average despite a switch off date of 2012, and Ireland, which in 2008 had a digital household adoption of 60 per cent but has fixed a late date for switchover. The deployment of DTT in Ireland has had a long history, with the first tests being carried out in 1998, but no public trials until August 2006. The system is not expected to fully launch until the end of 2009, although the state is committed to a 2012 analogue switch-off date.

Table 2: Top 10 European Countries by DTV Household Adoption (2008)

Ranking	Country	DTV penetration rate (%)
1	UK	89
2	Finland	75
3	Ireland	60
4	Iceland	59
5	Norway	57
6	Sweden	55
7	France	52
8	Spain	50
9	Italy	47
10	Malta	46

Source: Author's analysis based on the following market report: European and US Digital TV, by Strategic Focus, 16 July 2008.
Note: includes the four DTV platforms - satellite, terrestrial, cable and DSL.

It is clear that the European market in 2009–10 remains fragmented with regard to the adoption of technologies and there is little sign that Europe is developing a homogeneous digital TV industry. These variations in the national structure of the TV industry create a dilemma for EC regulators in terms of the feasibility of introducing common digital switch-off dates. The rationale of EC's involvement in the field is to create a workable internal market. Without doubt, switchover will bring about benefits to viewers and broadcasters, stimulate innovation and growth of the consumer electronics sector, and therefore contribute to the renewed Lisbon agenda. Hence the earlier the switchover process is started and the shorter the transition period, the sooner these benefits will be realized. However, the Commission's proposal for a common timescale may not be feasible, in view of the disparities of Member States' approaches and advances to digital switchover. The EC's proposal for the 2012 deadline for completing terrestrial analogue switch-off may lead some Member States to an ill-timed, insufficiently planned and unduly rapid introduction of DTT services to catch up with other more advanced territories (see Iosifidis, 2006; Iosifidis, 2011).

However, DTV in Western Europe was expected to reach a new record by 2012 with 165 million homes (up from around 105 million households subscribing to DTT, satellite, cable and Internet Protocol Television services at the end of 2006), according to a report by Datamonitor (2007), confirming earlier forecasts by market research Strategy Analytics (2006). The report suggested that by 2012 the most popular option for new users will be DTT, whereas satellite households will exceed 50 million. Digital cable is expected to show significant growth particularly as analogue cable is switched to digital. However the report said that IPTV, one of the most recent entrants into the pay-TV arena, will undergo the largest growth, with a forecast annual growth rate between 2006 and 2012 of 41.8 per cent (Datamonitor, 2007).

Terrestrial Broadcasters' New Digital Services—An Overview

The wide availability of DVT platforms has enabled a rapid expansion of digital channels globally. In 2006 US viewers had access to about 440 digital services, followed by the UK viewers who could watch some 416 channels. Meanwhile, the French, Italian, Spanish and German audiences could access 244, 205, 108 and 93 channels respectively, as the proliferation of DTV platforms in these territories prompted the entry of various channel operators. Terrestrial broadcasters have taken advantage of additional broadcasting capacity to launch channels that rely on their traditional source of revenue, such as free-to-air broadcasters expanding their advertiser-funded channel portfolios (for example, *France Télévisions* launching *France 4* and *Gulli* on the French DTT platform) (Ofcom, 2006). Table 3 presents an overview of the breadth of the terrestrial operator channel portfolios in a range of European countries and Table 4 shows the broad public service broadcaster portfolios in the countries under scrutiny (UK, France and Spain). Based on the data presented in these Tables the rest of the section focuses on the programming of digital services launched by public channels in these three large territories and compares them with the digital output of commercial terrestrial channels.

Table 3: Channel portfolios of terrestrial operators in sample European countries

Country	Broadcaster	Channel portfolio
UK	BBC	BBC One, BBC Two, BBC Three, BBC Four, BBC News 24, BBC Parliament, CBeebies, CBBC
	ITV	ITV1, ITV2, ITV3, ITV4, CITV, ITV Play, Men & Motors
	Channel 4	Channel 4, E4, More 4, Film Four
	Five	Five, Five Life, Five US
France	France Télévisions	France 2, France 3, France 4, France 5, Mezzo, Gulli, Euronews, Planete Thalassa, Ma Planete
	TF1	TF1, TF6, LCI, Eurosport, Serie Club, TV Breizh, Odyssee, Historie, TMC, TFOU, Ushiaia, Piwi, Eureka
	M6	M6, W9, Fun TV, Teva, M6 Boutique La Chaine, Paris Premiere, TF6, Music Hits, Music Black, Music Rock
Germany	ZDF	ZDF, ZDFtheaterjabakm ZDFFinfokanal, ZDFdocu kanal, 3Sat, Kinderkanal (with ARD)
	ARD	ARD, Das Erste, Eins Plus, Eins Extra, Eins Festival, Kika, 3Sa, Arte, Phoenix
	Pro7Sat1	Sat 1, ProSieben, Kabal eins, N24, Nine Life
	RTL	RTL, RTL2, Super, NTV, RTL Shop, Traumpatner
Italy	RAI	Pai Uno, Rai Due, Rai Tre, Rai Doc, Rai Utile, Rai News 24, Rai Sport Notixie, Rai Edu
	MediaSet	Canal 5, Boing, Italia 1, Retequattro
Spain	TVE	TVE1, La2, Teledeporte, Canal 24 Horas, Clan TVE, TVE 50 Anos
	Antena 3	Antena 3, Antena.Neox, Antena.Nova
	Telecinco	Telecinco, Telecinco Estrellas, Telecinco Sport

Country	Broadcaster	Channel portfolio
Sweden	SVT	SVT1, SVT2, SVT24, SVT Extra, Bamkalanen, Kinskapskanelen
	TV4	TV4, TV4 Plus, TV4 Film, TV400, TV4 Fakta
	Kanal 5	Kanal 5
	TV3	TV3, ZTV, TV8, TV6, TV1000, Nature, History, Crime, Explorer
Greece	ERT	CINE+, SPOR+, PRISMA+

Source: Ofcom, 2006; León 2006; Author research

Table 4: Public service broadcaster channel portfolios in the UK, France and Spain

Country	Operator	Services		Launch	Description
UK	BBC	BBC One	All homes	1932	Mixed genre
		BBC Two	All homes	1962	Mixed genre
		BBC Three	MC homes	2002	Mixed genre
		BBC Four	MC homes	2001	Arts & culture
		CBBC	MC homes	2001	Older children
		CBeebies	MC homes	2001	Younger children
		BBC News 24	MC homes	1997	News
		BBC Parliament	MC homes	1997	Political coverage
France	France Télévisions	France 1	All homes	1963	Mixed genre
		France 2	All homes	1972	Regional output
		France 4	MC homes	1996	Factual/ education
		France 5	MC homes	1994	Arts & Music
		Festival	MC homes	1996	French & EU Fiction
		Mezzo	MC homes	1998	Music service
		Ma Planete	MC homes	2004	Documentary
		Planete Thalassa	MC homes	2004	Marine life
		France Arte	All homes	1992	Franco-German arts
Spain	TVE	TVE1	All homes		Mixed genre
		La2	All homes		Mixed genre
		Canal24 Horas	MC homes	N/A	News service
		Teledeporte	MC homes	N/A	Sports
		Canal Clasico	MC homes	N/A	Classical music
		Clan TVE	MC homes	N/A	Children's
		TVE 50 Anos	MC homes	N/A	TVE archives

Source: Ofcom, 2006; León 2006; Author research

THE UK

The *British Broadcasting Corporation* has invested heavily in the area of digital television technology. Encouraged by the Labour government[2] which had a vision for an all-digital Britain, the BBC has launched an impressive portfolio of publicly funded niche digital services to ensure a smooth transition to digital broadcasting. More specifically, in 1997 it launched the digital news channel *BBC News 24* and the parliamentary service *BBC Parliament*. In September 2001 it re-launched its digital services, *BBC Knowledge* and *BBC Choice,* as *Cbeebies* (a service for children under 6), *CBBC* (another service for children aged 6–13), and *BBC Four* (aiming at 'anyone interested in culture, arts and ideas'). In 2002 the government approved another digital television service for young adults, dubbed *BBC Three* (see Table 4). These services are funded by the license fee and are available via digital terrestrial platforms, notably *Freeview*, digital satellite and digital cable. The cost of launching and operating these new digital services reached £115.8 million in 1999, the year that the corporation intensified its digital expansion strategy (7.9 per cent of the total allocation for television) and escalated to £270.5 million in 2002, the year that saw the completion of the above strategy with the launch of *BBC Three* (about 10 per cent of the total allocation for TV).

The corporation has specific obligations to promote DTV, notably, to develop the market for consumers who want DTV but do not want to subscribe to pay-TV services. The rationale for launching the *Freeview* platform was to provide an attractive free-to-view package, appealing enough to motivate consumers to invest in the necessary receivers. It is also required to offer affordable free-to-view receivers which consumers can buy with no subscription strings attached.

---

2 The government has recognized the central role which the BBC had to play in convincing people to switch to digital. The February 2000 funding settlement was intended to support the BBC in this role: allowing a balance to be struck between maintaining the quality of core services and investing adequately in new ones. More recently, in 2004, the Department of Culture, Media and Sport and the Department of Trade and Industry welcomed the BBC's commitment to "building digital Britain" and said that the BBC, alongside with commercial public service broadcasters would have to play the "lead role" in achieving digital switchover (DCMS and DTI, 2004).

Indeed, in 2006 digital terrestrial television set-top boxes were sold from as little as £30. In addition, the BBC is committed to promoting and marketing its digital services and catering to consumer awareness and information over digital services. According to a 2004 BBC report, the Corporation's investment in its digital channels and promotions for them "has played a strong role in exciting consumer interest in digital, tackling consumer confusion and assuaging fears," and that the continuing consumer enthusiasm for DTV during 2003 "makes achieving UK-wide digital switchover with the Government's timetable an achievable objective" (BBC, 2004, 1).

Research undertaken by Oliver & Ohlbaum (2004) confirms that the new BBC services have contributed greatly to overall digital take-up. While pay-TV take up has experienced some upheavals (particularly with the collapse of *ITV Digital*, but also with the financial problems of the two main cable operators *NTL* and *Telewest*—now merged and renamed *Virgin Media*), free-to-view DTV penetration has increased from 0.5 million households to about 3 million over a period of just two years since the launch of *Freeview*. Perhaps more importantly, evidence suggests that *Freeview* penetration has been largely additional to, rather than a substitute for, digital pay TV take-up (ibid, 17). Those considering getting subscription television services (most likely football fans) continued to do so, as evidenced by the rise of pay-TV (both cable and satellite) following the launch of *Freeview*, albeit at a slower rate than before. Without doubt, the healthy growth of *Freeview* reinforced competition between different platforms and established free-to-air digital reception as a viable alternative to pay-TV services. This may have reduced the share and reach of other digital platforms more rapidly than otherwise might have been the case. However, the relatively slow growth rate of subscription services may also be explained by the closure of the high profile digital terrestrial pay service *ITV Digital* in April 2002, as well as the stagnation and financial difficulties that the two main cable operators *NTL* and *Telewest* were facing at the time.

Analysis of the demographics of *Freeview* subscribers reinforces the notion that free-to-air digital customers are largely additional to pay-TV subscribers. A Quest survey in March 2003 gave demographic data on the types of households that were using each platform. It found that *Freeview* had a different profile to other platforms. In particular, the findings suggest that many of *Freeview's* customers are affluent, older people who have no interest in purchasing satellite or cable pay-TV services. Many of *Freeview* homes comprise of an age group of over 45, compared to satellite subscription television take up which is heavily skewed to the under 45s. The fact that the free-to-air package includes far less available channels made no difference to this group who has no interest in multi-channel TV (Quest Survey, 2003). In sum, *Freeview* appeals to those who reject satellite and cable pay-TV services and to whom, as a BBC report states (BBC, 2004, 10), "a terrestrial free-to-air service is a welcome bonus." According to Oliver & Ohlbaum (2004, 9) "the new BBC services have made a significant contribution to bringing forward the likely idea of analogue switch-off and the release of large amounts of spectrum."

A CRITIQUE OF BBC'S DIGITAL SERVICES—IS THE INVESTMENT JUSTIFIABLE?

A criticism often put forward regarding the new BBC services is that only a minority of viewers enjoys the full benefits of all BBC digital channels, whereas everybody pays the license fee. Indeed, at the end of 2003 the four new BBC services (*BBC Three, BBC Four, CBBC, CBeebies*) had a share of about 2.7 per cent of all day multi-channel viewing. This figure has hardly been improved by 2006. There is therefore a widespread perception that the BBC is spending disproportionate amounts of money (in 2003 the BBC spent £271 million on its digital channels, which represented about 9 per cent of its total budget of £2.5 billion) on channels to which few people have access. Is this investment justified?

The answer is largely positive. Regardless of audience share, a distinction should perhaps be drawn between services offered by public channels, required by their statute to address a wide range of public interest criteria, and those provided by private pay television consortia, driven by audience ratings. The BBC offerings entail more innovative and distinctive programs than those supplied by rivals. At the risk of simplifying what is a complex issue, a number of key things emerge from comparing the programming offered by commercial pay broadcasters with that of the BBC. First, the publicly-funded BBC has invested more on public service programming genres, such as news in peak, regional news, current affairs and other factual programming, original UK-made drama and comedy, children's shows, science, arts, religion and other minority programming. Second, the BBC provides a balanced TV diet of trusted and familiar programming with innovative, quality, original and high-risk output.

The assessment carried out by Oliver & Ohlbaum demonstrates the BBC's strong commitment to investing on original high quality, national and regional UK programming on its new DTV channels, which reflects and strengthens cultural identity. The study shows that each BBC television service is offering something distinctive to UK multi-channel audiences when compared with other thematic channels—and often to a distinct demographic. For example, the absence of advertising and imported animation on the BBC children's services is likely to have been attractive to families with children. This is evidenced by the relatively high levels of consumption of the *CBBC* and *Cbeebies* children channels, which had the highest absolute impact. The study goes on to show that *Cbeebies* utilises far less animation and shows more educational programming than its nearest rivals. *CBBC's* schedule has far more UK originated factual and current affairs programming than any near rival, and also more educational programming than its rivals except *Discovery Kids* whose educational output though is mostly non-UK originated.

In contrast to the channels addressed to children, the study found that the proportionate impact on digital adoption from *BBC 3* was relatively low as digital penetration in 2003 was already high among the 25 to 34 year old age group. Still, in terms of content, *BBC 3* has greater amounts of news, current affairs and factual programming than *E4*, *Sky One*, *ITV 2* and *Paramount*, and a greater variety of program types and genres across the whole schedule. The vast majority of its schedule is made up of UK originated material. Finally, according to the Oliver & Ohlbaum analysis, *BBC 4* has a far greater range of program genres and types than any factual, arts or performance focused thematic channel. In sum, the BBC digital channels content is qualitatively different to that offered by private pay television operators.

This is not to say that pay television consortia cannot provide programs that meet public service purposes. In addition to the *Discovery Kids* service mentioned above, other channels like *Sky News*, *Arts World* and the *History Channel* deliver value through stimulating learning and engagement in society. *More 4*, launched in September 2005 by the public service broadcaster *Channel 4*, centers around lifestyle, documentary and arts and competes successfully with the BBC's similar offering, *BBC Four*. However, these examples are the exception rather than the rule. Even in today's multi-channel digital world, there is under-provision of quality, original, innovative and hence high-risk programming, as pay operators often adopt a risk-averse approach in reducing innovation and marginalizing the specialist content that audiences tend to value less. This is evidenced by *ITV*'s content strategy to provide a great range of repeats or cheap imports and refrain from adhering to children's, religious and/or regionally-specific content, which is commercially undesirable. Digital channels *ITV2 and ITV3* show mostly repeats and soap operas that previously been aired on *ITV1*. *ITV4*, which replaced *Men & Motors* in November 2005, has a male-oriented line-up, including sport, cop shows and US comedies and dramas. It does not use *ITV1*'s archives, which would help it appeal to the elusive male audience.

Obviously *ITV*'s desire to be freed from these public service requirements is connected with its revenue-squeeze which costs the operator some £250 million per year. The relaxation of *ITV*'s regional news requirements is particularly alarming. Despite the wide availability of television news, there is now more uneven provision of regional news or news targeting younger viewers, areas where the *BBC*, and indeed for that matter, *Channel 4*, the other public service broadcaster, score high. This is a key area which as I argued previously should be protected, alongside the *BBC*'s significant role in the provision of children's TV (Iosifidis, 2007). Regarding the offering of the other main commercial terrestrial broadcaster *Five*, the new digital services *Five Life* and *Five US* launched in late 2006 are also commercially-oriented. *Five US* features a mix of America drama, films, documentaries, sport and comedy and *Five Life* broadcasts entertainment shows and drama series such as the Australian drama *Love My Way*. Viewers can also see backstage gossiping and special weekly omnibus of the Australian series *Home and Away*. In sum *Five*'s output does not seem to contribute greatly to programming diversity.

Returning to the BBC offering, in 2006 the corporation announced a change of its strategy with regard to how content is created and distributed in order to reflect the changing audience expectations and on-demand delivery. Director General (DG) Mark Thompson outlined this need for a change in thinking as follows: the BBC should aim to deliver more public value by making content available in many media and devices, either at home or portable; the BBC should form a new relationship with its audience by starting viewing them as partners and participants. New cross-platform content strategies have been put forward for journalism, sport, music, children's and teens, entertainment, drama, knowledge-building, comedy and music, which allow for more audience participation and different forms of access. The DG emphasized the informative function, which would focus on continuous services across different platforms, the education function, which would enhanced when the BBC opens up its archive, and the entertainment function, with the BBC continuing to invest in "distinctive British entertainment" (Thompson, 2006).

It can be seen that the BBC new digital services, alongside some of the niche services of other commercial terrestrial broadcasters, have accelerated DTV take-up and added consumer value. The new digital offerings by the public broadcaster have enhanced diversity in key areas such as children's, news and education and learning and they have stimulated creativity and cultural excellence. Backed by the license fee (the six-year settlement announced in January 2007 means that the cost of the TV license will rise from its current level of £131.50 to £151 by 2012), the BBC does not have to concern itself with how users are going to pay for new services, and it remains unaffected by the downturn in advertising revenues, placing it in a better position to take risks. However, most of the programming of the new services of terrestrial broadcasters pays strong emphasis on domestic content, with the notable exception of *E4*, which is operated by Channel 4 and shows primarily American films, and *Five US*, which was launched by Five. The problem is that pan-European programming is largely missing from the offerings, something that does not contribute to European cultural integration, as we shall see below. The other problem is that despite these strengths of PSB output, in the course of time the quality of programming is dropping owing to competition and market concerns, as evidenced by an Ofcom (2004) survey.

FRANCE

In France public broadcasters are increasingly dominated by commercial concerns and managed as private corporations. Their programming over the years tends to resemble those of their commercial counterparts, with the notable exception of *France 5* and *Arte* (EUMAP, 2005). Indeed, it is mainly *France 5* – which shares frequencies with the high-brow Franco-German joint venture channel *Arte*, which acts as a guardian of program quality and diversity, whereas the programming of the main terrestrial public channels *France 2* and *France 3* increasingly emulates that of private rivals. A pan-European study by León (2004) found that there are still some differences between French public and commercial broadcasters in the area of cultural programming. Using a wide concept of culture, the study showed that *France 2* and *France 3* had more cultural output than their competitors *TF-1* and *M6*, but in prime-time the public channels' programming showed a strong orientation towards entertainment, and information to a lesser extent.

The difficulty faced by *France Télévisions* to adjust to a continually changing television landscape and employ a clear and stable strategy is also reflected in its thematic portfolio. DTT in the country was only launched in March 2005, two years later than originally scheduled, owing to political upheavals, interminable conflicts on standards, and eternal differences between *France Télévisions, TF-1* and *Canal Plus*. The DTT service, in which the public broadcaster participates, is entitled *TNT* and the initial offering consisted of 14 free-to-air channels while in late 2005 two bouquets of pay-TV were added. Take-up of services exceeded expectations and by June 2007 about 8.2 million households were equipped to receive DTT, bringing the DTT penetration to 22 per cent of French TV households. This is significant given that DTT was only launched in March 2005. This early success was partly because the set-top boxes were made available from as little as 70 Euros, and partly because the offering was sufficiently convincing to make people forget the earlier hesitancy. In fact, the offering improved substantially with the launch of additional channels to match the variety offered by the satellite consortia.

However, apart from *France 5* and *France 4* the other services do not make a great impact as they attract negligible audiences. *Historie*, the thematic service broadcasting documentaries with a good audience share, was set up in 1997 but sold to *TF-1 Group* in 2002 due to the public broadcaster's financial difficulties. The launch of the thematic services would have been more successful and indeed diverse if *France Télévisions* had adapted the guiding principles identified by Philippe Chazal in a 1996 study on behalf of the public broadcaster. In more particular, the author argued that the following should be adhered to by the public sector in setting up thematic channels:

- The content of the thematic channels should consist of *France Télévisions*' extensive archive
- Thematic channels should focus on specialised topics that would meet the preferences of the twenty-first century viewer
- Emphasis should be placed on showing programs which, by definition, are not covered by the private sector (education, training, culture).

Most of Chazal's recommendations were inspired by Britain's *BBC*, but were not adopted by the then president of *France Télévisions*, Beauchamps, who believed that by launching niche services public channels could contribute to further fragmentation of society. However, the current digital offering of the French public broadcaster covers a wide range of genres. *France Télévisions's* new services consist of documentaries (*Ma Planete, Planete Thalassa*), music and arts (*Mezzo, France 5*), and factual/education (*France 4*). French and European fiction is depicted in the output of *Festival*, whereas *France Arte* shows Franco-German arts. But not many French citizens enjoy these services since the digital offerings in France are not as advanced as they are in the UK as the free-to-view digital services in the country only became available in 2005. Contrary to its British counterpart, whose digital services pioneered in the continent, *France Télévisions's* DTT offering has yet to make an impact. Despite the rapid take-up of DTT services their overall contribution to digital switchover is still minimal compared with other established platforms such as pay satellite and cable.

Leading commercial network *TF-1* controls the news channel *La Chaine Info (LCI)*, the documentary channel *Odyssee*, TF6, *Serie Club*, the regional channel *TV Breizh* and Eurosport, which broadcasts across Europe. It is also the majority shareholder in the pay digital satellite platform *TPS* with a 66 per cent stake (*M6* owns the balance). *M6*, the second most popular commercial channel, targets young audiences as well as housewives under the age of 50. In 1998 *M6* set up the thematic services *M6 Musique* and *Club Teleachat*. Table 3 shows that *TF-1* and *M6's* thematic portfolios are dominated by music hits, films and gossip.

However, the digital offerings of some of the French terrestrial broadcasters take a European dimension, in contrast to the UK's broadcasters whose digital portfolio is dominated by domestic output. In more particular, the public broadcaster is an owner (together with 19 more public channels) of *Euronews*, the Europe-wide satellite channel which broadcasts international news, and leading commercial operator *TF-1* makes available the pan-European sports service *Eurosport* and *Festival*. The provision of pan-European content is not surprising given France's concern about American cultural imperialism and advocacy of European culture and identity. The French are strong advocates of the TWF/AVMS Directive and the imposition of quotas to prevent US material dominating Europe. They claim that audiovisual works are the expression of an identity and audiovisual policy should therefore favor the emergence of a European conscience and a greater cohesion at the level of the continent.

SPAIN

In Spain the collapse of digital terrestrial pay-TV platform *Quiero TV* in 2002 retarded the process of implementation of free-to-view services. Following a lengthy period of negotiations between the government and main TV companies for the allocation of frequencies, finally in November 2005 eighteen free-to-air digital terrestrial channels began to broadcast. As Table 4 shows, public television broadcaster *TVE* launched five channels: *TVE1* and *La2* (the main channels which broadcast in analogue frequency); the 24-hour news service *Canal 24 Horas;* the 24-hour sports channel *Teledeporte;* the children's channel *Clan TVE* (which broadcasts from 7.00 am to 9.00 pm); and *TVE 50 Anos* (it shares the same frequency as *Clan* TVE and broadcasts programs from the *TVE* archives. Commercial broadcaster *Antena 3* broadcasts three channels: *Antena 3* (the same analogue channel); *Antena.Neox* (children and youth); and *Antena.Nova* (a family channel on lifestyle and entertainment). The other main commercial channel *Telecinco* also makes available its analogue service *Telecinco*, alongside *Telecinco Estrellas* (fiction) and *Telecinco Sport* (sports) (see Table 3).

According to León (2006) the new digital terrestrial services have not resulted in more programming diversity and/or novelty for the Spaniards, for they only managed to attract negligible audiences and offer content similar to that of the analogue services. The current DTT offering consists of channels previously available either on analogue free-to-air television (this is particularly the case with the new generalist channels) or on digital cable or satellite. These services cannot therefore be perceived as innovative, by means of developing new niche channels, specifically designed for the DTT platform. Programming diversity is enhanced by offering programming genres that are not adequately supplied by the analogue terrestrial channels and not by recycling or repeating material. But this is not the case in Spain as it is evidenced by comparing the top ranked programs of September 2003 with those of September 2006. The comparison demonstrates that in both years the leading genres were drama series and sports events, whereas reality shows only appear in 2003. León (2006) argued that this can be interpreted as a signal of tiredness of the audience with the reality shows, rather than an impact of the new services. Among the top programming genres appearing in both 2003 and 2006 are domestic and European league football matches, and American series such as *CSI Miami*.

It is apparent that the creation of attractive content is at the moment the weak side of the Spanish DTT offer, for it has not yet been a priority. Instead, emphasis has been given to the pay-TV market and the behaviour of the main players. According to León (2006) one of the reasons that could explain this deficit is that digitalisation in the country has so far been more an effort on behalf of the government and the main operators, rather than a priority for the Spanish people. The Spaniards are generally not involved in the digitalisation process as there are limited public forums and initiatives taken on behalf of the government on this front. Meanwhile the public TV broadcaster *TVE* has not really managed to adapt to the digital environment smoothly. It largely continues to behave as an analogue channel: most of its popular programs are not available on digital format; its digital and online services do not provide a public forum where viewers can engage in a dialogue and exchange information and ideas. As a result its thematic services greatly resemble those provided by its commercial rivals.

Has DTV Contributed to European Cultural Integration?

It can be inferred from the above cases that DTV has contributed to programming diversity only to a certain extent. But has EU policy in the area of digitalisation been significant in terms of promoting European cultural integration and creating a common European identity? Modern electronic devices and the proliferation of new networks seem the ideal instruments to promote an imagined European community and identity. The move to digital content and digital distribution is not just a simple technology shift (for example, a transfer from print to electronic formats), but brings with it a whole new way of thinking, cultural change and shift of the nature of the digital content landscape. Enhancing access to culture can be achieved through making the collections of cultural organizations (museums and galleries, libraries and archives) available online and use some of these materials to produce projects aimed at widening access to culture, particularly by hard to reach groups. Yet the EU policy stresses the competitiveness of the sector in terms of benefits it brings to businesses and industry, rather than pursuing the cultural element. This is demonstrated in the competitiveness indicators suggested in a 2005 Commission Working Paper. These indicators include among others: trade (imports, exports, the trade balance between production and consumption); productivity; turnover; employment; price of output; trends in advertising revenue; costs of production; innovation. Measures of cultural and political impact (for example, diversity, pluralism, access and quality) are getting less attention (EC, 2005).

European media (both traditional and new interactive media) play an important role in the development towards a more technologically integrated media culture operating to a still larger degree beyond the nation state and in relation to a European and even global market (Bondebjerg, 2001). Yet despite the process of globalization, the rapid development of the Internet and the proliferation of DTV channels across Europe, the media remain nationally entrenched and oriented towards national output. Broadcasting organizations (alongside public schools, the university and the Church) reflect deeply rooted national identities[3] which have a unique historic essence. Much European TV

---

[3] Price (1995, 40) defined national identity as the "collection of myths, ideas and narratives used by a dominant group or coalition to maintain power in a society." He argued that definitions of national identity provide the community with a sense of who belongs and who is differentiated, what is the norm and who is the "other" (ibid, 42).

material reflects and addresses the tastes, interests, events, cultural preferences and languages of viewers in individual countries. As can be seen from the channels' thematic portfolios outlined above, very few new services (notably *Euronews, Eurosport, Eureka* and *Festival*) deal with pan-European programming that would disseminate political or cultural information at a European level and would therefore encourage participation and exchange of ideas among European citizens. Also the Franco-German *Arte* offers arts output appealing to two large EU territories. Earlier empirical research by Bondebjerg (2001) shows that it is programs with national origin or US-origin that dominates in most European countries channels output. The study confirms that globalization of channel-supply has indeed taken place, but does not have a strong foothold among the viewers in Europe.

The media, especially television, provide the most important link between politics and the citizens (Entman and Bennett, 2001). However, what is missing from the offerings in the new digital environment is the existence of content which could contribute to a unitary and universal form of addressing all Europeans. It is specifically news and cultural material, rather than feature films and television fiction that can enable EU citizens to share information, participate in trans-national and borderless wide-reaching forums, and engage in a public debate and exchange views. The focus on factual programming is limited and it is only available in the digital output of public broadcasters, with services such as *BBC News 24* (*BBC*), *Canal 24 Horas* (*TVE*) and *France 4* (*France Télévisions*), but it is not realized in the content supply of the commercial terrestrial broadcasters *ITV, Channel 4* and *Five* in the UK, or those of *Antena 3* and *Telecinco* in Spain.

The broad absence of factual services with a clear pan-European content can be attributed to the national character of the television market, which has not changed much in this regard even after the introduction of digital TV services. The prevalence of popular American output in European digital TV networks is another factor inhibiting the dissemination of pan-European programming. US audiovisual material, particularly TV formats and Hollywood movies have succeeded in penetrating the European continent for a number of reasons: the export advantages attributed to the English language; the highly effective marketing and publicity; the dynamism of the American industry and the quality of much of its product. In Europe, on the other hand, cultural and linguistic diversity has resulted in demand for domestic, regional or local material which remains a strong feature of the content market in the digital era, alongside demand for certain 'global' products, such as blockbusters. The thematic services of most of the national terrestrial broadcasters are dominated to varying degrees by national and/or American material, while non-national European programming generally comes in a distant third place. As Bondebjerg (2001) put it there is a paradox in that we live in a local and national culture with global dimensions and we inhabit an American global culture as a natural part of our national and local culture.

The inadequate coverage of pan-European issues by DTV thematic channels reflects the absence of a unified, common media agenda that interests citizens throughout the Union and signals the lack of a united European public forum. This contradicts with the idea of a common European TV policy launched by the 1989 TWF Directive, aiming at creating a single market for TV broadcasts across Europe and a European public space that would promote European identity and vision. Channel abundance, brought about by DTV, has led to even greater market fragmentation and audience segmentation, thereby making it more difficult to form a common European identity. The EU policy seems to be seeking a common denominator across all markets, but this may not be achievable or even desirable due to differences in language, culture, population and market size. It will be difficult to achieve the aims of the TWF Directive to create a single market for European TV broadcasts, for the free movement of programming within the internal market has resulted in the dominance of US products.

Conclusion

Television is a cornerstone of modern democracy and cultural diversity, enhances our identity and capacity to live together and therefore contributes to social cohesion. The dominant audiovisual medium plays a major role in forming our cultural identity by determining not only what we see of the world, but also how we see it. Universally available terrestrial channels, particularly public bodies, have hitherto ensured high levels of investment in quality output, often taking risks with innovative programming and new forms of creativity. DTV offers a unique chance for the channels to continue this trend, carry programming from elsewhere in Europe and become active creators of both one's own and a European culture with the launch of numerous new services. New channels with new content appealing to a variety of tastes and interests—for example, services on education, art, current affairs, music, cinema, science and history—are necessary for the enhancement of our identity as well as the promotion of content diversity. Re-cycling material from old programs certainly wastes the opportunity offered by the new services to develop the nation and/or the continent's creativity via new and original content production.

This study of the content of the new digital services of established terrestrial broadcasters in sample EU countries had two primary goals. One was to establish whether the proliferation of digital services can enhance programming diversity. Diversity of TV supply can be defined as the availability of a whole range of content that can satisfy all viewers, including the minorities. The growing number of channels does not necessarily result in diversity of media or content. Yet, with the advent of digital broadcasting, media diversity remains a key policy objective that must be respected in the interests of democracy and societies' full cultural development (Council of Europe, 2002, 19). Another important aspect of diversity is granting consumer-citizens access to media services of their own choice on fair terms. From this point of view, the establishment of DTT is important, for it makes digital television accessible to a large part of the population, minimising the number of households which cannot access TV services when the switchover takes place. The UK is the world leader in establishing the *Freeview* DTT free-to-air platform in 2002 (that succeeded the bankrupt pay DTT platform *On Digital*, later renamed *ITV Digital*), whereas France and Spain are lagging behind. Public broadcasters generally have an important presence on the DTT free platform as a result of "must-carry" rules adopted by governments, but with the exception of the BBC, the rest of the public channels are still trying to adapt to their new role as leaders of digital television services and primary contributors to switchover.

Turning to the descriptive findings, with the exception of the *BBC* and *Channel 4* services and *France Télévisions* output to a lesser extent, the content of the new digital channels does not comfortably sit with the diversity ideal. In the UK, the digital services of the public broadcasters contribute more to the programming diversity compared with the offerings of the private terrestrial outlets. This is evidenced by the *BBC* new children's channels as well as the news services which convey everyday national and regional politics to the UK viewers. The *BBC*'s original domestic content and provision of high quality services can be attributed to the strong public service ethos, the wide availability of free-to-air digital services, and the guaranteed funding. In contrast in Spain, the lack of a clear digital strategy by the main terrestrial broadcasters, coupled with the financial difficulties of the public broadcaster *TVE*, had an adverse effect on programming diversity and consumer choice. The traditional tenets of public service media such as diversity, breadth of content, the representation of a wide range of opinions and universal access is more an illusion then reality in the digital services provided by the main Spanish channels.

The second goal of the study was to investigate the potential influence of the new digital channels to European cultural integration and the establishment of a "European public sphere." In terms of covering EU-related issues the findings suggest that the new digital services of all EU countries under scrutiny, with the exception of France, lack a clear commitment to European content. This verifies existing content analyses of the TV coverage of the EU (Norris, 2000; Kevin, 2003; Peter and de Vreese, 2004). European affairs, culture and politics are marginally represented in national digital networks, whereas the amount and prominence of American programming genres is more visible. The introduction of digital broadcasting has resulted in an explosion in demand for audiovisual content, but as Collins (2003) put it, "without a commensurate growth in broadcasting revenues." This has increased the proportion of foreign, often American, programs on European screens. The French exception in terms of EU coverage is to some extent due to their strong resistance to the American cultural domination and the commitment to promoting European culture. But the negligible coverage of European affairs reflects the absence of a communal and shared European culture and citizenship. It could be argued that Europe has made its presence felt only on an economic and monetary level, rather than on a cultural and social level.

For almost two decades now European media policy (including film and broadcasting policy) has been formulated to meet the challenges of global competition and market deregulation. On one front the objective has been to sustain and develop the production and distribution media processes across the continent to achieve a single market development of a unified Europe. On the other Information and Communication technologies and new digital media services have been set to improve the perspectives of digitalisation of culture, employment and education. However, EU media policy has not been very successful up to now in enhancing the tradition of a public service culture that can flourish and meet the challenges of a new global, digital world where media will no longer function as they do today. Unless there is a change of the EU media policy the development of the European media culture looks increasingly a distant dream rather than a reality. But as Bondebjerg (2001) mentions the development of the European media culture is not just a question of the changing media policy and cultural policy or the technological and economic aspects, but also a question of relating to a much bigger question of the European integration and gradual fragmentation of national cultures and identities in the light of globalization and the network society. Despite the potential for a new and more integrated European culture, the expansion of the nation state culture to an imagined European culture has not been achieved, partly due to the national character of the television industry and partly due to the dominance of American media products.

REFERENCES

BBC (British Broadcasting Corporation) (2004) *Progress Towards Achieving Digital Switchover*, Report to the Government (London: BBC, April 2004).
Bondebjerg, Ib. (2001) "European Media, Cultural Integration and Globalisation: Reflections on the ESF-Programme Changing Media—Changing Europe." *Nordicom Review* 22, no. 1 (June 2001). Available at: http://www.lboro.ac.uk/research/changing.media/Nordicom-2.htm (accessed December 2007).
Collins, R. (2003) *Identity & Television: Europe on Screen* (openDemocracy, 29 May 2003). Available at: http://www.openDemocrary.net (accessed December 2006).
Council of Europe (2002) *Media Diversity in Europe,* Report by the AP-MD (Advisory Panel to the CDMM on Media Concentrations, Pluralism and Diversity Questions), Strasbourg: Council of Europe, Media Division Directorate General of Human Rights, December 2002).
Datamonitor (2007) *European and US Digital TV, 2006–2012*. 19 July 2007.

DCMS (Department for Culture, Media and Sport) and DTI (Department of Trade and Industry) (2004) *Digital Television Project: Tessa Jowell Makes Announcement on the Progress of Digital Switchover,* Press Release (London: DCMS and DTI, 22 July 2004).

EC (European Commission) (2003) *Communication on Digital Switchover - Transition From Analogue to Digital Broadcasting, From Digital Switchover to Analogue Switch-off,* COM(2003) 541 final (Brussels: Commission of the European Communities, 22 September 2003).

EC (European Commission) (2005a) *Communication on Accelerating the Transition from Analogue to Digital Broadcasting,* COM(2005) 204 final (Brussels: Commission of the European Communities, 24 May 2005).

EC (European Commission) (2005b) *Staff Working Paper accompanying the Commission Communication on Scientific Information in the Digital Age: Access, Dissemination and Preservation* (Brussels: Commission of the European Communities, 22 September 2005).

Entman, R.M. and W.L. Bennett (2001) *Mediated Politics: Communication in the Future of Democracy.* Cambridge: Cambridge University Press.

EUMAP (EU Monitoring and Advocacy Program) (2005) *Television Across Europe: Regulation, Policy and Independence.* Brussels: OSI's EUMAP and Media Program, 11 October 2005. Available at: http://www.eumap.org/topics/media/television_europe (accessed October 2006).

Gilder, G. (1992) *Life After Television: The Coming Transformation of Media and American Life.* N. Y.: W.W. Norton.

Iosifidis, P. (2005) "Digital Switchover and the Role of BBC Services in Digital TV Take-up." *Convergence – The International Journal of Research into New Media Technologies* 11, no. 3 (August): 57–74.

Iosifidis, P. (2006) "Digital Switchover in Europe." *Gazette—The International Journal for Communication Studies* 68, no. 3 (May): 249–67.

Iosifidis, P. (2007a) "Public Service Broadcasting—Competition, Pluralism and Funding: The Case of Channel 4." *Broadcast* (25 October 2007a). Available at: http://www.broadcastnow.co.uk/opinion_and_blogs/blog_c4_and_psb.html (accessed December 2007).

Iosifidis, P. (2007b) *Public Television in Europe: Technological Challenges and New Strategies* London: Palgrave Macmillan.

Iosifidis, P. (2011) "Growing Pains? The Transition to Digital Television in Europe." *European Journal of Communication* 26, no. 1, forthcoming.

Kevin, D. (2003) *Europe in the Media: A Comparison of Reporting, Representation and Rhetoric in National Media Systems in Europe.* Mahwah NJ: Lawrence Erlbaum.

León, B. (2004) *Prime-time Programming in European Public Television: Information, Entertainment and Diversity.* Spain: University of Navarra, GLOBAPLUR Project.

León, B. (2006) *Personal Communication, informal interview by author.*

Murdock, G. (2000) "Digital Futures in the Age of Convergence." In *Television Across Europe,* eds. Wieten J, G. Murdock and P. Dahlgren, London: Sage 35–57.

Negroponte, N. (1995) *Being Digital.* N. Y.: Hodder & Stoughton.

Norris, P. (2000) *A Virtuous Circle: Political Communication in Post-industrial Societies.* Cambridge: Cambridge University Press.

Ofcom (Office of Communications) (2004) *Public Consultation on Quality.* London: Office of Communications (21 April 2004).

———(2006) *The International Communications Market 2006.* London: Office of Communications.

Oliver & Ohlbaum (2004) *An Assessment of the Market Impact of the BBC's Digital TV Services,* Report for the BBC's submission to the DCMS Review, London: Oliver & Ohlbaum Associates Ltd.

Peter, J. and C. H. de Vreese (2004) "In Search of Europe: A Cross-National Comparative Study of the European Union in National Television News." *The Harvard International Journal of Press/Politics* 9, no. 3: 3–24.

Quest Survey (2003). *Multichannel Quarterly, Q2 2003,* London: ITC. Available at: http://www.itc.org.uk/uploads/ITC_Multichannel_Quarterly_-_Q2_2003.doc.

Strategy Analytics (2006) *IPTV and DTTV Boost Western European Digital TV to Record* Growth (Strategy Analytics, 2 September 2006).

Thompson, M. (2006) *Creative Futures – The BBC Programmes and Content in an On-demand World.* Royal Television Society Fleming Memorial Lecture 2006, 25 April.

List of Contributors

MONICA ARINO, Principal, International Policy, Ofcom

DOMINIC BOYER, Associate Professor, Department of Anthropology, Rice University

FARREL CORCORAN, Professor, School of Communication, Dublin City University

PETER GROSS, Director, School of Journalism and Electronic Media, The University of Tennessee

ISTVÁN HEGEDŰS, Council of Europe

PETROS IOSIFIDIS, Reader in Media Policy Department of Sociology, School of Social Sciences, City University London

KAROL JAKUBOWICZ, Senior Adviser to the Chairman of the National Broadcasting Council of Poland

BEATA KLIMKIEWICZ, Assitant Professor, Institute of Journalism and Social Communication, Jagellonian University

INKA SALOVAARA-MORING, Associate Professor in Communication, University of Tallinn

KATERINA SPASOVSKA, Doctoral Student, School of Journalism and Electronic Media, The University of Tennessee

SLAVKO SPLICHAL, Professor of Communication and Public Opinion, Faculty of Social Sciences, University of Ljubljana

MIKLÓS SÜKÖSD, Associate Professor, Journalism and Media Studies Centre, University of Hong Kong

SABINA MIHELJ, Senior Lecturer, Department of Social Sciences, Loughborough University

GONZALO TORRES, Visiting Researcher, Center for European, Russian and Eurasian Studies, Munk Center for International Studies, University of Toronto

PETER J. VARGA, Journalist, Canada

Index